Nursing and the Law
Fifth Edition

Darlene M. Trandel-Korenchuk, RN, PhD
Director of Grants and Community Outreach
The Nalle Clinic
Charlotte, North Carolina

and

Keith M. Trandel-Korenchuk, JD, MPH
Attorney at Law
Davis Wright Tremaine LLP
Charlotte, North Carolina

AN ASPEN PUBLICATION®
Aspen Publishers, Inc.
Gaithersburg, Maryland
1997

This publication is designed to provide accurate and authoritative information in regard to the Subject Matter covered. It is sold with the understanding that the publisher is not engaged in rendering legal, accounting, or other professional service. If legal advice or other expert assistance is required, the service of a competent professional person should be sought. (From a Declaration of Principles jointly adopted by a Committee of the American Bar Association and a Committee of Publishers and Associations.)

Library of Congress Cataloging-in-Publication Data

Trandel-Korenchuk, Keith M.
Nursing and the law/Keith M. Trandel-Korenchuk and Darlene M.
Trandel-Korenchuk.—5th ed.
p. cm.
Rev. ed. of: Nursing & the law/Ann M. Rhodes, Robert D. Miller,
4th ed. 1984
Includes index.
ISBN 0-8342-0570-X
1. Nursing—Law and legislation—United States. I. Trandel
-Korenchuk, Darlene Marrie. II. Rhodes, Ann M. (Ann Marie).
Nursing & the law. III. Title.
KF2915.N8R46 1997
344.73'0414—dc21
97-36619
CIP

Orders: (800) 638-8437
Customer Service: (800) 234-1660

About Aspen Publishers • For more than 35 years, Aspen has been a leading professional publisher in a variety of disciplines. Aspen's vast information resources are available in both print and electronic formats. We are committed to providing the highest quality information available in the most appropriate format for our customers. Visit Aspen's Internet site for more information resources, directories, articles, and a searchable version of Aspen's full catalog, including the most recent publications: **http://www.aspenpub.com**
Aspen Publishers, Inc. • The hallmark of quality in publishing
Member of the worldwide Wolters Kluwer group.

Editorial Resources: Bill Fogle
Library of Congress Catalog Card Number: 97-36619
ISBN: 0-8342-0570-X

Printed in the United States of America

1   2   3   4   5

Dedicated to our children—
Michael, John, Thomas and Sarah Catherine

Table of Contents

Acknowledgments

We would like to thank our secretaries Sharilyn Craddock and Debi McCall for their invaluable assistance in the preparation of this book, for their patience with the process, and their unfailing good humor with the authors.

Preface

Over the last decade the healthcare system in general, and nursing in particular, have changed dramatically. Technology has brought tremendous advancement in patient care. At the same time, the healthcare system is undergoing a fundamental reorganization from a system characterized by an open access, fee-for-service decentralized system to one driven by managed care, where integrated systems and consolidated relationships are becoming the norm. As critical players in the healthcare system, nurses have been confronted with the opportunities and challenges that these fundamental changes have presented.

As nurses in all roles continue to be patient advocates and to provide care in a highly technological society, guidance is often necessary about the changing legal landscape that nurses increasingly confront. The fifth edition of *Nursing and the Law* has been prepared with the goal of putting into context the myriad legal changes that have occurred over the last few years. The present edition presents an evolving story of the legal changes that have occurred in a wide variety of areas, from organization of the healthcare system, to informed consent, to decisions being made near the end of life. All of these areas have undergone considerable evolution over the last few years, and are presented with significant challenges as they continue to perform the very critical task of caring for patients. In fact, the greatest challenge nurses may face is continuing to provide that high level of patient care as a patient advocate in an environment of organizational change, financial constraint, and competitive pressures.

CHAPTER 1

Introduction to Law

Chapter Objectives

1. To define the nature of law
2. To outline governmental organization and function
3. To discuss the sources of law
4. To outline the organization of the court system
5. To recognize other methods of resolving disputes
6. To present the anatomy of a trial
7. To examine the role of the expert witness

Many of the decisions that nurses make in the course of their practice are affected by legal principles and have potential legal consequences. Because it is impossible to obtain legal advice before each decision, nurses must develop an understanding of the laws that regulate and affect their practice. With the extension of nursing into independent practice, administration, expanded roles, and increased responsibility for decision making, a knowledge of fundamental legal principles becomes essential for three reasons: (1) to ensure that decisions are consistent with applicable legal principles, (2) to protect the nurse from liability, and (3) to protect the rights of the patient. This chapter provides basic information about law, the legal system, and the roles of the branches of government in creating, administering, and enforcing the law to serve as a foundation for nurses to understand the legal principles that affect their practice.

NATURE OF LAW

Law has been defined a variety of ways. The essence of most definitions is that law is a system of principles and processes by which individuals who live in a society attempt to control human conduct in an effort to minimize the use of force as a means of resolving conflicting interests. Through law, society specifies standards of behavior, the means to enforce those standards, and a system for resolving conflicts.

Law is not an exact science. Lawyers frequently are unable to provide a precise answer to a legal question or to predict with accuracy the outcome of a legal conflict. Much of the law is uncertain. Some questions have never been precisely addressed by the legal system. Even when questions have been answered, the legal system may change the laws in response to changing conditions or the answer may not be generally applicable to other situations. This lack of legal certainty concerning legal issues often creates uncertainty and anxiety for nurses who must function in that system.

There are many areas of legal uncertainty in nursing practice, resulting in part from the rapid increase in technology and the continuing development of nursing as a profession. When dealing with a system as complicated as the law and with a profession that has as many facets as nursing, uncertainty is inevitable. The advice of a lawyer still is valuable, however, because the attorney can apply knowledge of how the law has addressed similar questions and thus predict the most probable answer. After a dispute has arisen, a lawyer is essential in ensuring that the dispute resolution mechanisms of the law are used to the advantage of the client.

Laws govern the relationships of private individuals with each other and with government. The body of law that deals with the relationships between private individuals is called *civil law,* whereas that involving relationships between private individuals and the government is termed *public law* but are based on societal standards of behavior.

Civil law involves the recognition and enforcement of rights and duties of private individuals and organizations. It can be divided into contract law and tort law. Contract law involves the enforcement of certain agreements among private individuals (e.g., the terms of employment for a nurse or the payment of compensation or damages for failing to fulfill those agreements). Tort law is concerned with the definition and enforcement of duties and rights among private individuals that are not based on contractual agreements but are based on societal standards of behavior and include nursing malpractice.

Public law defines, regulates, and enforces the relationships of individuals with government and governmental agencies. One important segment of public law is criminal law, which proscribes conduct deemed injurious to the public order such as misuse of controlled substances and provides for punishment of those found to have engaged in such conduct. This punishment includes both monetary penalties and loss of freedom through incarceration. Public law also includes an enormous variety of regulations designed to enhance societal objectives by requiring private individuals and organizations to follow specified courses of action in connection with their activities, such as obtaining informed consent for patients in experimental protocols. Although noncompliance with these regulations can lead to criminal penalties, the basic thrust of public law is to obtain compliance and attain the goals of the law, not to punish offenders.

The law serves as a guide to conduct, because most disputes or controversies between persons or organizations are resolved without lawyers or courts. The existence of the legal system is a stimulus to orderly private resolution of disputes. The likelihood of success in court affects the willingness of persons to negotiate private settlements. Knowledge of the sources and application of the law, therefore, is important for nurses who may become involved in disputes or controversies, even if those disputes are unlikely to go to court.

GOVERNMENTAL ORGANIZATION AND FUNCTION

This section focuses on the structure of the three branches of government—legislative, executive, and judicial; how the functions of one branch relate to those of the two others; and the effect of each on nursing practice. Put succinctly, the legislature makes the laws, the executive branch enforces the laws, and the judiciary interprets the laws. Frequently, the functions of the branches overlap in practice.

A vital concept in the constitutional framework of the U.S. government and of the state governments is that of separation of powers. This means that no one of the three branches is clearly dominant over the two others; however, in the exercise of its functions, each may affect and limit the activities, functions, and powers of the others.

The concept of separation of power—the system of controlling the dispersion of powers or system of checks and balances—is illustrated in the relationships among the three branches in regard to legislation. On the federal level, Congress enacts a statute, but until the President signs it or it is passed over his veto by a two-thirds vote of each house in Congress, it does not become law, except when he allows it to become law without taking any action while Congress is in session. Thus, by his veto, the President can prevent a bill from becoming law temporarily and possibly prevent it from becoming law at all. At the same time, the President can suggest or promote a course of action by Congress but cannot compel such action. A bill that has become law ultimately may be declared valid or invalid by the U.S. Supreme Court, the top entity in the judicial branch of the government, because the Court decides that the law is not (or is) in violation of the Constitution.

Individuals nominated by the President for appointment to the federal judiciary, including the Supreme Court, must be approved by the Senate. Thus, over time, both the executive and legislative branches can affect the composition of the judicial branch of government. In addition, although a Supreme Court decision may be final with regard to the specific controversy before the Court, Congress and the President may generate revised legislation to replace the law that was held unconstitutional. The processes for amending the Constitution are complex and lengthy, but they too can serve as a method of offsetting or overriding a Supreme Court decision.

Functions of the Legislative Branch

Each of the three branches of government has a different primary function. The function of the legislative branch (Congress or state legislatures) is to enact laws that may amend or replace existing statutes or may be entirely new legislation. The legislature determines the nature and extent of the need for new laws and for changes in existing ones. Congress and legislatures use a committee system under which proposed bills are assigned or referred for study to committees with described areas of concern or interest. The committees conduct investigations and hold hearings, at which persons may present their views, to obtain information to assist their members in considering the bills. Some bills eventually reach the full legislative body where, after consideration and debate, they are either approved or rejected. Congress and every state legislature consists of two houses (except Nebraska, which has a unicameral body—only one house). Both houses must pass identical versions of a bill before it can go to the chief executive. Differences usually are resolved by a joint conference committee. Much of the legislation passed by Congress and state legislatures has greatly affected the way that nurses have performed their roles—from Medicare, to licensure of nurses, to major employment legislation effecting the workplace of nurses.

Functions of the Executive Branch

The primary function of the executive branch of government is to enforce and administer the law. The chief executive, either the governor of a state or the President of the United States, has a role in the creation of law through the power to approve or veto a legislative proposal. If the chief executive accepts a bill through the constitutionally established process, it becomes a statute, a part of the enacted law. If the chief executive vetoes the bill, it can become law only if the legislature overrides the veto.

The executive branch is organized on a departmental basis in which each department is responsible for a different area of public concern, and each enforces the law within its area of responsibility. Most federal law pertaining to nursing is administered by the Department of Health and Human Services. In the states, regulation of nursing practice is delegated to the state board of nursing. The state board of nursing establishes rules and regulations that provide oversight to the practice of nursing in a state. Most states also have separate departments for health and welfare matters that administer and enforce most state laws pertaining to health care. However, other departments and agencies of government also affect nursing care and practice. On the federal level, for example, laws relating to wages and hours of employment are enforced by the Department of Labor.

Functions of the Judicial Branch

The function of the judicial branch is adjudication, the resolution of disputes in accordance with law. How these suits are resolved provides guidance to others about their conduct. When a patient brings a suit against a hospital or nurse seeking compensation for harm allegedly suffered as the result of wrongful conduct, the suit is decided by the courts. Many other types of disputes involving hospitals come before the courts as well.

For example, hospitals resort to the courts to challenge exercises of authority by government agencies and departments, to dispute legislation affecting hospitals, to collect unpaid hospital bills, and to enforce contracts. Although news of litigation brought by patients or the government against hospitals receives the greatest attention from the public, very often the hospital initiates a suit to enforce a right or protect a legally recognized interest.

Many disputes and controversies are resolved without resort to the courts, such as by arbitration or informal nonbinding means such as mediation. In many situations, however, there is no way to end a controversy without submitting it to the adjudicatory process of the courts. A dispute brought before a court is decided in accordance with applicable law. This application of the law to dispute resolution is the essence of the judicial process. Although most nurses are never involved directly in the judicial process, the implication of many court rulings have greatly effected the practice of nursing

SOURCES OF LAW

The U.S. Constitution

The Constitution of the United States is the supreme law of the land. It establishes the general organization of the federal government, grants certain powers to it, and places certain limits on what federal and state governments may do. The Constitution establishes and grants certain powers to the three branches of the federal government and creates the separation of powers described earlier.

The Constitution is a grant of power from the states to the federal government. The federal government has only the power granted to it by the Constitution. These powers are both express and implied. The express powers include, for example, the power to collect taxes, declare war, and regulate interstate commerce. The Constitution also grants the federal government broad implied powers to enact laws "necessary and proper" for exercising its other powers.

The Constitution also places certain limits on what the federal and state government may do. The best-known limits on federal power are the first 10 amendments of the Constitution, the Bill of Rights. The Bill of Rights protects the right to free speech; free exercise of religion; freedom from unreasonable searches and seizures; trial by jury; and the right not to be deprived of life, liberty, or property without due process of law. The most famous limits on state power appear in the Fourteenth Amendment: ". . . nor shall any state deprive any person of life, liberty, or property, without due process of law; nor deny to any person within its jurisdiction the equal protection of the laws." These frequently are referred to as the due process clause and the equal protection clause.

The due process clause restricts state action, not private action. Actions by state and local governmental agencies, including public hospitals, are considered state actions and must comply with due process requirements. Actions by private individuals at the behest of the state also can be subject to these requirements. Private hospitals sometimes are considered to be engaged in state action when they are regulated or partially funded by government agencies.

The due process clause applies to state actions that deprive a person of "life, liberty, or property." This is interpreted to include such liberty and property interests as a physician's appointment to the medical staff of a public hospital and a nurse's licensure from the state. Thus, in some situations public hospitals must provide due process, and in other situations nurses are protected by the requirement that state and local governmental agencies provide due process.

The process that is due varies somewhat, depending on the situation. Its two primary elements are (1) the rules being applied must be reasonable and not vague and (2) fair procedures must be followed in enforcing the rules. Rules that are too arbitrary or vague violate the due process clause and are not enforceable. The primary procedural protections that must be offered are notice of the proposed action and an opportunity to present information on why the action should not be taken. The phrase *due process* in the Fourteenth Amendment also has been interpreted by the Supreme Court to include nearly all the rights in the Bill of Rights. Thus, state governments may not infringe on those rights.

State Constitutions

Each state has its own constitution. That document, as noted, establishes the organization of the state government, grants certain powers to it, and places certain limits on what it may do.

Statutes

Another major source of law is statutory law—measures that are enacted by a legislature. Legislative bodies include the U.S. Congress, state legislatures, and local legislative bodies such as city councils or county boards of supervisors. Congress has only the powers delegated to it by the Constitution, but those powers have been interpreted broadly. State legislatures have all powers not denied by the U.S. Constitution, by federal laws enacted under the authority of the federal government, or by the state constitution. Local legislative bodies have only those powers granted by the state.

The regulation of nursing practice is a function of state law. Consequently, the state legislature has the authority to pass the statutes that define and regulate nursing. Most nurses will have contact with state statutes through their licensure by the state. The nurse practice act of a state must be consistent with applicable constitutional and federal provisions to be valid. In practice, however, it is unusual for a state to pass a law regulating nursing that would violate some federal requirement. Accordingly, the states have great flexibility to regulate nursing practice.

Administrative Agencies: Decisions and Rules

The decisions and rules of administrative agencies are another source of law. Legislatures have delegated the responsibility and power to implement various laws to numerous administrative agencies. The example of the relationship between the legislature and the administrative agency that is most familiar to nurses is the state board of nursing, which implements and enforces the nurse practice act of a state. The powers of an administrative agency include the quasi-legislative power to adopt regulations and the quasi-judicial power to decide how the statutes and regulations apply to individual cases.

The legislature has delegated these powers because it does not have the time or the expertise to address the complex issues involved in many areas that it believes need to be regulated. Administrative agencies that have been delegated such powers include, for example, on the federal level, the Department of Health and Human Services and its agencies, the Food and Drug Administration, the National Labor Relations Board, and the Internal Revenue Service. On the state level, administrative agencies such as the board of nursing oversee the practice of the professions and regulate various aspects of commerce and public welfare.

All these agencies have the power to promulgate regulations and apply these to individual cases within their area of expertise. Many administrative agencies, such as state boards of nursing, seek to achieve some consistency in their decisions by following the position they adopted in previous cases involving similar matters. This is similar to the way that courts develop the common law (discussed later in this chapter).

Congress and many state legislatures have passed administrative procedure acts. These specify the procedures that administrative agencies must follow in promulgating rules or reaching decisions in contested cases, unless another law specifies different procedures. Generally, these laws provide that most proposed rules must be published to allow an opportunity for public comment before they are finalized. Many federal agencies must publish both proposed and final rules in the *Federal Register,* and many states have comparable publications in which, for example, a state board of nursing would publish rules regulating nursing practice.

Court Decisions

Judicial decisions are another source of law. These are the result of the role of the court in dispute resolution. In deciding cases, the courts interpret statutes and regulations, determine their validity under the appropriate constitution, and create the common law when deciding cases that are not controlled by statutes, regulations, or a constitution. These decisions act as guidelines for future action.

There frequently is disagreement over the application of statutes or regulations to specific situations. In some cases, an administrative agency has the initial authority to decide how they shall be applied; its decision usually can be appealed to the courts. Courts generally defer to such agencies in discretionary matters, limiting their review to whether the delegation of power to the entity was constitutional and whether it acted within its authority, followed proper procedures, had a substantial basis for its decision, and acted without arbitrariness or discrimination.

Whether or not an administrative agency is involved, the court still may have to interpret a statute or regulation or decide which of two or more conflicting ones apply. Courts have developed rules for interpretation of statutes. In some states, a statute specifies rules of interpretation that are designed to help determine the intent of the legislature in passing the law.

The courts also determine whether specific statutes or regulations violate the Constitution. All legislation and regulations must be consistent with the Constitution. The case of *Marbury v. Madison*[1] in 1803 established the power of the courts to declare legislation invalid when it is unconstitutional.

Many of the legal principles and rules applied by the courts in the United States are the product of the common law developed in England and, subsequently, in this country. The term *common law* is applied to the body of principles that evolves from court decisions resolving controversies. Common law is continually being adapted and expanded. During the colonial period, English common law applied uniformly. After the Revolution, each state provided for the adoption of part of or all of the then-existing English common law. All subsequent common law in the United States has been developed on a state basis, so on specific subjects the law may differ from state to state. Statutory laws are enacted to restate many legal rules and principles that initially were established by the courts as part of the common law. Many issues, particularly those pertaining to disputes in private law areas, still are decided according to common law rules. A state may change these rules by legislation modifying such principles or by later court decisions that establish new and different common law rules.

In deciding specific controversies, courts, for the most part, adhere to the doctrine of *stare decisis,* literally, "to stand by things decided" but usually called "following precedent." Applying the same rules and principles as in similar cases decided previously, the court arrives at the same ruling in the current case. However, slight differences in the situation presented may provide a basis for recognizing distinctions between precedent and a current case. Even when such factual distinctions are absent, a court may conclude that a particular common law rule no longer is in accord with the needs of society and may depart from the precedent.

One clear example of this departure from precedent in health care law was the reconsideration and elimination in nearly every state of the principle of charitable immunity, which had provided nonprofit hospitals and, accordingly, the nurses they employ with virtual freedom from liability for harm to patients resulting from wrongful conduct. In state after state over 30 years, courts found bases to overrule precedents that had provided immunity and, thereby, allowed suits against nonprofit hospitals. This has, in turn, expanded the liability of nonprofit hospitals for the acts of their nursing employees.

ORGANIZATION OF THE COURT SYSTEM

To understand the effect of court decisions as precedents, it is necessary to understand the structure of the court system. There are more than 50 court systems in the United States, including the system of the federal government, each state, the District of Columbia, Puerto Rico, and the territories. These courts do not all reach the same decisions on specific issues. Frequently, there are a majority approach and several minority opinions on each issue. Thus, careful review is necessary to determine which decisions of a particular court apply to any area of controversy and, if no decisions apply specifically, to predict which approach is likely to be adopted.

The federal and many state court systems have three levels—trial courts, intermediate courts of appeal, and a supreme court. Some states do not have intermediate courts of appeals.

State Court Systems

The trial courts in some states are divided into special courts that deal with specific issues such as family, juvenile, and probate and limited ones that deal only with lesser crimes such as misdemeanors or with civil cases involving limited amounts of money. Each state has trial courts of general jurisdiction that may decide all disputes not assigned to other courts or barred from them by state or federal law. The trial courts of general jurisdiction are where most nursing professional liability actions are heard.

At the trial court level, applicable law is determined and the evidence is assessed to determine what the "facts" are. The applicable law then is applied to those facts. It is the judge's role to determine what the law is. If there is a jury, the judge instructs the jury as to what the law is, and the jury determines what the facts are. In either case, the determination of the facts must be based on the evidence properly admitted during the trial, so the facts are not necessarily what actually happened.

In some cases, everyone agrees on the facts, and the only issues presented to the court concern what the law is. In other cases, everyone agrees what the law is, but there is disagreement over the facts. To determine the facts for purposes of deciding the case, the credibility of the witnesses and the weight to be given other evidence must be determined. Many cases involve both questions of law and questions of fact. The judge has significant control over the trial even when a jury is involved. If the judge finds that insufficient evidence has been presented to establish a factual issue for the jury to resolve, the judge can dismiss the case or, in civil cases, direct the jury to decide the case a specific way. In civil cases, even after the jury has decided, the judge can decide in favor of the other side.

Most state court systems have an intermediate appellate court. Usually, this court decides only appeals from trial court decisions. In some states, a few issues can be taken directly to the intermediate appellate court. When an appellate court is deciding appeals, it does not accept additional evidence but makes its decisions based on the evidence presented at the trial court and preserved in that record.

Appellate courts almost invariably accept the determination of the facts by the jury or judge in the trial court because they saw the witnesses and can better judge their credibility. Appellate courts usually base their decisions on whether proper procedures were followed in the trial court and whether it interpreted the law properly. However, an appellate court occasionally will find that a jury verdict is so clearly contrary to the evidence that it will either reverse the decision or order a new trial.

Each state has a single court at the highest level, usually called the supreme court (although in New York, the highest state level is the court of appeals). The highest court in each state decides appeals from the intermediate appellate courts or, in states without the intermediate level, from trial courts. The highest court frequently has other duties, including adopting rules of procedures for the state court system and determining who may practice law in the state, which includes disciplining lawyers for improper conduct.

Federal Court System

The federal court system has a structure similar to the states. The trial courts are the U.S. District Courts and special-purpose courts, such as the court of claims, which determines certain claims against the United States. Federal trial courts are fundamentally different from those in the states because they have limited jurisdiction. To be heard in federal court, a suit must either present a federal question or must be between citizens of different states. In many types of cases, the controversy must involve at least $10,000. Federal questions include cases on the application of federal statutes and regulations involving possible violations of rights under the Constitution. Actions regarding the application of federal equal employment opportunity laws to nurses as employees are examples of cases brought in federal court. When a federal trial court decides a controversy between citizens of different states, it is acting under what is called its "diversity jurisdiction," by using federal procedures but applying the law of the applicable state.

Appeals from the federal trial courts go to a U.S. Court of Appeals. The United States is divided into 13 areas, called circuits, numbered 1 through 12, plus the District of Columbia circuit.

The highest level is the U.S. Supreme Court. It decides appeals from the U.S. Court of Appeals and from the highest state courts if they involve federal laws or the Constitution. Sometimes, when the highest state courts or the courts of appeals decline to review a lower court decision, it can be appealed directly to the U.S. Supreme Court.

Generally, cases involving issues of nursing practice are not appealed to the Supreme Court because these issues emerge in actions involving either torts or licensing sanctions. Both of those types of cases fall under state law and usually do not involve constitutional principles.

The U.S. Supreme Court has the authority to decline to review most cases and accepts only a small percentage of those presented. With only a few exceptions, a request of review is made by filing a petition for a writ of certiorari ("cert.," as it is called). If the writ of certiorari is granted, the record of the lower court decision is transmitted to the Supreme Court for review. In most cases, the Supreme Court denies the writ of certiorari. Denial of a writ of certiorari does not indicate approval of the lower court decision; it merely means the Supreme Court declines to review that decision.

STARE DECISIS

The preceding description illustrates the complexity of the court system in the United States. When a court is confronted with an issue, it is bound by the doctrine of *stare decisis* to follow the precedents of higher courts in the same system that have jurisdiction over the geographic area where the court is located. Each appellate court, including the highest court, is generally also bound to follow the precedents of its own decisions, unless it decides to overrule the precedent because of changing conditions. The concept of *stare decisis* is applied vertically but not horizontally; thus decisions from equal or lower courts or from courts in other systems do not have to be followed. For example, an Illinois trial court would be bound by the decisions of the higher Illinois courts (i.e., the state appellate courts and supreme court) but would not be bound by decisions of other Illinois trial courts or by the decisions of out-of-state courts.

When a court is confronted with a question that is not answered by applicable statute or regulation and that has not been addressed by its court system or when it wants to reexamine its decision on a subject it has addressed, it usually will examine the solutions reached in the other systems to help decide the new issue. There is general tendency toward consistency. A clear trend in decisions across the country can form a basis for reasonable legal assessment of how to act even when the courts in a particular jurisdiction have not yet decided the issue. However, a court is not bound by decisions from other systems and may reach a different conclusion. When facts of a case vary from the precedent, courts can exercise flexibility in modifying the legal rules. Or the courts may decide to overturn their own earlier decisions completely, such as the Supreme Court of Pennsylvania, which overruled its own rule and precedent that had provided immunity from tort liability and, thereby, allowed suits against nonprofit hospitals and their staff in cases of negligence.[2]

Differences in statutes and regulations may force courts in different states to reach different conclusions on certain questions. Some decisions, therefore, are so specific to the statutory or regulatory law of the state that they would not be considered by other courts facing the same issue.

In summary, although it is important to be aware of trends in court decisions across the country, nurses should seek legal advice before taking actions based on decisions from court systems that do not have jurisdiction over the geographic area in which they practice.

OTHER METHODS OF RESOLVING DISPUTES

Two other methods in addition to the court system exist for resolving disputes. First, adjudication of legal rights as defined by administrative law is carried out by administrative agencies created by statute or constitution. Hence, many private disputes are not heard in the court system and are resolved through administrative law. For instance, when a nurse acts contrary to the regulations of the nurse practice act, the state board of nursing adjudicates the claim.

A second, more efficient and economic method of resolving disputes is through the use of arbitration or mediation. Both arbitration and mediation bypass the court system and use an impartial referee to settle the dispute. Decisions rendered in arbitration are usually binding on the parties. Mediation seeks to resolve disputes through a nonbinding process.

ANATOMY OF A TRIAL

As mentioned previously, court decisions emerge from the resolution of disputes through a lawsuit that is tried in court. The goal of a trial is to reach an orderly resolution of a dispute between two or more parties who have differing interests. The procedure is designed to ascertain facts by hearing evidence, determine which facts are relevant, apply the appropriate principles of law, and pass judgment based on the facts and the applicable law. The many procedural steps in a lawsuit can be divided into six major steps: commencement, pleading, pretrial, trial, appeal, and execution of judgment. This process would be followed in the typical nursing professional liability action.

Commencement of the Action

Lawsuits must be brought within a certain time limit that has been prescribed by law in a statute of limitations—a time span that varies with the cause of action. For example, in some states, a suit to recover damages for personal injury caused by nursing negligence of a nurse must be brought within two years of the injury. If a case is not brought within the prescribed time, the action is barred.

The first necessary element in the trial process is a person who believes a cause of action exists against another person. The first person, called the plaintiff, brings the action and makes the complaint; the defendant is the person against whom the suit is brought. Many cases have multiple plaintiffs and defendants, such as in personal injury actions where the patient and family members bring suit against the hospital, nurses, and physicians. Additional plaintiffs and defendants may be added as the lawsuit progresses.

The first step is to determine what kind of legal action may be instituted. If the controversy involves the performance of a contract, the proper action is for breach of contract, whereas if a person claims to have been injured by the negligent conduct of another, the correct action would be for negligence. The second step leading to trial is to determine where the suit will be filed. The choice depends on two factors: (1) which court has jurisdiction over the subject of the controversy and (2) which geographic district includes the area where one of the parties resides or where the alleged injury occurred.

There are two major methods by which a lawsuit may begin. First, in some courts an action is commenced by filing an order with the court clerk to issue a paper, called a writ or summons, to the sheriff (or other designated official). This orders the sheriff to inform the defendants that they must appear before the court on a particular date. In the second method, used in many states and in federal courts, suits are begun by filing and delivery of the complaint itself, which is called service.

On service of the summons or complaint, the defendant(s) such as a nurse should promptly notify his or her attorneys or insurance companies. The attorneys for the defendant will investigate, decide on a strategy, and respond to the complaint. Prompt notice by the defendant to the insurance company for professional liability actions also may be required as a prerequisite to coverage.

Pleading

Once the action is commenced, each party must present a statement of facts, or pleadings, to the court. The modern system of pleading requires a setting forth of the facts, which serves to notify the other party of the basis for the legal claim. The first pleading is the complaint, in which the plaintiff outlines the factual basis for the claim.

A copy then is served on the defendant, who must reply within a specified time period, usually 15 or 20 days. If the defendant fails to answer within that time, the plaintiff will win by default, and a judgment may be entered against the defendant. When particular circumstances exist, a default and a judgment may be entered against the defendant. In certain instances, a default judgment will be set aside if the defendant can demonstrate valid reasons for failing to respond.

On receiving a copy of the complaint, the defendant also has the right to file preliminary objections before answering the complaint. In these objections, the defendant cites possible errors that would defeat the plaintiff's case. For example, the defendant may object that the summons or complaint was improperly served, that the action was brought in the wrong county, or that there was something technically wrong in the document. The court may permit the plaintiff to correct the errors by filing a new or amended complaint; however, in some instances, the defects may be so significant that the case is dismissed.

The defendant also may present a motion to dismiss the action, alleging that the complaint does not set forth a claim or cause of action recognized by law. If the case is dismissed, the plaintiff has the right to amend the complaint or appeal the action of the lower court to an appellate court. However, if the court declines to dismiss the case, the defendant then is required to file an answer to the complaint.

In some cases, the defendant may have a claim against the plaintiff and will file a counterclaim. For example, the plaintiff may have sued a hospital for personal injuries and property damage caused by a collision of an automobile owned by the hospital and driven by a visiting nurse. The hospital may file a counterclaim on the grounds that its nurse was careful and that it was the plaintiff who was responsible for the accident and should be liable to the hospital for damages.

When the defendant has filed an answer, the plaintiff generally can file preliminary objections to that answer. The plaintiff may assert that the counterclaim is legally insufficient, the form of the answer is defective, or the counterclaim cannot be asserted in the court in which the case is pending. These objections are addressed by the court.

Pretrial Procedures

After the pleadings are completed, many states permit either party to move for a judgment based on the pleadings. The court then will examine the entire case and decide whether to enter judgment according to the merits of the case as indicated in the pleadings. In some states, the moving party is permitted to introduce sworn statements, called affidavits, showing that a claim or defense is false. This procedure cannot be used when there is substantial dispute concerning the matters presented by the affidavits.

In federal courts, as well as in most state courts, the parties have the right to discovery—the examination of witnesses before trial. It is during this process of discovery, which can last from several weeks to several years, that the nurse is most likely to become involved in the case, as either a witness or an expert witness.

The usual manner of conducting the discovery is to present questions to the opposing parties and witnesses. Interrogatories are questionnaires that are answered under oath, usually in writing, concerning the facts of the case. When the interrogatories are presented orally by an attorney, the answers, also given under oath, are called a deposition. The deposition not only is a method of discovering the strength of the other party's case, but it can also be used in court if a witness is unable to be present, and it can be used to impeach the testimony of a witness. For these reasons, nurses need to answer questions presented in the deposition very carefully and as if they were in a court of law. Nurses who are called for a deposition should meet with their attorney, who is often supplied by their employer. This preparation time in advance of the deposition is an important part of being a good witness.

Other methods of discovery include a court order by either party permitting the examination and reproduction of books and records such as medical records and nursing notes. A court order may be obtained to allow the physical or mental examination of a party when that condition is important to the case. This method of discovery is used when the physical or mental condition of a person is in dispute and good reason exists for such an examination.

The Trial

At the trial, as noted earlier, the facts of the case are determined through evidence presented, the principles of law relating to those facts are applied, and a conclusion is reached. Evidence presented consists of witnesses' answers to questions on direct examination or cross-examination; it also may include equipment, instruments, devices, and other tangible items that have a bearing on the case.

Generally, witnesses are persons who have a direct connection with some part of the case. A witness may have seen certain events take place or heard one of the parties say something. In highly technical cases, in which the ordinary layman is not qualified to appreciate or properly evaluate the significance of the facts, witnesses who qualify as experts in their particular field are called. This is typical in cases involving negligence claims in nursing or medical care. The expert witnesses state opinions in answer to hypothetical or theoretical questions.

At the start of the trial, a jury (if there is to be one) is selected. A number of apparently qualified individuals are selected as a panel, from which the jury is chosen and sworn. The attorneys then make opening statements. This practice may vary slightly from state to state, but usually the statement indicates what each side intends to prove.

The attorney for the plaintiff then calls the first witness for that side and direct examination begins. When the direct examination is completed, the opposing attorney may cross-examine the witness in an effort to challenge or disprove the testimony. The attorney for the plaintiff then may ask the witness additional questions in an effort to overcome the effect of the cross-examination. Subsequently, the other witnesses for the plaintiff are questioned. The attorney for the plaintiff also introduces other evidence such as documents and tangible items.

After the entire case of the plaintiff has been presented, the defendant may move for a directed verdict in its favor on the ground that the plaintiff has failed to present sufficient facts to prove the case or that the evidence does not supply a legal basis for a verdict in favor of the plaintiff. If the motion is overruled, the case of the defendant is presented in the same manner as the case of the plaintiff.

Either party then may ask the judge to rule that the claim has not been proved or that a defense has not been established and direct the jury to render a verdict to that effect. If these motions are overruled, the attorneys make oral arguments to the jury, and the judge instructs the jury on the appropriate law. This practice varies greatly from state to state and even from judge to judge. Some judges summarize the facts, integrate them with the applicable legal principles, and comment on the evidence as well. Other judges merely state the controlling legal principles. The jury then retires to a separate place to deliberate and reach a verdict; when it has done so, it reports to the judge, who then renders a judgment based on the verdict.

At the time the judgment is rendered, the losing party has an opportunity to move for a new trial. If a new trial is granted, the entire process if repeated; if not, the judgment becomes final, subject to a review of the trial record by an appellate court if the losing side appeals.

Appeals

An appellate court reviews a case on the basis of the trial record as well as written summaries of the applicable legal principles and short oral arguments by the attorneys. The court then takes the case under advisement while the judges consider it and agree on a decision. They then issue an opinion explaining their reasons. Appellate court decisions and opinions are usually published and are a source of continuing legal information for lawyers, who, relying in part on *stare decisis,* can prepare themselves to render advice to their clients by referring to similar cases that have been decided earlier.

Execution of Judgments

In lawsuits naming nurses or hospitals as defendants, a party generally will seek to recover money damages. Other forms of relief are available, such as an order or an injunction requiring the defendant to perform or refrain from performing an act. The jury decides the amount of damages, subject to review by an appellate court.

If, after the trial and final appeal, the defendant does not comply with the judgment in the suit, the plaintiff may cause the judgment to be executed. This means that if the defendant ignores an order to perform or refrain from performing an act, the failure to obey will be regarded as contempt of court and will result in a fine or imprisonment. If the judgment is for payment of money, the plaintiff may cause the sheriff or other judicial officer to sell so much of the property of the defendant as is necessary to pay the judgment and court costs.

THE EXPERT WITNESS

In court, the general rule is that witnesses must testify only to facts—their opinions and conclusions are inadmissible. However, it is obvious that some cases may involve information of a technical nature that is outside the knowledge and experience of the ordinary person. In such cases, an expert witness who has special knowledge, skill, experience, or training is called on to submit an opinion.

In negligence actions, expert testimony falls into two categories: (1) on the extent of damage and (2) on the standard of care. Both areas require specialized knowledge and experience for a witness to render an opinion. The questions of how much and what type of training and experience qualifies a person to be an expert witness is a difficult one. The American Law Institute suggests the following definition:

> A witness is an expert witness and qualified to give expert testimony if the judge finds that to perceive, know or understand the matter concerning which the witness is to testify requires special knowledge, skill, experience or training, and that the witness has the requisite special knowledge, skill, experience or training.

In practice, when it becomes evident that expert testimony is required, the attorneys for each side will obtain the services of experts. When testifying, the training, experience, and special qualifications of the experts are explained to the jury. The experts then are asked to give an opinion on hypothetical questions based on the facts of the case. It is up to the jury to decide which expert opinion to accept.

Increasingly, questions arise in malpractice litigation that involve both the appropriate scope of nursing practice and the standard of care. Expert testimony is used to clarify these issues for the jury. Nurses, especially those with specialized, supervisory, or teaching experience, may be asked to testify as experts. Supervisory nurses may be asked to describe the standard of nursing care when another nurse is being sued for negligence. This provides the jury with a standard against which to measure the conduct of the defendant nurse. The actual conduct will be established by documentary and testimonial evidence.

After answering questions for the party that called the expert, the individual may be questioned and challenged by the opposing attorney. The attorney who called the expert is expected to object to improper questions by the other attorney. In the event of an objection, the witness refrains from answering until the judge upholds or denies the objection and directs that the witness answer or until the attorney withdraws the question.

CONCLUSION

This chapter has described the nature and sources of law, the structure of the court system, and the anatomy of a trial and discussed briefly some of the ways in which nurses are likely to have contact with the legal system. Most commonly, a nurse will be involved in possible or pending litigation as a witness. The nurse may have been involved in or observed some incident or behavior that gives rise to a cause of action, or may have provided care to the patient before or after the incident took place. If this occurs, it is advisable that the employed nurse contact the attorney of his or her employer before discussing the case with either party.

If the case proceeds to a trial, expert testimony on the standard of nursing care will be required. Nurses with specialized education or extensive experience may be contacted to provide such testimony.

Another way a nurse may have contact with the legal system is by committing prohibited acts. This can subject the nurse to criminal liability under the criminal code of a state, civil liability, or licensing sanctions. These sanctions are described more thoroughly in Chapter 2.

FOOTNOTES

1. 5 U.S. (1 Cranch 137) (1803).
2. Flagiello v. Pennsylvania Hosp., 417 Pa. 486, 510-11, 208 A.2d 193, 205 (1965).

Licensure, Certification, and Scope of Practice

Chapter Objectives

1. To examine individual licensure
2. To discuss private credentialing
3. To look at hospital credentials for advanced practice nurses
4. To compare physician assistants and the nursing profession

---

A complex system of licensing and credentialing has developed in an attempt to ensure that qualified individuals are engaged in the practice of the health care professions. All states require licensure for individuals who wish to practice nursing, and most have instituted licensing mechanisms for advanced or specialized nursing practice. The primary purpose of licensure and credentialing is to protect the public health by helping identify qualified providers and by prohibiting unqualified ones from engaging in practices that require expertise.

There are many public and private credentialing methods. The public method is individual licensure—the method used to ensure at least minimal competence in nursing practice in all states. Private methods include accreditation of educational programs, certification of individuals, and credentialing by institution. This chapter discusses state licensure of nurses, the statutory definitions of nursing, and the role of nursing state boards in the implementation of the public credentialing method. Private credentialing is examined as it relates to nursing education programs, health care institutions, and professional nursing organizations.

INDIVIDUAL LICENSURE

Licensure can be defined as the process by which a legal authority grants permission to a qualified individual or entity to perform certain activities that are declared to be illegal without a license. In the context of health care delivery, licensure is the process by which state-authorized licensing agencies grant the legal right to practice a health profession such as nursing to individuals who meet predetermined standards.

There is considerable variation in the occupations licensed by each state, but nurses are licensed in all states. In many states, physicians and dentists were the first health professionals to be licensed, with nurses generally next. Pharmacists also are licensed in all states. Many other professionals and technicians are licensed in many states, including physical therapists, psychologists, audiologists, emergency medical technicians, and radiologic technicians. In some states, staff members of certain types of hospitals are exempt from some licensure requirements.

Most nurse practice acts provide for the imposition of a penalty for practicing without a license, including a fine and/or imprisonment. The term *scope of practice* refers to the legally permissible boundaries of practice for the health care provider and is defined in each state to statute, rule, or a combination of the two. Mandatory licensure laws reserve a certain scope of practice for those who obtain a license. The definition and evolution of the scope of practice for nurses have been controversial, focusing on two broad issues: (1) who may make the judgment that certain procedures may be performed? and (2) who may perform the procedures?

The nurse generally determines what nursing care is required by the patient's status and condition and when care is insufficient so that medical attention or instructions must be sought. Nursing practice is different from medical practice, and this distinction has been recognized in state statutes for some time.

Definition of Nursing Practice

The entry of nurse practitioners and nurse specialists into the health field, advances in nursing education, and the changing role of the nurse in performing functions previously considered the practice of medicine have stimulated revision of nurse and medical practice acts. States have been updating the definition of professional nursing in nurse practice acts. Additional legislative changes granting authority to nursing have been made.

Historical definitions illustrate that nurses' orientation is to the promotion of the well-being of the people being served, whether that involves care of the sick or promotion of health. A 1980 definition that incorporates the concept of care for persons at all levels of wellness is: "Nursing is the diagnosis and treatment of human responses to actual or potential health problems." This definition appears in the American Nurses Association (ANA) *Social Policy Statement.*[1] In 1955, the ANA adopted the following definition, which has become the basis for many states' nurse practice acts:

> The term "practice of professional nursing" means the performance, for compensation, of any acts in the observation, care, and counsel of the ill,

injured, or infirm, or in the maintenance of health or prevention of illness in others or in the supervision and teaching of other personnel, or
the administration of medications and treatments prescribed by a licensed physician or dentist, requiring substantial specialized judgment
and skill and based on knowledge and application of the principles of
biological, physical, and social science.[2]

There are three general approaches to the statutory definition of nursing. The
first, or traditional, approach is based on that 1955 model definition. The traditional definition of nursing does not encompass diagnosis, prescription, or treatment. Generally, this approach is used in states that have not addressed the issue of
scope of practice for the advanced or expanded practitioners. The approach is relatively rare as most states have adopted statutes or rules regulating advanced practice. The second approach in effect in a few states authorized nurses to perform
additional acts beyond the traditional definition and typically allows them to practice under standing orders or under the supervision of the physician. A few states
have corresponding "delegatory amendments" to the medical practice act that authorize nurses to perform delegated medical tasks under the physician's supervision. The third approach, which most states use, is administrative. This includes a
definition of nursing that expands upon the ANA statement and allows nurses to
perform such additional acts as may be authorized by appropriate state regulatory
agencies.

Nurse practitioners and nurses practicing in expanded roles are regulated by the
nurse practice act in each state or by rules adopted by the state licensing agency.
Many statutes specifically prohibit nurses from performing "medical" acts such as
medical diagnosis and prescription of treatment, but there is a growing trend toward amending the laws to permit the performance of medical acts or "additional
acts" recognized as proper by the nursing profession. These amendments generally grant authority to the state board of nursing to promulgate regulations as to
requirements for nurse practitioners and what tasks they may perform. The regulations then are administered and enforced by the board of nursing.

The legal authority for advanced practice nurses continues to expand. Nearly
one-third of the states have given the state board of nursing authority to regulate
practice of advanced practice nurses with no requirement for physician collaboration or supervision. This is a growing trend in the law. A number of other states,
nearly one-half, give the board of nursing authority to determine the scope of practice but contain a requirement for physician collaboration or supervision. Approximately four states have scope of practice issues jointly authorized by the
board of nursing and the board of medicine. The remaining states do not have
specific regulations for advanced practice nurses, but nurses in those states practice under a broadly interpreted Nurse Practice Act.[3]

The ability of advanced practice nurses to prescribe has also expanded greatly. Nearly one-half of the states now authorize advanced practice nurses to prescribe drugs, including controlled substances, based on physician supervision and collaboration. Approximately one-third of the states grant this authority for prescription with required physician supervision/collaboration but exclude controlled substances. Only a few states grant advanced practice nurses complete and independent authority to prescribe drugs, including controlled substances, and only two states have given advanced practice nurses complete and independent authority to prescribe, excluding controlled substances.[4]

Clearly, the evolution of nurse practice acts continues with an ever-increasing focus on clarifying and expanding the role of nursing practice with both legislative and regulatory efforts. It can be anticipated that this effort will continue, as nurses in the expanded role provide cost-effective alternatives to physician care on an increasingly managed care-driven health care delivery system.

The Board of Nursing

Each nurse practice act creates a regulatory agency, usually called the board of nursing. The legislature delegates to that board the authority to implement and enforce the statute. The board is responsible for determining eligibility for initial licensing and relicensing, approving and supervising educational institutions, enforcing the statute, and promulgating rules that regulate nursing practice. The board must follow the procedures specified by state law.

The governor of the state generally appoints the board members, with the categories of representatives often being specified in the legislation. Because they are expected to have expertise in nursing, the selections usually are made from a list of names submitted by professional nursing organizations. Some statutes require this advisory input from the professional organizations, but most governors solicit such recommendations even when not statutorily required to do so.

The number of board members ranges from 3 to 20, although most have no more than 10. Members usually are selected to represent some area or specialty in nursing and have a direct interest in those fields. The statute often stipulates that members must have practiced nursing in the state for a minimum number of years. Boards in some states also include one or more nonprofessional members.

The nursing licensing board, like other administrative agencies, exercises several types of authority: (1) legislative, by developing rules and regulations that govern nursing practice and are binding on all licensees; (2) quasi-judicial, to hear and decide cases involving violations of professional standards or rules; and (3) licensure control.

Nursing Licensure

The objectives of licensing laws are to limit and control admission into the health occupations and to protect the public from unqualified practitioners by promulgating and enforcing standards of practice within the profession. Nursing, along with other groups aspiring to professional status at the end of the nineteenth century, viewed licensure as a means of gaining control over the membership of the emerging profession.[5] There now is less public support for limiting the size of professions through the law, so most licensing laws must be justified on the basis of public protection. All states regulate nursing practice.

Requirements for Licensure

Because the goal of licensure is to ensure the competence of practitioners, requirements generally focus on the characteristics that are thought to ensure that the applicant is at least minimally competent. These characteristics include academic and clinical training, satisfactory performance on a licensing examination, and personal attributes.

Formal training is necessary for nursing licensure in all states. Course requirements vary, but all courses must be completed at board-approved schools or institutions. Although many state boards still adhere to their own standards for accreditation, an increasing number now accept standards established by national accrediting agencies (e.g., National Association of Pediatric Nurse Associates and Practitioners, American College of Nurse Midwives). This trend has tended to standardize the instruction program at nursing schools.

Each state requires that the applicant pass an examination for nurse licensure, which is a national standardized test. The licensing statutes also typically specify certain personal qualifications such as a minimum age, good moral character, and citizenship or an appropriate visa.

Special Licensing Procedures

Because each state has its own act, boards have had to address the issue of licensing nurses who have qualified in other states. There are four methods by which boards license such nurses: reciprocity, endorsement, examination, and waiver.

Reciprocity is a formal or informal agreement between two states that the board of each agrees to recognize licenses of the other. The initial licensing requirements of such states usually are essentially equivalent. The concept of reciprocity also is recognized in licensing sanctions. For example, in 1983 a Pennsylvania court upheld the state board's revocation of a nurse's license based on the fact that her license had been revoked in Florida under a provision similar to Pennsylvania law.[6]

Under endorsement, boards issue a license to a nurse licensed in another state if the individual's qualifications were equivalent to their own state's requirements at the time of the original licensure. As a condition for endorsement, many states require that the qualifying examination taken in the other state be comparable with their own. As with reciprocity, endorsement becomes much easier when uniform qualifications are required by the different states.

Examination and waiver are much less common than licensing by reciprocity and endorsement. Some states will not recognize prior licensure by another state and require all applicants to pass the regular examination as well as fulfill the other requirements for initial licensure. However, when applicants do not meet all the requirements for licensure but have equivalent qualifications, some of the specific educational, experience, or examination requirements may be waived.

Most states grant temporary licenses while an application or a regular license is processed or to nurses in other states who tend to be in the state for a limited time. Most commonly, temporary licenses are granted to new graduate nurses pending the outcome of the required licensing examination.

Rule Making

Boards generally have broad authority to regulate the professions they license. This authority is exercised through *rule making*—the process by which rules and regulations are promulgated to regulate and define the practice of nursing. When developing and approving rules, the board must follow the procedures specified by state law. Generally, the proposed rule must be published, and members of the profession and others must be given an opportunity to comment. Rules are valid only if they are within the authority granted to licensing boards by the legislature.

Some rules have been challenged on the ground that they are beyond the authority of the board. For example, the Washington State Nurses Association challenged a regulation of the Board of Medical Examiners that authorized physician's assistants to issue prescriptions and write medical orders for patient care. In 1980, the Washington court upheld the regulation and found that it did not exceed the board's statutory authority.[7] Some controversial rules have been found to exceed the scope of the regulatory agency's authority and have been held to be invalid on that basis. It is important for nurses to be familiar with the current positions of the board of nursing in states where they practice.

Discipline and Due Process

Licensing boards have broad authority to discipline professionals who violate the standards specified in the law or the board's rules. The discipline may be suspension or revocation of the license or a probationary period during which certain conditions must be met. Most licensing boards have been given the authority to impose various conditions, including prohibiting certain types of practice or requiring substance abuse rehabilitation efforts, consultation or supervision for various procedures, or satisfactory completion of special education programs.

Disciplinary proceedings against a nurse can be initiated in several ways, described in each state's statutes or rules. Typically, a written complaint to the board of nursing is required, setting forth the basis for the disciplinary action. The complaint can be made by anyone, including physicians, patients, and other nurses. In some states, nurses are required to report actions of other nurses that could lead to discipline.[8] Occasionally, the board of nursing initiates a complaint. Complaints are screened by the board, and if appropriate, an investigation is instituted.

The board has the authority to determine which charges to pursue and investigate. For example, in one case a patient filed a complaint demanding the revocation of the licenses of several nurses. The board said the evidence did not warrant disciplinary action. On appeal, a Pennsylvania court held that the action of the board in determining not to pursue the charges was a valid exercise of the agency's prosecutorial discretion.[9]

In disciplinary proceedings, the board's authority is limited to the areas defined by statute. In 1981, the Tennessee Court of Appeals held that the board of nursing had no jurisdiction over a licensed nurse who provided services as a lay midwife. Noting that the Tennessee Nurse Practice Act did not deal with midwifery and that midwifery was excluded from the statutory definition of medicine, the court found that the board had acted beyond the scope of its authority in revoking the nurse's license.[10]

Before imposing disciplinary sanctions, the licensing board must provide due process to the professional, including at least notice of the alleged wrongful conduct and an opportunity to present information regarding the allegations. Many states impose stricter requirements that must be followed for the board's action to be valid. Failure by the board to comply with the requirements of due process or state law can result in a court decision reversing the board's action. For example, the Colorado Supreme Court ordered a nurse's license reinstated, in part because the statute required the full licensing board to attend the hearing concerning the revocation of her license and the full board had not done so.[11] Most laws do not require the full board to be present, but if that is the law, it must be followed. Typically, a quorum of the board must either attend the hearing or review the testimony.

Another element of due process is that the licensed professional must have adequate notice that the questioned conduct is prohibited. The courts usually rule that a prohibition of "unprofessional conduct" gives adequate notice that a wide range of inappropriate behavior is forbidden. It is not considered too vague as long as it is applied to conduct that is widely recognized as unprofessional. The Oregon Supreme Court upheld the revocation of a nurse's license for "conduct derogatory to the standards of professional nursing."[12] She had instructed, recommended, and permitted her daughter to serve as a registered nurse, knowing that the daughter was not licensed as a nurse.

However, unprofessional conduct is not adequate notice for all possible violations. An Idaho nurse challenged a six-month suspension of her license for unprofessional conduct. The board of nursing had found that she had discussed laetrile treatment in a hospital with a leukemia patient on chemotherapy without the approval of the physician, interfering with the physician–patient relationship. The board considered this unprofessional conduct. The Idaho Supreme Court ruled that the board could have prohibited this conduct by rule but that a prohibition of unprofessional conduct did not give the nurse adequate warning that this conduct was prohibited. The court ordered the reinstatement of the nurse's license.[13]

A Texas court upheld a one-year suspension of a nurse's license for "unprofessional and dishonorable conduct . . . likely to deceive, defraud or injure patients."[14] The nurse had failed to check the vital signs of a patient with obvious cardiac distress and instructed the person to go to a hospital 24 miles away. The patient died en route. The court found that the nurse's behavior violated both the statute and a rule of the Texas Board of Nursing. Many licensing boards are now specifying by rule more detailed grounds for disciplinary action. Nurses should monitor these efforts closely and participate in the rule-making process to ensure that the rules do not inadvertently prohibit appropriate existing practices.

State law generally sets forth the basic grounds for disciplinary action against nurses: fraud in obtaining a license; unprofessional, illegal, dishonorable, or immoral conduct; performance of specific actions prohibited by the act; conviction of a felony or crime of moral turpitude; and drug or alcohol addiction rendering the individual incapable of performing duties. Many recent licensing cases involve drug-related offenses committed by nurses, often involving the theft or use of controlled substances from their place of employment.

The statutory authority for disciplinary action, in these cases, usually is found in the prohibition of "unprofessional conduct" in most nurse practice acts. Many courts have held that unprofessional conduct gives legally adequate notice to professionals as to what conduct is prohibited. A Minnesota court defined unprofessional conduct as "conduct which violates those standards of professional behavior which . . . have become established by the consensus of the expert opinion of the members as reasonably necessary for the protection of the public interest."[15]

The grounds for disciplinary action vary widely from state to state, so nurses must inform themselves of the general basis for license suspension or revocation in the states in which they practice. Many state boards also have developed rules to define what behavior is subject to disciplinary action. Some statutes specifically authorize judicial review of board proceedings. This right may be limited to a review of the fairness and legality of the board's action, or it may permit a complete new hearing, depending on the jurisdiction.

Most courts defer to the determination of the nursing board in disciplinary proceedings. If the board acted within the scope of its statutory authority, the action was supported by the evidence presented, and the decision does not appear to be unreasonable, it will be upheld. Appellate courts have criticized trial courts for substituting their judgment for that of the board.

However, in some cases courts have found that the evidence did not justify the disciplinary action that the board imposed. A Pennsylvania court reversed the board's action in reprimanding a nurse for allegedly slapping a patient.[16] The court, after examining the evidence, said that the evidence clearly showed that the nurse "tapped" the patient's arm to induce him to let go of her hand, that other means had been used to persuade the patient to release her, and that the patient was in danger of falling when the nurse tapped his hand. The court also said that the violation was not a "willful or repeated" violation as required by the Pennsylvania statute to justify a reprimand.

Usually, the nurse practice act designates which state court may hear appeals of nursing board actions. If the statute does not specifically authorize judicial review, this right is presumed. All opportunities for administrative appeals must be exhausted before a case can go to court.

Disciplinary proceedings before an administrative board differ substantially from those in court. Differences include the level of formality of the hearing, the type and scope of evidence that is acceptable, and the level of proof that is required to impose a punishment on the licensee. Nurses and other professionals involved in disciplinary proceedings before licensing boards do not receive the same procedural protections as are available to defendants in court.

PRIVATE CREDENTIALING

A wide variety of private credentialing methods has been developed. Educational programs are accredited, individuals are certified, and hospitals and other institutions investigate the credentials of prospective staff members before permitting them to practice in the institution.

Accreditation of Educational Programs

Private professional organizations sponsor programs that establish criteria to evaluate educational programs in their disciplines. For nursing, the National League for Nursing (NLN) assumes this role. Periodically, the NLN sends an individual or a team to investigate educational programs that have applied for accreditation; it then accredits programs that meet its criteria. Although accreditation is voluntary, most educational programs make a significant effort to obtain and retain accreditation from established bodies. The NLN also has assumed a role in the establishment and upgrading of standards of nursing practice through the promotion of a national standard for educational programs as well as of research, consultation, and publication.

Certification

Private professional organizations sponsor programs to certify that individuals meet certain criteria and are prepared to practice in the discipline. Certification recognizes the attainment of advanced, specialized knowledge and skills beyond what is required for safe practice. Some forms of certification have become so widely accepted that it may be difficult to practice without certification.

The development of certification standards in nursing has focused primarily on practice in expanded roles. Controversy has surrounded efforts to develop certification programs within the specialty areas of nursing. Most of the states mandate completion of a formal nursing educational program of specified length that is approved by the respective boards. Some states require certification for expanded practice licenses by a national certifying agency such as the American Association of Nurse Anesthetists, the American College of Nurse Midwives, the National Association of Pediatric Nurse Associates and Practitioners, or the ANA. The trend is toward the development of state requirements for expanded practice, often based on obtaining a graduate degree.

Institutional Credentialing

Hospitals that desire accreditation by the Joint Commission on Accreditation of Healthcare Organizations (the Joint Commission) are required to have a formal statement adopted by the medical staff delineating the "qualifications, status, clinical duties, and responsibilities of specified professional personnel."[17] The Joint Commission's *Accreditation Manual for Hospitals* does not specify which personnel fall into this category, but its surveyors have focused on clinical psychologists, nurse anesthetists, and physician's assistants The Joint Commission does not require individual review of these professionals by the medical staff. However, the hospital should have a method for ensuring that the qualifications are met.

Some nursing specialists and other professionals are seeking authorization to practice in some hospitals on an independent or quasi-independent basis without being hospital employees. These groups include nurse anesthetists, psychiatric nurse specialists, and a variety of nurse practitioners. In nearly all states, hospitals have the authority to establish whether these services will be provided in the facility and, if so, whether they may be provided by nonemployees. A hospital that decides or is required to permit nonemployees to practice in the facility adopts a procedure for verifying their qualifications, obtaining their commitment to abide by all applicable hospital and department rules, defining their scope of practice, ensuring appropriate supervision and evaluation of their performance, and providing for terminating their permission to practice if warranted.

HOSPITAL CREDENTIALS FOR ADVANCED PRACTICE NURSES

The growth of technology and advances in the complexity of curative and restorative techniques have vastly increased the importance of advanced practice nurses. Unlike physicians, who traditionally have been held capable of exercising a general supervision over the care of the patient, advanced practice nurses have been restricted by law or custom to treating one specialized area of the human body or one particular type of health care problem or to providing some specialized care of service under the supervision of a physician. Hospitals have increasingly assumed responsibility for granting credentials to advanced practice nurses to practice on the hospital premises.

Practice Considerations

Central to the provision of credentials to advanced practice nurses is the consideration of what services such practitioners are trained to provide and the extent to which they are capable, legally and professionally, of practicing independently. Those practitioners who are permitted by state law to provide specialized health care services to patients without physician direction or supervision are independent practitioners. The following are the principal types of advanced practice nurses who have obtained credentials:

1. Nurse practitioners who are licensed registered nurses with additional training and experience that enable them to provide a range of diagnostic and therapeutic services involving significant independent judgment to a degree not customary in the traditional practice of nursing.
2. Nurse anesthetists, also licensed registered nurses with additional training, who provide surgical anesthesia services, including intubation, induction, and intrasurgical and postsurgical monitoring of patients. Their practice is often subject to the supervision of a physician qualified in anesthesiology.
3. Nurse-midwives are licensed registered nurses who not only deliver babies but also provide prenatal monitoring, counseling, and education, as well as postpartum care and follow-up.

Some state statutes prohibit arbitrary disqualification of a class of practitioners on the ground that they are not physicians but permit denial on the basis of competence or other factors related to the quality of care.[18] It would seem that antidiscrimination statutes of this type confer no more "right" to admit patients to hospital facilities than physicians have. In a New Jersey case, for example, a public hospital's denial of medical staff privileges to a nurse certified in psychiatric nursing was found reasonable.[19] The nurse sought a court order compelling the hospital to consider her application for membership on the hospital's adjunct medical staff, but the court denied her request, holding that the hospital's refusal to entertain her application was nondiscriminatory and was reached in the normal course of conducting the affairs of the hospital.

The Joint Commission medical staff standards now permit, but do not require, hospitals to include advanced practice nurses as members of the medical staff. It is discretionary under the standards as to whether a hospital will grant such practitioners medical staff membership or clinical privileges only, but in either instance, these practitioners are subject to medical staff and departmental bylaws, rules, and regulations and are subject to quality assurance review.[20]

Expanded role nursing practitioners have not generally been granted the protection of legislation prohibiting discrimination among schools of practice, so there seems to be no widespread belief in a right to institutional practice. In the District of Columbia, however, legislation grants qualified nurse anesthetists, nurse-midwives, and nurse practitioners the right to apply for clinical privileges and staff membership at D.C. health care facilities.[21]

Credentialing Procedures

The granting of hospital privileges to advanced practice nurses is, with only minor limitations, a matter of institutional policy established by a hospital's governing body on recommendation of its medical staff. The Joint Commission neither precludes nor requires delineated hospital clinical privileges for advanced practice nurses. The decision whether to grant clinical privileges appears to be optional, but if a hospital decides to do so, the Joint Commission requires mechanisms for delineation of such privileges.[22]

Advanced practice nurses who, in accordance with established hospital policy set forth in the medical staff bylaws, may be eligible for clinical privileges should be required to complete an application form eliciting the same type of information as that sought from physician applicants to the medical staff. Once the completed application is received, procedural mechanisms established in the bylaws are followed. Like physician staff members, the applicant goes through a series of steps (e.g., credentials committee approval, medical staff department approval, medical staff executive committee approval or full staff approval, recommendation to the governing body, and finally governing body approval).

Physician's Employees

When the medical staff bylaws provide for granting credentials to advanced practice nurses who are employees of physician members of the medical staff, the hospital often develops an application procedure less complex than that for medical staff membership and privileges. The application often contains

1. detailed information on the practitioner's education, training, and experience
2. proof that the practitioner is duly licensed or certified in the jurisdiction
3. a detailed description of the procedures the practitioner is expected to perform

4. the practitioner's agreement to abide by the medical staff and hospital by-laws, rules, and regulations
5. the physician employee's agreement to accept all legal responsibility for the practitioner's practice in the institution
6. the practitioner's agreement that, in the event of termination of privileges, he or she shall have recourse only to those due process rights explicitly granted to practitioners by the hospital bylaws, not those accorded physician members of the medical staff

Procedures regarding credentials usually include a mechanism whereby the physician-employer can be held responsible to the medical staff for the actions of the employee-practitioner. Bylaw provisions often make the physician-employer subject to medical staff disciplinary action, including termination of privileges for the improper or inadequate performance of the employee.

Hospital Employees

Hospitals have traditionally employed a variety of expanded role nursing practitioners without reference to the granting of credentials. Because these practitioners as hospital employees are subject to control by the hospital administration and because formal procedures to grant privileges are intended to implement institutional control over practitioners, the process of providing credentials was deemed unnecessary. State regulations in some jurisdictions that require credential procedures for these practitioners seem to have changed this to some degree. As the employer of nursing practitioners, the hospital may be held legally responsible for their actions under the doctrine of respondeat superior. By contrast, the doctrine generally does not render the hospital liable when the practitioner is an employee of a staff physician.

To adhere to the standard set by the Joint Commission when granting clinical privileges and to comply with state regulations, the hospital usually establishes mechanisms of delineating the privileges of hospital employees that are slight modifications of the procedures used for a physician's employees.

PHYSICIAN ASSISTANTS AND THE NURSING PROFESSION

The provision of credentials to physician assistants in the hospital may bring to the forefront a dispute between physician assistants and the nursing profession.

The most common symptom of the dispute is a controversy over whether nurses are to carry out orders written by physician assistants. The position of nurses and their licensing boards has been that only physicians may give nurses orders for treatment. In Florida, where the issue was submitted to the state attorney general, physician assistants were held to be agents of their supervising physicians and the transcribed orders to be those of the physicians so nurses violate no provision of the nurse practice act in carrying them out.[23] In Washington state, the state nurses' association challenged a rule of the board of medical examiners that permitted physician assistants to issue prescriptions and write orders for care in specified circumstances. The court refused to invalidate the rule, finding that the physician assistant orders are, for all purposes, those of the physician.[24] In Pennsylvania, however, nurses are not required to administer medication or carry out treatment orders prescribed by a physician assistant, according to a formal opinion of the Pennsylvania attorney general.[25]

The granting of privileges to nurses in independent practice is often a source of controversy. A nurse anesthetist was not entitled to practice at a hospital without a contract, the Mississippi Supreme Court has ruled.[26] For many years, a certified registered nurse anesthetist (CRNA) operated as an independent contractor, providing services to patients at a hospital as requested by physicians. She operated under a series of written and verbal agreements with the hospital. After a drop in patient census and subsequent efforts to reduce expenses, the hospital properly terminated the CRNA's contract with the intent to renegotiate the contract at a lower rate. The CRNA refused, stating that she would practice anesthesia on her own by working for two physicians at the hospital who performed approximately 80 percent of the surgery. She contended that she had submitted her credentials to the hospital and medical staff for review, that her credentials went through standard medical staff channels for review and approval, that her credentials were reviewed annually for 20 years, that she met the requirements to practice her profession, and that she was therefore entitled to medical staff privileges and the right to practice as an independent contractor. The hospital then asked a court to determine whether the CRNA could practice at the hospital without a contract.

The court ruled that she could not. It pointed out that the hospital and medical staff bylaws make no provision for medical staff membership for CRNAs and that she therefore did not meet the criteria to be on the medical staff. Even qualified physicians cannot practice in hospitals where they are not staff members, the court noted. If CRNAs or any other practitioners could practice their specialty without a contract or without even consulting the hospital, chaos would result, according to the court. It therefore concluded that the CRNA could not practice in the hospital without a contract.

CONCLUSION

The practice of nursing is regulated by all of the states through a board of nursing. This regulation process is designed to protect the public from harm while at the same time ensuring that the process is fair to nurses. The scope of nursing has expanded dramatically over the past two decades and will continue to expand at the turn of this century as managed care becomes the way in which most Americans receive their health care. To accommodate this expanded scope of nursing, both private and public credentialing bodies have sought to regulate the multi-specialty practices of nurses. Because licensure and credentialing can vary from state to state, the nurse is encouraged to be familiar with his or her state/professional regulations on practice.

FOOTNOTES

1. AMERICAN NURSES ASSOCIATION, NURSING, A SOCIAL POLICY STATEMENT (1980).
2. *ANA Board Approves a Definition of Nursing Practice,* 55 AM. J. NURSING 1474 (1955).
3. *Annual Update of How Each State Stands on Legislative Issues Affecting Advanced Nursing Practice,* THE NURSE PRACTITIONER, January 19, 1994, at 11–15.
4. *Id.*
5. Shannon, *Our First Licensing Laws,* 75 AM. J. NURSING 1327 (1975).
6. Schoenhair v. Pennsylvania, 459 A.2d 877 (Pa. 1983).
7. Washington State Nurses Ass'n v. Board of Med. Exam'rs, 93 Wash. 117, 605 P.2d 1269 (1980).
8. *E.g.,* IOWA CODE § 258A.9(2).
9. Frawley v. Downing, 364 A.2d 748 (Pa. Commw. Ct. 1976).
10. Leggett v. Tennessee Bd. of Nursing, 612 S.W.2d 476 (Tenn. 1981).
11. Colorado State Bd. of Nursing v. Hohu, 129 Colo. 195, 268 P.2d 401 (1954).
12. Ward v. Oregon State Bd. of Nursing, 226 Or. 128, 510 P.2d 554 (1973).
13. Tuma v. Board of Nursing, 593 P.2d 711 (Idaho 1979).
14. Lunsford v. Board of Nursing Exam'rs, 648 S.W.2d 391 (Tex. Civ. App. 3rd Dist. 1983).
15. Rayburn v. Minnesota State Bd. of Optometry, 247 Minn. 520, 78 N.W.2d 351 (1956).
16. Leukhardt v. Pennsylvania, 44 Pa. Commw. Ct. 318, 403 A.2d (1979).
17. JOINT COMMISSION ON ACCREDITATION OF HEALTHCARE ORGANIZATIONS, ACCREDITATION MANUAL FOR HOSPITALS (1995).
18. *See* Fritz v. Huntington Hosp., 348 N.E.2d 547 (App. Div. 1976); New Hampshire Podiatric Med. Ass'n v. New Hampshire Hosp. Ass'n, 735 F. Supp. 448 (D.N.H. 1990) (challenge based on equal protection rejected); Silverstein v. Gwinnett Hosp. Auth., 861 F.2d 1560 (11th Cir. 1988) (hospital bylaw requiring specific postgraduate training does not violate equal protection, due process, or state antidiscrimination law, despite its impact on osteopathic physician).
19. Vrable v. Community Hosp., 517 A.2d 470 (N.J. Super. Ct. App. Div. 1986).
20. JOINT COMMISSION, *supra,* Medical Staff.
21. D.C. Bill 5-166, enacted Oct. 28, 1983.
22. JOINT COMMISSION, *supra,* Medical Staff.
23. Op. Fla. Att'y Gen., No. 077-96 (1977).
24. Washington State Nurse Ass'n v. Board of Med. Exam'rs, 93 Wash. 2d 117, 605 P.2d 1269 (1980).
25. Op. Pa. Att'y Gen. (July 23, 1982).
26. Wicker v. Union County Gen. Hosp., 152 So. 2d 2975 (Miss. 1989).

CHAPTER 3

The Nurse as Employee

Chapter Objectives

1. To examine the employer–nurse relationship
2. To explore AIDS and employment issues
3. To review equal employment opportunity laws
4. To examine compensation and benefit laws
5. To consider occupational safety and health issues
6. To outline labor–management relations
7. To discuss state laws for workers' compensation
8. To address state laws for unemployment compensation
9. To look at laws for public employees

Most nurses work as employees of health care institutions, public or private agencies, private practitioners, or businesses. This chapter discusses the rights and responsibilities of nurses as employees and their employers. A significant determinant of whether good-quality compassionate care is provided to patients or clients is the quality and performance of the nurse and the relationship between the nurse and the employer.

Employers must be careful in selecting, training, supervising, and disciplining nurses and other employees. Nurses need to know the rights and the responsibilities of employees and employers to understand and respond to actions concerning their employment. Detailed state and federal regulations control many aspects of employee relations, including equal employment opportunities, compensation and benefits, occupational safety, labor–management relations, and other matters. The National Labor Relations Act (NLRA) is the dominant influence in the labor field, and the trend is toward increased preemption of state laws in labor relations.

EMPLOYER–NURSE RELATIONSHIP

Selection of Employees

Employers must exercise care in selecting their employees. Employers should verify any required licenses and check references and other information provided to confirm that it is reasonable to believe the applicant is qualified for the position. Nurses should expect this verification to occur. It is not because a prospective employer has doubts concerning the individual applicant or nurses in general; it is a prudent step that helps protect patients from unqualified nurses and helps protect qualified nurses from being assigned to work with unqualified ones. Selection also must be in compliance with applicable equal employment opportunity laws (discussed in this chapter).

Health Screening

Health care employers should screen nurses and other employees to identify conditions, such as contagious diseases, that may constitute a risk to patients and take appropriate steps to ensure that persons who constitute a risk do not have contact with patients or objects that could transmit their condition. Employers that choose to perform health screening of applicants before hiring must require it for all applicants for covered positions. Selective screening of individual applicants violates section 504 of the Rehabilitation Act of 1973.[1]

Training and Supervision

Employers are liable for injuries caused by the negligence of their employees. To optimize patient care and minimize liability exposure, health care employers must ensure that employees receive necessary training and supervision. It is important for nurses to participate in continuing education to maintain and improve their skills. Although employers should facilitate continuing education, in most states there is no obligation to provide it without cost to the employee or during compensated time.

Discipline and Dismissal—Employment At-Will

A long-standing rule in the United States, taken from English common law, is that an employer can fire an employee at any time, with or without reasonable cause. As one court stated, employers "may dismiss their employees at will . . . for good cause, for no cause or even for cause morally wrong."[2] That means that employers may terminate employees at will at any time without cause unless there is a contract that specifies a specific period of employment or a statute that lists criteria or procedures for termination.[3] Conversely, an employee is free to terminate his or her employment relationship at any time. It is estimated that approximately two-thirds of American workers are employed at-will.[4] Although the employment-at-will rule is still dominant in the United States, it has been seriously eroded in recent years by federal and state law and court decisions.

Health care employers have a responsibility to take steps to enforce institutional policies to maintain patient care and the integrity of the institution or agency. It is important that proper procedures be followed and that the action be based on legally permissible grounds. Some nurses have attempted to convince courts that their states' nursing licensing law created procedural rights, but courts have rejected this contention.[5]

Most courts will require health care employers to follow their own procedures when pursuing disciplinary measures or dismissal.[6] However, courts have disagreed on what constitutes an enforceable policy or procedure. The Delaware Supreme Court ruled that statements in employee handbooks do not change an employee's at-will status unless they specify a definite term of employment.[7] A Florida appellate court ruled that hospital personnel policies might be enforceable and ordered a trial court to reconsider the matter.[8] Some public employees are covered by civil service laws that require certain procedures.

When employees are covered by individual employment contracts or collective bargaining agreements, the procedures they specify should be followed. Such contracts do not have to be in writing to be enforceable. A Louisiana court found a hospital liable for breaching an oral promise to five certified registered nurse anesthetists that they would be given a six-month notice of termination. The court awarded payment of salary for the six months, less the amount they actually earned during the six months.[9] This illustrates the principle that courts generally will not order employees reinstated unless a statute authorizes it; instead, they will order that employees be paid for their lost wages and other damages when they are wrongfully discharged.

Several federal laws create limitations on an employer's ability to discharge employees. For instance, federal equal employment opportunity laws forbid employment discrimination on the basis of race, sex, religion, national origin, age, handicap, and Vietnam-era veteran status.[10] State laws also restrict employers' ability to fire employees with impunity. In fact, the employment laws of several states provide more extensive employee protection than is available under federal law.[11]

Provisions in collective bargaining agreements specifying that discharges must be for good cause constitute another limitation on the employment-at-will doctrine, as do similar provisions included in individual employment contracts.

Finally, the employment-at-will rule has been eroded by judicial decisions in several states. The courts of more than 30 states currently recognize exceptions to employment at-will.[12] There are three major exceptions to the rule: the public policy exception, the implied contract exception, and the good faith and fair dealing exception. Although these exceptions are becoming more widely accepted, it should be noted that in most wrongful discharge cases, the courts have upheld the employer's right to discharge.

Courts have recognized the public policy exception when an employee is discharged for refusing to commit an unlawful act. A nurse who claimed she was fired when she refused to falsify medical records can also sue the hospital for wrongful discharge, because requiring an employee to engage in such conduct violates public policy, the Arkansas Supreme Court has ruled.[13] An appeals court in Missouri has ruled, however, that an at-will director of nursing at a psychiatric hospital who alleged that her employer requested management to prepare "bogus" minutes of committee meetings to satisfy Joint Committee accreditation standards may not sue under the policy exception to the at-will employment doctrine.[14] Obviously, preparing minutes of meetings that did not occur should not be done.

In *Wright v. Shriners Hospital for Crippled Children,*[15] a survey team from a hospital's national headquarters visited the facility in response to criticisms it had received from a former head nurse regarding the hospital's medical staff and administration. The assistant director of nursing told the survey team that there were communication problems between the physicians and the nurses and gave specific examples of patient care problems. Several months later, the hospital terminated the director for "patient care issues that had arisen as a result of the survey." The director sued the hospital, claiming that it had terminated her at-will employment in retaliation for criticizing patient care and that her discharge violated public policy. A trial court agreed, and a jury awarded the director $100,000 in damages.

On appeal, the director in *Wright v. Shriners Hospital for Crippled Children* argued that a state board of nursing regulation stating that a registered nurse should communicate and collaborate with other health care providers was sufficient evidence of public policy to support her claim for wrongful discharge. The high court refused, however, to hold that a regulation governing a particular profession is a source of well-defined public policy sufficient to modify the at-will employment rule. Although the provision of good medical care is in the public interest, the court concluded that this does not change the at-will employment rule for health care employees who report on issues that they think are detrimental to health care.

In *Pearson v. Macon-Bibb County Hospital Authority,*[16] after an incident involving contaminated surgical instruments that were left unattended in the hospital operating room, a black senior staff nurse with supervisory duties received an oral reprimand. The nurse subsequently attended a seminar where she criticized the failure of her supervisors to adequately supervise the cleaning responsibilities of operating room nurses and sent a letter to her supervisor asking for a clarification of duties. Because of the nurse's disruptive behavior, the hospital removed her from operating room duties and told her to resign or transfer to another department in the hospital. When the nurse did not succeed in finding another position in the hospital, the hospital terminated her. She sued, claiming that the hospital had retaliated against her for her comments about operating room cleanliness and had therefore violated her right to free speech. She also sued under Title VII, arguing that the hospital had discriminated against her on the basis of race.

The nurse argued that because her statements concerned operating room conditions that were potentially hazardous to patients in a publicly funded facility, they were of public significance. The court refused to endorse this view, finding that the nurse's complaints pertained to the assignment of cleaning responsibilities in the operating room and the assignment of blame when those duties were neglected. The court in *Pearson v. Macon-Bibb County Hospital Authority* did, however, allow her to proceed to trial, concluding that she had initially established that three similarly placed white employees who had been involved in the contaminated instruments incident were not discharged.

Discharge for breach of an implied contract of employment constitutes the second exception to the employment-at-will rule. Employment may be terminated only "for cause" if there is an express or implied agreement to that effect or if the employee gives some type of consideration in addition to the contemplated service.

The Supreme Court of Arizona held that an employer's representations in a personnel manual can become terms of the employment contract and can limit an employer's ability to discharge other employees.[17] In that case, a nurse who was discharged after requesting a transfer to a subordinate position sued her employer, alleging breach of contract. Although the court found that manuals can become part of employment contracts, it was careful to point out that not all personnel manuals will become part of employment contracts. The court added that employers are free to issue no personnel manual or to issue one that clearly states that the manual is not part of the employment contract, in which cases the employment relationship is terminable at will.

One issue that is receiving increasing attention is whether employees should be protected from retaliatory discharge for certain conduct. Some statutes specifically forbid retaliatory discharge of employees who make certain reports to governmental agencies,[18] and some courts have extended such protection to employees who make other reports (e.g., workers' compensation claims).[19] There may be some protection for employees or other staff members of public institutions who are discharged for exercising their rights of free speech,[20] but this does not extend to employees of private employers. For example, an Illinois court ruled that even if a nurse had been terminated solely in retaliation for reporting incidents to a newspaper, she would not be entitled to any more protection than other at-will employees of private employers.[21]

Some provisions of the NLRA also apply when employees are not represented by a union. The equal employment opportunity laws described later in this chapter apply to all aspects of employment, including discipline and dismissal, so they may offer recourse for nurses in actions with a discriminatory basis.

Certain grounds for dismissal are not considered just cause by state unemployment compensation agencies, so employers are required to pay unemployment compensation to the dismissed nurse. (Unemployment compensation issues are discussed later in this chapter.)

Communications about Former Staff

Many types of employers, including hospitals, have been sued for libel or slander by former staff members based on statements in unfavorable evaluations, termination notices, and responses to inquiries from prospective employers. Some supervisory personnel have been reluctant to communicate deficiencies accurately because of limited understanding of what they may legally say. It is essential that nursing supervisors understand what they may legally say. It is essential that supervisors understand what they can communicate so present and prospective employees can obtain accurate evaluations with minimum legal risk.

In general, there can be no liability based on libel or slander for communicating the truth. However, because it often is difficult to prove the absolute truth of a statement, the law extends a "qualified privilege" or protection of certain communications. This means that there is no liability as long as the communication was not made with malice. The qualified privilege applies to communications to certain persons who have a legitimate interest in the information given, as long as the information is limited in scope commensurate with the legitimate interest and is provided in a proper manner so that others do not learn of it inappropriately. Courts generally have recognized that an employer or prospective employer has a legitimate interest in employment-related information.[22] The best way to avoid exceeding the qualified privilege is to limit the communication to factual statements and avoid comments concerning personality or personal spite. Neutral factual statements can communicate the deficiencies that need to be expressed without creating the appearance of malice.

AIDS AND EMPLOYMENT ISSUES

The Rehabilitation Act of 1973 prohibits discrimination on the basis of handicap by employers who receive federal financial assistance.[23] Hospitals that receive Medicare and Medicaid funds are therefore bound by this law. The Health and Human Services regulations implementing the Act are broad enough to apply to physical impairments associated with acquired immune deficiency syndrome (AIDS).[24] Also, because the regulations refer to those "regarded as having an impairment" as handicapped, they may be interpreted as applying to those who are human immunodeficiency virus (HIV) infected and asymptomatic but encounter discrimination because of fear of contagion.

In a significant ruling on the issue of AIDS as a handicap under the Rehabilitation Act, the Fifth Circuit Court of Appeals has found that a hospital did not violate the Act when it terminated a nurse for his refusal to divulge the results of his HIV test.[25] On learning that a male nurse was the roommate of a patient who had been diagnosed as having AIDS, a hospital requested that the nurse undergo HIV antibody testing. The nurse informed his supervisor that he had already undergone such testing and that he would submit the results when they became available. When the nurse subsequently refused to disclose the test results, the hospital suspended and ultimately terminated him. The appeals court dismissed the nurse's claim that the hospital had discriminated against him on the basis of a perceived handicap because he had failed to establish that the hospital's sole reason for terminating him was the possibility that he was infected. Hospital policy requires employees to report any exposure to infectious diseases, the court observed, and the nurse was terminated for his failure to abide by this policy.

About two-thirds of the states also recognize AIDS as a handicap under state law. Some state laws cover impairment from illness or disease but do not specifically mention AIDS, whereas others specifically prohibit discrimination based on AIDS.[26]

Employers must, under federal law, accommodate handicapped employees who are otherwise qualified and pose no threat to others. In determining if a person with a contagious disease is otherwise qualified, such facts as the nature, duration, and severity of the risk and the probability that the disease will be transmitted and cause varying degrees of harm must be considered.

The final step is to determine whether the employee can be reasonably accommodated. What constitutes reasonable accommodation will vary with the job and the individual's health. Reasonable accommodation may include part-time work or a restructured job or work schedule. A hospital might reassign an employee to a comparable position with less direct patient contact if there is a danger of transmitting the disease, but with the current medical evidence, that would be difficult to substantiate. In one case that was settled by consent decree, a hospital was prohibited from taking action against a physician simply because he had AIDS.[27] The physician was required to comply with Centers for Disease Control (CDC) guidelines, follow hospital policies concerning monitoring of employees with AIDS, and wear two sets of gloves for certain procedures. This is the first reported case of judicially supervised accommodation of a physician with AIDS.

In some instances, the safety of the employee with AIDS might be a reason for removing the employee from a direct patient care position. The CDC recommendations indicate that health care workers with impaired immune systems are at an increased risk of acquiring or experiencing serious complications of infectious diseases.[28] Employees may be reasonably accommodated by transfer to a position that does not expose them to such risks.

EQUAL EMPLOYMENT OPPORTUNITY LAWS

Congress has enacted laws to expand equal employment opportunities by prohibiting discrimination on various grounds. The measures include Title VII of the Civil Rights Act of 1964, the Equal Pay Act of 1963, the Age Discrimination in

Employment Act, and sections 503 and 504 of the Rehabilitation Act of 1973. Numerous state laws also address equal employment opportunities.

Title VII of the Civil Rights Act of 1964

Title VII of the Civil Rights Act of 1964[29] prohibits disparate employment treatment based on race, color, religion, sex, national origin, or pregnancy. It applies to hiring, dismissal, promotion, discipline, terms and conditions of employment, and job advertising. It applies to nearly all employers; governmental agencies were included by the 1972 amendments. One of the few exemptions permits religious institutions to consider religion as a criterion in their employment practices.

The primary enforcement is the Equal Employment Opportunity Commission (EEOC) and its general counsel. Charges of discrimination are processed by one of the EEOC's 22 district or area offices. If a charge cannot be conciliated or settled and the EEOC decides that it merits litigation, it is transferred to one of the EEOC's litigation units. Private litigants also are entitled to bring individual or even class action lawsuits.

Three legal theories are used as the basis for finding employment discrimination. The first, the disparate treatment theory of employment discrimination, says that employers are prohibited from treating applicants or employees in a different—or disparate—manner because of their race, color, religion, sex, or national origin. Most instances of disparate treatment involve employee discipline and discharge. These cases involve a fairly straightforward type of comparative analysis. If a work rule or employment practice is not applied in a consistent fashion, disparate treatment exists. If such treatment affects any of the groups protected by Title VII, it is a violation. Most cases of disparate treatment are proved by using direct evidence such as individual testimony and work records.

In the second theory of discrimination, *disparate impact* or *adverse impact*, the test is whether an employer's practice, even though it may appear nondiscriminatory, disproportionately affects individuals of a protected group. The classic example of an employment practice that may have an adverse impact on minorities is the use of standardized written employment tests. Although the same tests may be given to minorities and nonminorities, the minorities may not score as well and, thus, may be hired in fewer numbers than the nonminority test takers. If such a test is not job related (i.e., does not test for qualities necessary to the successful performance of the job), the employer will be found to have violated Title VII.

The third theory of employment discrimination, *past discrimination carried over,* encompasses the purely social aspects of Title VII and is otherwise known as the rightful place doctrine. This theory maintains that had there been no discrimination before the passage of Title VII, members of minorities would have been in different positions. Proponents of the theory argue that affected individuals should be, as nearly as possible, put in the positions they would have obtained had employment discrimination not been practiced. In other words, they should be placed in their rightful places.

Discrimination Based on Race and Gender

Employers are prohibited from retaliating against employees who oppose discrimination by engaging in reasonable activities. In 1984, a federal court of appeals found that a hospital had violated this provision when it fired a black registered nurse who had complained about black patient care.[30]

The prohibition against discrimination based on gender under Title VII applies equally to males and females.[31] Sex discrimination complaints have been filed by men who have been denied access to jobs traditionally thought of in the health care industry as "women's jobs" (i.e., nursing). The EEOC has issued comprehensive guidelines on most of the issues related to sex discrimination.

If a hospital can demonstrate that sex "is a bona fide occupational qualification reasonably necessary to the normal operation" of its business, the general prohibition against sexual preference under Title VII will be waived.[32] A federal court in Michigan, for example, ruled that sex can be a bona fide occupational qualification (BFOQ) for mental health care workers because same-gender caretakers are required to protect the privacy rights of mentally ill patients.[33] The EEOC, however, continues to interpret the BFOQ exception in an extremely limited manner. Therefore, assumptions based on "employment characteristics of women"[34]; stereotypical characteristics based on sex; and preferences of employers, coworkers, or clients generally are not considered BFOQs.

In 1981, a federal court ruled that it was not illegal sex discrimination for a hospital to employ only female nurses in its obstetrics gynecology department.[35] The court noted that the policy was based on the patients' privacy rights, not just their preference.

Hospitals cannot merely assert that patients prefer one gender or the other to provide patient care. Numerous cases have rejected nursing home and hospital contentions that patients prefer one gender over the other. Even assuming that a hospital could establish the existence of such a preference, the EEOC would require a showing that the preference was universal or nearly so.

In 1978, Title VII was amended to prohibit discriminatory treatment of pregnant women for all employment-related purposes. No special considerations are required. However, for example, if leaves are offered for disabilities, similar leaves must be offered for maternity. Mandatory maternity leaves that are not based on inability to work violate Title VII. Pregnancy itself is not considered a disability, but if a pregnant worker becomes unable to work, then disability benefits offered for other disabilities must be offered to such a woman. Basically, there is no statutory requirement that an employer do anything more for pregnant women than the employer does for other employees. An employer who does not provide paid sick leave or disability benefits to other employees is not required to provide them for pregnant employees.

Court opinions indicate that Title VII does not protect employees who allege discrimination on the basis of sexual preference. Courts have held that a company's refusal to hire an effeminate male does not constitute sex discrimination under Title VII.[36] In a related case, a court held that a hospital did not violate Title VII by discharging an employee who intended to have a sex change operation.[37]

Evidence that an employer asked family-oriented questions only of a female job applicant is not sufficient to support a claim of intentional sex discrimination, the Seventh Circuit has ruled.[38] In this case, an employer who was hiring for a paramedic position asked a female applicant how many children she had, whether it was time to have more children, what she had arranged for child care, and what her husband thought about her working 24-hour shifts. Acknowledging that these questions were based on sex stereotypes, the court ruled that the woman must still prove that the employer relied on her gender in making his decision to hire a male for the position. In this case, the employer demonstrated that he was concerned about the family circumstances of any applicant where both husband and wife work 24-hour shifts.

The area of sexual harassment in the workplace has taken on increasing importance. In response to several courts' opinions, the EEOC published guidelines on sexual harassment. According to these guidelines, an employer is liable for the sexual harassment of employees by supervisory and managerial staff. In addition, an employer is liable for the sexual harassment of employees by coworkers or nonemployees if the employer knew of, or should have known of, such actions.

The U.S. Court of Appeals for the Sixth Circuit has further defined the parameters of a sexually hostile work environment case.[39] It ruled that to prevail in such an action, an employee must prove that he or she was subject to sexual harassment consisting of verbal or physical conduct of a sexual nature; that the harassment unreasonably interfered with work and created an intimidating, hostile, or offensive work environment that seriously affected the employee's psychological well-being; and that the employer was liable. When an employee alleges a sexually hostile work environment because of the conduct of peers rather than of a supervisor, the court ruled, the employer is liable if the employee proves that the employer knew or should have known of the sexual harassment and failed to take prompt and appropriate corrective action.

Some groups have sought to convince the courts that Title VII requires the adoption of a comparable worth doctrine. This doctrine would require employers to revise wage scales so pay is based on the comparable worth of the work performed by persons in different job classifications when work categories that are predominantly filled with females have been assigned lower wage scales. This comparable work doctrine goes beyond the Equal Pay Act (discussed in the following section) that requires equal pay for essentially identical work.

Nursing groups have been in the forefront of the effort to establish the comparable worth doctrine. However, courts generally have ruled that Title VII does not require wage scales based on comparable work.[40] One exception is a federal court decision in 1983 involving a broad range of public jobs in the state of Washington. The court applied comparative worth principles to find the state's wage scales in violation of Title VII.[41]

Discrimination Based on Religion

An employer must make some attempt to accommodate an employee's religious beliefs, the Fourth Circuit has ruled in a non–health care case, even if the employee flatly refuses to work on Sundays.[42] The U.S. Supreme Court has ruled, however, that an employer's duty to reasonably accommodate the religious beliefs of its employees does not require the employer to adopt the accommodation preferred by an employee.[43]

In hospital settings, courts differ as to whether particular accommodations impose an undue hardship on employers. For example, one court held that it would not be an undue hardship for a hospital to accommodate a nurse's religious belief that precluded her from assisting in abortions.[44] However, because a hospital would incur substantial costs in overtime for other nurses or suffer decreased efficiency by rearranging a work schedule to accommodate a nurse's religious beliefs that forbade Saturday work, the hospital was found to be justified in terminating her employment.[45]

Equal Pay Act of 1963

The Equal Pay Act[46] is designed to prohibit discriminatory compensation policies based on sex. The act requires that employees who perform equal work receive equal pay. Equal work is broadly defined as work that requires "equal skill, effort and responsibility, and that [is] performed under similar working conditions."[47] The act also recognizes that wages may be unequal as long as they are based on a factor other than sex.[48]

Jobs are considered equal if they involve (1) equal skill, (2) equal effort, and (3) equal responsibility and (4) are performed under similar working conditions. If jobs are unequal with respect to any one of these four factors, then a wage differential may be justified. However, *equal* does not mean *identical*. To determine whether two jobs are of an equal nature, the previously mentioned four factors must be measured on a similar scale.

The courts have ruled that each equal pay case must be decided on its own merits and cannot be applied on an industry-wide basis.[49] Thus, hospitals have been involved in innumerable cases on the issue of equal pay for nurse's aides and orderlies and equal pay for maids and porters. It is therefore not surprising that some courts in the aide–orderly cases have reached diametrically opposite conclusions on similar facts; however, the courts have, so far, generally agreed that maids and porters perform equal work.

In one case, a federal trial court held that a hospital had not violated the Equal Pay Act by compensating female nurse practitioners at a rate significantly lower than a male physician assistant.[50] The court explained that its ruling did not concern the relative education, competence, or skills of nurse practitioners and physician assistants in general. In this case, however, although the jobs were substantially similar in terms of effort and working conditions, the physician assistant possessed greater skills, had more responsibility, and could legally perform a wider range of services than the nurse practitioners.

Age Discrimination in Employment Act

The Age Discrimination in Employment Act[51] (ADEA) prohibits discriminatory treatment of persons older than 40 for all employment-related purposes. In 1986, Congress eliminated the upper age limit on coverage under the ADEA.[52] The law now protects workers older than the age of 40 in matters such as hiring, compensation, job security, and other terms and conditions of employment.

In 1990, Congress adopted the Older Workers Benefit Protection Act (OWBPA) to amend the ADEA. Title I of OWBPA adopts the equal benefit or equal cost rule. In general, an employer may not discriminate on the basis of age in employee benefits. If the cost of providing the same benefit is greater for older workers than for younger workers, however, the employer may offer a lesser benefit to the older workers, provided that the cost is the same as the benefit provided to younger workers. Some common benefit arrangements are allowed, however. These include early retirement incentive plans (as long as they are voluntary and consistent with the purposes of the ADEA), subsidized early retirement, and social security bridge payments.

There are exceptions for bona fide occupational qualifications for seniority systems or employee benefits plans, mandatory retirement ages, and reasonable factors other than age (e.g., physical fitness).

Rehabilitation Act of 1973

The Rehabilitation Act of 1973 prohibits discrimination on the basis of handicap.[53] The most controversial and difficult aspect of the Vocational Rehabilitation

Act and its amended regulations deals with the definition of who is handicapped. The present regulations emphasize that the term *handicap* is to be defined in a broad manner. The statute and regulations have divided such a definition into three parts:

> [I]ndividual with handicaps means any person who (i) has a physical or mental impairment which substantially limits one or more of such person's major life activities, (ii) has a record of such an impairment, or (iii) is regarded as having such an impairment.[54]

Each of these statutory categories is further defined in the regulations. For example, "physical or mental impairment" specifically includes cosmetic disfigurement, any physiologic condition, mental illness or retardation, and learning disabilities.[55] One may have a record of an impairment event if it is based on a misdiagnosis.[56] Further, a person's handicap may result solely from the attitudes and perceptions of others.[57]

In addition, the statute enunciates the status of current and former alcoholics and drug users.[58] Current alcoholics and drug addicts are specifically excluded from the definitions of "individual with handicaps," whereas those who have recovered from their impairments are covered. Current users of illegal drugs are also excluded. The law is sensitive to employer concerns regarding the hiring of alcoholics and drug users, by providing that only qualified handicapped persons are protected by the law.

In a case dealing with a hospital's decision to discharge a nurse because he refused to divulge the results of his HIV virus test, a federal trial court held that because he did not meet the definition of handicapped under Section 504, the hospital had not discriminated against the nurse.[59] The nurse had argued that he was handicapped because the hospital perceived him as HIV-positive and Section 504 defines handicapped persons to include those regarded as impaired. The trial court ruled, however, that the hospital fired the nurse because he refused to comply with its infection control policy and not because it perceived him as HIV-positive. An appeals court upheld this ruling, finding that the nurse had failed to establish that the hospital's sole reason for terminating him was the possibility that he was infected.[60] Section 504 deals only with discrimination against qualified handicapped persons. The regulations define a qualified handicapped person as one who, "with reasonable accommodation, can perform the essential functions of the job in question."[61] Therefore, a hospital may not insist that a handicapped employee perform *all* aspects or functions of the job, but only those that are "essential."

Because the courts are only beginning to define "reasonable accommodation," it is difficult to provide specific examples to illustrate the term. Accommodation could be achieved by a health care employer if such employer modified work schedules, restructured jobs, and embarked on physical modifications or relations of particular offices or jobs. Although the regulations recognize that "undue hardship" might be related to the cost of making the accommodations, they do not specifically spell out such an exemption.

The U.S. Supreme Court has reviewed Section 504 in several cases. In *Southeastern Community College v. Davis,*[62] for example, the Court made a narrow interpretation of the statutory phrase "otherwise qualified handicapped individual." The Court found that a community college covered by Section 504 was not required to admit a deaf individual to an RN training program. The Court held that "an otherwise qualified person is one who is able to meet all of a program's requirements in spite of his handicap." The Court stated that physical qualifications may be considered as part of a program's requirements in a proper situation.

Section 504's regulations prohibit *any* inquiry on an employment application or in an employment interview about an applicant's handicaps. However, the regulations do permit a hospital to ask whether the applicant is able to perform the job in question. Furthermore, the regulations provide that an employer may not subject handicapped applicants for employment to physical examinations unless all applicants for the job are required to take the same physical examination.

Americans with Disabilities Act of 1990

The Americans with Disabilities Act (ADA),[63] representing a landmark in civil rights legislation, became law on July 26, 1990. The ADA prohibits discrimination against individuals with disabilities in private employment, public services and transportation, public accommodations, and telecommunications services.

The law specifically protects persons who have communicable diseases such as AIDS or HIV, as well as persons who are undergoing rehabilitation for substance abuse. Current users of illegal drugs are not protected, however, and employers are free to test applicants for drug use.

Under Title I, an employer must reasonably accommodate disabled individuals who are otherwise qualified to do a job, unless making reasonable accommodations would impose an undue hardship on the employer. An employer will be liable for discrimination by denying job opportunities to a qualified individual with a disability if the denial is based on the need to make reasonable accommodation. Examples of "reasonable accommodation" in the ADA include making existing facilities readily accessible to disabled individuals, structuring jobs, providing qualified readers or interpreters, and purchasing or modifying equipment.

Title III of the ADA prohibits any private entity that owns, leases, or operates a place of public accommodations from discriminating against an individual on the basis of disability. *Public accommodation* is broadly defined and includes most privately owned businesses that serve the public. Both hospitals and the professional offices of health care providers fall within this definition.

COMPENSATION AND BENEFIT LAWS

Several federal laws regulate employee compensation and benefits, including the Fair Labor Standards Act. In addition, numerous state laws address these issues.

Fair Labor Standards Act

The Fair Labor Standards Act (FLSA)[64] establishes minimum wages and maximum hours of employment. Employees of all nonprofit and proprietary hospitals are covered by this act, and hospitals must conform. Not every person working in a hospital is covered by the FLSA. Congress has chosen to exempt hospital volunteers, independent contractors, private duty nurses, interns (medical students working in a hospital as part of their training), and in some narrowly defined instances, trainees.[65]

Even in some employment situations, the FLSA has been amended to provide specific exemptions. Most FLSA regulations (e.g., wage and hour provisions) do not apply to persons employed in a bona fide executive, administrative, or professional capacity. All three exemptions require that the individual be compensated on a salary basis. In addition, these employees are protected by the equal pay provisions of FLSA.

Hours of Work

Section 7(a)(1) of the FLSA states that, with certain exceptions, "no employer shall employ any of his employees . . . for a workweek longer than forty hours unless such employee receives compensation for his employment in excess of the hours above specified at a rate not less than one and one-half times the regular rate at which he is employed."

The hours worked are, quite simply, those hours that the employee is required to give the employer. The workweek ordinarily includes all the time that the employee is required to be "on the employer's premises, on duty or at prescribed work place."[66] One federal court has ruled that time spent by hospital employees changing into and out of hospital uniforms must be included in the hospital's hours-worked records and that the employees must be compensated for that time.[67]

Usually, waiting time that occurs during normal duty hours (i.e., the idle hours the employee spends standing in "readiness to serve"[68]) is considered working time. For example, any idle time spent by nurses in an operating room waiting for the scheduled patient to be brought in would be considered working time. Short rest periods, such as 15-minute coffee breaks or snack times, are considered working time. They may not be offset against compensable waiting time or compensable on call time.

Meal periods need not be considered working time if the employee is completely relieved of duty and is permitted to leave the premises and if the time permitted is at least 30 minutes. If the employee is required to perform any duties, to be on call for emergencies, or to remain at the work station for work, then the mean period is compensable work time.

Overtime

The FLSA provides that the health care employer and the employee(s) can agree that the work period will be 14 consecutive days instead of the traditional seven. This is permitted if two conditions are met. First, the agreement must be reached before any work is performed. Second, the employee must be compensated at a rate of one and one-half the regular rate for all hours in excess of eight hours in a workday and for all hours in excess of 80 hours in the 14-day period.[69] The overtime rate is one and one-half times the regular rate.[70]

Although some salaried employees may qualify for the exemptions provided for executive, administrative, or professional employees, this is not the case for all salaried employees. The nonexempt salaried employee is entitled to overtime compensation.

The wage and hour administrator has ruled that employers may require employees who work overtime to take compensatory time off in lieu of paying monetary overtime.[71] However, this paid compensatory time off must be granted during the same pay period in which the overtime was earned and at the rate of one and one-half times the number of overtime hours worked.

OCCUPATIONAL SAFETY AND HEALTH

Congress enacted the Occupational Safety and Health Act (OSH Act)[72] of 1970 to establish standards and to provide for their enforcement. Standards developed for various industries are mandatory for all covered employers. The statute provides that when no federal standard has been established, state safety rules remain in effect. The OSH Act applies to health care institutions, in addition to other industries.

The federal act mandates that each state enact legislation to implement the standards and procedures promulgated by the Department of Labor. Litigation has arisen over inspections by federal and state officials to enforce the OSH Act standards. The courts have held consistently that an employer may refuse an inspection unless the inspector obtains the consent of a duly authorized agent of the employer or has a valid search warrant issued in accordance with state law. The Supreme Court ruled as unconstitutional an OSH Act provision that permitted "spot checks" by Occupational Safety and Health Administration (OSHA) inspectors without a warrant.[73]

OSH Act issued a final bloodborne pathogens standard to protect more than 5.6 million workers from bloodborne infections, including AIDS and hepatitis B virus (HBV).[74] The standard applies to all employees who could be "reasonably anticipated" to face contact with blood or other potentially infectious body fluids as the result of performing their job duties. It requires employers to identify in writing tasks and procedures as well as job classifications where occupational exposure to blood occurs without regard to the use of personal protective clothing and equipment. Universal precautions (treating body fluids as if they are infectious) are now mandatory, with emphasis on engineering and work practice controls. In particular, the standard stresses handwashing and requires employers to provide facilities and ensure that employees use them after exposure to blood. Employers must also provide, require employees to use, and replace as necessary personal protective equipment such as gloves, gowns, masks, and mouthpieces. Postexposure evaluations and follow-ups, including any laboratory tests, must be available at no cost to all employees who have had exposure incidents.

The rule requires that HBV vaccinations be available to all employees with occupational exposure to blood within 10 working days of assignment. Employees who choose not to be vaccinated must sign a declination form and may later opt to receive the free vaccine.

Under the law of some states, employers are charged by statute with the duty of furnishing employees with a safe place to work. Of course, even in the absence of such statutes, employers are liable for most injuries workers suffer as a result of employment. In most situations, the employee must pursue compensation through workers' compensation rather than through the courts.

In addition to provisions relating to unsafe conditions in the workplace, other state statutes require the presence of certain facilities there. These facilities, such as lavatories, are to be provided for the convenience and safety of employees. Ordinances and laws of the city and county in which an employer is located also may include requirements such as sanitary and health codes to promote and safeguard the safety and health of employees and others. In most instances, these laws do not exempt institutions because of their charitable status. However, in most states, state institutions are exempt from local regulation unless state law grants local government the authority to encompass such institutions.

LABOR–MANAGEMENT RELATIONS

Unions have become a significant factor in relations between health care institutions and their employees in many parts of the country. Several different types of labor organizations now are recognized as collective bargaining representatives for groups of hospital employees: craft unions, whose primary organizing efforts are devoted to skilled employees such as carpenters and electricians; industrial unions and governmental employees' unions that seek to represent large groups of relatively unskilled or semiskilled employees; and professional and occupational associations and societies (e.g., state nurses' associations) that represent their members. The professional organizations are labor unions to the extent that they seek goals directly concerned with wages, hours, and other employment conditions and engage in bargaining activities on behalf of employees.

Labor–Management Relations Act

The Labor–Management Relations Act,[75] which defines certain conduct of employers and employees as unfair labor practices and provides for hearings on complaints alleging that such practices have occurred, explicitly exempts governmental employees from its coverage. This act consists of the National Labor Relations Act (NLRA) of 1935,[76] the Taft-Hartley amendments of 1947,[77] and numerous other amendments, including the Labor–Management Reporting and Disclosure Act of 1959.[78] The Act is administered by the National Labor Relations Board (NLRB). The NLRB (1) investigates and adjudicates complaints of unfair labor practices and (2) conducts secret-ballot elections among employees to determine whether they wish to be represented by a labor organization and, if so, which one.

The exemption for governmental hospitals has been interpreted by the NLRB to apply only to hospitals that are owned and operated by governmental agencies. For example, a municipal hospital operated under contract may be considered a private entity subject to the NLRB if overall daily control is by a private contractor. Exempt governmental hospitals usually are subject to state laws concerning governmental employees.

Unfair Labor Practices

Section 7 of the NLRA established four fundamental rights of employees: (1) the right to self-organize; (2) the right to engage in concerted activities for the purpose of collective bargaining or other mutual aid or protection; (3) the right to engage in collective bargaining; and (4) the right to refrain from union activities.

Employer Unfair Labor Practices

An employer commits an unfair labor practice through (1) interference with any of the four rights recognized in section 7; (2) domination of a labor organization; (3) discouragement or encouragement of union activity; (4) discrimination against employees who file charges or testify in an NLRB proceeding; or (5) violation of the other obligations, including good faith bargaining, specified in section 8(a) of the NLRA.

Employees' rights to engage in concerted activities for the purpose of mutual aid or protection can apply to isolated incidents. For example, the NLRB ruled that a small group of unorganized staff were protected when they left their work station to complain to hospital officials concerning work conditions.[79]

A hospital committed an unfair labor practice when it attempted to comply with its guarantee to nonstrikers that they would be placed in the positions of their choice once the strike ended, even if they had not worked in those positions during the strike, the Second Circuit has ruled.[80] During a strike, a hospital decided to reopen several units and began hiring new nurses and crossovers to staff these units. The hospital offered the nonstrikers their choice of positions and promised that the positions would be permanent even if the positions were in departments that were not operating during the strike. When the conflict ended, the hospital refused to reinstate strikers whose positions had been filled or promised to nonstrikers. The union filed unfair labor practice charges arguing that the hospital should return all the strikers to their former positions.

The Second Circuit endorsed the NLRB finding that two groups of nonstrikers had not acquired permanent replacement status. An employer faced with an economic strike is entitled to hire replacements only to the extent needed to preserve production. In this case, the court found, the employer did not have to offer the nonstrikers a choice of permanent positions to ensure continued operations during the strike. Accordingly, only the nonstrikers who had occupied or who had received training for their chosen positions were entitled to retain these jobs as permanent strike replacements. Those who had neither worked nor trained in their current positions during the strike were not permanent replacements, the court concluded, and the hospital's refusal to return strikers to these jobs was unlawful.

Employee Representation

A labor organization seeking representation rights for employees may petition the NLRB for a secret-ballot election. The petition must make a "showing of interest" supporting the petition—that is, at least 30 percent of the workers who ultimately will make up the bargaining unit must support it and show their interest by signing union authorization cards.

In 1989, the NLRB issued a final rule delineating eight bargaining units to be recognized in acute care hospitals.[81] This rule represented the first time the Board had promulgated bargaining unit rules for a single industry. The eight units include

1. all registered nurses
2. all physicians

3. all professionals except registered nurses and physicians
4. all technical employees
5. all business office clerical employees
6. all skilled maintenance employees
7. all nonprofessional employees, except technical employees, skilled maintenance employees, business office clerical employees, and guards
8. all guards

Under the rule, these eight bargaining units would be the only units appropriate for collective bargaining in an acute care hospital, unless a facility is able to claim and prove "extraordinary circumstances."

Bargaining Status of Nurses' Associations

In a major policy decision, the NLRB has announced the standards by which it will determine the bargaining status of nurses' associations.[82] After reviewing its prior decision, the Board decided to change its standards of review in this type of case. The new standards are

1. The Board no longer conditions certification of nurses' associations on the delegation of their bargaining authority to autonomous chapters or locals.
2. Participation of supervisory nurses in a state nursing association is virtually irrelevant in determining its status as a valid labor organization. Thus, as long as nurse-employees participate in the association and one of the association's purposes is to represent employees in collective bargaining, a nurses' association meets the definition of labor organization in section 2(5) of the act.
3. The role of supervisors in the association may, however, disqualify it from collective bargaining. If there is a clear risk of a conflict of interest that would interfere with the collective bargaining process, the association is not allowed to represent employees for the purposes of collective bargaining.
4. The burden of proving that there is a danger of conflict of interest rests entirely on the employer.

Solicitation and Distribution

Most hospitals have rules concerning solicitation of employees and distribution of materials in the hospital to avoid interference with patient care. The NLRB examines each policy on a case-by-case basis. Some general guidelines can be derived from past decisions. Nonemployees generally may be prohibited access to the facility for solicitation or distribution. Employees can be prohibited from solicitation or distribution during work time. Solicitation or distribution can be limited to nonpatient care areas at all times.[83] In general, a genuine likelihood of patient disturbance is necessary, so areas where visitors have general access such as cafeterias and lounges usually cannot be prohibited.

Collective Bargaining and Mediation

After a labor organization has been recognized as the exclusive bargaining agent, the employer and union both have a duty to negotiate in good faith. Collective bargaining is usually defined as the bilateral process of reaching an agreement between an agent representing employees and an employer with respect to wages, hours, and other terms and conditions of employment. They may bargain on other permissive subjects but are not legally obligated to do so. It is unlawful to bring negotiations to an impasse, to strike, or to lock out employees over permissive subjects.

The most complex and subtle requirement of the federal law is that the parties negotiate in "good faith." The NLRB and courts have said that a good faith attitude is one in which the parties have an open mind and a sincere desire to reach agreement.[84] The NLRA defines the obligation to bargain in good faith:

> The performance of the mutual obligation of the employer and the representative of the employees to meet at reasonable times and confer in good faith with respect to wages, hours, and other terms and conditions of employment, or the negotiation of an agreement, or any question arising thereunder, and the execution of a written contract incorporating any agreement reached if requested by either party, but such obligation does not compel either party to agree to a proposal or require the making of a concession. . . .[85]

When a union has been certified by the NLRB as the exclusive bargaining agent, the parties are mandated to engage in bargaining for a first contract. It is generally believed that the single most important labor contract that an institution will ever negotiate is its first collective bargaining contract, for this establishes the environment and attitudes that will shape future relations between the parties. Moreover, experience proves that language inserted in the initial contract often becomes deeply embedded and is hard to eliminate.

Several special notice, mediation, and conciliation safeguards were built into the law for the health care industry to avoid strikes when possible. For example, 90 days' notice is required if a party intends to terminate or modify a bargaining agreement, and the Federal Mediation and Conciliation Service (FMCS) must be given 60 days' notice. When notified, the FMCS is required to attempt to bring about an agreement, and all parties must participate fully and promptly in meetings called by the agency to aid in a settlement. In the event of a threatened strike, the FMCS, under certain conditions, can establish an impartial board of inquiry to investigate the issues and provide a cooling-off period of up to 30 days.

Strikes

For private hospitals, the NLRA protects the right of employees in private hospitals to engage in *concerted activities,* a phrase that includes the right to strike. However, Congress has provided a special strike notice and cooling-off feature for the hospital industry to minimize the impact of strikes on patients.

When employees engage in a lawful primary strike against their employer, they may not be disciplined or discharged *because* they have engaged in such activity. It is precisely this protection that the Taft-Hartley Act grants to employees, because it had not been granted under the laws of most of the 50 states.

Another special provision for health care institutions is a 10-day advance notice of intention to engage in concerted economic activities including strikes, picketing, or any other joint refusal to work. This provision is designed to allow a hospital to make plans for continuity of patient care in the face of a work stoppage. Some courts have ruled that individual unorganized employees do not have to give a 10-day notice. One federal court ruled in 1980 that two physicians who walked out of the hospital and joined the picket line of a lawful strike by other employees did not have to give the notice.[86] The court noted that the action was inconsiderate and ethically suspect but protected.

Administering the Contract

After negotiating a labor agreement, the hospitals and labor organizations should spend no less care on its administration. Rights that have been established at the bargaining table, sometimes at a high price, can be eroded or entirely lost through inattention. Employees should be knowledgeable concerning their rights and responsibilities. The entire managerial team, especially first-line and second-line supervisors, should know the aspects of the contract applicable to their responsibilities. Of particular importance is the problem of discipline. They must be trained to ensure that discipline is administered for the right reasons and by the appropriate procedures under the contract.

STATE LAWS—WORKERS' COMPENSATION

Every state has some form of workers' compensation legislation that is designed to ensure that employees will be compensated for losses resulting from accidental on-the-job injuries. These acts replace the common-law remedy that required the employee to sue the employer for negligence, which usually was unsuccessful. Most employers are subject to the act, although some states provide exceptions. In cases not routinely paid by the insurance carrier, the matter will go to hearings before a state commission to determine questions of liability.

State statutes define employee, injury, and other terms and have comprehensive schedules stating payment amounts for types of injuries. Where the workers' compensation law applies, the employee is barred from suing the employer for the injury. The only way courts become involved is if there is an appeal concerning the decisions of the state official or agency administering the law.

Considerable litigation takes place in each state to settle the question arising in the many situations in which employees are injured. One sensitive area involves whether the injury occurred "out of and in the course of employment," a key phrase in qualifying for compensation. A related issue is whether the injury was truly caused by an "accident" or was instead the "natural and probable result of that particular job." Numerous exclusions are stated for preexisting or congenital physical conditions, as well as injuries caused by horseplay and other causes not incidental to employment.

Initially, an employee must give written notice of the injury to the employer. This and the report of the medical treatment provided ordinarily constitute the basis for compensation. Usually employees cannot receive compensation under workers' compensation laws (1) if the injury was caused by the intoxication of the injured worker(s); (2) if the injury was caused by the worker's willful intent to injure him- or herself or another; or (3) if (in some states) the injury was caused by the willful act of another directed against the employee for personal reasons.

STATE LAWS—UNEMPLOYMENT COMPENSATION

State law generally provides for payment of unemployment compensation to many unemployed individuals. Generally, persons who have been discharged for misconduct forfeit all or part of the compensation they would have received otherwise. Thus, there is considerable litigation concerning what constitutes misconduct.

For example, the Pennsylvania Supreme Court found a nursing assistant guilty of misconduct for smoking in a patient's room contrary to hospital rules. Therefore, she was denied unemployment compensation after her discharge.[87] However, the Vermont Supreme Court ruled that a nurse who had been discharged for giving a patient medications by intravenous push instead of intravenous drip was entitled to unemployment compensation because her error had been in good faith.[88]

PUBLIC EMPLOYEES

Because the NLRA does not apply to employees of state and local agencies, the relations between these public employees and their governmental employers are controlled by state law, which often varies from the federal act. There is significant variation among the states. Some prohibit collective bargaining by public employees, so that workers' rights are determined by state civil service laws and individual agency policies. Many states authorize representation by a labor organization and collective bargaining. A state agency similar to the NLRB usually is established to administer the authorizing law. State laws frequently limit the subjects that may be determined by collective bargaining. Many states prohibit strikes by all or some public employees and require that an arbitration procedure be used to resolve impasses.

CONCLUSION

The laws regulating the employment relationships with nurses are exceedingly complex. Generally, nurses are often considered employees "at-will," which means they can be discharged at any time without cause. The employment relationship is, however, subject to a myriad of federal legislation that prohibits discrimination of various kinds. Union activity is a major part of the health care scene that is affected by both federal and state legislation. Although most nurses as employees should be familiar in general with this legal landscape, they do not need intimate knowledge of these laws. Nurses in an administrative or supervisory capacity, however, need to be intimately knowledgeable about selecting, training, supervising, and disciplining nurses and other employees in this complex and evolving area of the law.

FOOTNOTES

1. 29 U.S.C. § 794 (Supp. V 1981).
2. Payne v. Western Atl. R.R. Co., 81 Tenn. 507 (1884).
3. *E.g.,* Lampe v. Presbyterian Med. Ctr., 590 P.2d 513 (Colo. Ct. App. 1978) (head nurse terminated for inability to follow staffing procedures and stay within budget).
4. Note, *Protecting At Will Employees against Wrongful Discharge: The Duty to Terminate Only in Good Faith*, 93 HARV. L. REV. 1916 (1980).
5. *E.g., Lampe*; Kurle v. Evangelical Hosp. Ass'n, 88 Ill. App. 3d 45, 44 Ill. Dec. 357, 411 N.E.2d 326 (1980).
6. *E.g.,* People *ex rel.* Miselis v. Health & Hosp. Governing Comm'n, 44 Ill. App. 3d 958, 3 Ill. Dec. 536, 358 N.E.2d 1221 (1976).
7. Heideck v. Kent Gen. Hosp., 446 A.2d 1095 (Del. 1982) (dismissal for failure to heed patient's plea for privacy on bedside commode).
8. Falls v. Lawnwood Med. Ctr., 427 So. 2d 361 (Fla. Ct. App. 1983) (alleged abuse of patient).
9. Herbert v. Woman's Hosp. Found., 377 So. 2d 1340 (La. Ct. App. 1979).
10. Civil Rights Act of 1964, 42 U.S.C. § 2000e; Age Discrimination in Employment Act, 29 U.S.C. §§ 621–634 and 663(a); Rehabilitation Act of 1973, 29 U.S.C. § 794; Vietnam Era Veterans' Readjustment Assistance Act, 38 U.S.C. §§ 2021–2028.

11. *See, e.g.*, Michigan Fair Employment Practices Act, Mich. Stat. Ann. § 3.548 (101); Pa. Stat. Ann. tit. 43, § 955.

12. Annotation, 12 A.L.R. 4th 544 (1982).

13. Webb v. HCA Health Servs. of Midwest, Inc., 780 S.W.2d 571 (Ark. 1989).

14. Crockett v. Mid-America Health Servs., 780 S.W.2d 656 (Mo. Ct. App. 1989).

15. Wright v. Shriners Hosp. for Crippled Children, No. SJC-5613 (Mass. Sup. Jud. Ct. April 16, 1992).

16. Pearson v. Macon-Bibb County Hosp. Auth., 952 F.2d 1274 (11th Cir. 1992).

17. Leikvold v. Valley View Community Hosp., 688 P.2d 170 (Ariz. 1984). *See also* Duldalao v. Saint Mary of Nazareth Hosp. Ctr., 505 N.E.2d 314 (Ill. App. Ct. 1987); Land v. Michael Reese Hosp. & Med. Ctr., 505 N.E.2d 1261 (Ill. App. Ct. 1987); Watson v. Idaho Falls Consol. Hosp., Inc., 720 P.2d 632 (Idaho S. Ct. 1986). *But see* Johnson v. National Beef Packing Co., 551 P.2d 779 (Kan. 1976); Heideck v. Kent Gen. Hosp., A.2d 1095 (Del. 1982); Mau v. Omaha Nat'l Bank, 299 N.W.2d 147 (Neb. 1980), in which the courts held that employer representations in a personnel manual do not modify an employment-at-will relationship.

18. *E.g.,* Iowa Code § 135C.46 (reports by employers of health care facilities to the facility licensing agency).

19. Kelsay v. Motorola, Inc., 74 Ill. 2d 172, 23 Ill. Dec. 599, 384 N.E.2d 353 (1979).

20. Hitt v. North Broward Hosp. Dist., 387 So. 2d 482 (Fla. Dist. Ct. App. 1980) (private duty nurse put flyers concerning nursing group on public hospital bulletin board).

21. Rosier v. St. Mary's Hosp., 88 Ill. App. 3d 994, 44 Ill. Dec. 144, 411 N.E.2d 50 (1980); *see also* Manus v. National Living Ctrs., Inc., 633 S.W.2d 675 (Tex. Civ. App. 1982) (discharge of nurse's aid by nursing home for complaints to superiors concerning patient care).

22. *E.g.,* Gengler v. Phelps, 589 P.2d 1056 (N.M. Ct. App. 1978), *cert. denied* 92 N.M. 353, 588 P.2d 544 (1979) (communication concerning nurse anesthetist).

23. 29 U.S.C. § 794.

24. 45 C.F.R. § 84.1.

25. Leckelt v. Board of Comm'rs Hosp. Dist. 1, 909 F.2d 850 (5th Cir. 1990).

26. *See, e.g.,* Conn. Gen. Stat. Ann. § 46a-15(15); N.J. Stat. Ann. § 10:5-5.

27. Doe v. County of Cook, No. 87 C 6888 (N.D. Ill. Feb. 24, 1988).

28. Centers for Disease Control, Recommendations for Preventions of HIV Transmission in Health-Care Settings.

29. 42 U.S.C. §§ 200e-200e-17.

30. Wrighten v. Metropolitan Hosp. Inc., 726 F.2d 1346 (9th Cir. 1984).

31. *But see* Patee v. Pacific Northwest Bell Tel. Co., 803 F.2d 476 (9th Cir. 1986), which held that male employees cannot sue under Title VII as persons injured because of sex-based wage discrimination against women.

32. *See* Backus v. Baptist Med. Ctr., 510 F. Supp. 1191 (E.D. Ark. 1981), and EEOC v. Mercy Hosp. Ctr., No. 80-1374-W (W.D. Okla. Feb. 2, 1982) (male nurses were lawfully barred from assignment in labor and delivery areas because a sex-based job qualification in those locations was justified by nondiscriminatory business reasons or patients' privacy rights). *See also* Jones v. Hinds Gen. Hosp., 666 F. Supp. 933 (S.E. Miss. 1987).

33. American Fed'n of State, County & Municipal Employees Local 567 v. Michigan, 635 F. Supp. 1010 (E.D. Mich. 1986).

34. 29 C.F.R. § 1604.2(a) (1) (i).

35. Backus v. Baptist Med. Ctr., 510 F. Supp. 1191 (E.D. Ark. 1981), *vacated as moot,* 671 F.2d 1100 (8th Cir. 1982).

36. *See, e.g.,* Smith v. Liberty Mut. Life Ins. Co., 395 F. Supp. 1098 (N.D. Ga. 1975).

37. Vayles v. Ralph K. Davis Med. Ctr., 403 F. Supp. 456 (N.D. Cal. 1975); *see also* Willingham v. Bacon Tel. Publ'g Co., 507 F.2d 1084 (5th Cir. 1975).

38. Bruno v. Crown Point, Ind., 950 F.2d 355 (7th Cir. 1991).

39. Rabidue v. Osceola Ref. Co., 805 F.2d 611 (6th Cir. 1986).

40. *E.g.,* Lemons v. City of Denver, 620 F.2d 228 (10th Cir. 1980); Briggs v. City of Madison, 536 F. Supp. 435 (W.D. Wis. 1982).

41. A.F.S.C.M.E. v. Washington, 578 F. Supp. 846 (W.D. Wash. 1983).

42. EEOC v. Ithaca Indus., 849 F.2d 116 (4th Cir. 1988).

43. Ansonia Bd. of Educ. v. Philbrook, 107 S. Ct. 367 (1986).

44. Brener v. Diagnostic Ctr. Hosp., 673 F.2d 141 (5th Cir. 1982); Kenny v. Ambulatory Ctr. of Miami, Inc., 400 So. 2d 1262 (Fla. App. 1981); North Shore Univ. Hosp. v. State Human Rights Appeals Bd., 439 N.Y.S.2d 409 (Sup. Ct. App. Div. 1981).

45. Murphy v. Edge Mem'l Hosp., 550 F. Supp. 1185 (M.D. Ala. 1982). *See also* Pennsylvania State Univ. v. Commonwealth, 505 A.2d 1053 (Pa. Commw. Ct. 1986); Baz v. Walters, 782 F.2d 701 (7th Cir. 1986).

46. 29 U.S.C. § 206(d).

47. 29 U.S.C. § 206(d)(1).

48. *Id.*

49. Hodgson v. Golden Isles Nursing Home, 468 F.2d 1256 (5th Cir. 1972).

50. Beall v. Curtis, 683 F. Supp. 1563 (M.D. Ga. 1985).

51. 29 U.S.C. §§ 621–634 and 663(a).

52. Pub. L. No. 99-592.

53. 29 U.S.C. §§ 701-794.

54. 29 U.S.C. § 706(8)(b).

55. 45 C.F.R. § 84.3(j)(2)(i).

56. 45 C.F.R. § 84.3(j)(2)(iii).

57. 45 C.F.R. § 84.3(j)(2)(iv).

58. Pub. L. No. 101-336 § 512(a), July 26, 1990.

59. Leckelt v. Board of Comm'rs of Hosp. Dist. 1, Civ. No. 86-4235 (E.D. La. Mar. 15, 1989).

60. 909 F.2d 820 (5th Cir. 1990).

61. 45 C.F.R. § 84.3(k).

62. 442 U.S. 397 (1979).

63. Pub. L. No. 101-336.

64. 29 U.S.C. §§ 201–219.

65. Marshall v. Baptist Hosp., Inc., 668 F.2d 234 (6th Cir. 1981) (FLSA not applicable to trainees in a two-year X-ray technician program).

66. Anderson v. Mt. Clemens Pottery Co., 328 U.S. 680 (1946).

67. Brock v. Mercy Hosp. & Med. Ctr., No. 84-1309g(m) (S.D. Cal. May 6, 1986).

68. 29 C.F.R. § 785.7.

69. Note that an employer who fires employees because they demand compensation for overtime violates the FLSA, the Second Circuit has ruled. Brock v. Casey Truck Sales, 839 F.2d 872 (2d Cir. 1988).

70. A hospital can lawfully pay on-call night shift employees overtime at a rate of one and one-half the minimum wage instead of one and one-half the employee's regular rate, according to a federal trial court. Townsend v. Mercy Hosp., 689 F. Supp. 503 (W.D. Pa. 1988).

71. Wage and Hour Opinion Letter, December 27, 1968.

72. Pub. L. No. 91-596, 84 Stat. 1590 (1970) (codified as amended in 29 U.S.C. §§ 651–678 and scattered sections of 5, 15, 18, 29, 42, and 49 U.S.C.).

73. Marshall v. Barlow's, Inc., 436 U.S. 307 (1978).

74. Occupational Exposure to Bloodborne Pathogens, 56 Fed. Reg. 64,004 (1991).

75. 29 U.S.C. §§ 141–187.

76. Act of July 5, 1935, ch. 372, 49 Stat. 449.

77. Act of June 23, 1947, ch. 120, 61 Stat. 136.

78. Pub. L. No. 86-257, 73 Stat. 519.

79. *E.g.,* Mercy Hosp. Ass'n, Inc., 235 N.L.R.B. 681 (1978).

80. Waterbury Hosp. v. NLRB, L.R.R.M. 2005 (2d Cir. Dec. 3, 1991).

81. 54 Fed. Reg. 16,336 (1989).

82. Sierra Vista Hosp., Inc., and California Nurses Ass'n, 242 N.L.R.B. No. 107, 100 L.R.R.M. 1591 (1979).

83. NLRB v. Baptist Hosp., 442 U.S. 773 (1979).

84. *See, e.g.,* NLRB v. Montgomery Ward & Co., 133 F.2d 676 (9th Cir. 1943).

85. 29 U.S.C. § 158(d) (A).

86. Montefiore Hosp. and Med. Ctr. v. NLRB, 621 F.2d 510 (2d Cir. 1980).

87. Selan v. Unemployment Comp. Bd. of Review, 433 A.2d 1337 (Pa. 1981).

88. Porter v. Department of Employment Sec., 139 Vt. 405, 430 A.2d 450 (1981).

CHAPTER 4

The Nurse as Independent Contractor

Chapter Objectives

1. To compare practice arrangements
2. To consider the scope of practice
3. To discuss reimbursement for services
4. To address clinical privileges
5. To examine liability

With the emergence of nursing specialities and certification for advanced practice, many nurses have begun the independent practice of a specialty. Nurse practitioners, nurse anesthetists, and clinical nursing specialists are examples of those who may practice independently or contract with an agency (e.g., a clinic or hospital) to provide service. Others, including nurse anesthetists, nurse-midwives, pediatric and family nurse practitioners, and mental health practitioners, often practice independently or under the supervision of a physician.

Generally, nurse practitioners and nurse anesthetists are registered nurses who have completed a practitioner program of specialized clinical and academic preparation, often with but not necessarily leading to a master's degree, whereas clinical nursing specialists are registered nurses who have received a master's degree. Increasingly, states are requiring that specific criteria be met before nurses can represent themselves as qualified to practice in an expanded role. For instance, many states are requiring a master's degree for nurse practitioner licensure. Many states have developed separate licensing for advanced practice.

The opportunities for nurses to practice in expanded roles have grown as a result of increased nursing knowledge and specialization, shortages of physicians in some areas, consumers' demands for primary caregivers, and their cost-effective use in managed care settings. Nurses have assumed a greater role in providing patients with services such as health maintenance and promotion, education, information about diseases and treatment, and anticipatory guidance, often in nontraditional health care settings such as schools, factories, and clinics as well as in hospitals, nursing homes, and doctors' offices.

The expanded role refers to the enlargement of the individual's functions in using all aspects of problem-solving processes: delineation of the field of the problem, assessing and implementing care, and evaluating outcomes. The result is a qualitative change in the nurse's delivery of patient care services.

Role expansion is based on theory, using natural and behavioral sciences that give direction to nursing action. Knowledge and skill are applied to decision making as well as to performance. The nurse assumes or shares the responsibility for the health care services delivered to the patient and establishes plans and goals alone or in consultation with other professionals.[1]

A nurse functioning in an expanded role acts on knowledge that reflects theory (e.g., determining the need for a Pap smear, dealing constructively with the behavioral factors that inhibit the patient from taking the recommended action, and making referrals when appropriate under established protocols).

This chapter addresses some of the legal issues associated with nurses engaged in expanded or independent practice, covering three basic patterns of practice: (1) nurses who maintain their own practice, (2) nurses who engage in expanded practice and contract to provide services to an agency, and (3) nurses who function in an expanded role under the supervision of another health professional. Some of the legal issues covered include the types of practice arrangements, scope of practice, payment and collections, clinical privileges, and liability.

PRACTICE ARRANGEMENTS

Nurses engage in expanded practice in several types of settings, with wide variation in their job functions and responsibilities. Typical responsibilities of the nurse practitioner or expanded practitioner include history taking, physical examination, identification of problems, counseling, and referral. Some states allow nurse practitioners to prescribe treatments and drugs, and many permit them to prescribe within standing orders or protocols. Most nurse practitioners work in a clinic or office, but they also are found in hospitals, in industrial settings, and as consultants. Some work independent of an agency or supervisor, on a fee-for-service basis. The most common ways in which an independent practice can be structured are described below.

Sole Proprietorship

In a sole proprietorship, an individual has sole responsibility for all aspects of the enterprise, including hiring employees, collecting fees, liability, and policy determination and decision making. The sole proprietor may hire employees on salary. The income from the business will be taxed by the federal government at the same rate as income from any other job. The owner is personally liable for all aspects of the business, including the actions of the employees. If the owner dies or leaves the business, it does not automatically continue.

General Partnership

When two or more individuals enter into a business enterprise, sharing both the responsibilities and the profits or losses, a general partnership exists unless the business is incorporated. Each partner is responsible for the management and liabilities. If the partnership does not have sufficient assets to meets its obligations, the partners may be required to use their personal assets. If one partner is found liable for negligence arising out of the partnership, all the partners will be responsible for the damages. One partner can bind the other partners to an agreement. Income from a partnership is taxed as personal income, and a partnership usually ends when one of the partners dies or leaves the partnership.

Limited Partnership

A limited partnership consists of two types of partners: general partners whose rights and obligations are the same as those in a general partnership, and limited partners who have made an investment in the business and whose liabilities extend only to the extent of that investment. Limited partners do not participate in the management or operations of the business.

Business Corporation

The business corporation is a legal entity, organized under the laws of the state, with the same power as a natural person to engage in acts consistent with its stated purpose. The corporation is organized under a board of directors, which manages the corporation, and is owned by shareholders. There are several advantages to the corporate form of business. Because the law recognizes the corporation as a separate entity, it can own property, make binding agreements, and exist indefinitely, independent of the individuals who own or operate it. The shareholders also have limited liability if the corporation is found liable for negligence.

The income of a corporation generally is taxed at the corporate level, and the profits are taxed again at personal income rates whenever they are distributed to stockholders. The corporation can offer some tax-free fringe benefits to its employees, but these are being increasingly restricted. The corporation must comply with the laws and regulations governing corporations in the state, limiting management flexibility of the practice to some extent.

Professional Corporation

An increasingly popular type of business organization in the health care field is the professional corporation. It has many of the features of a business corporation. In many states, all the members must be licensed in the same profession, but some states permit multiple professions to form one corporation. In some states, all members are jointly liable for malpractice committed within the practice of the professional corporation, but in many other states, unlike partners, individual members are not liable for malpractice of others in the corporation. Liability for matters not related to the professional practice generally is limited to the investment.

Limited Liability Company

A new type of organization is the limited liability company. Authorized by legislation that has been adopted in nearly every state, these organizations are a hybrid that combine the best features of corporations and partnerships. Limited liability companies have the limited liability attributes of a corporation. In addition, they are taxed as partnerships, meaning that, like partnerships, only the individuals, not the entity, pays tax on its income.

Independent Practice

A nurse entering independent practice should be familiar with the advantages and disadvantages of each type of business organization and should review the state laws pertaining to each. It is important to consult an attorney when making any practice agreements. There are several disadvantages to independent practice arrangements, including the necessity of hiring employees, bookkeeping, interaction with government agencies, arranging third-party payment, and financial risks.

Many nurse practitioners engage in a modified independent practice in which they contract with a physician or agency to provide services The services usually are in the nature of expanded practice, and the nurses have a significant measure of independence. They are liable for their own acts of negligence and may be liable for those of others acting under their direction even if not their employees. An agreement between a nurse and an agency should indicate clearly what provisions exist for liability coverage, payment of fees, and referral.

In the most common practice arrangement, the nurse practitioner is employed by an agency or a physician to provide expanded services to a group of patients. Typically, there is indirect supervision over the nurse, who practices within a list of protocols. Protocols attempt to standardize the diagnosis and management of specified patient complaints.

SCOPE OF PRACTICE

One major legal issue is the legally permissible scope of practice for nurses in an independent role. Traditionally, the nurse's responsibilities were ministerial and administrative in nature, and the physician had sole responsibility for diagnosis, treatment, and prescription. Developments in nursing and in legislation have expanded the scope of practice and blurred the distinction between the activities of nurses and physicians in some areas.

There is no dispute that nursing practice still includes the traditional elements of ministerial care of patients, including meeting their needs for safety, comfort, and carrying out prescribed treatments and other orders. The scope of the nurses' role in defining, prescribing, and monitoring treatment has expanded, however, and can be expected to continue to grow.

This has taken two forms: (1) the expansion of the definition of basic nursing practice through nurse practice acts, regulations, and judicial decisions; and (2) the trend toward advanced practice licensure.

A review of state statutes shows that most states have laws that authorize nurses to diagnose and treat patients and that recognize nurse practitioners.[2] The scope of practice also may be defined through the state medical practice act, judicial decisions, and attorney generals' opinions. Nurses should be familiar with each of these sources in the state in which they practice.

An example of the relationship of all these sources to the scope of practice is the prescription of medications by nurses, which was prohibited by early acts. When states began to authorize expanded practice, they frequently left it to the boards of medicine and nursing to work out the details of the changes. Many assumed that if the statute allowed nurses to diagnose and treat patients, it inferentially authorized nurses to prescribe. Idaho, the first state (in 1971) to authorize expanded practice, took this approach.[3] In some states the statute specifically authorizes nurses to prescribe medications, some grant prescriptive authority by rule, and some specify that it be authorized by contract with an agency or health department. Several states' attorney generals (e.g., Michigan, New York) have issued opinions that describe circumstances under which nurse practitioners can prescribe medications.

A judicial definition of the appropriate scope of nursing practice is found in *Sermchief v. Gonzales*.[4] The case involved two certified family nurse practitioners who were providing services in a family planning clinic. The services included breast and pelvic examinations, Pap smears, gonorrhea cultures, blood serology, birth control methods, pregnancy testing, and information and education. The services were provided according to standing orders and protocols agreed on jointly by the nurse practitioners and the five physicians with whom they worked.

A written complaint was filed with the Missouri Board of Registration for the Healing Arts, alleging that the nurse practitioners were practicing medicine without a license. After an investigation, the Board recommended criminal prosecution of the two. The Circuit Court of St. Louis County ruled that the two nurses were not practicing nursing but were practicing medicine without a medical license. The court stated that determining the existence or nonexistence of contraindications to the use of contraceptives required an individual to draw on education, judgment, and skill based on knowledge and application of principles in addition to and beyond biologic, physical, social, and nursing sciences. The court also found that by authorizing the use of protocols, the physicians were abetting the unlawful practice of medicine.

On appeal, however, the Missouri Supreme Court overturned the ruling, holding that the Missouri legislature, in passing the Nursing Practice Act in 1976, indicated its intent to avoid statutory constraints on the evaluation of new functions for nurses delivering health services and that those performed by the practitioners were clearly within their scope of practice as defined by the Act. The court stated, "We believe the acts of the nurses are precisely the types of acts the legislature contemplated when it granted nurses the right to make assessments and nursing diagnoses."[5] On the question of the distinction between a nursing diagnosis and a medical diagnosis, the court said:

> There can be no question that a nurse undertakes only a nursing diagnosis, as opposed to a medical diagnosis, when she or he finds or fails to find symptoms described by physicians in standing orders and protocols for the purpose of administering courses of treatment prescribed by the physician in such orders and protocols.[6]

The court also stated:

> The broadening of the field of practice of the nursing profession authorized by the legislature and here recognized by the court carries with it the profession's responsibility for continuing high educational standards and the individual nurse's responsibility to conduct herself or himself in a professional manner. The hallmark of a professional is knowing the limits of one's professional knowledge. The nurse, either upon reaching the limit of his knowledge or upon reaching the limits prescribed for the nurse by the physician's standing orders and protocols, should refer the patient to the physician.[7]

The Missouri court thus determined that professional nurses in Missouri had a right to practice within the limits of their education and experience. It also said nurses had a professional duty to make a timely referral of patients whose needs exceed the scope of the practitioners' expertise.

REIMBURSEMENT FOR SERVICES

Payment

Payment to nurses in private or expanded practice is important both in terms of professional status and in ensuring the viability of a business enterprise. For those reasons, the issue of reimbursement of third-party payers for nursing services has become important. Traditionally, payments for nursing services provided in an institution or in the home have been made to the employing organization. Nurses now are seeking to receive reimbursement for services directly from Medicare, Medicaid, and private insurers rather than through a physician or other organization.

The Medicare and Medicaid programs provide for some reimbursement for nurse practitioners. For example, Medicare Part B provides for direct reimbursement of nurse practitioners and nurse-midwives practicing in rural areas.[8] The authority for Medicaid, the joint federal-state program, is Title XIX of the Social Security Act[9] and individual state statutes. Federal Medicaid regulations authorize payment to licensed practitioners within the scope of their practice as defined by the law of the state, which undoubtedly includes nurses in expanded roles.

A large part of health care is paid for by third-party payers other than the government, including Blue Cross and Blue Shield, commercial insurance companies, self-funded health insurance plans of some industries, health maintenance organizations, and other alternative delivery systems. Blue Cross covers hospital and related services, and Blue Shield covers physician and related services. Blue Cross and Blue Shield plans cover local regions and have widely different practices concerning payment and other matters. Consequently, there is wide variation among regions as to the reimbursement of nurses and nurse practitioners, with an increasing number of states recognizing the appropriateness of this payment.

Collections

A difficult area for any health care provider is the collection of payments for services. Although third-party payments may constitute a portion of nurses' accounts receivable, collection from individual patients remains an important source of revenue. To ensure that a bill can be pressed to its legal limits for collection, it must be accurately prepared and maintained. The correct name and address of the patient and the name of the person responsible for payment must be obtained, services provided and dates clearly described, and the recording of any payments or other credits promptly reflected on the account.

An unpaid bill for professional services frequently is turned over to a collection agency. Practitioners usually enter into a written agreement with one or more collection agencies specifying the terms and conditions for their activities to ensure compliance with the law.

A bill for services is evidence of a contract to pay for care provided and is enforceable by legal action. Although small bills usually are not worth the cost of judicial proceedings, legal collection actions sometimes serve to educate patients about their obligation to pay medical bills just as they pay other bills. A court judgment can be obtained against a debtor and enforced through several mechanisms such as garnishment of wages.

Several state and federal laws regulate collection practices, including the Consumer Credit Protection Act,[10] the Federal Debt Collection Practices Act,[11] and federal bankruptcy laws. Independent practice nurses engaged in the collection of bills should consult with an attorney to make sure that the legal requirements are met.

CLINICAL PRIVILEGES

Some nurses in expanded or independent practice seek to obtain hospital privileges. Before they may practice in a hospital, they must be granted clinical privileges by its governing board. Some boards delegate the responsibility for granting privileges to an administrative official or committee. Practitioners may provide only the services for which they have clinical privileges, and the board has the responsibility to exercise its discretion in determining whether to grant an appointment and the scope of privileges. Some institutions grant nurse practitioners hospital privileges, some give limited privileges to function under a sponsoring physician, and some have decided not to admit them. When a hospital does decide to accept such nurses, it must consider the criteria and procedures for determining whether any specific practitioner will be granted privileges.

LIABILITY

The expansion of nursing practice into some areas traditionally defined as medical in nature has led to an increased risk of liability. In addition to the standard liability principles (discussed in Chapters 14 and 15, applicable to nurses generally), those practicing in an expanded role may be at increased risk of civil liability to patients for their expanded treatments and for failing to refer a patient in a timely manner.

Changes in the scope of practice make it difficult to say with certainty when a practitioner has a duty to refer a patient to a specialist. Physicians and other health care providers have long been recognized to have a duty to refer. Generally, providers have a duty to disclose to the patient the advisability of seeking other treatment if they know or should know that the ailment is beyond their ability to treat. In other words, a general practitioner has a duty to refer a patient to a specialist when the condition demands it.[12] It is likely that this duty will be applied to nurse practitioners.

CONCLUSION

Increasingly, nurses who practice independently will be challenged to organize their businesses and operate them successfully. Three important issues that must be considered in creating an independent practice are (1) the proper form of business, (2) the permissible scope of practice, and (3) reimbursement and liability concerns.

FOOTNOTES

1. AMERICAN NURSES ASSOCIATION, NURSING: A SOCIAL POLICY STATEMENT. PT. 3. SPECIALIZATION IN NURSING PRACTICE.
2. *Annual Update on How Each State Stands on Legislative Issues Affecting Advanced Nursing Practice,* 19 NURSE PRAC., 17 (1994).
3. IDAHO CODE § 54-1413, as amended 1971; IDAHO BOARD OF NURSING AND BOARD OF MEDICINE, GUIDELINES FOR NURSING PRACTITIONERS WRITING PRESCRIPTIONS; MINIMUM STANDARDS, RULES, AND REGULATIONS FOR THE EXPANDING ROLE OF THE PROFESSIONAL NURSE (June 1972).
4. Sermchief v. Gonzales, 600 S.W.2d 683 (Mo. *en banc* 1983).
5. *Id.* at 689.
6. *Id.* at 689–690.
7. *Id.* at 690.
8. 42 C.F.R. part 405.2401–405.2430.
9. 42 U.S.C. § 1396a-1936p as amended by Pub. L. No. 97-35, 95 Stat. 785 (1981) and Pub. L. No. 97-248, 96 Stat. 367 (1982).
10. 15 U.S.C. §§ 1671–1677.
11. 15 U.S.C. §§ 1692–1692o.
12. *E.g.,* Manion v. Tweedy, 257 Minn. 59, 100 N.W.2d 124 (1960).

CHAPTER 5

Health Care Organizations and Their Business

```
Chapter Objectives

1. To compare the types of hospitals
2. To examine governing boards
3. To review federal income taxation of medical organizations
4. To recognize the responsibility for charges for health care
   services
5. To compare managed care programs
```

Health care systems have become big businesses. As managed care programs replace the traditional indemnity insurance and fee-for-service systems, nurses must find new ways of operating within the hospital organization as well as developing new roles in the health care marketplace. In an environment of cost containment, cost control, and cost reductions, nurses must be knowledgeable about the business operations of the health care system to be successful in functioning within such a system while delivering high-quality nursing care. Moreover, increasingly nurses are becoming "case managers" in managed care programs; in such a role, it is necessary that he or she be familiar with fundamental managed care principles to implement nursing care strategies effectively. This chapter discusses the basic organizational and business issues that confront health care organizations to assist the nurse to operate within the health delivery system in a variety of roles.

TYPES OF HOSPITALS

Hospitals may generally be divided into three major types based on ownership: voluntary, public, or investor-owned. Nurses, of course, work in all three types of institutions so it is important to understand the differences.

70

Voluntary Hospitals

A voluntary hospital is one that is nonprofit and nongovernmental. It is thus a private rather than a public institution. It is often organized as a charitable corporation. A definition of charitable hospital is "one which does not deny treatment to persons unable to pay though it charges those able to pay."[1] From a legal standpoint, the most important feature of the voluntary hospital is that it is a not-for-profit organization (i.e., none of its net earnings inure to the benefit of any private shareholder or individual).[2]

Today, in most states, there are detailed nonprofit corporation acts under which charitable corporations may be organized, and new voluntary hospitals are normally organized under these acts. The awareness of the special problems of nonprofit corporations that has led states to enact nonprofit corporation laws has also led to scrutiny of the conduct of such corporations. Generally, a greater degree of stewardship and scrupulous observance of the proper mode of conducting business are demanded of charitable corporations, their officers, and their governing boards.

A major characteristic of voluntary hospitals is their tax-exempt status. Nonprofit organizations that qualify under section 501(c)(3) of the Internal Revenue Code are exempt from federal taxes, and all voluntary hospitals seek to fulfill the requirements of the code for exemption from taxes.

The charter and bylaws of the hospital corporation provide for a governing board. Members of this board may be elected by the full membership, appointed by some outside authority, or appointed by the governing body itself. Representation along geographic or other lines may be required, and the corporate instruments may set qualifications for governing board membership.

Public Hospitals

Public hospitals may be defined as those that are owned and operated by government. The Department of Veterans Affairs, Public Health Service, Indian Health Service, and the military all operate federal hospitals. Most states have a system of state-owned mental hospitals; some states administer hospitals for the treatment of chronic diseases or other purposes. Public hospitals may exist as units within hospital districts, or authorities, created by general or special act or by legislative charter. The hospital district or authority may contain from one to several hospitals.

Like voluntary hospitals, public hospitals are generally under the direct control of a governing body. The governing body may be responsible for one hospital, or in the case of hospital districts or authorities, the governing board may control several institutions. Members of the governing bodies of the public hospitals may be selected by general election, or they may be appointed by state or local officials.[3] When a hospital is established by a county or city, hospital governing body members are usually appointed to their posts by the county commission or city council. Governing board members of hospitals created as independent units of government are often elected, although a county commission or city council or a governor may have powers of appointment. Whatever the mechanism, public hospital governing board members are selected by the public, either at the polls or through elected public officials.

Investor-Owned Hospitals

A growing number of hospitals are privately owned and operated with the objective of generating a profit to be divided among shareholders or owners. Such hospitals, if corporate in organization, are subject to the general business corporation laws of the state in which they are located, so the authority, duties, and responsibilities of their governing boards are basically the same as those of the board of directors of any other business corporation. Additional duties and responsibilities may be imposed, however, by state licensure acts and, if the hospital is a Medicare provider, the Conditions of Participation.

Governing body members of investor-owned hospitals are elected by the shareholders or owners, in accordance with the provisions of the corporate charter and the corporation's bylaws.

GOVERNING BOARDS

Authority and Its Limitations

Governance of a hospital is important for nurses to understand as the organizations in which they work are all directed by governing boards. Members of the governing board of a hospital have a legal duty to exercise reasonable care and skill in the management of hospital affairs and to act at all times in good faith and with undivided loyalty to the institution.[4] The general duty of due care and loyalty requires that any individual who accepts membership on the governing board of any hospital must fulfill the functions of a member of such a board and must fulfill those functions personally. This duty requires that the member attend meetings and participate in the consideration of matters within the province of the board.

The governing board's authority is limited by factors outside the corporate charter and applicable statutes. In the voluntary hospital, the members customarily elect the governing board. Membership dissatisfaction with the performance of the governing board may result in the ousting of board members. Similarly, board members in public hospitals may be removed by an appointing official or at the polls if they exercise authority that, even though legally acceptable, is displeasing to the electorate. The extent to which governing board authority may be exercised is clearly subject to restraints imposed by the membership or shareholders, primarily through the mechanism by which governing board members are selected and retained.

The governing board of a hospital must look to the collective professional judgment of the medical staff in approving rules and regulations relative to professional practice in the institution and in ascertaining the quality of care provided to patients. This relationship between the governing board and medical staff is unique to hospitals. Because the medical staff possesses the professional expertise necessary for effective decision making by members of the governing board, the medical staff can exert considerable influence in the board's defining and regulating of professional medical matters, which may pose some limitation on governing board authority.

If the governing board refuses to adopt recommendations of the medical staff relative to equipment, supporting personnel, and procedures that, in the opinion of the medical staff, are needed to meet the prevailing professional standard of care, there is a possibility that the institution may be found liable if an injured patient can demonstrate that the failure of the governing board to listen to the medical staff resulted in a lack of some service or item of equipment that, if available, would have prevented or lessened the injury and the same is found to be a breach of the applicable standard of care. Liability would, of course, be predicated on whether the provision of such service or equipment was within the acceptable standard of care in hospitals generally. The influence of health planning limitations on acquisition of new services and capital expenditures would be another factor for consideration.

Establishing Policy

Because the governing board has broad authority to establish hospital policy, it follows that the board has a corresponding duty to establish hospital policy. All these policies affect the working environment of many nurses.

Fundamental policies of the hospital are usually contained in the bylaws of the institution. A great deal of hospital policy is not set forth in the institution's bylaws. Policies and procedures for day-to-day operation are often established by the hospital administration, which is under the direction of a chief executive officer. The governing board normally delegates the authority to manage operations to that person and may actively or passively acquiesce to rules established by the administration.

The operational policies and procedures established by the chief executive officer and his or her assistants are, of course, subject to the approval of the governing board, although approval of each item may not be explicit. The volume of management policies and procedures is so great that it is usually impractical for the governing board to consider and approve each one individually. In practice, the board delegates authority to make operational policy to the chief executive officers, who, in large hospitals, further delegate authority to assistants. The governing board usually becomes directly involved with such policies and procedures when it disapproves of them.

Maintaining the Quality of Patient Care

The governing board of a hospital has been recognized as having ultimate responsibility for the quality of care provided in the institution, including nursing care.[5] Review of the quality of care provided by physicians within the institution is carried out almost exclusively by the medical staff. The governing board, however, has final responsibility and the power to intervene if circumstances demand it. Joint Commission standards require that the governing board act on recommendations concerning medical staff appointments, reappointments, terminations of appointments, and the granting of clinical privileges within a reasonable period of time, as specified in the medical staff bylaws. In addition, any differences in recommendations must be resolved within a reasonable period of time by the governing body and the medical staff.[6]

The Joint Commission requires hospitals to maintain an ongoing, facility-wide quality assurance (QA) program to monitor and evaluate the appropriateness of patient care and resolve identified problems.[7] Clinical and administrative staffs must be actively involved in the QA program and report information to the governing body. There must be operational linkages between the risk management functions concerning clinical aspects of patient care and safety and QA functions.

The Joint Commission requires the medical staff to perform surgical case review, drug usage evaluation, medical record review, blood usage review, and pharmacy and therapeutics function review.[8] The quality and appropriateness of patient care in specific services must also be monitored and evaluated. The Joint Commission also requires hospitals to review infection control, utilization, accident injuries, patient safety, and safety hazards.

FEDERAL INCOME TAXATION OF MEDICAL ORGANIZATIONS

In most recent years, federal income tax authorities have developed a significant body of law concerning tax-exempt organizations. Also, the practice of medicine has come to be conducted to an increasing extent through professional corporations, health maintenance organizations (HMOs), clinics, hospitals, and medical schools that employ medical staff on a full-time basis, and professional staffs organized into charitable organizations that support hospitals and medical schools.

The federal income tax status of these organizations is vital to their existence and to their ability to assist the hospital community.

Requirements for Exemption of Health Care Facilities

After World War II, the economic, social, and political circumstances surrounding the delivery of health care in the United States changed rapidly. Public financial support through the federal government, rather than private philanthropy, became the dominant force in medical research and health care financing.

In 1969, the Internal Revenue Service (IRS) changed its position concerning the requirements for tax-exempt status for a hospital. Revenue Ruling 69-545 specifically states that "the promotion of health . . . is one of the purposes of the general law of charity." In Revenue Ruling 69-545, the IRS listed the specific factors that would be used to determine whether a hospital was operated to serve a public rather than a private interest:

1. the operation of an active emergency department
2. control of the hospital by a board of trustees composed of independent civic leaders
3. maintenance of an open medical staff with privileges available to all qualified physicians
4. a policy of leasing available space in the hospital's medical building to members of the active medical staff
5. the use of surplus funds from operations to improve the quality of patient care, expand facilities, and advance the hospital's medical training, education, and research programs

Section 501(c) (3) of the Internal Revenue Code exempts from federal income tax organizations that are organized and operated exclusively for charitable, educational, or scientific purposes, providing that no part of the net earnings benefits any private shareholder or individual, subject to restrictions on various types of political activities.

According to Treasury Regulations on income tax, the term *charitable* includes relief of the poor and distressed, advancement of education and science, and the promotion of social welfare designed to accomplish any of these purposes. Revenue Ruling 69-545 explicitly states that the promotion of health is an established objective under the general law of charity and is recognized by the IRS as a charitable purpose within the meaning of section 501(c) (3) of the Internal Revenue Code. Treasury Regulations state that the term *educational* as used in section 501(c) (3) relates to the instruction or training of individuals for the purposes of improving or developing their capabilities. Treasury Regulations define a scientific organization as one carrying on scientific research in the public interest, such as research to discover a cure for a disease or to aid in the scientific education of college or university students.

RESPONSIBILITY FOR CHARGES FOR HEALTH CARE SERVICES

Nurses, particularly those in administrative or independent roles, should be aware of the basic rules concerning the financial responsibility of patients. This section provides a brief overview of those financial guidelines. A conscious adult patient who is neither mentally incompetent nor intoxicated on admission is responsible for the payment of his or her bill based on their promise to pay. If there is no express promise from the patient at the time of admission, the liability is based on an implied contract, meaning that by consenting to the admission, the patient has made an implied promise to pay for services rendered.

Medicare Payments

Medicare is the federal program of health insurance for the elderly and disabled. Funded by special "hospital insurance" payroll taxes analogous to Social Security taxes, Medicare provides basic health insurance coverage for most Americans older than 65 years. Individuals younger than 65 are also covered by Medicare if they are entitled to Social Security or Railroad Retirement disability benefits or if they have been determined by a physician to suffer from end-stage renal disease (ESRD) (and have applied for benefits).

Persons qualifying for Medicare benefits automatically receive coverage under Part A of the Medicare Act[9] and thus are entitled to hospital and other institutional health services. To receive coverage for physician services, a Part A beneficiary must enroll (or be deemed to have enrolled) in Medicare Part B.

Even for covered individuals, Medicare may not pay for services if the program's "secondary payer" rules are applicable. Those rules are most likely to apply when the patient (or the patient's spouse) is employed, when the patient's illness or injury is job-related and thus may be covered by workers' compensation insurance, or when the patient has been involved in an automobile accident or other traumatic injury in which liability insurance may be available.

Medicare is administered at the federal level by the Health Care Financing Administration (HCFA). The Social Security Administration also is involved in the program, mostly to assist in eligibility determinations. Local administration of the Medicare program is provided by Blue Cross or private insurance companies under contract with HCFA, which deal directly with hospitals and other providers and act as a buffer against government involvement. These agencies are known as "intermediaries" under Part A and "carriers" under Part B. Medicare intermediaries and carriers adjudicate claims and provide support services such as professional relations, financial accounting, and statistical activities.

Medicare—Part A

Medicare Part A pays primarily for hospital and other institutional health services needed by program beneficiaries. A person is considered to be an inpatient if admitted with the expectation of occupying a bed and remaining at least overnight. Customarily, Medicare reimburses only for semiprivate accommodations. It pays the same amount for hospital inpatient services whether the patient has a private room that is medically necessary, a private room that is not medically necessary, a semiprivate room, or ward accommodations. To the extent that the services are covered by Medicare, the patient receives the services at the program rate.

Medicare's coverage of inpatient hospital services is time-limited. Beneficiaries are entitled to up to 90 days of inpatient care during a "spell of illness," with a possible extension of up to 60 "lifetime reserve" days. The benefit period begins with admission to the hospital and ends when the patient has not been an inpatient in a hospital or skilled nursing facility for at least 60 days. During the first 60 days of coverage, the patient is liable only for the Part A deductible. Coinsurance is payable for days 61 through 90. If the hospitalization extends beyond 90 days, lifetime reserve days will be used, unless the patient has exhausted them or unless the patient elects not to use them. The coinsurance amount for lifetime reserve days is twice the amount payable during days 60 through 90.

Medical or surgical services provided in a hospital by a physician, resident, or intern are excluded from coverage under Medicare Part A as inpatient care unless they are offered by interns or residents under teaching programs in medicine or surgery approved by the American Medical Association or American Osteopathic Association, in dentistry approved by the American Dental Association, or in podiatry approved by the American Podiatry Association. They are paid for under Part B. Dental services generally are excluded from Medicare coverage. However, they will be covered if the individual, because of an underlying medical condition, requires hospitalization and the performance of the dental services.

Medicare Part A also covers

- emergency inpatient and outpatient services, if provided in a participating hospital, or if provided by a nonparticipating hospital if that institution is the most accessible to provide emergency care
- kidney transplantation, when performed in a renal transplantation center approved under the provisions for coverage of ESRD services
- heart transplantation, if performed in a hospital meeting specific criteria
- ambulatory surgical services provided by a hospital or a freestanding ambulatory surgical center
- hospice services. Medicare beneficiaries with a life expectancy of six months or less may opt for hospice services by waiving other Medicare benefits
- home health services. Medically necessary home health care is a covered service under both Parts A and B

Medicare—Part B

Part B of the Medicare program provides for a voluntary supplementary medical insurance plan. Benefits under Part B supplement services offered under Part A such as the costs of covered physicians' medically necessary treatments, home health care, and other medical and health services.[10] Persons entitled to Part A benefits automatically are enrolled and covered for Part B benefits unless they decline to participate.

Physicians, hospitals, and other providers are reimbursed for physicians' care, certain ancillary services, and items such as braces, prosthetic devices, and durable medical equipment under Part B when the articles are supplied to individuals who have enrolled in Part B. However, the program does not pay the complete cost of covered services. Generally, the beneficiary must pay a deductible amount for the cost of such services in each year (which changes every year) and ordinarily 20 percent of the remaining cost.

Medicare Prospective Payment System

The Medicare prospective payment system (PPS) was enacted in Title VI of the Social Security Amendments of 1983. Under PPS, each patient's case (discharge) is classified into a diagnosis-related group (DRG). The federal government has set urban and rural payment rates for each DRG.

The statute provides that payment for Part A is based exclusively on the DRG system in accordance with a federally determined payment rate for each DRG. Within the same locale, two hospitals generally will receive the same payment rate for the same DRG regardless of their costs. However, even within the same locale, hospitals may receive different DRG payments based on adjustments for the indirect costs of medical education or service to a disproportionate number of low-income patients.

Reasonable Cost Reimbursement under Medicare Part A

Psychiatric, long-term, children's, rehabilitation, and cancer hospitals are exempt from PPS, as are distinct-part psychiatric and rehabilitation units in general hospitals. For such hospitals and distinct-part units, Part A services continue to be reimbursed based on reasonable cost principles. Hospital outpatient costs, while covered under Part B, are also reimbursed by using reasonable cost principles.

Methods of Payment under Part B

Physicians and other providers under Medicare Part B historically were reimbursed on the basis of reasonable charges, as determined by the carrier.[11] On January 1, 1992, a new Medicare physician payment system took effect, signaling the most significant change in Medicare payments to physicians, practitioners, and suppliers since the program began.[12] Instead of the former charge-based system, the new reimbursement scheme uses a resource-based relative value scale to determine payments. The total relative value units (RVUs) for a service are the sum of the RVUs associated with three elements: (1) the physician work required for the service, based on the time required to furnish the service, the intensity of the effort, and the technical skills required; (2) practice expenses such as office rent, office staff salaries, and supplies; and (3) professional malpractice liability premiums. Medicare fee schedule amounts will be adjusted to reflect the variation in practice costs in different geographic areas. There is a geographic practice cost index for every Medicare payment locality for each of the three components of a procedure's RVU (work, practice expenses, and malpractice). The new system entailed a five-year transition period. Since 1996, all providers' services are paid under the full Medicare fee schedule.

"Antidumping" Rules

Participating hospitals with emergency departments are required to conduct an appropriate medical screening of any individual (whether or not a Medicare beneficiary) who applies to that department requesting examination or treatment.[13]

The hospital is required to determine whether or not an emergency medical condition exists or if the individual is in active labor and to provide stabilizing treatment or, unless the patient refuses, to transfer the patient to another medical facility if a transfer is appropriate. A patient may not be transferred until stabilized unless a physician (or if a physician is not available, another qualified person) certifies in writing that the benefits of transfer outweigh the increased risks to the individual's medical condition. When a patient is transferred, the receiving facility must have available space and qualified personnel, and it must have agreed to accept the patient and to provide medical treatment. Appropriate medical records of the examination and treatment provided by the transferring facility must be provided to the receiving facility.

The Omnibus Budget Reconciliation Act of 1989, P.L. 101-239, expanded requirements for hospitals and rural primary care hospitals participating in Medicare to assess, stabilize, and treat patients in the emergency department. These obligations included

- adopt and enforce a policy ensuring compliance with the antidumping provisions
- provide medical screening examinations without causing delay by inquiring whether the individual has insurance coverage
- before transfer, provide such treatment as is within the capacity of the hospital
- maintain medical and other records on persons transferred to or from the hospital for a period of five years

- have policies and procedures that ensure protocols for the screening, treatment, and stabilization/transfer of emergency patients
- maintain a list of physicians who are on call after the initial examination
- post signs specifying the rights of individuals to emergency treatment

Failure of a hospital to meet those requirements, either intentionally or negligently, may result in termination or suspension of its Medicare provider agreement. In addition, negligent failure to comply with these requirements may subject the hospital and any provider employed by or under contract with it who has professional responsibilities regarding that patient's examination, treatment, or transfer to a civil monetary penalty of up to $50,000 for each violation. If such a penalty is imposed, the provider also may be barred from participation in the Medicare program.

The antidumping law also provides that a person who suffers personal harm, or any medical facility that suffers a financial loss, as a result of the violation of these provisions may bring a civil action for damages and other appropriate relief against the participating hospital up to two years after the violation occurs.[14]

Medicaid

Medicaid is a cooperative state–federal program to provide direct payment to providers, practitioners, and others from certain medical and health services to the financially needy. The Medicaid program is state-operated under a specific set of federal requirements established by Title XIX of the Social Security Act.[15] This statute, and the federal regulations implementing it, set forth a number of fairly specific minimum requirements and provide the basis for federal matching of a portion of the state funds paid in the program. This state–federal share varies according to a formula based on the state's per capita income, from a top of 50–50 sharing to an almost 80–20 federal–state ratio in the poorer states.

Each state government designates the single state agency responsible for the administration of the Medicaid program. Each state determines its own Medicaid benefits and its own eligibility requirements as long as they are consistent with minimum federal guidelines.

Each state is required to provide these Medicaid insurance payments on behalf of persons who are covered by such federal programs as Old-Age Assistance, Aid to Families with Dependent Children, Aid to the Blind, and Aid to the Disabled. In addition, a state may, if it chooses, expand its program to include the medically needy, defined as persons who would qualify in the mandatory coverage group as being in receipt of cash public assistance or Supplemental Security Income (under Social Security) but whose income is above that for the essentials of living although still not sufficient to cover these basics plus medical costs.

The services that are paid for under the medical assistance program vary substantially from state to state. The following 24 services are those that *may* be included in a state's Medicaid program. Numbers 1 through 9 *must* be available to those who are mandatorily covered by Medicaid, the so-called categorically needy. If a state also provides benefits for the additional group, the medically needy, these individuals also must receive a specified number of the listed services. The other services, for both the categorically and medically needy groups, are optional. These services are

1. inpatient hospital services other than those in an institution for tuberculosis or mental diseases
2. outpatient services provided by hospitals, rural health clinics, and other federally qualified health centers
3. laboratory and X-ray services
4. nursing home services
5. physicians' services
6. home health services
7. nurse-midwife services and pediatric nurse practitioner services
8. transportation to and from health care providers
9. early and periodic screening, diagnosis, and treatment of physical and mental defects in eligible individuals younger than 21; family planning services
10. medical care, or any other type of remedial treatment recognized under state law, furnished by licensed practitioners within the scope of their practice
11. private duty nursing services
12. clinic services
13. dental services
14. physical therapy; speech therapy; occupational therapy
15. prescribed drugs, dentures, and prosthetic devices; eyeglasses prescribed by a physician or an optometrist
16. other diagnostic, screening, preventive, and rehabilitative services
17. inpatient hospital services and nursing facility care for individuals 65 or older in an institution for mental diseases
18. intermediate care facility services in an intermediate care facility for the mentally retarded
19. inpatient psychiatric hospital services for individuals younger than 21
20. hospice care
21. case management services
22. respiratory care services
23. Christian Science sanitoria or nurses' services, emergency hospital services; personal care in the patient's home

24. home and community-based care for functionally disabled elderly persons; community-supported living arrangements services

Military Health Programs

CHAMPUS and CHAMPVA pay for health care services provided by nonmilitary health care institutions and physicians to the spouses and dependent children of active members of the armed forces and certain disabled veterans. In addition, the Department of Veterans Affairs (DVA) may authorize eligible veterans to receive care, in certain circumstances, from nonfederal hospitals.

The DVA will pay for hospital care provided to a veteran by a nonfederal facility only if there has been a preadmission authorization by that agency. All hospitals certified by the Joint Commission or certified as a provider under the Medicare program are deemed to be authorized providers by the DVA.

CHAMPVA is a relatively small program in which the DVA underwrites the health care of the spouses and dependent children of certain disabled veterans. The DVA contracts with the Department of Defense to administer CHAMPVA. Hence, CHAMPUS regulations also apply to CHAMPVA.

All Medicare hospitals are required to participate as authorized providers in CHAMPUS, CHAMPVA, and the DVA's medical program. Thus, they must bill CHAMPUS, CHAMPVA, or the DVA and accept the government's payment as full compensation for their services (less applicable deductible, patient cost-share, and noncovered items).

CHAMPUS has adopted a prospective payment system for inpatient hospital care.[16] The CHAMPUS PPS closely resembles Medicare's. Payment is based on federal–national rates, with capital (at cost minus 7 percent) and direct medical education costs being treated as pass-throughs if the hospital makes a written request for such payment. Payment for indirect medical education costs is calculated by a formula that differs from Medicare's. DVA-authorized care provided to veterans by nonfederal hospitals is generally reimbursed through a prospective payment system that is based on Medicare's.[17]

MANAGED CARE PROGRAMS

Changing economic conditions in the health care marketplace have provided the catalyst for developing managed care programs as an alternative to the traditional indemnity insurance and fee-for-service health care payment methodologies. By adopting managed care programs, private and public sector payers hope to institute cost containment, cost control, and cost reduction systems to prevent the continuation of dramatic increases in national health care expenditures. As significant players in the health care system, nurses should be aware of fundamental managed care principles as this growing trend will affect the work of all nurses regardless of the role a particular nurse performs.

What Is "Managed Care"?

Managed care is a continuously evolving concept. Managed care initially operated as, and was perceived to be, simply an organized group of providers that offered health care services at discounted rates and limited retrospective utilization review services.

Prompted by demands of employers, insurers, and other public and private payers for true management of health care, "managed care" developed into a more sophisticated system. The following definition of managed care reflects the transition from the provision of health care at discounted prices to the actual management of medical care: "Managed care is providing the patient with the appropriate care at the appropriate level of care and coordinating such care."[18] Based on the premise that a system providing patients with appropriate care in the appropriate setting reduces cost irrespective of price, this definition of managed care reduces the global costs, but not necessarily the incremental prices, charged by medical providers for health care services.

Forms of Managed Care

A variety of structures currently are used to provide managed care, including HMOs, preferred provider organizations (PPOs), utilization management companies, and hybrids of each type.

Health Maintenance Organizations

Generally, an HMO is a prepaid health plan that combines health insurance and centralized management, administration, and service utilization functions, with the actual delivery of medical care to enrollees through providers. Participating practitioners may be directly employed by, or under independent contractor arrangements with, the HMO.

There are several models of HMOs, including the staff model (generally a single organization that directly employs and pays a salary to providers), the group model (generally, the HMO contracts with one or more medical groups or individual providers who provide services on a capitated basis), and the independent practice association (IPA) model (generally, the HMO contracts with an IPA and reimburses providers on a discounted fee-for-service basis).

In the IPA model and some group model HMOs, the participating medical group or IPA agrees to share with the HMO entity a designated portion of the financial risk of providing medical care. Such risk-sharing arrangements usually are accomplished through the creation of, and provider participation in, a contingency reserve fund or risk pool. The reserve fund is created by the HMO withholding a certain percentage of provider fees or payments. The HMO reconciles the amount budgeted for enrollee service utilization with actual figures on an annual basis. Depending on the results of the annual reconciliation, participating providers may receive none, all, or a portion of the risk pool remaining after the annual reconciliation. Some HMOs also require providers to contribute pro-rata to any risk pool deficiency.

Preferred Provider Organizations

A PPO is a separate entity that assembles a provider network to deliver medical care, similar to the IPA model HMO. The PPO does not deliver health care services directly. Members of the provider network deliver care pursuant to provider participation agreements that contain special compensation arrangements such as fee schedules, discounted usual and customary rates, and/or contingency reserve funds. The PPO establishes or contracts for a utilization management program that is available to payers, or the payers implement their own utilization management system. PPO network providers are contractually bound to participate in, and accept the determinations of, the utilization management system. The PPO enters into agreements with payers under which the payers are granted access to the provider network and to the special financial and other provider arrangements. The payers, in turn, have a designated beneficiary group that exercises free choice of providers, although financial and other incentives are generally used to encourage beneficiaries to use the services of the PPO network. Thus, PPOs preserve the concept of fee-for-service medicine and patient choice.

There are three basic models of PPOs:

1. The *open panel PPO* allows the beneficiary to obtain the services of both network and non-network providers. However, benefit plans usually encourage beneficiaries to use the PPO network providers through incentive-based reimbursement formulas.
2. The *gatekeeper plan* requires the beneficiary to select a primary care physician from among those in the PPO provider network. The selected primary care physician oversees the beneficiary's medical care and provides prior authorization for specialist and other provider referrals. Failure by the beneficiary to obtain the primary care physician's authorization before using non-network providers often results in financial penalties to the beneficiary.
3. In the *exclusive provider organization (EPO)* model the beneficiary is permitted to select either the EPO network providers (in exchange for greater benefits or lower premiums) or non-network providers (resulting in reduced benefits or higher premiums).

Utilization Management Companies

The provision of utilization management and quality assurance is an essential element of every managed care program. However, due to the ability of utilization management companies to contain rising health care costs, these companies have also become significant independent factors in the managed care market. Utilization management companies generally contract with payers, PPOs, HMOs, insurers, and providers to offer utilization management services concomitantly with a managed care program. Properly operated, utilization management companies do not govern the level of care provided to a patient or otherwise practice medicine. Rather, utilization management companies monitor the medical appropriateness of the services performed by providers. The companies advise payers of medical necessity and medical appropriateness determinations regarding specific services proposed for, or rendered to, managed care program enrollees. Payers generally rely on such determinations in making payment decisions.

Sponsors of Managed Care Entities

Sponsors of managed care programs may include insurance companies, hospitals or hospital alliances, physician or medical groups, physician and hospital joint ventures, employers, independent investors, third-party administrators, or HMOs. Insurance companies may either design and offer their own program or use existing networks under a marketing and utilization agreement. Regardless of the arrangement, insurance companies usually provide their own administrative services, claims processing, utilization review (although this may also be accomplished through a separate contract), marketing services, and provider participation agreements. Hospital or group medical staff sponsors frequently become actively involved in the research, development, design, and implementation of the managed care program, particularly in the utilization review and provider participation criteria. The employer-sponsored PPO arises from the increase in self-insurance and the desire to exert greater control over service utilization and costs.

Managed Care Provider Network

A critical element of managed care is the ability of the system to both establish and control an effective provider network to render medical care pursuant to a benefit plan. A properly composed network enables the managed care program to coordinate all providers and provider services and to control the allocation of benefits, ensuring that the patient receives the appropriate level of care. The program's established network must therefore include a sufficient number of, and the requisite variety in specialty and type of, physicians, hospitals, ancillary care providers, and other facilities.

The key to actually managing health care is quality, cost-efficient physicians. In addition to amassing the appropriate number and type of providers in a managed care network, the managed care program must establish and enforce physician selection criteria that ensure that only qualified physicians participate in the system. The managed care program must adopt a written provider credentialing and recredentialing program that is based on specific criteria. The managed care program must comply with its credentialing program without exception, unless a reasonable written justification for deviation has been established.[19]

As noted above, utilization management is an essential element of managed care. Utilization management permits the managed care program to coordinate providers and provider services by monitoring treatment quality, identifying quality and cost-efficient providers, identifying and minimizing inappropriate use of services or facilities, and making medical necessity determinations on which payers rely to make coverage and payment decisions. Managed care programs use several utilization management techniques to accomplish these objectives, including prospective, concurrent, and retrospective review, treatment and discharge planning, mandatory second surgical opinions, and case management activities.

Although today's managed care market achieves cost-effectiveness by managing medical services rather than simply providing health care at discounted prices, incentive payment systems continue to play an integral role in the relationship between managed care programs and providers. Incentive payment systems arguably also include coverage and payment provisions applicable to enrollees, such as the availability of higher reimbursement or lower premiums in exchange for using only network providers. These and similar financial options encourage cost-consciousness among beneficiaries.

However, the traditional approach to, and the basic theory behind, incentive payment systems that link provider compensation to the furnishing of quality, cost-effective health care encourages providers to render only necessary, efficient, and appropriate care. The typical managed care incentive payment system therefore usually consists of financial risk–sharing arrangements between the managed care entity or payer and the provider. Incentive payment systems applicable to providers take a variety of forms, including contingency reserve funds, discounted fee-for-service, per diem, per case, capitation, and percentage of premiums.

A successful managed care program includes not only a quality, cost-effective provider network but also financially sound payers who, in turn, have a defined beneficiary group that will enroll in the managed care program and use the services offered through the managed care network. Verifying (1) the existence of, (2) the extent or volume of, and (3) the type (e.g., elderly population versus mixed characteristics) of the enrolled beneficiaries is a significant step that must be completed by the managed care program and its contracting providers to determine the true net value of the payer contract. For example, a defined enrollment of 1,000 or more employees, most of whom are young or middle-aged, married with young dependents, may command a more aggressive fee schedule because the beneficiary group (and thus the aggregate premiums) is relatively large, and the risks and costs of providing care to this group may not be as great as those inherent in an enrolled population consisting only of elderly beneficiaries who have Medicare or Medicaid as their primary or secondary payer. Determining these factors will also likely be important to the managed care program, both on a contract-by-contract basis and on a system-wide basis, taking into account all payers associated with the managed care program.

A managed care program capable of providing a full range of health care services (covering the entire continuum of health care necessary to serve enrollees) generally will offer its payers a detailed benefit plan that may include all or only a portion of the health care services available through the managed care network. The plans usually include specific benefits (generally listed and defined in the plan agreement as "covered services") that are tailored to the peculiar needs of each payer and each payer's beneficiary group. The delineation of specific benefits is important to the managed care program, to the payer and its enrolled population, and to the provider because each party must know what type of service and what level of service may be accessed and paid for through the managed care program before initiating a particular course of treatment.

Managed Care Liability Issues/Limitations on Services

Managed care programs generally limit payment for services (rather than the actual services) patients may receive from hospitals, physicians, and other providers. The fact that a particular procedure is not a "covered service" under a benefit plan or that prior authorization for coverage is denied precludes payment by the managed care program but (theoretically) does not prohibit the patient from obtaining the medical care. Although this may represent a distinction without a practical difference for many patients, it can become a critical distinction when interpreting contractual language allocating liability for patient care between the managed care program, the utilization review contractor, and the provider.

Recent court decisions have addressed the potential liability exposure of managed care programs for utilization review decisions resulting in medical treatment payment denials.[20] In *Wickline,* the California court stated that although in that particular case the patient's medical care was the responsibility of the treating physician, a third-party payer could be found liable for injuries resulting from an arbitrary or unreasonable decision disapproving requests for payment of medical care. The court warned that although "cost consciousness has become a permanent feature of the health care system, it is essential that cost limitation programs not be permitted to corrupt medical judgement."[21] This decision resulted in the proliferation of provider participation contract language imposing sole responsibility for medical treatment decisions on the provider.

The California courts recently expanded the *Wickline* language in *Wilson v. Blue Cross of Southern California*.[22] In *Wilson*, the court held that a utilization management firm that contracted with a health insurance company could be found liable for a patient's injury if a jury found that the conduct of the utilization reviewer contributed to the death or injury of the patient. The court noted that liability would exist if the utilization reviewer's actions were negligent and were a substantial factor in the patient's injury.

CONCLUSION

The business of health care has evolved rapidly. Hospitals, whether they be voluntary, public, or investor-owned have governing boards that must make decisions in the best interests of their facilities. The financial issues related to these institutions are largely driven by third-party payers: the government, insurance companies, and increasingly, a variety of managed care organizations. Nurses should be aware of the way that the organizations in which they work operate and the financial implications placed on these entities; it is these factors that increasingly determine where nurses work, the functions they perform, and the method by which they deliver quality care to patients.

FOOTNOTES

1. BLACK'S LAW DICTIONARY 296
2. *See* 26 U.S.C. § 501(c) (3).
3. *See* State v. Burroughs, 487 So. 2d 220 (Miss. 1986), in which the Mississippi Supreme Court struck down a statute that provided two methods for appointment of hospital trustees, one for a particular county and another for the rest of the state.
4. Ray v. Homewood Hosp., 27 N.W.2d 409 (1947).
5. Darling v. Charleston Community Mem'l Hosp. 211 N.E.2d 253 (Ill. 1965), *cert denied*, 343 U.S. 946 (1966); Joiner v. Mitchell County Hosp. Auth., 186 S.E.2d 307 (Ga. App. 1971), *aff'd*, 189 S.E.2d 412 (Ga. 1972); Corleto v. Shore Memorial Hosp., 350 A.2d 534 (N.J. Super. 1975).
6. JOINT COMMISSION, ACCREDITATION MANUAL FOR HOSPITALS (1995).
7. *Id.*, Quality Assurance.
8. *Id.*
9. Title XVII of the Social Security Act, 42 U.S.C. § 1395.
10. 42 U.S.C. §§ 1395j–1395m.

11. 42 C.F.R. § 501.

12. 56 Fed. Reg. 59,502 (November 25, 1991).

13. 42 U.S.C. § 1395dd.

14. 42 U.S.C. § 1395dd.

15. 42 U.S.C. § 1396.

16. *See* 52 Fed. Reg. 32,991 (Sept. 1, 1987); revisions (effective Oct. 1, 1988) published at 53 Fed. Reg. 33,461 (Aug. 31, 1988).

17. 55 Fed. Reg. 42,848 (Oct. 24, 1990), effective November 23, 1990.

18. *See* ELDEN & SCHLUETER, PREFERRED PROVIDER AND OTHER MANAGED CARE AGREEMENTS: CONTRACTING ISSUES. HOSPITAL CONTRACTS MANUAL. (Aspen Publishers 1990).

19. *Id.*

20. Wickline v. State, 228 Cal. Rptr. 661, *rev. granted,* 231 Cal. Rptr. 560 (1986), *rev. dismissed and remanded,* 239 Cal. Rptr. 805 (1987).

21. *Id.* at 670.

22. 271 Cal. Rptr. 876, *rev. denied* (1990).

CHAPTER 6

Antitrust in Health Care

Chapter Objectives

1. To review antitrust statutes
2. To examine antitrust in the health care industry
3. To consider contracts and other agreements
4. To discuss mergers and acquisitions
5. To explore antitrust enforcement
6. To consider staff privileges

Of the variety of legal issues currently faced by the health care industry, antitrust liability is one of the greatest concerns. The structure of the industry and its historical practices raise a number of antitrust issues. These legal concepts are complex and generally not well understood. Each case must be evaluated on its own because differences in the market and in structuring arrangements may result in different judicial or administrative determinations. The consolidation underway in the health care industry raises a number of antitrust issues. Because these issues arise so often, this chapter presents a brief overview of what is a very difficult and complex area of law. Nurses, as participants in the health care delivery system, should be cognizant of the widespread impact antitrust laws have on the health care delivery system. In the traditional role of the nurse, antitrust issues were of little concern to nurses. Now, however, as nurses expand their professional presence into more independent practices, these laws may be more applicable. Increasingly, nurse practitioners and nurses practicing in an expanded role may look to antitrust laws to remedy situations in which they are denied hospital or staff privileges. Such adverse actions could be construed as anticompetitive.

The basic antitrust statutes are the Sherman Act, the Clayton Act, and the Federal Trade Commission Act. Because the statutes are so general, interpretations have been developed in the following 100 years by a large number of judicial decisions.

ANTITRUST STATUTES

The Sherman Act

The Sherman Act passed by Congress in 1890, provides, in part, that

every contract, combination in the form of trust or otherwise, or con-
spiracy, in restraint of trade or commerce among the several States, or
with foreign nations, is hereby declared to be illegal.

Every person who shall monopolize, or attempt to monopolize, or
combine or conspire with any other person or persons, to monopolize
any part of the trade or commerce among the several States, or with
foreign nations, shall be deemed guilty of a felony.[1]

Under the Sherman Act, the government was granted the authority to initiate
criminal prosecution against parties to restrictive agreements and monopolies. In
addition, the government was granted the power to seek injunctive relief. These
provisions, which are almost constitutional in scope, have provided the judiciary
with a great deal of flexibility in interpretation.

The Clayton Act

By 1914, Congress had determined that additional legislation was required to
complement the broad prohibitions of the Sherman Act. With the passage of the
Clayton Act, certain specific practices of single entities—price discrimination, tying
arrangements, and mergers—that would tend to lessen competition or create a monopoly were declared to be illegal. Significantly, under the Sherman Act, an activity
generally must have an actual adverse effect on competition before it is considered
illegal; under the Clayton Act, however, an activity that might substantially lessen
competition may be illegal. Thus, the Clayton Act addresses practices in their incipi-
ence that, if carried to their logical conclusion, would lead to a monopoly.

Perhaps most important, Congress authorized in the Clayton Act private antitrust enforcement and enacted the treble damages remedy. By granting injured
persons the right to sue and recover treble damages if successful, Congress provided a powerful financial incentive to refrain from anticompetitive behavior.
This remedy is applicable to violations of both the Sherman and Clayton acts.

The Federal Trade Commission Act

Also in 1914, Congress enacted the Federal Trade Commission (FTC) Act,[2]
which declared "unfair methods of competition" to be illegal. This broad proscrip-
tion was intended to ensure that antitrust enforcement would not be limited to the
specific activities prohibited by the Clayton Act. Not surprisingly, the FTC Act
has been interpreted as broader than the Sherman or Clayton acts.[3]

The FTC was created to enforce the substantive provisions of both the FTC Act and the Clayton Act. The commission's jurisdiction has since been extended to include matters such as advertising and consumer loans. The FTC is empowered, among other things, to investigate and order the cessation of unfair methods of competition. It has characterized its role as that of a public watchdog and has engaged in numerous activities in the health care industry.

THE HEALTH CARE INDUSTRY IS SUBJECT TO THE ANTITRUST LAWS

The antitrust laws have been applied increasingly to activities of health care professionals and facilities, their professional associations, other self-governing bodies, and at times, advanced nursing practitioners. Several social and economic reasons, including physician oversupply and cost-containment, have been suggested as casual factors for this trend.

For a long time, the health care industry was widely believed to be exempt from the antitrust laws. The activities of individual health care providers such as physicians were considered outside the scope of the antitrust laws, because they involved "learned professions," as distinguished from trade or business. Over the years, the scope of this "exemption" was limited, and its validity was often challenged. These challenges reflected a growing public perception that the activities of those in learned professions were not entirely different from the activities of those in trade or business and that some such activities were anticompetitive in purpose and effect. It was not until 1975, however, that the Supreme Court, in *Goldfarb v. Virginia State Bar*,[4] abolished any remnants of a blanket exemption from the federal antitrust laws for the learned professions. Although *Goldfarb* involved the activities of lawyers, its reasoning has been applied to other professions, including health care.[5]

Since the Supreme Court's decision in *Goldfarb*, there have been many government and private antitrust actions instituted against professionals. Probably the greatest number of these cases have involved the health care industry. This is not surprising because, to some extent, economic conditions in the health care sector parallel economic conditions of the late 19th and early 20th century in the industrial sector.

CONTRACTS AND OTHER AGREEMENTS

Although particular joint practices, such as mergers, are covered specifically by the Clayton Act, the antitrust risk of most joint activities must be determined under the Sherman Act. A literal interpretation of the Sherman Act would result in the prohibition of virtually all contracts, as every contract restrains trade in one way or another. Merely purchasing syringes from one vendor, for example, effectively precludes another vendor from supplying syringes to the same hospital at that time. The courts, however, have recognized that Congress intended to prohibit only unreasonable restraints of trade.

In *Chicago Board of Trade v. United States,* the Supreme Court set forth the basic rule for analysis under the Sherman Act:

> The true test of legality is whether the restraint imposed is such as merely regulates and perhaps thereby promotes competition or whether it is such as may suppress or even destroy competition. To determine that question the Court must ordinarily consider the facts peculiar to the business to which the restraint is applied; its condition before and after the restraint was imposed; the nature of the restraint and its effect, actual or probable. The history of the restraint, the evil believed to exist, the reason for adopting the particular remedy, the purpose or end sought to be obtained, are all relevant facts. This is not because a good intention will save an otherwise objectionable regulation but because knowledge of intent may help the court to interpret facts and to predict consequences.[6]

This test, which has come to be known as the "rule of reason," can be applied to virtually every allegedly anticompetitive practice. Indeed, other analytical rules that have been developed can be considered merely applications of the rule of reason. Analysis under the rule of reason requires that an activity be evaluated on the basis of its intent, competitive impact, and breadth in view of the need. A court assesses the motive for the activity and weighs its procompetitive effects against any anticompetitive effects. Alternatively, a court might determine whether the restraint is ancillary to a procompetitive purpose.

The comprehensive nature of the rule-of-reason analysis renders it difficult to administer, and prosecution of cases under the rule of reason is expensive and time-consuming. Moreover, its predictive value to guide future conduct is limited because decisions under the rule of reason depend largely on the particular facts of each case. Thus, the courts have recognized that some restraints are so inimical to competition and so unjustified that they are conclusively presumed to be illegal (i.e., per se violations). As stated by the Supreme Court:

> There are certain agreements or practices which because of their pernicious effect on competition and lack of any redeeming virtue are conclusively presumed to be unreasonable and therefore illegal without elaborate inquiry as to the precise harm they have caused or the business excuse for their use.[7]

The per se rules are rules of judicial economy, permitting courts to find a violation on simple proof of an agreement. The primary effect of the per se rules, therefore, is to dispense with the need for elaborate proof concerning the competitive
and economic effects of the challenged practice.

Three types of arrangements among competitors (horizontal agreements) have
been held to be per se illegal under the Sherman Act: price fixing, market allocation, and group boycotts. In addition, tying arrangements (vertical agreements),
which involve the exercise of market power by a single firm, have been held to be
per se illegal under the Clayton Act when they restrain a substantial amount of
commerce. All other types of arrangements that arguably restrain trade are evaluated under the rule of reason.

Price Fixing

The Sherman Act forbids, as per se illegal, any agreement among competitors
that has the effect of raising, depressing, fixing, pegging, or stabilizing the price of
a commodity. Even if the agreement affects the pricing mechanism only indirectly, the agreement is illegal. Even if the prices agreed on are reasonable, the
agreement is illegal. Thus, price fixing includes joint action to set minimum or
maximum prices, as well as any agreement that tends to stabilize prices. Other
arrangements that affect price less directly (e.g., agreements on bidding, limiting
production, and advertising prices) have also been characterized as per se illegal
price fixing.

Establishment of maximum or minimum fee schedules by competitors clearly
falls within the prohibition against price fixing. The case of *Arizona v. Maricopa
County Medical Society*[8] involved two foundations for medical care (FMC) that
had been organized by medical societies to promote fee-for-service medicine and
to provide the community with a competitive alternative to existing health insurance plans. The foundations allowed their physician members to establish the
maximum fees that a physician could claim in full payment for health services
provided to policyholders of FMC-sponsored insurance plans. Arizona sued the
foundations on the ground that such arrangements constituted price fixing and
were, therefore, per se unlawful under the Sherman Act. The Supreme Court, in a
four-to-three decision, held that the maximum fee schedules established by the
FMCs were indeed per se illegal under the antitrust laws. In its opinion, the Court
rejected the contention that procompetitive justifications for the fee arrangements
made the per se rule inapplicable.

Market Allocation

Arrangements that allocate portions of the market among competitors are typically viewed as per se illegal. Thus, any agreement to direct patients to particular

hospitals based on geographic location, services required, or a method of payment may be characterized as per se illegal market allocation. Similarly, an agreement among competing hospitals that one will provide cardiac care, one will provide orthopedic care, and so on or that only one will seek a certificate of need to obtain a computerized axial tomography scanner would probably be considered illegal market allocation.

Market allocation that is ancillary to an otherwise legitimate arrangement may be permitted. For example, joint ventures effectively allocate the market among participants. If the joint venture enables the participants to enter a new market that they would not have entered by themselves, the arrangement will often be permitted. If it appears that market allocation is a principal goal of the venture, however, the arrangement will be held to be per se illegal.

Group Boycotts

Although any single entity may unilaterally refuse to deal with any other business, the refusal becomes unlawful when two or more entities so agree. Traditionally, all group boycotts have been considered inherently anticompetitive and, therefore, characterized as per se violations of the Sherman Act.

Exclusive Agreements

In response to increased competition and a changing reimbursement system, hospitals are more frequently using exclusive agreements to obtain better services, higher-quality goods, greater efficiency, and lower prices. As the use of these exclusive arrangements has proliferated, challenges to their legality by disgruntled competitors have increased.

To determine whether an exclusive agreement is permissible, it is necessary to consider its effect on competition, market characteristics, and business justifications. The Supreme Court has enunciated the applicable test as follows:

> It is necessary to weigh the probable effect of the contract on the relevant area of effective competition, taking into account the relative strength of the parties, the proportionate volume of commerce involved in relation to the total volume of commerce in the relevant market area, and the probable immediate and future effects which preemption of that share of the market might have an effective competition therein.[9]

Market share is the most probative factor in this analysis, and courts vary the weight given to other factors according to the market share involved. When the market share foreclosed is small, other measures of market performance are more likely to be weighted to determine the overall effect of the restraint on competition. Similarly, when the market foreclosure is neither clearly de minimis nor clearly significant, the courts focus on other factors, including any proffered justifications, to determine the legality of the exclusive arrangement.

Generally, the shorter the duration of the exclusive arrangement, the more likely that it will be upheld. By contrast, the longer the term of the exclusive arrangement, the more likely that the arrangement's restrictiveness will be found to outweigh any business efficiencies or legitimate benefits it produces.

The courts also consider whether the market foreclosure produced by the exclusive arrangement raises barriers to entry or drives competitors from the market. If there are no barriers to entry, any anticompetitive effects of the agreements are unlikely to persist over a long period of time. Further, the economic justifications for an exclusive dealing arrangement must be evaluated to determine whether the arrangement promotes or suppresses competition. In most cases, hospitals have multiple justifications for such agreements; for example, exclusive arrangements could (1) benefit patients by reducing costs and making quality control more effective, (2) enhance competition among local hospitals, or (3) result in better and more efficient services.

MERGERS AND ACQUISITIONS

Perhaps the most restrictive kind of joint activity is that which completely eliminates a competitor. Thus, consolidations of hospitals or other health care facilities that unduly increase concentration in any market are held to violate the antitrust laws.

A horizontal merger involves similar or identical businesses at the same level of the market. Recognizing a congressional intent to preserve competition by preventing undue market concentration, the courts have focused primarily on the likelihood that the consolidation will substantially lessen competition. In this regard, the competitive evil of a horizontal merger is that it places great economic power in the hands of a few businesses, which in turn forecloses business opportunities for smaller firms. Ultimately, however, the primary concern is the impact of the merger on market conditions. Thus, the market share controlled by a merged firm is a critical factor, as is the degree of concentration in the market.

If there are few barriers to market entry, mergers that result in large market shares may have little or no anticompetitive effect. However, in a concentrated industry or in an industry (e.g., the hospital industry) in which there are regulatory barriers to entry, even a small increase in market share through merger is more likely to be challenged.

Trends toward market concentration in the industry are also considered. Thus, even if the market would remain competitive after a merger, courts will invalidate the merger if it appears to be one of a series of events that will lead to concentration in the industry over time. In an attempt to simplify the analysis, the Supreme Court has adopted the following rule:

A merger which produces a firm controlling an undue percentage share of the relevant market, and results in a significant increase in the concentration of firms in that market is so inherently likely to lessen competition substantially that it must be enjoined in the absence of evidence clearly showing that the merger is not likely to have such anticompetitive effects.[10]

The Justice Department's antitrust charges against two proposed nonprofit hospital mergers have resulted in two very different outcomes. In *United States v. Rockford Memorial Hospital Corporation,* a federal court in Illinois ruled that a hospital merger violated section 7 of both the Clayton Act and the Sherman Act.[11] The case involved the proposed merger of two nonprofit, nonstock, acute care hospitals. The relevant product market, according to the court, was acute inpatient hospital services. It did not consider outpatient services to be part of the product market. If the merger were approved, the hospitals would control 90 percent of the inpatient hospital business in the area. The court further determined that there were significant barriers to the entry of new competitors. It concluded that the hospitals had not shown that there would be a net economic benefit for consumers and that the merger would be likely to substantially lessen competition. The court therefore prohibited the hospitals from carrying out the proposed merger.

A federal court in Virginia, however, held in *United States v. Carilion Health System* that section 7 of the Clayton Act does not apply to mergers of nonprofit entities and that the proposed hospital merger that it was reviewing did not unreasonably restrain trade.[12] The case involved one nonstock, nonprofit hospital that owned several nonprofit and for-profit facilities and another nonstock, nonprofit hospital. The FTC does not have jurisdiction over nonprofit entities (e.g., the hospitals in this case), the court explained. Turning to the alleged Sherman Act violations, the court found the product market to be broader than acute inpatient hospital services because hospitals also compete with outpatient providers. The court also defined a broad geographic market. It concluded that the merger would not constitute an unreasonable restraint of trade because the competition in the area outweighs the increased market share that the merged facilities would obtain.

HMOs AND OTHER PREPAID PLANS

Hospitals may enter into joint ventures with other health care institutions and professionals to form a health maintenance organization (HMO) or other prepaid plan. The antitrust implications of such a joint venture, which are largely dependent on the extent of provider control, were discussed at length in a policy statement issued by the FTC in 1981.[13] In general, the FTC believes that HMOs and other prepaid plans have significant potential both to promote competition in the health care marketplace and to restrain competition, because they usually involve a combination of physicians and institutions. As a result of their procompetitive potential, however, the FTC has stated that the activities of prepaid health plans should be governed by the rule of reason and should not be declared per se illegal.

The FTC distinguishes between nonprovider-controlled plans and provider-controlled plans. Nonprovider-controlled plans are treated as single entities, raising antitrust concerns only when they (1) take concerted action with third parties, (2) attempt to monopolize, or (3) exercise monopoly power. By contrast, actions taken by provider-controlled plans are viewed as concerted activity subject to the antitrust laws. As a result, a provider-controlled plan may be found to violate the antitrust laws merely by establishing plan policies.

PREFERRED PROVIDER ORGANIZATIONS

Unlike HMOs, preferred provider organizations (PPOs) do not perform any insurance function. Moreover, in most PPOs, the providers themselves do not assume any risk, as they are reimbursed on a fee-for-service basis. In evaluating the antitrust risk associated with the operation of a PPO, it is necessary to distinguish between provider-controlled PPOs and payer-controlled PPOs.

Antitrust analysis of the activities of provider-controlled PPOs is similar to that of the activities of provider-controlled HMOs if the providers have a stake in the success of the PPO as a competitive entity. Thus, if the hospitals and physicians forming a PPO have invested risk capital in the venture and have integrated marketing, claims administration, billing, and other functions, the provider-controlled PPO is likely to be characterized as a legitimate joint venture rather than as a mere subterfuge enabling competing providers to fix prices. In addition, a PPO is likely to be characterized as a legitimate joint venture if provider participation is limited; agreements among the controlling providers with respect to fees for services provided to patients enrolled in the PPO may be characterized as ancillary to the activities of the venture. Similarly, limitations on the number of providers allowed to participate in the PPO may be permissible when the PPO does not possess undue market power.

In *Ball Memorial Hospital v. Mutual Hospital Insurance, Inc.,*[14] 80 Indiana acute care hospitals failed to stop the implementation of a new PPO offered by Blue Cross and Blue Shield. The hospitals claimed that the Blues' purpose in offering the PPO was to exclude other PPOs from the market, to extract unreasonable discounts from health care providers through coercion, and to extend its own market position. Charging that this conduct violates federal and state antitrust laws, the hospitals asked a federal court to halt the initiation of the new PPO. The Seventh Circuit refused to delay the PPO's implementation, however, finding that the Blues do not possess sufficient market power to warrant antitrust scrutiny of the PPO. Market power results from the ability to cut back the market's total supply and then raise prices due to consumer demand for the product. In this case, the court found that the Blues do not have such power because they furnish a product, health care financing, that other people can and do supply easily. The market in health care financing is competitive because the customers can readily switch companies, new suppliers can enter the market quickly, and existing suppliers can expand their sales rapidly, the court explained. Rather than finding the proposed PPO to be an antitrust threat, the court found that blocking its implementation would have an anticompetitive effect. Without the PPO, the court explained, buyers of health care financing will have fewer options, and competitors will have one fewer entity to compete with.

Significant antitrust implications for providers may arise in regard to negotiations with PPOs. Although no significant antitrust issues are raised when a PPO negotiates and contracts with providers on an individual basis, negotiations with provider groups carry an antitrust risk for the providers. Because the providers do not have a financial stake in the venture, the bargaining process would be viewed simply as an agreement among providers to negotiate collectively.

ENFORCEMENT

To evaluate an entity's degree of antitrust exposure accurately, it is necessary to consider whether the potential plaintiffs are likely to bring suit. The potential plaintiffs that must be considered include the Justice Department, the FTC, state attorneys general, and individuals harmed by anticompetitive actions. The likelihood that either a government or private suit will be initiated depends on statutory limitations or the degree of the potential plaintiff's interest in the particular activity. Thus, each activity must be evaluated on the basis of its particular facts.

Justice Department

The antitrust division of the Justice Department has primary responsibility for enforcing federal antitrust laws. This responsibility includes investigation of possible violations of both the criminal and civil provisions of the Sherman, Clayton, and Robinson-Patman acts.

The Justice Department investigates possible criminal violations of antitrust laws by initiating a proceeding before a grand jury. The grand jury has broad investigative power; it may compel witnesses to testify and may require the presentation of books, documents, records, and other information. Unlike trial juries, which determine guilt or innocence, a grand jury merely determines whether a party charged with violating an antitrust law should stand trial. If, after the examination of witnesses, documents, and other information, the grand jury finds probable cause to believe that a criminal antitrust violation has occurred, it returns an indictment setting forth the practices alleged to be in violation of the law.

If the indictment results in a conviction under the Sherman Act, a corporation may be fined a maximum of $10 million. Individuals, partnerships, and unincorporated associates are subject to imprisonment not exceeding three years and/or a maximum fine of $350,000.[15] The penalties that may be imposed under the Clayton Act are considerably smaller; the maximum fine provided under the Clayton Act is $5,000, and the maximum length of imprisonment is one year.[16]

The Justice Department may also initiate civil investigations pursuant to the Civil Process Act[17] to determine whether a party has violated any civil provision of the antitrust laws. If the civil investigation indicates that a violation has occurred, the Justice Department may institute a civil suit, seeking an injunction or damages. In civil enforcement actions instituted by the Justice Department, only actual damages may be recovered.

Federal Trade Commission

The FTC is authorized to enforce section 5 of the FTC Act, which prohibits unfair methods of competition and unfair or deceptive acts or practices. Together with the Justice Department, the FTC also enforces the Clayton Act sections that prohibit discrimination (e.g., in price), exclusive dealings and similar arrangements, certain corporate acquisitions of stock or assets, and interlocking directorates.

In 1993, the Justice Department and the FTC announced a refinement in their system for dividing antitrust enforcement responsibilities. The main element in deciding which agency will pursue an investigation that falls within the jurisdiction of both agencies is which agency has gained the most expertise in the product involved. The written procedures are expected to expedite the initiation of investigations.

Before an adjudication on the case's merits, an FTC investigation may be terminated by the entry of a consent order. Like consent decrees, consent orders that are entered before adjudicative proceedings are conducted have the same force and effect as a court order.

The FTC is also authorized to institute civil penalty actions against those who knowingly violate the FTC Act and to petition a court for a temporary restraining order or a preliminary injunction in appropriate circumstances. Courts have generally interpreted this power as authorization for the FTC to seek any equitable remedy judicially appropriate. The FTC does not, however, have the power to seek damages for antitrust violations.

State Attorneys General

Both state and federal antitrust laws are enforced by state attorneys general. State officials responsible for antitrust enforcement usually have available an array of enforcement procedures comparable with those of the federal agencies. The types of penalties imposed by state antitrust law parallel those imposed by federal antitrust law, but they vary in severity from state to state. Several states impose only fines and/or imprisonment as the penalties for antitrust violations. Most states, however, provide for injunctive relief, ouster of out-of-state corporations, or the forfeiture of corporate charters or property, as well as for fines and/or imprisonment.

Private Enforcement

The universe of potential private plaintiffs is large, and the exposure to treble damages (the amount of actual damages multiplied by three) can be disastrous. Hospitals and physicians, as well as vendors, are likely antitrust plaintiffs. To assert an antitrust claim, a private plaintiff is required to demonstrate three "standing" requirements:

1. a violation of the antitrust laws
2. injury to its business or property or, in the case of injunction, threatened loss or damage
3. a causal relationship between the antitrust violation and the injury

Private plaintiffs that are successful in treble damage actions or that substantially prevail in injunctive actions are entitled to the ordinary and reasonable costs of the suit, including attorneys' fees. Costs and attorneys' fees resulting from unsuccessful claims, including those that are part of an otherwise successful action, are not recoverable, however. Furthermore, if the court believes that the unsuccessful suit was initiated in bad faith, it may award attorneys' fees to the defendant.

STAFF PRIVILEGES

Historically, cases involving hospital staff privileges have been decided on the basis of state or constitutional law. Increasingly, however, health care providers have looked to the antitrust laws to remedy adverse decisions in regard to hospital privileges. One reason for this trend is that the antitrust laws provide a useful framework for the analysis of exclusive agreements and competitively motivated denials of staff privileges. Just as important, the fact that providers often lost suits on state or constitutional law grounds was a powerful incentive to test new legal theories. Antitrust is a particularly attractive theory because of the availability of treble damages.

Health care practitioners may view any adverse action taken with respect to a hospital staff member or an applicant for staff membership as anticompetitive. Cases have been brought under the antitrust laws to challenge exclusions, expulsions, and suspensions from staffs, as well as other limitations placed on practitioners' use of hospitals' facilities. In addition, alleged exclusions from referral lists have been challenged, as has exclusion from an emergency department on-call roster. Any action that impinges on a practitioner's unfettered right to practice may be the subject of an antitrust challenge.

Restrictive hospital staffing decisions should, for the most part, be considered under the rule of reason.[18] The difficulty with cases involving staff privileges is that hospitals and their staffs may have independent interests in restricting staff privileges. For example, a hospital may want to restrict the practice of nurse anesthetists for quality-of-care reasons, whereas the medical staff may want to restrict the practice of nurse anesthetists for anticompetitive reasons. It is not always clear whether the interest of the hospital or the interest of the staff predominates in staff restrictions. The rule of reason is particularly well suited to situations (e.g., the credentialing process) in which many different interests are at stake.

A health care provider alleging an antitrust violation must establish the relevant product and geographic markets. The product market is typically defined by the specialty in which the provider practices but may be broader if other types of providers provide similar services. The geographic market will vary, depending on the scope of the provider's practice.

In determining anticompetitive effect, the focus is on the entire marketplace. If there are other facilities at which the provider can practice and there are other providers to whom patients can go, there will be no finding of anticompetitive effect.[19]

A provider-plaintiff who has proved that an antitrust violation has caused an injury to his or her business or property can recover damages.[20] In addition, if a plaintiff can show a threatened or continuing violation of the antitrust laws, an injunction may be issued to prohibit further anticompetitive conduct.[21]

In lawsuits involving staff privileges, the party most likely to be sued is the hospital itself. The members of the medical staff who participate directly in the adverse action may be named co-conspirators in an antitrust suit. It is possible that the officers and directors of a hospital could be held personally liable for antitrust damages as the result of staff privileges decisions. Because it appears that officers and directors (or trustees) will be held liable only when the activity is inherently unlawful and its purpose is clearly anticompetitive, personal liability is unlikely to be imposed in very many staff privileges cases.

The Health Care Quality Improvement Act

The Health Care Quality Improvement Act of 1986 (HCQIA) was enacted partially as a response to numerous antitrust suits against participants in peer review and credentialing activities.[22] Congress passed the Act to encourage continued participation in these activities. The purpose of the HCQIA is to provide those persons giving information to "professional review bodies" and those persons assisting in review activities limited immunity from damages that may arise as a result of adverse decisions that affect a physician's medical staff privileges. The immunity does not extend to civil rights litigation or litigation filed by the United States or an attorney general of a state.

Entities covered by the immunity provisions in the Act include hospitals as well as entities that provide health care services and professional societies if those entities engage in formal peer review activities intended to promote the quality of care. The immunity provision, however, applies only if the following requirements have been satisfied:

- The challenged peer review action must have been taken in the reasonable belief that the action was in the furtherance of quality health care.
- The action must have been taken after reasonable efforts to obtain the facts of the matter.
- The entity must have afforded the affected provider adequate notice and hearing procedures.
- There must be a reasonable belief that the action was warranted.

In the first case to apply the immunities of the HCQIA, the Ninth Circuit ruled that a physician peer review committee had met all the due process requirements under the HCQIA and was therefore shielded from antitrust liability.[23]

Exclusion of Particular Health Care Professionals

In recent years, there has been increasing competition among physician specialists, as well as between physicians and other health care professionals. Although they are often competitive allies, there has on occasion been fierce competition between allopathic and osteopathic physicians. Moreover, other health care professionals (e.g., podiatrists, chiropractors, nurse anesthetists, nurse practitioners, physicians' assistants) may also be significant competitors for physicians.

Osteopathic physicians were the first group to challenge their exclusion from hospital staffs, and they have been the most successful in obtaining hospital privileges. Nevertheless, there is still evidence of restrictive attitudes toward osteopaths. In *Weiss v. York Hospital,*[24] a jury found that the plaintiff would have been granted staff privileges at the hospital "but for the fact that he was an osteopathic physician rather than an allopathic physician."[25] Significantly, the jury reached this conclusion despite the fact that, of the eight osteopaths who had applied for staff privileges, six had been accepted and one application was pending. In reviewing the case on appeal, the Third Circuit held that the discrimination by the hospital's allopathic medical staff against osteopathic physicians applying for staff privileges constituted a per se illegal boycott.

Podiatrists have typically had more difficulty than osteopathic physicians in obtaining staff privileges. For example, in *Cameron v. New Hanover Memorial Hospital, Inc.,*[26] the court dismissed the suit of two podiatrists who alleged antitrust violations and wrongful denial of privileges; the court found that there was nothing to suggest that the staff physicians had coerced the hospital into withdrawing privileges.

Nevertheless, it can be expected that courts will closely scrutinize the reasons behind denials of staff privileges to podiatrists. Although denials for legitimate quality-of-care reasons are likely to be upheld, denials for anticompetitive reasons are likely to be invalidated.

Chiropractors have had considerably less success in obtaining staff privileges than either osteopathic physicians or podiatrists. This is to be expected in view of the differences in philosophy and treatment between chiropractors and allopathic physicians. In some instances, however, chiropractors have sought limited privileges at hospitals to obtain radiology and laboratory services. Generally, courts have refused to overturn hospital denials of staff privileges to chiropractors.[27]

Nurse practitioners, nurse anesthetists, midwives, and physicians' assistants can be expected to initiate legal action to gain access to hospitals. In *Bhan v. NME Hospitals, Inc.*, the Ninth Circuit ruled that a hospital's practice of excluding certified registered nurse anesthetists (CRNAs) in favor of physician anesthesiologists was not a per se violation of the Sherman Act.[28] The court held that the policy of excluding nonphysicians does not necessarily have an anticompetitive effect. It also acknowledged a hospital's right to exercise control over staff privileges to ensure quality of care. Further, it found no violation under the rule of reason, finding that the CRNA failed to meet his burden of showing that the practice substantially restrained competition in the relevant market.

If a hospital denies allied health care practitioners the limited privileges they need to perform treatment for which they are qualified, these health care professionals may be able to persuade the courts that their exclusion as a class is motivated by the anticompetitive interests of physician-dominated medical staffs. Such an argument would be particularly persuasive if made by a nurse practitioner or midwife, whose license typically permits him or her to perform certain services without physician supervision.

CONCLUSION

The antitrust laws are a complex collection of statutes and case and enforcement activities. The main federal statutes are the Sherman Act and Clayton Act, with the main enforcement agencies being the Department of Justice and the FTC. For most nurses, the principal reason to be aware of the antitrust laws is the widespread impact that these laws have on the health care delivery system. For advanced practice nurses, their ability to practice may be affected by their competitors, which may bring into direct application antitrust principles.

FOOTNOTES

1. 15 U.S.C. § 2.
2. 38 Stat. 717 (1914), 15 U.S.C. § 41-51.
3. Federal Trade Comm'n v. Brown Shoe Co., 384 U.S. 316, 321 (1966).
4. 421 U.S. 775 (1975).
5. *See, e.g.,* Arizona v. Maricopa County Med. Soc., 102 S. Ct. 2466 (1982).
6. 246 U.S. 231, 238 (1918).
7. Northern Pac. Ry. Co. v. United States, 356 U.S. 1, 5 (1985).
8. 102 S. Ct. 2466 (1982).
9. Tampa Elec. Co. v. Nashville Coal Co., 365 U.S. 320 (1968) at 329.
10. United States v. Philadelphia Nat'l Bank, 374 U.S. 321 (1963).
11. 717 F. Supp. 1251 (N.D. Ill. 1989), *aff'd*, 898 F.2d 1278 (7th Cir.), *cert. denied*, 111 S. Ct. 295 (1990).
12. 707 F. Supp. 840 (W.D. Va. 1989), *aff'd*, 892 F.2d 1042 (4th Cir. 1989).
13. This policy was originally published at 46 Fed. Reg. 48,982 (October 5, 1981).
14. 603 F. Supp. 1077 (S.D. Ind. 1985).
15. 15 U.S.C. § 1.
16. 15 U.S.C. § 24, 15 U.S.C. § 13(a).
17. 15 U.S.C. § 1311–1314.
18. *See, e.g.,* Goss v. Memorial Hosp. Sys., 789 F.2d 353 (5th Cir. 1986).
19. *See, e.g.,* Anesthesia Advantage, Inc. v. Metz Group, 759 F. Supp. 638 (D. Colo. 1991).
20. 15 U.S.C. § 15.
21. 15 U.S.C. § 26.
22. 42 U.S.C.A. §§ 11101–11152.
23. Austin v. McNamara, 979 F.2d 728 (9th Cir. 1992).
24. 548 F. Supp. 1048 (M.D. Pa. 1982).
25. *Id.* at 1051.
26. 293 S.E.2d 901 (N.C. Ct. App. 1982).
27. *See* Kentucky Ass'n of Chiropractors v. Jefferson County Med. Soc'y, 549 S.W.2d 817 (Ky. 1977); Aasum v. Good Samaritan Hosp., 542 F.2d 792 (9th Cir. 1976); Boos v. Donnell, 421 P.2d 644 (Okla. 1966). These cases were decided on constitutional rather than antitrust grounds.
28. 929 F.2d 1404 (9th Cir. 1991).

CHAPTER 7

Beginning and Ending the Patient Relationship

Chapter Objectives

1. To examine the nurse–patient relationship
2. To explore the physician–patient and nurse practitioner–patient relationship
3. To outline the hospital–patient relationship

The legal relationship between a nurse and an institutional patient is unique because of the continuous personal responsibility during the period that the nurse is on duty coupled with the ending of that responsibility when a replacement takes over at the end of the duty period. The legal relationship between nurses in independent practice and their patients is similar to the physician–patient relationship. There have not been many court decisions discussing the beginning and ending of the nurse–patient relationship; instead, nearly all the decisions have focused on physicians and hospitals.

This chapter discusses the ways the nurse–patient relationship begins and ends. It also explores the physician–patient and hospital–patient relationships, because it is important for nurses to understand the responsibilities of physicians and hospitals and the responsibilities that may be imputed to nurses practicing in the expanded role. In addition, it is important for nurses to understand their obligations to the patient regardless of the role the nurse plays in health care delivery.

NURSE–PATIENT RELATIONSHIP

The nurse–patient relationship shares characteristics of both the physician–patient and the hospital–patient relationships. Most nurses in institutional or other employment relationships assume responsibility for a designated group of patients during a specified time period, a shift. Unlike the physician who is expected to be physically present only episodically, the nurse has continuous responsibility for monitoring and caring for those patients during the shift. However, unlike the physician who continues to be individually responsible for the patient around the clock, the nurse is expected to transfer the care of the client to another nurse at the end of the assigned period. Of course, the nurse cannot abandon the patient at the end of that period if the replacement does not arrive on time but must continue to provide care until other coverage can be arranged. After the appropriate transfer of responsibility, the nurse is not legally responsible to return to care for the patient while off duty unless the contract with the employer requires it. The physician is legally responsible to return whenever personal attendance is required.

Nurses are expected to allocate their time properly while on duty and to be knowledgeable concerning the anticipated workload involving both existing patients and expected additional admissions. Nurses can be legally liable for taking a break or leaving a unit at a time when they should know that the demand for care on the unit will require their presence, if a patient is harmed because of their absence.[1]

Nurses are expected to exercise professional judgment concerning the needs of the patients to whom they are assigned and not to abandon any who need their services. In a 1983 California case, a circulating nurse left the operating room to assist with another surgery before the first patient was transferred to the recovery room. One of the responsibilities of the circulating nurse was to monitor the patient and assist the anesthesiologist. After the nurse left, the patient went into cardiac arrest and suffered a severe loss of oxygen, resulting in permanent, total paralysis and a semicomatose state. The only defense raised by the nurse was that she was angrily told to leave her position. The court ruled that the abandonment of a patient by the nurse at a life-endangered time is so obviously negligent that no expert testimony was required to establish liability. The nurse's employer, the hospital, was ordered to pay $982,000, under the doctrine of respondeat superior, which finds the employer responsible for actions of the employee in the course of the employee's duties.[2]

Failure to be present for a scheduled shift without adequate excuse has not generally been viewed as nursing malpractice. This is another indication that the law has not viewed the legal nurse–patient relationship as extending beyond each assigned shift. Of course, a nurse who is absent without adequate excuse may be subject to employment sanctions and, in some states, discipline by licensing agencies.

If the institution assigns a nurse to care for a different group of patients on subsequent shifts, it does not violate the legal nurse–patient relationship with those the nurse cared for on previous shifts unless there is a special contract promising that a particular nurse will continue to care for a particular patient. Although many nurses establish meaningful relationships with individual patients that extend over an entire period of hospitalization, the legal relationship does not extend as such; instead, it ends when the patient is transferred to another unit or to the care of another nurse after the end of the shift. The legal relationship is recreated each time the nurse reports for a shift and is assigned to the patient. Employed nurses generally are not authorized to make promises to patients concerning being present during future shifts, so they must avoid such promises unless the officials responsible for scheduling give them special authorization and the nurses are willing to accept the responsibility for fulfilling the promise.

The contracts of institutional nurses and most other employed nurses include an express or implied agreement to provide care to all patients to whom they are assigned. This is similar to the contract most employed physicians enter. Thus, employed nurses generally do not have the right to refuse to care for patients to whom they are assigned. Many employers attempt when feasible to accommodate severe personality incompatibilities, but as every experienced nurse knows, some patients are difficult for anyone to care for so the only accommodation possible may be a rotation of responsibility.

Advanced practice nurses in private practice may create a relationship similar to the physician–patient relationship described in the following section unless the contract with the patient or client limits their responsibility. Advanced practice nurses in private practice have the same latitude as other independent professionals to decide whether to accept a particular patient or client, unless the nurse has entered a contract to care for a certain population. The advanced practice nurse may assume a 24-hour-a-day responsibility to provide personally necessary services. When such a relationship has been established, the nurse has the same options for ending it as does the physician.

THE PHYSICIAN–PATIENT AND NURSE PRACTITIONER–PATIENT RELATIONSHIP

Beginning the Relationship

Generally, a physician has the right to accept or decline establishing a professional relationship with any person. A nurse practitioner (NP), like a physician, does not have a legal responsibility to diagnose or treat anyone unless there is an express or implied agreement to do so. Likewise, an individual does not have an obligation to accept diagnosis or treatment from any particular physician unless the situation is one in which the law authorizes that the person be cared for involuntarily.

There are three ways that a physician or NP can establish a patient relationship: (1) by contracting to care for a certain population and to have one of that population seek care, (2) by entering an express contract with the patient or the patient's legal representative by mutual agreement, or (3) by engaging in conduct from which a contract can be implied.

A physician or NP who enters a contract to care for members of a certain population must provide care for them to the extent required by the contract. For example, physicians enter contracts with hospitals to care for emergency patients or to provide certain services such as radiology or pathology. Usually, these contracts include restrictions on the freedom of the physician to refuse to care for individual hospital patients requiring those services. Physicians frequently enter contracts with other institutions and organizations (e.g., athletic teams, schools, companies, prisons, jails, nursing homes, and health maintenance organizations) that include an agreement to provide certain kinds of care to all members of certain populations.

The most frequent way that the physician–patient or NP–patient relationship is begun is by mutual agreement of the physician or NP and the patient or the person's representative, such as the parent or guardian of a minor or the guardian or next of kin of an incompetent adult. The physician or NP may limit the scope of the contract and not assume responsibility for all the health care needs of the patient.

For example, the services can be limited to a particular specialty, so that an internist can refuse to perform surgery.[3] An obstetrician can refuse to participate in home deliveries.[4] Physicians may limit the geographic area in which they practice—they are not obligated to travel to another town to see a patient who becomes ill while visiting out of town.[5] A consulting physician who examines a patient at the request of the primary physician can limit the involvement to the consultation and not accept continuing responsibility as long as this limitation is made clear to the patient and the primary physician.

Some limitations on the scope of the contract are not permissible. For example, an admitting physician assumes the responsibility to examine the patient and offer appropriate treatment until the physician–patient relationship is terminated. In a 1975 Florida case, a physician who was at home recovering from an illness had agreed to admit a patient to the hospital as a favor to a friend but attempted to limit his contract solely to the act of admission by making it clear he could not treat the patient. The patient died of an undiagnosed brain abscess within a few days. The physician never saw her. The court ruled that there was a physician–patient relationship that included a duty to see the patient, so the father of the patient could sue the physician for malpractice.[6]

Sometimes a relationship with all its attendant responsibilities is inferred from the conduct of the physician. If the physician commences treatment of a person, the courts generally will find a physician–patient relationship. However, some courts have found a relationship from lesser contact. The Iowa Supreme Court ruled that a physician–patient relationship was established when a physician told a patient he would perform surgery.[7] A New York court based an implied contract on the fact that the physician had listened to a recital of the patient's symptoms over the telephone.[8] Thus, physicians or NPs who do not wish to assume the responsibility of a relationship should limit telephone calls to advising the caller to seek medical assistance elsewhere.

In some situations, very limited conversations may not be interpreted as creating a relationship. For example, a Georgia hospital employee sued the hospital medical director for giving her erroneous medical advice when he responded with a few suggestions to her questions while stopped in the hospital hallway. The court found that this was not enough to conclude that the physician had agreed to treat her or advise her as a physician.[9]

Although some specialists such as pathologists and diagnostic radiologists seldom see their patients, a physician–patient relationship is still established. This does not usually include the responsibility for continuing care that is one of the elements of most relationships, but it does include responsibility for consequences of intentional or negligence errors in providing pathology or radiology services.

Ending the Relationship

A physician or NP has a duty to continue to provide medical care until the relationship is terminated legally. A physician or NP who discontinues care before that occurs can be liable for abandonment. The relationship can be ended if (1) health care no longer is needed, (2) the patient withdraws from the relationship, (3) the care of the patient is transferred to another provider, (4) the physician or NP gives the patient ample notice of withdrawal, or (5) the physician or NP is unable to provide care.

If the patient withdraws from the relationship, the physician or NP has a duty to attempt to warn the person if further care is needed and on request should advise the successor physician, if any, of information necessary to continue treatment. If care still is needed, the physician or NP usually should request the patient to provide written confirmation of the withdrawal, realizing that in many situations the patient will decline to do so.

The care of a patient can be transferred to another physician or NP. It is recognized that professionals attend meetings, take vacations, and have other valid reasons that they cannot be available. A physician or NP can fulfill the duties of the relationship by providing a qualified substitute. A physician or NP can withdraw without providing a substitute by given reasonable notice in writing with sufficient time to locate another physician or NP willing to accept the person if continuing care is required. Some of the reasons for withdrawal are noncooperation or failure to pay bills when able to do so.

Finally, a physician or NP can be excused from the responsibilities of the relationship when unable to provide care. A physician or NP who is ill should not accept additional responsibilities and should attempt to arrange for a substitute. However, it is recognized that sometimes physicians or NPs become too ill to be able to arrange a substitute. It also is recognized that a physician or NP cannot be with two patients simultaneously. Thus, the necessity of attending another patient may provide a valid excuse as long as the physician or NP has exercised prudence in determining the priority. The physician or NP cannot entirely give up one patient to attend another. The frequency of attendance of each patient will be an important factor in assessing whether one patient has been abandoned.

A physician or NP who fails to see a patient with whom there is a relationship without an acceptable reason may face liability for breach of contract or, if the patient is injured as a result, malpractice. Physicians or NPs do not have to be with the patient continuously to satisfy their responsibility. They can leave orders for others to administer medications or other care, as long as they return at intervals appropriate to the condition of the patient. When admission to a hospital is not indicated, the patient usually can be sent home with instructions to call if further care is needed. The patient then has the responsibility to call. It is not abandonment if the patient fails to return or follow instructions; however, if the individual has a know debility, it may be necessary to follow up if the patient does not return. When the patient and those responsible for the individual are unable to provide the needed care in the home, the physician or NP should then have arrangements made for other assistance or placement.

HOSPITAL–PATIENT RELATIONSHIP

This section addresses the responsibilities of a hospital to persons who are not in need of emergency care, responsibilities to persons who need emergency care, and issues concerning discharge. Because nurses are employed by hospitals, it is important for nurses to have a basic understanding of the relationship that exists between hospitals and patients.

Nonemergency Patients

Under common law, a person who does not need emergency care usually does not have a right to be admitted to a hospital. The hospital can legally refuse to admit any person unless one of three broad categories of exceptions applies: (1) the common law, (2) contractual exceptions, and (3) statutory exceptions. Several statutes forbid discriminatory admission policies but do not grant a right to be admitted. All these rights to be admitted are contingent on the necessity for hospitalization, appropriateness of the hospital for the needs of the patient, and availability of space.

A person generally has a right to be admitted when the hospital is responsible for the original injury that caused the need for hospitalization. In some circumstances, a person who becomes ill or injured in the hospital buildings or on the grounds may have a right to be admitted even if the facility is not otherwise responsible for the problem. If a hospital begins to exercise control of a person by examining or beginning to provide care, that may start a hospital–patient relationship, entitling the patient to be admitted.

If a hospital has made a contractual promise to accept members of a certain population, then they have a right to be admitted when they need care that the institution is able to provide. Some hospitals have entered contracts with employers to provide services to their employees or with health care insurers such as Blue Cross or health maintenance organizations, agreeing to accept patients covered by the insurer.[10]

Hospitals that accepted Hill-Burton construction grants or loans agreed to a "community service" obligation. The regulations defining this obligation specify that no person residing in the area served by the hospital will be denied admission to the portion of the facility financed by Hill-Burton funds on any grounds other than the individual's lack of need for services, the availability of the needed services in the hospital, or the ability of the individual to pay.[11] These regulations have also established limits to this uncompensated care obligation.

Inability to pay cannot be a basis for denial when the person needs emergency services or the facility still has a Hill-Burton uncompensated care obligation. Emergency patients who are unable to pay and for whom services are not available under the uncompensated care obligation may be discharged or transferred to another facility that is able to provide the necessary service. However, there must be a medical determination that the discharge or transfer does not substantially risk deterioration in the medical condition of the patients.

Some hospitals, especially governmental ones, are obligated by statute to accept all patients from a certain population that may be defined in terms of geographic area of residence, inability to pay for care, or a combination of both. Several state statues and judicial opinions take the position that no one should be denied admission to a hospital on the basis of an inability to pay for services provided by the facility.[12]

A number of courts have also considered the right of the needy to be admitted to a hospital for care without regard to the ability to pay for such services. To deny a person treatment or admission solely because he or she has no demonstrable way of paying for such services has been seen by some courts as an unlawful, arbitrary action by an institution charged with the responsibility of serving the community in which the facility is located.[13]

Several states still follow the common law principle that a hospital does not have a responsibility to admit or treat a person in a nonemergency situation.[14] Yet, differentiating emergency from nonemergency matters is not a simple task. Denial of care based on such a distinction can result in civil litigation charging wrongful denial of care. Given the developing trend of extending the duty of a hospital in a nonemergency situation, it is necessary for institutions to develop guidelines that require the emergency department personnel to evaluate the seriousness of a complaint of injury or illness without first assessing ability to pay for care. A hospital and its employees are charged with the responsibility of exercising reasonable care under the circumstances. If nonemergency treatment or admission is warranted, steps could then be take to determine whether the person has any means of paying for care. Deposits may be requested at this point, or transfer to another facility may be warranted. In this way, the hospital would be acting reasonably in meeting its duty of care to nonemergency patients.

Public hospitals are subject to the Equal Protection Clause of the Fourteenth Amendment, which has been interpreted to mean that race is an unlawful criteria for restricting or denying hospital care.[15] In addition, public hospitals are subject to federal laws such as the Civil Rights Act of 1964 that prohibit discrimination based on race, color, and national origin.[16] Private hospitals that receive federal funds are subject to Title VI of the Civil Rights Act of 1964.[17] The Hill-Burton Act regulations also preclude an applicant for construction funds from denying use of the facility on the basis of color, creed, or race.[18] In addition, many states have enacted laws that preclude institutions serving the public from discriminating on the basis of race or ethnic background.[19]

The Age Discrimination Act of 1975 prohibits discriminating on the basis of age by facilities whose programs or activities receive federal funds.[20]

According to the Rehabilitation Act of 1973, individuals cannot be excluded from participating in or receiving the benefits of a federally financed program or activity solely because they have handicaps.[21] Hospitals receiving Medicare or Medicaid funds or a Hill-Burton grant cannot deny hospitalization or treatment of a person merely because that person has handicaps. In addition, hospitals receiving funds from federal programs are subject to regulations that require nondiscrimination in federally funded programs.[22]

Title III of the Americans with Disabilities Act of 1990 (ADA) prohibits places of public accommodation from discriminating against the handicapped in the provision of goods and services.[23] Acquired immune deficiency syndrome (AIDS) patients and those infected with human immunodeficiency virus are considered handicapped under the ADA.[24] In addition, several courts have ruled that AIDS is a protected handicap under the Rehabilitation Act.[25]

The Comprehensive Alcohol Abuse and Alcoholism Prevention, Treatment, and Rehabilitation Act of 1970 prohibits private and public general hospitals and outpatient facilities that receive federal funds from discriminating against alcoholics solely because of their alcoholism or alcohol abuse.[26] Similarly, the Drug Abuse Office and Treatment Act of 1972 prohibits discrimination by such facilities against drug abusers solely because of their drug abuse.[27]

Every state has a mandatory reporting law that obliges physicians and NPs who have reason to believe that a child has been abused to report their findings to a designated state agency (e.g., a child welfare bureau).[28] A failure to exercise reasonable care in diagnosing child abuse or laxity in complying with the mandatory reporting laws may result in liability being imposed on an errant physician, NP, or hospital. This was illustrated in the California case of *Landeros v. Flood,*[29] in which a physician in the emergency department of a hospital treated an 11-month-old child with a fractured leg, a fractured skull, and multiple bruises about the body. The child's mother gave no explanation for the injuries. Three months later, the child was taken by her mother to another hospital with puncture wounds on her leg and back, severe bites on her face, and mutilated hands. The physician at the second hospital diagnosed the child's condition as battered child syndrome, and the child was placed in foster care. A suit was brought on behalf of the child against the first physician and hospital for negligence in failing to diagnose the child abuse syndrome and to report the child battery pursuant to California's mandatory reporting laws.

In a 1985 Michigan case, a court reviewed a physician's liability for reporting child abuse when it was later proved that the charges were not true. Instead, the child had a disease that caused the bones to be brittle and easily broken. The court held that the parents could not recover for erroneous abuse charges because the physician was acting in good faith and was therefore entitled to statutory immunity.[30]

Although only a few state statutes require hospitals to provide treatment for sexually abused persons,[31] many hospital licensure acts imply that facilities with emergency departments are obliged to care for such individuals. Illinois also has legislation requiring hospitals to provide emergency care for rape victims.[32] Some hospitals have rape crisis units staffed by specially trained physicians, nurses, psychologists, and social workers, who provide the medical and psychosocial support that a patient needs after an assault.

When treating sexually abused persons in the emergency department, it is important that the nurses be acquainted with the collection of specimens and other evidence necessary for prosecution of the offender. A number of groups, including many local prosecutors' offices, willingly provide so-called "rape evidence kits," along with instructions and training programs on their use.

Even when a person otherwise has a right to be admitted to a hospital, several reasons are generally recognized as justifying nonadmission. First, if hospitalization is not medically necessary, there is no right to admission. A hospital is not a hotel; it is an institution for the provision of necessary medical services. Second, if the hospital does not provide the services that the patient needs, it does not have to admit the patient. If the patient needs emergency care to prepare for transfer to an appropriate facility, the hospital usually will be expected to provide such care. Thus, a hospital may turn away those for whom there are inadequate facilities and may decline to accept for care those whose medical problems are minor.

Generally, when space is not available, the hospital may refuse to admit a patient. This rule usually applies even when a court orders admission.[33] However, not all courts adopt this realistic position,[34] so court orders should not be violated except on advice of legal counsel knowledgeable concerning local law.

Emergency Patients

In the past, the general rule was that persons did not even have a right to emergency care in a hospital except in the circumstances discussed earlier in which they would be entitled to any necessary hospital services. In many states, the rule now is that there is a special right to hospital care in actual emergencies. In states that have not yet formally adopted the rule, hospitals that maintain an emergency department should provide necessary emergency care because it is unlikely that many courts will rule today that such care may be denied.

Hospitals that participate in the Medicare program are now subject to the emergency care requirements enacted in the Consolidated Omnibus Budget Reconciliation Act of 1985 (COBRA).[35] This statute is discussed later in this chapter.

If a hospital cannot provide the care that the patient needs, it has a duty to attempt to arrange a transfer. A California court found a hospital and treating physician liable for the negligent care of a severely burned patient in part because the hospital did not have the facilities to care for severe burns.[36]

If a transfer is required, the hospital has a duty to prepare the patient properly for the move and to make arrangements for it. Preparation of the patient includes an appropriate examination and stabilization. In a Mississippi case, a veteran who went to a community hospital emergency department bleeding profusely had been transferred to a Veterans Administration hospital by an emergency nurse who made no effort to stop the bleeding.[37] The community hospital was found liable for the death because the nurse did not obtain information concerning his condition from the individuals who presented him, did not tell the physician on call of the extent of the bleeding, and did not do anything to stop the bleeding.

Appropriate transfer arrangements include appropriate attendants and appropriate speed. When ambulances and helicopters staffed with emergency medical technicians, emergency nurses, or physicians are available, it will be difficult to convince a court of the appropriateness of an interhospital transfer of a critically ill patient in an unequipped vehicle that is not staffed with specially trained personnel.

However, emergency department staff members can take actions based on the reasonably available information. They do not have to be able to foresee the future in the absence of information. For example, a Florida hospital was sued by the wife of a man who had been stabbed by a person who had been seen briefly in the emergency department. A grandmother had taken her grandson to the emergency department because she suspected he had taken LSD, but the hospital did not have the testing facilities to determine the presence of the substance. While the grandmother was driving the grandson to another hospital, he jumped out of the car, ran into a building, and fatally stabbed the plaintiff's husband. The court found that the hospital was not liable because the patient had exhibited no behavior there that would have led the personnel to suspect a risk of this outcome.[38] If there had been reason to suspect this, other arrangements would have had to be made for transport.

Other Health Care Institutions

Similar rules apply to relationships between patients and other health care institutions such as skilled nursing and intermediate care facilities. Although it is unlikely that medical circumstances will arise compelling emergency admissions to such facilities, there are circumstances after admission that may require transfer to a hospital. Questions then arise concerning the scope of the right to be readmitted when hospitalization no longer is required. The scope of the right will vary depending on state licensing rules, transfer agreements between the health care institution and the hospital, contracts between the patient and the health care institution, and applicable rules of the agency paying for the patient's care.

Application of Good Samaritan Statutes to Hospital Emergency Departments

Over the years, many nurses have expressed a concern as to what standard of care would be expected of them if they went to the aid of an accident victim. Given the unavailability of emergency medical equipment, would the standard be the same as that applied in other settings? Legislatures in most states and the District of Columbia recognized these concerns and enacted legislation, known as "Good Samaritan" statutes, designed to reduce the health care provider exposure to liability for medical attention provided under such circumstances.

Although the exact elements of the Good Samaritan legislation vary from state to state, these statutes do have a number of common requirements. An individual will be immunized from liability if

- Care is rendered in an "emergency" situation.
- The rescuer is a licensed physician, nurse, or other licensed health care provider. In some states, *anyone* who "voluntarily" goes to the aid of another in distress is protected by such legislation.
- Any harm inflicted in an attempt to assist the imperiled persons must be unintentional. The "rescuer" who willfully or intentionally harms the accident victim is not immunized. This is sometimes phrased that the person must have acted in "good faith."
- The aid provided is rendered without expectation of compensation. If a physician goes to the aid of a person in distress with the idea of sending a bill later, the immunity provided by the Good Samaritan statues is inapplicable.

Although most statutory language would suggest that Good Samaritan legislation does not apply to care provided in the emergency department, several courts have held that such legislation is applicable to care rendered in this setting.[39] However, the seemingly majority view is that the protection of these Good Samaritan statutes is unnecessary in the hospital emergency department because immediate care is part of the normal course of practice for emergency physicians and nurses.

Patient Information on Admission: Patient Self-Determination Act

The Patient Self-Determination Act requires all federally funded facilities to inform patients of their rights under state law to accept or refuse medical treatment.[40] The law affects hospitals, health maintenance organizations, nursing homes, home health care or personal service entities, and hospices that receive Medicare or Medicaid funds. It states that such institutions must provide written information to patients at the time of admission about their rights under state law to accept or refuse medical treatment. The institution must also describe its own policies regarding the exercise of these rights. Examples of such advance written instructions include living wills and durable powers of attorney for health care.

The decision of a patient to provide an advance directive must be documented in his or her medical record. Often, a nurse may be involved in providing a patient information about living wills or durable powers of attorney. Federally funded health care facilities may not condition the availability of care or otherwise discriminate against a patient based on whether the patient has given an advance directive. The law also states, however, that it does not override state legislation allowing health care providers to refuse to implement living wills or durable powers of attorney on the basis of conscience.

In some hospitals, it is an internal policy to provide each patient with a pamphlet detailing the patient's rights while hospitalized in the facility. This "bill of rights" typically includes a recognition of the patient's right to privacy and informed consent, as well as an explanation of hospital costs attributed to the patient. Nurses may find themselves confronted with questions of patients regarding these sensitive issues. In some states, legislatures have enacted patient bill-of-rights statutes. In Rhode Island,[41] for example, the rights of patients are deemed to be standards that a licensed health care facility must follow to comply with applicable licensure provisions.

Discharge and Transfer from an Institution

A number of legal considerations arise in the discharge or transfer of patients. Discharging a patient in need of further care, in certain circumstances, can lead to liability, as can preventing patients who desire to do so from leaving the facility. Certain responsibilities confront the hospital and staff when patients needing further treatment leave against medical advice. This section examines these and other problem situations arising from the release, discharge, and transfer of patients.

Hospitals' Responsibilities in Discharging and Transferring Patients

The advent of prospective payment as the method of reimbursement for Medicare claims focused new attention on patient discharges and transfers. Because hospitals are reimbursed a set amount for each diagnosis, they have a financial incentive to discharge patients as soon as medically indicated. Keeping a patient hospitalized longer than necessary costs hospitals money.

Patient Transfer—Federal Law (COBRA). Hospitals have been charged with transferring patients to other facilities because of the patient's inability to pay, even though such transfers were not medically indicated (patient dumping). Congress addressed this problem through COBRA.[42] Hospitals that participate in the Medicare program are subject to COBRA, which set forth parameters regarding the treatment and transfer of all patients, whether or not they are eligible for Medicare.

If an individual comes to the emergency department and the individual or someone acting on his or her behalf requests examination or treatment for a medical condition, the hospital and staff must provide for an appropriate medical screening examination within the capability of its emergency department, including ancillary services routinely available to the emergency department, to determine if an emergency exists. A hospital cannot delay a medical screening examination, further medical examination, or treatment to inquire about the individual's method of payment or insurance status. If an emergency exists, the hospital staff must either treat the individual or arrange for an appropriate transfer to another facility. If the hospital staff determines that an individual has an emergency medical condition, the physicians and nurses must either stabilize the patient's medical condition or transfer the individual to another medical facility.

If a hospital and staff offer the individual further medical examination and treatment and inform the individual of the risks and benefits of the examination or treatment but the individual refuses to consent, the hospital will have fulfilled its obligation under the law. The hospital and staff must take all reasonable steps to secure the individual's written informed consent to refuse treatment. Similarly, if a hospital and staff offer to transfer the individual and inform the individual of the risks and benefits of the transfer but the individual refuses to consent, the hospital and staff will have fulfilled their obligation under the law. The hospital must take all reasonable steps to secure the individual's written informed consent to refuse the transfer.

A transfer is considered appropriate if

- the transferring hospital and staff provide the medical treatment within their capacity that minimizes the risks to the individual's health or the health of the unborn child in case of labor
- the receiving facility has available space and qualified personnel to treat the individual and has agreed to accept the transfer and provide treatment
- the transferring hospital sends to the receiving facility all medical records (or copies) related to the emergency condition, available at transfer, including observations of signs or symptoms, preliminary diagnosis, and treatment provided; results of any tests and the informed consent to transfer or the physician's certification; and the name and address of any on-call physician who has refused or failed to appear within a reasonable time to provide necessary stabilizing treatment
- the transfer meets any other requirements the Secretary of Health and Human Services finds necessary to the health and safety of the individual

A hospital that has specialized capabilities (such as burn units or neonatal intensive care units) cannot refuse to accept an appropriate transfer of an individual who requires such specialized capabilities if the hospital and staff have the capacity to treat the individual.

Patient Instruction on Discharge

Hospitals are required by federal law to provide discharge planning for Medicare patients.[43] Under this law, hospitals are charged with identifying patients who will need posthospital services in their hospitalizations to ensure that appropriate arrangements for posthospital care will be made before actual discharge. Hospitals must also provide discharge planning for other patients at the request of the patient or the attending physician. Patient discharge plans must be developed by a professional nurse or social worker.

Staff nurses or hospital personnel must give patients certain information concerning referrals to certain physicians.[44] If hospital personnel or staff refer a patient to a nonparticipating physician for further medical care on an outpatient basis, the personnel or nurse must inform the patient that the physician is a nonparticipating physician and, whenever practical, must identify at least one qualified participating physician, as listed in a directory of participating physicians.

At discharge, many hospital emergency department nurses provide patients with a sheet of instructions detailing the manner in which they should care for their wound or injury and what to do if certain conditions or problems are manifested later. If it is an established hospital policy to give patients these instruction sheets at the time of discharge and there is a failure to do so, any harm that occurs to the patient as a result of not having this information may lead to a judgment of negligence against the hospital and nurse. A California case is illustrative of this principle.[45]

An 11-year-old boy had sustained a blow to the head in a schoolyard scuffle. He was in obvious distress, and his father took him to a hospital emergency department for treatment. An intern, pediatric resident, and two nurses examined the child. It was suspected that the child had suffered a head injury, and it was decided to admit the child for observation. The intern was incorrectly informed that the child could not be admitted because he was not under the care of an attending physician with staff privileges. The pediatric resident asked the director of the hospital's pediatric clinic to assist in getting the child hospitalized. Without examining the child, but after speaking with the boy's father, the clinic director determined that the child could be returned home in his father's care. He told the father to make sure that the boy's pupils did not become dilated and that the child could be easily aroused from sleep.

It was a hospital policy to provide parents with a detailed instruction sheet in the case of a child with a possible head injury. This was not done. The child was taken home but returned 90 minutes later after the father had read a first-aid book and learned that a slowing pulse rate in the case of a possible head injury was indicative of bleeding within the skull. The boy's pulse had slowed measurably in a five-minute period. Emergency surgery was performed, but the intracranial bleeding had created such severe pressure that it caused permanent brain damage. The appeals court affirmed a jury verdict of $4.5 million for the child, who was left paralyzed from the neck down.

Instruction sheets supplied by hospitals at the time of discharge usually contain an instruction that patients should contact their attending physician or the emergency department in the event of a sudden or unusual change in condition. A failure to respond properly to patients who contact the emergency department pursuant to such instructions may result in liability. It is important, therefore, that hospital nurses and staff be instructed on the appropriate dissemination of and response to discharge instruction information.

False Imprisonment

False imprisonment is holding persons against their will without lawful authority. Physical restraint or a physical barrier is not necessary. Threats leading to a reasonable apprehension of harm can provide enough restraint to establish false imprisonment.

An action for false imprisonment can be entertained for the detention of a voluntarily committed patient beyond a statutory period without benefit of a court proceeding.[46] Similarly, preventing a voluntary nursing home patient from using the telephone, receiving visitors, or leaving the premises and using physical restraint provide a sufficient basis for a false imprisonment action.[47]

If a hospital and their staff are on notice that a patient presents a danger and do not take steps to prevent the patient's escape or wrongfully discharges the patient, the hospital and staff can be held liable for any harm to the patient or a third party.

The principle that providers have a duty to warn identifiable potential victims of violent patients was established and modified in California. It now appears that in California a duty to warn arises only when there is a "special relationship"—an ongoing contract that allows a reasonable inference of the patient's dangerousness—between the health care provider and the patient or the potential victim. Thus, a hospital was relieved of liability for failure to warn the eventual victim of a mentally disturbed and dangerous emergency department patient who was released for transfer to another facility; the emergency department physicians had established no special relationship with either the patient or the decedent.[48] The special relationship doctrine imposes a duty to warn even when the intended victims are identifiable only as a class of persons, such as small children living in the patient's neighborhood. The type of warning owed potential victims apparently varies with how specifically they can be identified.[49]

Many states have enacted legislation stating that health care providers shall not be liable for failure to warn any person against a mentally ill patient's violent behavior. For example, Colorado law provides immunity in this situation except when the patient has communicated to the therapist a serious threat of physical violence against a specific person.[50] In Alaska, the law now requires that immediate notification of an involuntarily committed mental patient's unauthorized absence from a treatment facility be given to any person known to have been threatened by the patient, as well as to the patient's family or guardian.[51]

Physicians and hospitals have authority under the common law to temporarily detain and even restrain disoriented medical patients without court involvement. This responsibility generally can be delegated to nurses to the extent necessary to deal with emergencies in which there is insufficient time to contact the physician before restraints are initiated.

The authority of physicians and hospitals to detain and restrain is inferred from the cases in which institutions have been found liable for injuries to patients because they were not restrained during temporary disorientation. This common-law authority does not apply when the patient is being detained for treatment for mental illness or substance abuse. The applicable statutory procedures should be followed in those cases. This common-law authority also does not apply when the patient is fully oriented, but the hospital usually can maintain custody long enough for the person's status to be determined if there is reasonable doubt.

If parents try to take children out of the hospital when removal presents an imminent danger to their life or health, most states either authorize the health care provider to retain custody or provide an expeditious procedure for obtaining court authorization to retain custody. Some states give only physicians or hospital administrators authority to retain custody, so nurses must get an appropriate order before doing so. Most parents will agree to an acceptable treatment or at least postpone precipitous withdrawal when advised that these procedures will have to be invoked.

An adult patient who is neither disoriented nor committable generally has a right to leave unless it is one of the other unusual situations when courts will order treatment. Interfering with this right can lead to liability. Honoring the patient's wishes to leave can cause nurses and other staff members great distress. For example, nearly all physicians or nurses are distressed when an oriented patient with a spinal fracture insists on leaving the hospital, risking paralysis or even death that probably could be prevented by appropriate care in the hospital. This distress does not change the right of the patient to leave. It will affect the efforts to convince the patient to stay and to explain the risks of leaving.

Patients who decide to leave against medical advice should be advised of the risks, if possible, and should be urged to reconsider if further care is needed. The explanation should be provided by the physician, if possible, and should be documented. Patients should be asked to sign a release form that they are leaving against medical advice and that the risks have been explained to them. However, they cannot be forced to sign. If they do refuse, the explanation and refusal should be documented in the medical and nursing record by the staff persons involved.

Discharge of Patients Needing Additional Care

A patient should be discharged only with a written order of a physician familiar with the person's condition or decision to leave against medical advice. This helps to protect the patient from injury and the hospital and nurses from liability for premature discharge.

Most premature discharge cases arise from misdiagnosis, but sometimes they result from releasing patients who are ready to leave but for whom adequate arrangements have not been made. It is essential for children, the infirm aged, and others unable to care for themselves to be discharged only to the custody of someone who can take care of them. A California physician was found liable for discharging an abused 11-month-old child to the abusing parents without first giving the state an opportunity to intervene.[52]

If a patient becomes sufficiently difficult or disruptive, it is permissible in some situations for the hospital to discontinue providing care. In 1982, a California court refused to order a physician and several hospitals to continue to provide chronic hemodialysis to a noncooperative, disruptive female patient who had even refused to comply with the conditions of a court order that provided for continued treatment during the litigation.[53] The physician had given her due notice of his withdrawal from the physician–patient relationship with ample time for her to make other arrangements. The court clearly was troubled by the possibility that the patient would not be able to receive necessary care but concluded that several alternatives were available.

Courts are more comfortable with discharges when the condition of a patient is not so severe. For example, an Arizona court rules that the physician and hospital were not liable for discharging a difficult patient who had been admitted for treatment of lesions on his lips.[54] The court observed that the patient was uncomfortable but not helpless, and the hospital nurses had done nothing to actively retard his treatment or worsen his condition.

Any discharge of a patient in need of continued care could become controversial, so most hospitals usually limited these releases to situations that interfere with the care of other patients or threaten the safety of staff members. Hospital administration usually reviews each case to minimize legal liability and other adverse effects on the institution. When the attending physician desires an inappropriate discharge, the hospital may have to arrange for the transfer of the care of the patient to another physician or to discuss with the physician the compatibility of the proposed discharge with the hospital's standards for continued membership on the medical staff.

Refusal to Leave

Patients and their representatives do not have the right to insist on unnecessary hospitalization. If patients refuse to leave, or their representatives refuse to remove them after the physician's discharge order, the patients are trespassers and the hospital can take appropriate steps to effect their removal. If the situation is simply a delay in discharge because of difficulties in arranging placement, hospitals usually make reasonable efforts to assist in making arrangements. However, if patients and their representatives will not cooperate, it may be necessary to use reasonable force to remove them or to get a court order. In North Carolina, there is a statute[55] that specifically makes it a criminal trespass for a patient to refuse or fail to leave a hospital once the patient has been directed to do so by the superintendent or administrator of the facility. A determination to discharge the patient must be based on the medical judgment of two physicians. If patients are found guilty of criminal trespass, they may be fined or imprisoned. As with the discharge of noncooperative and disruptive patients, hospital administration should make decisions concerning forcible removal after appropriate review.

Temporary Releases

Sometimes children, incompetent adults, cooperative committed patients, or competent adults who need continuing supervision or care ask to leave the hospital for a short time. This is permissible in many situations and may assist the care of the patient. Because there is a possibility of liability, certain precautions should be taken. Should it be determined that a temporary release is medically acceptable, the hospital should take steps to limit the patient's exposure to harm during this absence from the facility. This could be accomplished by the nurse providing the patient and the family or friends with a set of instructions detailing the limitations on the activity of the patient during this period, medications to be taken, diet to be followed, and a notification that should complications arise, the attending physician should be contacted. Hospital policies should be followed, which usually include the following precautions:

- There should be a written authorization from the attending physician indicating that the temporary release is not medically contraindicated.
- There should be written authorization from competent adult patients or from the parent or guardian of other patients acknowledging that the hospital is not responsible for the care of the patients while the person is out of the custody of the hospital.
- There should be release (of patients who are not able to take care of themselves and are not a danger to others) only to an appropriate adult who has

been instructed concerning the needs of the patient, such as medications and wheelchair use, and how to contact the hospital for information or assistance if needed. If arrangements are made for such patient needs, the risks associated with temporary releases are minimized.

If patients who are a danger to themselves or others are temporarily released and are harmed or harm others, the hospital could be liable. For example, a Florida court ruled that the hospital could be sued by a person who was injured in an automobile accident caused by a patient on a temporary release because the hospital should have known she would attempt to operate an automobile and could not do so safely.[56] This illustrates the significance of careful review by the physician and nurses before authorizing the release.

Escape

Hospitals and nursing staff frequently are sued when patients who have escaped either commit suicide, are injured or killed in accidents, or injure or kill others. The courts usually focus on (1) how much those involved in the care of the patient knew or should have known about the dangerousness of the patient to self or others and (2) the appropriateness of the precautions taken to prevent escape in the light of that knowledge.

Generally, if the injury was not foreseeable, there is little likelihood of liability for failure to take additional precautions. If the injury was foreseeable, courts will examine the reasonableness of the precautions, and liability will be more likely. However, many courts have recognized the therapeutic benefits of more open patient care units and found them to be reasonable even for some patients at risk. In other cases, the precautions have been found to be inadequate, and liability has been imposed.

CONCLUSION

Nurses, physicians, and hospitals all establish and end patient relationships. For most nurses, the patient care obligations apply to patients cared for during their shift. For advanced practice nurses and physicians, however, this treatment obligation continues beyond the shift or episode of care. Although advanced practice nurses and physicians can terminate most patient relationships on reasonable notice, these practitioners and hospitals do face legal restraints on inappropriately discharging patients.

FOOTNOTES

1. *E.g.,* Laidlow v. Lions Gate Hosp., 8 D.L.R. 3d 730 (B.C. Sup. Ct. 1969).
2. Czubinsky v. Doctor Hosp., 139 Cal. App. 3d 361, 188 Cal. Rptr. 685 (1983).
3. Skodje v. Hardy, 47 Wash. 2d 557, 288 P.2d 471 (1955).
4. Vidrine v. Mayes, 127 So. 2d 809 (La. Ct. App. 1961).
5. McNamara v. Emmons, 36 Cal. App. 2d 199, 97 P.2d 503 (1939).
6. Giallanza v. Sands, 316 So. 2d 77 (Fla. Dist. Ct. App. 1975).
7. McGulpin v. Bessmer, 241 Iowa 1119, 43 N.W.2d 121 (1950).
8. O'Neil v. Montefiore Hosp., 202 N.Y.S.2d 436 (N.Y. App. Div. 1960).
9. Buttersworth v. Swint, 53 Ga. App. 602, 186 S.E. 770 (1936).
10. *E.g.,* Norwood Hosp. v. Howton, 32 Ala. App., 375, 26 So. 2d 427 (1946).
11. 42 C.F.R. §§ 124.601–124.607.
12. N.C. Gen. Stat. § 131E-7(a)(6).
13. Williams v. Hospital Auth., 168 S.E.2d 336 (Ga. Ct. App. 1969). *See also* Tabor v. Doctors Mem'l Hosp., 501 So. 2d 243 (La. Ct. App. 1987).
14. Tabor v. Doctors Mem'l Hosp., 544 So. 2d 849 (La. Ct. App. 1989).
15. In the seminal case of Simkins v. Moses Cone Mem'l Hosp., 323 F.2d 959 (4th Cir. 1963), *cert denied,* 84 S. Ct. 793 (1964), the Fourth Circuit applied the same state action concept to a private hospital. By participating in the Hill-Burton program, the court stated, the hospital was engaged in sufficient "state" activity to bring it under the Fourteenth Amendment prohibition against race as a criterion for denying a person admission to a hospital.
16. 42 U.S.C. §§ 2000.
17. 42 U.S.C. §§ 2000d.
18. 42 C.F.R. § 124.603.
19. *See, e.g.,* M.M. Stat. Ann. § 28-1-7(F); N.J. Stat. Ann. § 10:5-4.
20. 42 U.S.C. §§ 6101.
21. 29 U.S.C. § 794.
22. 45 C.F.R. § 85.3; 42 C.F.R. § 124.9.
23. Pub. L. No. 101-336, § 302 (1990).
24. 42 U.S.C. § 2101.
25. *See, e.g.,* Chalk v. United States Dist. Ct., 840 F.2d 701 (9th Cir. 1988); Ray v. School Dist., 666 F. Supp. 1524 (M.D. Fla. 1987).
26. 42 U.S.C. § 290dd.
27. 42 U.S.C. § 290ee.
28. *E.g.,* Fla. Stat. Ann. § 415.502; Mass. Gen. Laws Ann. ch 119, § 51A; Utah Code Ann. § 78-36-3.
29. 131 Ca. Rptr. 699 (1976).

30. Awkermann v. Tri-County Orthopaedics, 373 N.W.2d 204 (Mich. Ct. App. 1985).

31. *See, e.g.,* Pa. Stat. Ann. tit. 35, § 810171; R.I. Gen. Laws § 823-17-26.

32. Illinois Rape Victims Emergency Treatment Act, Ill. Comp. Stat. Ann. ch 111½ §§ 87-1 to 87-9.

33. *E.g.,* People *ex rel.* M.B., 312 N.W.2d 714 (S.D. 1981).

34. *E.g.,* Pierce County Office of Involuntary Commitment v. Western State Hosp., 644 P.2d 131 (Wash. 1982).

35. 42 U.S.C.A. § 1395dd.

36. Carrasco v. Bankoff, 220 Cal. App. 2d 230, 33 Cal. Rptr. 673 (1963).

37. New Biloxi Hosp. v. Frazier, 245 Miss. 185, 146 So. 2d 882 (1962).

38. Nance v. James Archer Smith Hosp., 329 So. 2d 377 (Fla. Dist. Ct. App. 1976).

39. McKenna v. Cedars of Lebanon Hosp., 155 Cal. Rptr. 631 (1979); Hamburger v. Henry Ford Hosp., 284 N.W.2d 155 (Mich. Ct. App. 1979); Storch v. Silverman, 231 Cal. Rptr. 27 (Cal. Ct. App. 1986); Thornhill v. Detroit, 369 N.W.2d 871 (Mich. Ct. App. 1985); Gordon v. William Beaumont Hosp., 447 N.W.2d 793 (Mich. Ct. App. 1989).

40. Pub. L. No. 101-508 (1990).

41. R.I. Gen. Laws § 23-1-19.1.

42. 42 U.S.C. § 1395dd.

43. Pub. L. No. 99-509, § 9305.

44. 42 U.S.C. § 1395cc(a) (1) (N) (ii).

45. Niles v. City of San Rafael, 116 Cal. Rptr. 733 (Cal. App. 1974).

46. Johnson v. Greer, 477 F.2d 101 (5th Cir. 1973).

47. Big Town Nursing Home, Inc. v. Newman, 461 S.W.2d 195 (Tex. App. 1970); Big Town Nursing Home, Inc. v. Reserve Co. Inc., 492 F.2d 523 (5th Cir. 1974).

48. McDowell v. County of Alameda, 151 Cal. Rptr. 779 (Cal. Ct. App. 1979).

49. Thompson v. County of Alameda, 614 P.2d 728 (Cal. 1980).

50. Colo. Rev. Stat. § 13-21-117. *See also* Ky. Rev. Stat. Ann. § 202A.400; Minn. Stat. Ann. §§ 148.975 and 148.976.

51. Alaska Stat. § 47.30.790.

52. Landeros v. Flood, 17 Cal. 3d 399, 551 P.2d 389 (1976).

53. Payton v. Weaver, 131 Cal. App. 3d 38, 182 Cal. Rptr. 225 (1982).

54. Modla v. Parker, 17 Ariz. App. 54, 495 P.2d 494 (1972), *cert. denied,* 409 U.S. 1038 (1972).

55. N.C. Gen. Stat. § 131E-90.

56. Burroughs v. Board of Trustees of Alachua Gen. Hosp., 328 So. 2d 538 (Fla. Dist. Ct. App. 1976).

CHAPTER 8

Collection and Disclosure of Patient Information

> **Chapter Objectives**
>
> 1. To discuss health care records
> 2. To look at access of records
> 3. To discuss disclosure

Hospitals and health professionals including nurses must collect a large amount of sensitive information about patients to provide appropriate diagnosis, treatment, and care. The health care record, including the nursing notes, is a critical piece of evidence in determining the standard of care provided to the patient. Because this record can be used as evidence in a variety of legal actions, nurses should be familiar with complete and accurate charting techniques. This chapter discusses the recording of patient information and its uses, as well as the law concerning confidentiality and the circumstances in which disclosure is prohibited, permitted, or mandated.

HEALTH CARE RECORDS

Since the introduction of Medicare and Medicaid in the mid-1960s, the hospital industry has experienced an exponential growth in government regulation, together with an expanding consumer movement and an increased emphasis on patient rights. Health care facilities are now subject to a multiplicity of laws, rules, and regulations governing medical records management.

Once required to be a written document, the medical record increasingly is becoming a computer record immediately available to authorized personnel and reduced to written form only after the patient's discharge from the hospital. Whether written or in computer code, the medical record is a complete current record of the history, condition, and treatment of the patient and the results of the patient's hospitalization.[1]

The medical record is used not only to document chronologically the care rendered to the patient but also to plan and evaluate the patient's treatment and to facilitate communication among the patient's physician, nurses, and other health care professionals in the hospital. The record also provides clinical data for medical, nursing, and scientific research. In addition, those participating in medical and nursing audit and peer review programs evaluate the quality of care given hospitalized patients by reviewing treatment documented in hospital medical records.

Hospital medical charts are more than patient care records, however; they are also important legal documents that are essential to the defense of professional negligence actions. Because such actions are often litigated two to five years after the plaintiff received the treatment in question, the hospital chart is frequently the only detailed record of what actually occurred during the hospitalization. Persons who participated in the plaintiff's treatment may not be available to testify on behalf of the defendants or may not remember important details of the case. A good chart enables the hospital to reconstruct the patient's course of treatment and to show that the care provided was acceptable under the circumstances.[2] The contents of the hospital record are usually admissible as evidence for or against the hospital and physician.

Contents

A variety of statutes and regulations require hospitals to maintain health care records. Hospitals that participate in the Medicare program must comply with minimum content requirement.[3] State hospital licensing laws and regulations addressing health care records can be divided into three groups: (1) those detailing the information required, (2) those specifying the broad areas of information required, and (3) those stating simply that the health care record shall be adequate, accurate, or complete. In some cities, municipal codes require certain information not otherwise specified by state law or regulation.[4]

The Joint Commission on Accreditation of Healthcare Organizations (the Joint Commission) also specifies standards concerning health care records that hospitals must meet to be accredited. The Medical Records chapter of the *Accreditation Manual for Hospitals* lists specific items to include. They are designed to ensure the patient is identified, the diagnosis is supported, the treatment is justified, and the results are documented accurately. Although many of the items apply only to inpatients, the general standards apply to all, including ambulatory care patients, emergency cases, and those served in a hospital-administered home care program.[5]

Accuracy and Timely Completion

The medical record is often the single most important document available to a hospital and staff in the defense of a negligence action and ordinarily is admissible as evidence of what transpired in the care of the patient. Without a legible and complete medical record, the hospital and nursing staff may be unable to defend itself successfully against allegations of improper care.

Medical and nursing record entries should be made in clear and concise language that can be understood by all professional staff attending the patient. An illegible record is often worse than no record, because it documents a failure of the hospital and professional staff involved to maintain a proper record and may impair the ability of staff to provide proper treatment to the patient. Moreover, an illegible record entry introduced as evidence in a court action against the hospital may create suspicion in the minds of the jury that the entry was improper and may thereby weaken the hospital's defense.

Nurses making entries should place their signatures and positions after each entry. The hospital and the patient's attending physician must be able to determine who participated in the patient's care should the need arise to consult on a treatment question or to reconstruct the hospitalization in defense of a professional negligence action.

The medical record should be a complete account of the treatment given the patient. The statutes and regulations of several states require hospitals to maintain "a complete record" of the care rendered to a patient during hospitalization.[6] In addition, the Joint Commission requires accredited hospitals to maintain complete records of the care they provide.[7]

State hospital licensing statutes and regulations and Joint Commission standards require accurate records. An inaccurate record may increase the hospital's exposure to liability by destroying the credibility of the entire record. In a 1974 case,[8] the court found that a clear discrepancy between what the health care record stated and what actually happened to the patient could justify a jury finding that, if the record was erroneous in part, it could be erroneous in other parts as well and thus be considered generally invalid.

Failure to make a complete record may lead to a finding that the hospital was negligent in its treatment of the patient. In *Collins v. Westlake Community Hospital,*[9] the plaintiff alleged that the hospital's nursing staff negligently failed to observe the condition and circulation of his leg during the time it was in a cast and that their failure caused the patient to lose the leg. The Illinois court examined the patient's medical record and concluded that the absence of nursing notes documenting observations of the leg during seven critical hours, particularly in view of the physician's order to "watch condition of toes," could reasonably have led the jury to infer that no observations were made during that time.

The hospital's nurses testified in *Collins* that nurses do not always record observations on the chart when patients are checked, that usually they record only abnormal findings, and that this procedure is consistent with the principles of problem-oriented medical records, which many hospitals have adopted. Nonetheless, the court allowed the jury to draw an inference from the absence of documented observations that no observations had been made. As some courts have not kept pace with recent trends in medical records charting, nurses must be certain that, in cases for which careful observation is essential, nursing staff document their contacts with patients. The hospital's and nurses' interest in increased efficiency should not prevent nursing staff from keeping records sufficiently detailed to show the treatment rendered. Some hospitals use flowsheets and checklists to document frequent periodic patient observations in a manner that requires no narrative chart entry.

Complete records can protect the hospital and nursing staff in many situations. In a 1961 Kentucky case, a hospital was found not to be liable for the death of a patient 13 hours after surgery because the health care record included documentation of proper periodic observation by the nursing staff, contacts with the physician concerning management of the patient, and compliance with the physician's directions.[10] Compliance with the physician's directions does not protect the hospital and the nursing staff when the directions are clearly improper. However, when they are within the ambit of acceptable professional practice, compliance and documentation of compliance provide substantial protection from liability.

Record entries usually should be made when the treatment is given or the observations made. Entries made several days or weeks later have less credibility than those made during or immediately after hospitalization. Medicare conditions of participation require completion of hospital records within 15 days after the patient's discharge.[11] The Joint Commission accreditation standards require the hospital's medical staff regulations to state a time limit for completion of the record after discharge. Persistent failure to conform to a medical staff rule requiring the physician to complete records promptly was held in one case to provide a basis for suspension of the staff member.[12] Under Texas law, a government hospital may be liable for negligent use of personal property for failing to properly record a patient's condition, an appeals court in that state has ruled.[13] A patient who had suffered severe brain damage broke his hip at sometime in the 24 hours after his admission to a hospital's rehabilitation unit, but there was no indication in his medical record that such an injury had occurred. The parents noticed scratches on his arm, a progressive redness and swelling on his hip, and a deterioration of his mental condition. They requested that these observations be noted in the patient's chart, but the entries were never made. Four days after the patient's admission, a physical therapist recommended a radiograph of the right hip. A radiograph taken five days after the recommendation revealed the broken hip. A trial court found that the hospital's failure to accurately record the patient's condition resulted in the failure to diagnose the injury until approximately nine days after it had occurred and that the hospital was liable for the negligent use of medical records. The hospital appealed, arguing that the failure to record an essential entry in a medical chart is not negligent use of personal property and that the incomplete record was not the cause of the patient's injuries. The appeals court upheld the damage award against the hospital.

In some situations, inaccurate records can be a crime. In 1978, a New York court ruled that a nurse and surgeon could properly be charged with the crime of falsifying business records when they failed to enter in the operating room log the fact that an unlicensed salesman had assisted in the surgical implantation of a total hip prosthesis.[14]

Who May Make Entries?

The number of people making entries in patient charts, particularly in large teaching hospitals, can create potentially serious legal hazards. Extraneous entries can give rise to negligence liability exposure, problems involving unlicensed persons practicing nursing or medicine, and poor patient relations.

Numerous professional personnel including licensed physicians, professional nurses, practical nurses, and physical therapists may make entries in a medical chart. Most states do not specify the type of professionals who may write entries in the chart; who may do so is a matter of individual hospital policy.[15]

The entries of nursing students should be countersigned by a licensed professional nurse if such entries document the practice of professional nursing as defined by the state's nursing licensure act. Without evidence of proper supervision, a nursing student practicing professional nursing could be held in violation of the state's nursing licensure act, unless the act specifically authorizes nursing students to practice nursing in the course of their studies toward a registered nurse degree. Professional nurses who sign such entries are responsible for supervising that the actions of the student nurse were appropriately performed.

A physician's verbal orders and other instructions generally considered by the medical staff to be associated with any potential hazard to the patient must be transcribed in the medical record and signed by the physician within 24 hours.[16] Joint Commission accreditation standards and hospital-licensing regulations in some states require all physician orders to be written in the patient's medical record.[17] A physician's signature on a transcribed verbal order authenticates the order and indicates that it is correct. Who may receive and transcribe a physician's verbal order is a matter of hospital policy, usually set forth in the medical staff rules and regulations.[18]

In view of the increased potential for error in verbal orders, hospitals should discourage all verbal orders except those issued by telephone. Physicians giving orders on the patient care unit should be able to write their orders in the patient charts. If circumstances require other personnel to transcribe a physician's orders, they should ask the physician to authenticate the orders before leaving the unit. Nursing or house staff in most hospitals receive and transcribe telephone orders from attending physicians. Although not practical in all cases, having a second person at the hospital on the telephone to witness the conversation reduces error and controversy concerning the order given. For especially sensitive orders, such as do-not-resuscitate orders, hospitals should require a witness to the order.

Corrections and Alterations

Hospitals and health care professionals should give attention to the method by which they correct errors in health care records. Improper alterations can reduce the credibility of the record, exposing the hospital to an increased risk of liability.

Generally, there are two types of errors made in health care records: (1) minor ones in transcription, spelling, and the like, and (2) more significant errors involving important test data, physician medication orders, inadvertently omitted progress notes, and similar substantive entries. Persons authorized by hospital policy to make record entries may correct minor errors in these entries when errors are discovered soon after the original entry is made. A physician or administrative or nursing staff supervisor should be present when substantive errors and those discovered some time after the original entry are corrected, preferably by the person making the error. If the original entry is likely to have been read by others who could be misled by the error, the physicians, nurses, and others likely to be relying on it should be notified of the change.

The person correcting the error should place a single line through the incorrect entry, enter the correct information, initial or sign it, and enter the time and date. Mistakes in the record should not be erased or obliterated, because such changes can create suspicion in the minds of jurors concerning the original entry.

After a claim has been made or a lawsuit has been threatened or filed against the hospital or a nursing staff member, changes should not be made in the records without first consulting defense counsel. In a 1979 New York case, after physicians had won a malpractice case, it was discovered that a page of the record had been replaced not long before the beginning of the suit, so the court ordered a new trial.[19]

In a 1980 Connecticut case in which a hospital's nurses rewrote an entire section of the patient's medical record after the patient's injury in the hospital, the court held in the subsequent negligence action that *the revision indicated a consciousness of negligence.*[20]

Altering or falsifying a health care record for purposes of wrongfully obtaining reimbursement is a crime. In some states, a practitioner who improperly alters a record is subject to licensure revocation or other discipline for unprofessional conduct.

Some patients request modification of records. Because the records are the best evidence of what occurred and were relied on in making decisions concerning the care provided, hospitals usually should not modify records except to update the identity of patients whose names are changed. If a patient disagrees with an entry, there are two approaches to modifications. (1) Some hospitals permit the physician or nurse supervisor to make amendments in the same manner as corrections of substantive errors, if the physician concurs in the appropriateness of the change. The amendment should include a note that it is being made at the request of the patient, so that the patient will be responsible for explaining the change if it is questioned later. (2) Some hospitals, instead of changing the original, permit the patient to add a letter of explanation to the record. If the staff concurs with the statement, that can be noted on the letter. This approach clearly documents the source of the change.

Retention of Records

Because the facility's record is maintained primarily for the use of the institution and its staff in providing better patient care, the decision concerning the length of time it shall be retained should be made on the basis of sound hospital and professional practice. However, the decision as to the retention period cannot be made on this basis alone. In several states, regulations specify the minimum length of time all records must be retained; in others, these provisions apply to certain records only, for example, radiographs and clinical laboratory test reports. Medicare requires records to be kept for the longer of five years after the filing of the hospital's cost report or the period in which suits may be filed. Several states insist that records be kept permanently, but more now are requiring that they be retained for the period in which suits may be filed for breach of contract or personal injuries. Several states provide that records cannot be destroyed without the approval of a regulatory agency.

The American Hospital Association (AHA) and the American Medical Record Association have adopted a policy on record retention that recommends retaining records for a period of 10 years after the most recent patient care usage and retaining certain parts of the record permanently.[21]

When there are no controlling regulations, the retention time after records are not needed for medical and administrative purposes should be determined by the hospital administration with the advice of legal counsel. The factors taken into account should include whether microfilming is feasible or practical, storage space, future needs for the records, and the legal considerations of having them available in the event a patient sues the hospital or a third party. Hospitals in which extensive research is conducted may prefer a longer retention period to facilitate retrospective studies.

Charting Tips

The health care record is used as evidence in a variety of legal actions, including workers' compensation, personal injury actions, and will contests. Generally, nurses are most concerned about the use of records in negligence actions.

The record, including nurses' notes, is a critical piece of evidence in the determination of the standard of care provided. The notes should reflect, accurately and completely, the patient's condition, progress, and nursing activities for the period that the charting covers. Nurses should keep in mind that charts can be a defense against a negligence allegation and that good charting can protect them from liability.

Nurses should be familiar with the hospital policy on charting. The hospital should review each element of the policy periodically to ensure that its requirements are realistically designed to promote accuracy and efficiency. It may be advisable to use graphic sheets or charts that summarize numerical and objective data to facilitate ease and completeness of charting. In addition to saving time, a well-designed flowsheet can make it easy to find information and identify needs and changes in patients' conditions.

Specific recommendations for charting include

1. Charting must be done as soon as possible after the events occur. The notes must include the time events occurred. Doing all charting at the end of the shift should be avoided, as details, times, and incidents are likely to be omitted.

2. Observations charted should lead to nursing diagnosis and describe the patient's behavior, appearance, and symptoms. Patient quotes and statements should be used. Conclusions should not be charted without supporting objective data.

3. An error in charting should not be obliterated; rather, the entry should be crossed out and "error" written above it. An obliterated entry could be construed as a cover-up or as an error that injured the patient. Other nurses' notes should not be recopied if an error is made. If a treatment or medication is discontinued, the entry should be crossed out and "D/C" or "discontinued" written in.

4. A late entry is better than no entry. The date and time that the note is made should be charted with a notation that it is a late entry. A note should not be squeezed into a small space or the margin of the page.

5. Chart entries should be clear, and correct grammar and spelling should be used. It is not always necessary to use complete sentences, but nurses should not expect an attorney or jury to fill in the gaps left by "shorthand charting."

6. The writing must be legible; only abbreviations that are on the institutional approved list should be used.

7. It is not necessary to describe everything as "appears" or "seems." Every nurse is capable of documenting observations without these qualifiers. The only time it may be advisable to use *appears* is when the patient appears to be sleeping.

8. Once is enough; it is not necessary to repeat data that can be found elsewhere in the chart, such as intake and output, medications, or activity, unless it is indicative of a change in the patient's condition.
9. Changes in the patient's status, especially signs that indicate deterioration, should be documented with extra care, along with the steps taken by the nursing staff to respond to the change.
10. "Routine" checks of a patient's status should be charted, including the assessment and the results, even if they are "normal." Failure to enter normal data can lead to the inference that the patient was not checked at all. This practice should be evaluated as well with the trend to only chart changes. Institutional policy should be reviewed on this issue.
11. Inaccuracies are totally impermissible in charting. If discovered, they can cast doubt on the credibility of the record and the nurse.
12. It is imperative to document steps taken to respond to changes in a patient's condition, such as "M.D. notified. Order for oxygen obtained. Patient placed in 40% oxygen." The results of the intervention also must be charted.
13. Diagnostic tests and treatments, who performed them, and the patient's response all should be charted.
14. The writer should be identified by name and title at the conclusion of each chart entry.
15. Charts must not be destroyed or recopied.

A clear factual account of the patient's condition and care can protect the nursing staff from liability for negligence. Nurses should keep in mind that the charting should reflect compliance with the appropriate standard of care for that patient.

Ownership

The hospital owns the records. They are the hospital's business record. The hospital's ownership is stated explicitly in the statutes and regulations of some states. Courts have recognized the hospital's ownership.[22] If the physician maintains separate records, they are the property of the physician; however, the physician still has a responsibility to maintain complete hospital records.

The health care record is an unusual type of property because physically it belongs to the hospital, which must exercise considerable control over access, but patients and others have an interest in the information it contains. One way of viewing this is that the hospital owns the paper or other material on which the information is recorded but is just a custodian of the information. Thus, patients and others have a right of access to the information in many circumstances but not to possession of the original records.[23] In a 1935 Michigan case, the court ruled that the patient did not have a right to radiograph negatives.[24] The patient does not purchase a picture; the patient purchases the professional service of interpreting the radiograph. Thus, the patient could not use the physician's retention of the radiograph as a defense to a physician's suit to collect his professional fee.

Although hospitals may have a duty to permit a patient and his or her representative to inspect and copy the patient's medical record, hospitals are not obligated to do so free of charge.[25] Fees charged by hospitals for reproduction of medical records should be reasonably related to the hospital's actual cost in removing the record from the record library and duplicating the portions requested.

Computers

Taking advantage of automated data processing techniques, hospitals have developed new methods for handling health care record information. Several legal questions are raised by these new techniques. In states that require physicians' signatures as authentication of their entries and orders, some accommodation will be necessary; because a completely automated system provides no conventional written record for a period of time, that produced in an automated system may not suffice. In some states, there may be a question of court admissibility of information generated by the system.

Although the mechanics of storage and access in an automated records system may differ from those in a manual one, the rules governing confidentiality of information in a computerized system are the same as those in a traditional record system. The unauthorized release of patient information, whether by means of a photocopied medical record or a printout at a remote computer terminal, is actionable.

Questions of confidentiality may arise because of the potential access to information by a larger number of people. However, a properly designed computer access security system may provide more confidentiality protection than the traditional hospital record because (1) there are few points of access to the computer, (2) it is possible to restrict each person's access to a limited scope of information, and (3) it is possible to monitor continuously or selectively the information being sought using individual access codes, making misuse easier to detect. Of course, the security system depends in part on educating staff members that disclosure of their personal access codes is equivalent to disclosure of confidential health care information and thus subject to the same sanctions by the hospital.

Confidentiality

It is generally accepted that the record is a confidential document and that access to it should be limited to the patient, the patient's authorized representative and attending physician, and hospital and nursing staff members who have a legitimate interest in the record. There are several exceptions to this general rule, however, each of which permits individuals other than those listed to review the medical record. The exceptions include disclosures that are made pursuant to the federal Freedom of Information Act (FOIA); those required by federal and state reimbursement regulations; those necessary to meet peer review organization (PRO) requirements, as well as other review and state statutory reporting requirements; and those made to law enforcement agencies or other governmental agencies for appropriate purposes.

The primary rationale for confidentiality is to encourage candor by patients and their associates to optimize diagnosis and treatment. Confidentiality also respects patient privacy; individuals should not have to broadcast details of their bodily condition to obtain health care. Confidentiality also can promote candor by those caring for the patient.

Persons outside the hospital seek to obtain this information. There is much interest in the health condition of individuals and the care they receive. Family members are interested in the condition of relatives. Some patients can have a significant effect on affairs of business and state, so their condition is valuable information. There also is a general interest in unusual health conditions and the condition of those involved in public events, so media attention focuses on health information. The health condition is an important element of many insurance coverage determinations and legal proceedings, criminal and civil.

The tension between access and secrecy has existed since the beginning of medicine. Most health professions in addressing the issue have incorporated confidentiality mandates in their ethical standards. For example, the Hippocratic Oath of physicians states: "And whatsoever I shall see or hear in the course of my profession, as well as outside my profession in my intercourse with men, if it be what should not be published abroad, I will never divulge, holding such things to be holy secrets."[26] These codes led to tensions as legal requirements of disclosure evolved. For example, some physicians challenged early laws requiring reporting of births and deaths.

Most modern codes recognize that professionals have an obligation to comply with legal mandates regarding disclosure. The American Medical Association code as amended in 1980 states: "A physician . . . shall safeguard patient confidences within the constraints of the law."[27] Nursing has adopted a similar balanced standard. The American Nurses Association *Code for Nurses* states: "The nurse safeguards the client's right to privacy by judiciously protecting information of a confidential nature."[28]

ACCESS TO HEALTH CARE RECORDS

Access for Intrahospital Use

There are many needs for access to information within the hospital, including direct patient care, administrative uses, research, and billing purposes.

Those involved in patient care must have timely access to the records, or the communication function of the record is defeated to the detriment of proper treatment. In some states, this rule is established by statute[29] or regulation,[30] which often restrict access to those who directly participate in a patient's medical treatment.[31] In addition, Joint Commission accreditation standards permit access to medical records by hospital staff for purposes of treatment, quality control activities, official surveys, education, research, and the like.[32] Records must be located where they are readily accessible for patient care, even though this may increase the risk of unauthorized access by others, for treatment of the present condition and for future care. Although confidentiality is an important goal that hospitals and health professionals should strive to achieve, unauthorized access results in less exposure to liability than does improper patient care because of unavailable records.

A New Jersey hospital was liable for failing to protect the confidentiality of a diagnosis of acquired immune deficiency syndrome (AIDS) in a staff physician who had been treated at the facility, a trial court in that state has ruled.[33] When the physician became ill, he was hospitalized at the facility where he held staff privileges. A bronchoscopy and a blood test subsequently revealed he had AIDS. Although the treating physician and the laboratory personnel initially preserved the confidentiality of the diagnosis, the test results were placed in the physician's medical chart, which was kept at the nurses' station on the floor where the physician was an inpatient. There were no restrictions on access to the record. Within hours of the diagnosis, the physician's condition was widely known within the hospital. Soon thereafter, several of the physician's patients learned of his condition and many refused to seek further treatment from him. The physician sued the hospital, claiming that it had breached its duty of confidentiality.

Medical records also are key elements of the business records of the hospital. Many staff members must have access to operate the hospital. Hospitals have the authority to permit internal access by professional, technical, and administrative personnel who have need to do so for such functions as auditing, filing, billing, replying to inquiries, and defending potential litigation.

These administrative uses are so widely understood that they seldom have been addressed in reported court decisions. The few cases have been decided in favor of administrative access. In one case, the court authorized a trustee to examine records of patients involved in a controversial research project.[34] The court observed: "Actually, the supposed strict secrecy does not really exist as to qualified persons since these records have been seen, read and copied by numerous staff members and employees of the hospital and cooperating institutions."[35]

Courts have upheld the authority of hospitals to review records for quality assurance purposes[36] and to permit their insurers and lawyers to have access to prepare to deal with patient claims.[37]

In most hospitals, medical and nursing staff members may examine medical records for any of the purposes established by the hospitals' medical records policies. One legitimate purpose for staff inspection of patient records is nursing research. In determining how much control to impose on staff access to medical records, the hospital must balance the patients' interest in protecting their privacy against the practitioners' interest in advancing nursing science for the general welfare.

The responsibility for evaluating the risk to the patient and the potential good to society rests in most hospitals with an institutional review board (IRB) or a committee of the medical staff. Hospitals that are federal grantees or contractors and that conduct medical research with human subjects are required by federal regulations[38] to establish an IRB to evaluate proposed research protocols and to determine whether they constitute appropriate research and whether adequate safeguards are available to protect the human subjects at risk.[39] In some hospitals, a medical staff committee makes these determinations in accordance with the definition of appropriate research set forth in the staff's rules and regulations.

The criteria by which an IRB or other committee evaluates proposed medical records studies should be established as hospital policy. Although patient consent for disclosure of record information is certainly desirable, it is seldom possible to obtain for retrospective studies. This fact is recognized in the federal regulations,[40] and IRBs generally need not require patient consent to disclosures in which it is impossible or impractical to obtain. The IRB or research committee should require that the following safeguards be in place before authorizing disclosure of medical records information to medical investigators:

- The information will be treated as confidential.
- The information will be communicated only to qualified investigators pursuing an approved research program designed for the benefit of the health of the community.
- The results of the investigation will be presented in a way that prevents identification of individual subjects.[41]

Patient Authorization

In general, all patients have a right of access to their records. One of the clearest sources of authority to release information to nonhospital personnel is the authorization of a competent patient.

The courts in many states have recognized the right of patients or their authorized agents to have access to their medical records. Competent patients generally can authorize their own access to records concerning their care. Some states have statutes that establish patients' rights to access to records on their own care and establish procedures for doing so. A common-law right of access has been recognized by several courts. In cases over the past two decades, patients generally have been held to have a right of access.[42] Courts also have said that if a patient wants a copy of the record, the hospital may require that a reasonable charge be paid for it.[43]

Several of the statutes that authorize a patient or patient's representative to inspect records do not permit inspection of records until after the patient has been discharged from the hospital.[44] The question is frequently raised by nurses as to whether the hospital must allow patients to examine their records while they are still hospitalized. In the absence of a statutory or common-law right of access during hospitalization, the hospital is not obligated to permit patients to inspect their records while on the hospital's patient care units. However, a patient who is not allowed to examine his or her chart in the hospital may become hostile and more difficult to treat and may file a claim against the hospital if treatment ends in a poor result. Therefore, unless the patient's attending physician can establish a reasonable basis for an opinion that disclosure of the inpatient medical record would be harmful to the patient, the hospital should allow the patient to review the record.

In some states, the rules governing access to the medical records of mental health patients differ from those applicable to medical records generally. In the past, mental health patients in most states, even in those states that granted a right to access to non–mental health patients, could not access their medical records. It was widely believed that authorizing such patients to review their records would be injurious to their health. Today, however, mental health patients in some states have the same right to inspect their records as do other patients. Some courts have recognized the right of mental health patients or their representatives to review their medical records.[45]

There is little specific guidance in the law concerning who may have access to or authorize the release of the records of minor patients. In the absence of statutory or common-law authority on this point, the generally accepted rule is that a hospital may disclose the medical record of a minor patient only on the authorization of one of the patient's parents, unless a legal guardian has been appointed for the minor, and that a minor's parents may be allowed access to such records on request. A few states have statutes that permit the release of such records with the consent of either the patient's parent or the patient.

In California, a patient who is a minor may only authorize the release of medical information if the information relates to services to which the minor is legally authorized to consent. A minor's legal representative may authorize the disclosure of all other types of medical treatment information. A minor's authorization would appear to be sufficient to release his or her hospital records for any purpose, including those for which a parent's consent is allowed.

Other state statutes, however, simply are not clear on questions of parental control of access to a minor's records. Most statutes permit access to records with the consent of "the patient"[46] or "the person."[47] In these states, hospitals follow the general rule and obtain the authorization of the patient's parent before disclosing records to third parties. In some situations, statutes authorize certain categories of minors (e.g., those who are pregnant, parents, married, or suffering from drug abuse) to consent to their own medical care. It is a logical extension of these statutory rules to allow such minors to consent to disclosure of their medical records, but there is no clear authority for such a position.

Access by Others

When patients may authorize their own access, they may authorize access by others. In an Oklahoma case, the court ruled that insurers of the patient have a right to copy the hospital's records upon proper authorization of the patient.[48] The court found the hospital's refusal to provide a copy to be unlawful interference with the insurer's business.

There is implied consent to keep the immediate family informed of the patient's progress unless the person expressly directs that no information be released or a statutory prohibition applies, such as the federal substance abuse confidentiality rules discussed later in this chapter. In a 1963 Louisiana case, the court found that the husband had a right of access to information concerning his wife's care even though they were separated and he was pursuing a divorce.[49] It is doubtful whether many courts would extend the right of access that far today. Thus, the most prudent practice would be to require express patient consent or court authorization before releasing information when estrangement is known.

In a 1982 New York case, the court stated that a spouse should not be told psychiatric information even where there is no estrangement unless the patient authorizes the disclosure or there is a danger to the patient, spouse, or another person that can be reduced by disclosure.[50] Some statutes authorize the disclosure of psychiatric information to the spouse in other circumstances.[51] Thus, release of psychiatric information is subject to special restrictions in some jurisdictions.

Exceptions

Some courts have recognized exceptions to the general rule in favor of access. They recognize that there may be situations when the release of information would be against the best interests of the patient's health. However, as illustrated by a 1979 case, the courts generally have insisted that medically contraindicated information be made available to the patient's representative, frequently an outside professional acting on behalf of the patient.[52]

This case addressed the withholding of information from patients preparing for hearings challenging their transfer to facilities that provide a lower level of care.

The court ruled that it was not enough for the state to offer to release the information to a representative when the patient did not have a representative. The state was permitted to withhold medically contraindicated information from the patient only when the person actually had a representative, provided by the state if necessary. In a 1965 case, the court stated that records that would be adverse to the patient's health could be withheld from insurance companies.[53] It is doubtful whether this rule would be applied today, given the widespread understanding of third-party payment.

Releasing Information in the Patient–Provider Context

The AHA Patient's Bill of Rights focuses on release of information by the physician rather than by the hospital.[54] It states that patients should be able to obtain complete information from their physician except when disclosure is not medically advisable, and then the information should be given to an appropriate person on the patient's behalf. When patients will accept information from their physician, this approach is preferable to having the person read the health care record. Thus, physicians should be encouraged to provide information to their patients.

However, in many situations, patients still wish to see the record. Access is recommended because in many situations, patient curiosity and concerns will be satisfied, dispelling any appearance of a cover-up and avoiding the need for the patient to hire an attorney or file suit to obtain the records. A 1980 study that analyzed patient reactions found:

1. One-third of the patients who read their charts had self-induced or factitious illness and were angry to have been uncovered.
2. One-third had believed their physicians to be unsympathetic to their symptoms, and some found their suspicions confirmed but others gained renewed confidence.
3. One-third were worried about their prognosis, fearing the physician was not telling them the severity of their illness; and all these patients were reassured.[55]

Another good reason to provide prompt access is that in some cases courts have ruled that the period from the request until the release does not count toward exhausting the statute of limitations period in which suits must be brought if that span is unreasonably long.[56] Thus, resistance to disclosure can reduce the protection of the statute of limitations.

Authorization by Patient's Representative

When the patient is unable to authorize access because of incompetency, minority, or death, someone else must be able to authorize access.

In general, guardians of mentally incompetent patients are entitled to access to records to which the patients would have access if competent. However, some courts have stated they will suppress portions of the record on a determination they contain family confidences or information that may upset the patient severely.[57]

When a mentally incompetent patient does not have a guardian, the hospital probably is safe in relying on the authorization of the next of kin or other responsible person who is authorizing medical treatment, especially for access by the responsible person or by others for continuity of patient care or payment of charges. When the mental incompetence is temporary and release of the information can reasonably wait, it usually is most prudent to wait for the patient's authorization.

The scope of parent and guardian access to records of minors is less clear. For instance, in California, a parent does not have an absolute right of access to a minor child's medical records, and a court may deny access to such records if a therapist determines that access is detrimental, an appeals court has ruled.[58] In a juvenile dependency proceeding, a parent requested that the child's therapist testify about alleged molestation by the parent. The parent contended that he is entitled to access the child's confidential communications to the psychotherapist because as a parent, he has the right to receive information concerning the medical condition of his child.

The court reviewed California's access to medical records statutes and noted that one statute specifically denies access by a parent if the health care provider determines that access to the patient records would damage the provider's professional relationship with the minor patient. In this instance, the court found that access could cause substantial harm to the child, who might refuse to be open with the therapist out of fear of disclosure to the parent. The court also found that the child had a substantial privacy interest at sake.

Some state statutes specify that information regarding certain types of treatment, such as venereal disease and substance abuse, may not be disclosed without the minor's consent. Some states specify by statute that parents must be informed before minors may obtain certain kinds of services. For example, Utah requires parents to be informed of abortions. In a 1981 Supreme Court case, the Court found the Utah reporting law not to violate the Constitution but declined to rule on whether the law would be constitutional if it were applied to mature minors.[59]

When minors are permitted under state law to consent to their own care, it is likely that parents would not have a right to information concerning the treatment. If the minor fails to pay for the care and relies on the parents, the parents then may be entitled to more information. However, providers can release information concerning immature minors to parents without substantial risk of liability, unless state statutes expressly prohibit it. When a mature minor wants information withheld from parents, the provider must make a professional judgment except in the few circumstances in which the law is settled, such as when a statute requires or forbids notification. A circumstance that clearly permits disclosure is when there is likelihood of harm to the minor or others, such as a contagious disease, that requires parental involvement to avoid.

After the death of a patient, if there is an executor of the estate, authorization by that source usually should be sought. If there is no executor, authorization should be obtained from the next of kin, such as a surviving spouse[60] or child.[61] If there is known conflict among next of kin, it is most prudent to obtain the authorization of all the nearest kin available. In such cases, a surviving spouse could authorize release alone, but if there is no spouse, the authorization of all the available children should be obtained if reasonably possible under the circumstances.

In a few states, the legal responsibility to maintain confidentiality ends with the death of the patient. However, it still is prudent to insist on appropriate authorization to avoid compromising the interests of the surviving family.

Access by Law

Even if the patient or representative opposes release of information, the law requires hospitals and health care professionals to permit access in many circumstances. Some governmental agencies have specific authority to examine medical records. The law grants parties in lawsuits access through subpoenas and other mechanisms to discover evidence. The law requires health care providers to report a variety of patient conditions to law enforcement or public health authorities or to give certain persons access if they request the information.

Some governmental agencies have specific authority to examine hospital medical records. Although governmental authority to access medical records has been challenged, most courts have refused to strike it down.[62] Hospitals participating in Medicaid programs must submit medical record information to the state's Medicaid agency and to the Secretary of Health and Human Services (HHS) upon request.[63] When patients have challenged state agency reviews of records, the courts have held that access to records is a federal law requirement of state Medicaid plans and is necessary to ensure quality of service and detection of fraud and does not infringe on the provider–patient relationship.[64]

Several states have enacted statutes that authorize or require the release or disclosure of medical records without the patient's consent. Medical records may be released when a patient is transferred to another health care facility,[65] when they are required by the state's board of medical examiners,[66] when state health department inspectors[67] or county medical examiners[68] request them, or when the hospital closes and must send its patient records to another institution.[69] These statutory provisions authorizing release of medical records vary from state to state.

Subpoenas and Other Discovery Mechanisms

In lawsuits and many administrative proceedings, the court or agency has the authority to issue orders to assist one side to gain access to information that is in the control of others. Lawyers call this the discovery process. The most frequent discovery orders are called subpoenas, which require a person to appear at a specific place on or before a certain time, frequently bringing certain documents. Other discovery orders can require a person to submit to a physical or mental examination or to permit someone to inspect land, buildings, or other property.

A subpoena may order that health care records (or copies) be provided to the court or to the other side in a suit. A subpoena may order a nurse to submit to formal questioning under oath before the trial. This question-and-answer session is called a deposition and often is used as testimony if the person cannot be at the trial. If the person is at the trial and gives different testimony, the deposition can be used to cast doubt on what is said at trial.

Under the current liberal discovery practices, health care records nearly always can be subpoenaed if the mental or physical condition of the party is possibly relevant to the suit. When records can be subpoenaed, those who provided the health care such as nurses usually can be ordered to give depositions.

In most circumstances, courts will not permit the discovery of information concerning the care of persons who are not parties. Some attorneys have sought the information to establish what happened when similar treatment was given to other patients. Providers have resisted these attempts on the basis that it invades the patient's privacy, violates the provider–patient privilege (discussed in the section on limitations on disclosures), and is not relevant because of the uniqueness of the condition and reaction of each patient.

The only widely accepted exceptions to the general rule not permitting discovery have been in cases involving billing fraud by, or professional discipline of, the health care provider. However, in recent years, some courts have permitted access to records of nonparties in malpractice suits but have required all "identifiers" to be deleted.[70] There is no clear trend because several courts have reaffirmed the traditional rule and declined to order access.[71]

Some attorneys have attempted to bypass the rule on nondisclosure of nonparty records by seeking the names of nonparty patients and obtaining their permission to get the records. Providers have resisted these attempts for reasons similar to those for resisting discovery of their records. Most courts have not permitted the discovery of the names of nonparties.

For example, in a 1964 case, the court ruled that the names of patients were protected by the physician–patient privilege.[72] However, in 1976, the court held that privilege does not protect patients' names in Arizona but still refused to order release of other names because it did not consider them relevant to the case.[73] Thus, there is a risk that records obtained without identifiers could be linked later to patient names through another exception.

Law Enforcement Agencies

As a general rule, nurses should not release medical records or other patient information to law enforcement personnel without the patient's authorization. In the absence of statutory authority or legal process, a police agency has no authority to examine a medical record.

There are several exceptions to the rule, however. The law enforcement agency may be authorized by a specific statute to inspect medical records without patient consent, as in South Carolina, where the medical records confidentiality statute states that medical record information may be disclosed without patient authorization when "[d]isclosure is necessary in cooperating with law enforcement agencies."[74] Law enforcement personnel also may be authorized to obtain medical record information in connection with child abuse reports or investigations[75] or if a patient is suspected of driving while intoxicated.[76] A law enforcement agency may compel disclosure of records pursuant to a subpoena or court order.

Certain types of cases (e.g., those involving rape or other crime victims) create routine police inquiries. When possible in these cases, hospitals should seek, preferably during the admitting process, the patient's consent to release of information to law enforcement agencies. Where a report to police is required by statute or ordinance, as in cases involving gunshot wounds, patient consent is not required.

DISCLOSURE

Statutory Duty to Disclose

Reporting Laws

The law compels disclosure of health care information in many contexts other than discovery or testimony. A variety of reporting laws have been enacted that require many kinds of information to be reported to governmental agencies: vital statistics, communicable disease, child abuse, and wound reporting. Familiarity with these and other reporting laws is important to ensure compliance and to avoid making the report to the wrong agency. Reports to the wrong agency may not be legally protected, resulting in potential liability for breach of confidentiality.

All states require the reporting of births and deaths. Courts have ruled as far back as 1882 that these laws are a valid exercise of the state's police power.[77] Many states also require the reporting of some fetal deaths and abortions. In a 1976 Missouri case, the Supreme Court upheld some abortion reporting requirements.[78]

Communicable disease reporting laws that require hospitals and practitioners to inform public health authorities of infectious disease cases are among the oldest compulsory reporting statutes in many states. The statute or regulation usually lists diseases that should be reported and directs practitioners to give local public health officials the patient's names, age, sex, address, and identifying information, as well as the details of the patient's illness.[79]

1. The sensitive nature of an individual's human immunodeficiency virus (HIV) status has prompted a number of states to enact specific legislation regarding the confidentiality of HIV test results. There is legislation that enunciates confidentiality rules for health records that contain personal identifying information with respect to AIDS or that prohibits disclosure of test results except under specific circumstances.
2. Most states have enacted legislation prohibiting disclosure of test results for the presence of the AIDS antibody except to the test subject and to others under carefully defined circumstances.[80]

Legislation in many states imposes specific duties on health care providers to disclose AIDS-related patient information to designated agencies or individuals. In all 50 states, confirmed cases of AIDS constitute a reportable condition, and in some states, cases of HIV infection must also be reported.[81] Other states either require or allow licensed health care providers treating a patient who is subsequently diagnosed as having AIDS to contact the emergency medical personnel who treated or transported the patient.[82] In addition, legislation in many states allows disclosure of a patient's HIV test results to health care workers who, in the course of their occupational duties, would have significant exposure to the infection.[83] Numerous states also give discretion to a provider who orders an AIDS antibody test to disclose the results to the patient's sexual partner, and many of these statutes grant immunity to providers who make such a disclosure.[84] Other states allow disclosure to a patient's sexual partner or intravenous drug use partner only if the patient is deceased[85] or restrict disclosure to the patient's spouse.[86]

A trial court correctly allowed a hospital to disclose the identity of an AIDS-infected obstetrics/gynecology resident to patients who had been treated by the resident, a Pennsylvania Superior Court has ruled.[87] During an invasive internal procedure, a physician sustained a cut through his surgical glove and exposed a patient to his HIV-infected blood. Two hospitals where the physician had worked requested court permission to disclose the physician's name and some medical information to more than 200 patients who had been associated to some degree with the physician in the course of their treatment. Although Pennsylvania legislation specifically provides for the confidentiality of AIDS-related patient information, the hospitals argued that they have a duty to disclose the physician's identity to patients and health care workers who were potentially affected by contact with him. The trial court agreed and authorized limited disclosure.

The status of state law on AIDS reporting requirements is still evolving rapidly, and consequently nursing practices must respond to numerous changes. Nurses should be aware of current legislation that governs the release of this type of information and should be sensitive to the fact that the law on this issue is still developing.

A few states require hospitals and providers to report abortions they perform[88] and any complications that may develop.[89] Other states require hospitals to report fetal deaths, including those resulting from abortions.[90] Courts have held these requirements to be rationally related to a compelling state interest in maternal health and not to be an infringement on the physician–patient relationship, the right to an abortion, or any personal right of privacy.[91]

A few states require disclosure of information from the records of cancer patients to central state or regional tumor registries.[92] These registries usually contain information about patients who suffer from the same or similar disease and are designed to provide raw data for studies concerning incidence of a disease in the population; long-term prognosis of the disease; type, duration, and frequency of treatment rendered to patients with the disease; and other indicators of the health care industry's ability to manage the disease.

Most states require the reporting of suspected cases of child abuse or neglect. Some professionals, including nurses, are required to make reports and thus are called mandatory reporters. Usually, anyone who is not a mandatory reporter may make a report as a permissive reporter. Any report arising out of diagnosis or treatment of a child in an institution usually must be made through the administration. Most child abuse reporting laws extend some degree of immunity from liability for mandatory or permissive reporters who make their reports through proper channels.

For instance, the California legislation that grants immunity to health care providers when they make mandated reports of child abuse also protects providers from liability when they make reports that are not required but merely authorized under the law.[93] A hospital treated a child for injuries sustained by falling down stairs. After the child died, the treating physician filed a report of suspected child abuse as required under state law, but he also gave statements about the case to investigators and attorneys who were following up on the initial report. The parents sued the hospital and the physician for damages, but a trial court ruled that the reporting legislation provides absolute immunity to medical providers who report child abuse.

There usually are criminal penalties for mandatory reporters who do not make required reports, but there have been few prosecutions. A mandatory reporter who fails to report child abuse is at greater risk of civil liability. Some state statutes specify that a mandatory reporter who fails to make a required report is civilly liable for future injuries to the child that could have been avoided if a report had been made.[94] In one case, the California Supreme Court ruled that there could be civil liability under the common law when the statute did not address whether there should be civil liability.[95] A few states have enacted similar adult abuse reporting laws.

Under the National Childhood Vaccine Injury Act of 1986,[96] all health care providers and hospitals must record each administration of any vaccine to a child and report any illness, disability, or death resulting from the administration of the vaccine to HHS. A hospital staff nurse that administers a vaccine listed in the vaccine injury table[97] must record in the patient's permanent medical record:

- date of administration of the vaccine
- vaccine manufacturer's name and lot number of the vaccine
- name and address and, if appropriate, title of the health care provider administering the vaccine
- any other information required pursuant to federal regulations

The hospital staff must also report any injury, disability, illness, condition, or death resulting from the vaccine as listed in the vaccine injury table and aids to interpretation provision[98] that occurs within seven days of administration or as specified in the table. Any contradicted reaction listed in the manufacturer's package insert must also be reported. Reports on illnesses resulting from the vaccine, but not indicated reactions, must specify the time period after the administration of the vaccine that the illness occurred, in addition to the manufacturer's name and the lot number of the vaccine.

Many states require the reporting of certain wounds. Some states specify that all wounds of certain types must be reported—in New York, wounds inflicted by sharp instruments that may result in death and all gunshot wounds.[99] Other states limit the reporting requirement to wounds caused under certain circumstance—in Iowa, for wounds that apparently resulted from a criminal act, so those that clearly are accidental or self-inflicted do not have to be reported there.[100]

Some states require the reporting of other types of information (e.g., drug abuse, poison, or industrial accidents), so it is important to be familiar with the requirements of local law. Several national reporting laws apply to hospitals involved in manufacturing, testing, or using certain substances and devices. For example, fatalities from blood transfusions must be reported to the Food and Drug Administration (FDA).[101] Sponsors of investigational medical devices must report to the FDA when their use produces unanticipated adverse effects.[102]

Access Laws

A second type of statute does not mandate reporting but authorizes access on request to certain individuals or organizations or to the general public without the permission of the patient.

Workers' Compensation. Some state statutes specify that all parties to a workers' compensation claim have access to all relevant health care information after a claim has been made.[103] In states that do not authorize access by statute, health care records should not be released unless patients or their representatives so authorize or the records are legally subpoenaed by an administrative agency or court. One exception is in states where the courts have ruled that filing a workers' compensation claim is a waiver under the common law of the right to confidentiality of relevant health care information.[104]

Freedom of Information Act. The federal FOIA[105] applies only to federal agencies. A hospital does not become a federal agency by receiving federal funds. Thus, the act applies to few hospitals outside of the Veterans Administration and Defense Department. When it does apply, health care information is exempted from disclosure only when that would "constitute a clearly unwarranted invasion of personal privacy." Thus, there is only limited protection of the confidentiality of health care information in the possession of federal agencies.

State Public Records Laws. Many states have public records laws that apply to public hospitals. Some statutes explicitly exempt hospital and medical records from disclosure.[106] In a 1974 case, Colorado's law was interpreted as not permitting a publisher to routinely obtain all birth and death reports.[107] However, in a 1978 Ohio case, the state law was interpreted to require access to the names of all persons admitted to a public hospital and the dates of admission and discharge.[108] In states that follow the Ohio rule, it is especially important to resist discovery of nonparty records because removal of "identifiers" does not offer much protection because dates in the record can make it possible to identify the patient by comparison with the admission list. It is important for those associated with public hospitals to be familiar with local law on records access.

Peer Review Organization Program. The PRO program became effective in 1985.[109] The law requires that PROs disclose, in accordance with procedures established by the Department of HHS, review information (1) to state or federal fraud and abuse agencies; (2) to state licensure or certification agencies; and (3) to federal and state agencies responsible for identifying cases involving risks to the public health.[110]

Although PROs are not permitted to release patient- and physician-specific information to consumers, information concerning utilization and quality of care may be released if the identity of the practitioner, patient, or reviewer would not be obvious to persons with an understanding of the PRO area.

Common-Law Duty to Disclose

In addition to these statutory requirements, the common law has recognized a duty to disclose health care information in several circumstances. Persons who could have avoided injury if the information had been disclosed have won civil suits against providers who failed to disclose the information.

There is a duty to warn persons at risk of the presence of contagious disease. Hospital staff, family members, and others caring for the patient must be warned. In a 1978 case, the court ruled that a physician could be liable for the death of a neighbor who contracted smallpox while assisting in the care of the physician's patient who had smallpox because the physician failed to warn the neighbor of the contagious nature of the disease.[111] However, there is no duty to warn all members of the public individually, although in a California case the court observed that liability to the general public might result from failure to make a required report to public health authorities.[112]

In California, a patient who, for the purpose of alerting a health care provider to take necessary precautions, informed the provider that he was HIV-positive, sued the provider based on the state's constitutional right to privacy for disclosing his HIV status.[113] During a medical examination, the patient told the physician's nurse to be careful because he was HIV-positive. The patient claimed that he made it clear to the nurse that he was disclosing this information in confidence. The physician's report mentioning AIDS as a possible source of the patient's symptoms was sent to the insurance company's attorney, who in turn sent copies to the patient's attorney, the insurance carrier, and the workers' compensation appeals board. An appeals court held that when a patient makes clear that he is communicating the fact that he is HIV-positive solely for the purpose of protecting health care professionals, the communication is entitled to constitutional privacy.

The courts of a few states have ruled that there is a duty to warn an identified person whom a patient has made a credible threat to kill. The first time this duty was imposed was in a 1976 case in which the parents of a murder victim sued the California Board of Regents for the death of their daughter.[114] The court found the employer of a psychiatrist liable for his failure to warn the daughter that his patient had threatened to kill her. The court ruled that he should have either warned the victim or advised others likely to apprise the victim of the danger.

Four years later, the court clarified the scope of this duty in California by ruling that only threats to readily identified individuals create a duty to warn.[115] There is no duty to warn a threatened group. Some courts have declined to establish a duty to warn even readily identified individuals.[116] The more prudent practice today is to warn identified individuals of credible threats when the patient is not detained.

Courts have recognized other situations in which there is a duty to disclose. One example is the duty of referral specialists to communicate their findings to the referring practitioner.[117] A competent patient can waive this duty by directing the referral specialist not to communicate with the referring physician.

Limitations of Disclosure

Several statutory and common law limitations on disclosure have evolved that help preserve confidentiality and impose sanctions for some violations.

Many states' laws prohibit certain health care professionals from testifying as witnesses concerning certain information gained in the professional relationship with a patient. Health care professionals did not have a privilege from testimonial disclosure under English common law. Nearly all American courts also have adopted this position, so with few exceptions the privilege exists only in states that have enacted privilege statutes. One exception is Alaska, which established a common-law psychotherapist–patient privilege for criminal cases.[118]

Approximately two-thirds of the states have enacted a statutory physician–patient privilege, and a few have nurse–patient privilege. Privilege statutes address only situations in which the professional is being compelled to testify, such as in a deposition, an administrative hearing, or a trial. There is a widespread misperception that privilege statutes apply to other disclosures, but in most states, this is not true. The duty to maintain confidentiality outside of testimonial contexts is grounded on other legal principles (discussed in the later section on common-law limitations). Thus, privilege statutes usually are of concern only when responding to legal compulsion.

The privilege applies only when there is a bona fide professional–patient relationship. Thus, for example, it usually does not apply to court-ordered examinations or others solely for the benefit of third parties such as insurance companies.

The scope of the privilege varies among the states. For example, Pennsylvania limits the privilege to communications that tend to blacken the character of the patient,[119] whereas Kansas extends it to all communications and observations,[120] Michigan limits it to physicians,[121] and New York extends it to dentists and nurses.[122]

When a nurse is present during a confidential communication between physician and patient, some states extend the physician's privilege to the nurse, whereas others rule that the communication no longer is privileged for the physician. Generally, the privilege extends to otherwise privileged information in the hospital record.[123] However, information required to be reported to public authorities generally has been held not to be privileged, unless those authorities also are privileged not to disclose it.

The patient may waive the privilege, permitting the professional to testify. In nearly all states, the privilege can be waived by contract, such as in an insurance contract. A variety of other actions constitute implied waiver. If a patient introduces evidence disclosing details of a health condition or fails to object to testimony by a professional, most courts find these actions to be an implied waiver.

Most courts also have ruled that authorization of disclosure outside the testimonial context does not waive the privilege.[124] Thus, the patient could authorize other parties to have access to health care records outside of court and still successfully object to having them introduced into evidence unless other actions had waived the privilege. A few courts have adopted the opposite position, so in those states authorization of any disclosure to opposing parties waives the privilege.[125]

Waiver of the privilege usually permits only formal discovery and testimony, not informal interview. This rule requires express patient consent before informal interviews are permitted.[126] However, other courts have permitted informal interviews based on waiver.[127] The most prudent practice is for providers to limit disclosures to formal channels unless there is express patient consent.

Other Limitations on Disclosure

Some federal and state statutes such as federal substance abuse confidentiality laws and state licensing and confidentiality laws limit access to health care information.

Access to records of alcohol and drug abuse patients is severely limited and strictly controlled by the Comprehensive Alcohol Abuse and Alcoholism Prevention, Treatment, and Rehabilitation Act of 1970,[128] the Drug Abuse Office and Treatment Act of 1972,[129] and federal regulations issued pursuant to these acts.[130] These pronouncements, particularly the regulations, impose strict confidentiality requirements on patient records that are maintained in connection with any federally assisted drug or alcohol abuse program. This includes hospitals and general medical care facilities that have an identified unit providing alcohol or drug abuse diagnosis, treatment, or referral for treatment.[131]

The regulations explicitly preempt any state law that purports to authorize disclosures contrary to the regulations but do permit states to impose tighter confidentiality requirements. The rules apply to any disclosure, even acknowledgment of the patient's presence in the facility. Information may be released with the patient's consent if the consent is in writing and contains all of the following elements:

1. name of the program to make the disclosure
2. name or title of the person or organization to receive the information
3. name of the patient
4. purpose of need for the disclosure
5. extent or nature of the information to be disclosed
6. a statement that the consent may be revoked and when it will expire automatically
7. date signed
8. patient's signature

The regulations also stipulate how the consent requirements apply to minors. If under relevant state legislation a minor patient has the legal capacity to obtain drug or alcohol abuse treatment, the minor patient acting alone may authorize disclosure of medical information relating to such treatment. If, however, state law requires that a parent or guardian consent for a minor to obtain drug or alcohol abuse treatment, written consent for disclosure must be given by both the minor and the person authorized to act in the minor's behalf.[132] Disclosures may be made without the patient's consent in medical emergencies; in connection with research, audit, and evaluation activities; and in compliance with an appropriate court order.

A court order, including a subpoena, does not permit release of information unless all the requirements of the regulations have been met. The regulations require a court hearing and finding that the purpose for which the order is sought is more important than the purposes for which Congress mandated confidentiality. Fortunately, the regulations have been interpreted to permit hospitals or other providers to tell the court why they cannot comply with the order until after a hearing.

It is important that staff members be oriented to rules involving substance abuse records. In one case, a nurse successfully challenged her discharge for failure to report a fellow employee's theft of health care records by establishing the reasonableness of her belief (which actually was erroneous) that these federal regulations prohibited the report.[133]

Professional licensing laws or regulations frequently specify that breach of confidentiality is unprofessional conduct and grounds for discipline by the licensing board.[134] Hospital licensing laws and regulations frequently require that confidentiality of records be maintained.[135]

Some state statutes establish a general responsibility to maintain confidentiality of records,[136] whereas some address only records of treatment for certain conditions. For example, chapter 140 of the Iowa Code specifies the confidentiality of information concerning venereal disease.[137] Thus, it is important to be familiar with local statutes and regulations.

Accreditation Standards

The Joint Commission medical records standards specify that hospitals have the responsibility of protecting the record and the information it contains "against loss, defacement, and tampering, and from use by unauthorized individuals."[138] If a hospital accepts this responsibility through its own rules to become accredited, many courts will require the facility to follow those rules and impose liability for injuries that result from violations.

Common-Law Limitations

As discussed in the prior section on professional–patient privilege, common law does not provide any protection from disclosure in testimonial contexts except in a few states such as Alaska. Courts have uniformly refused to impose liability for testimonial disclosures.[139] Health care professionals are not obligated to risk contempt of court to protect confidences (except for substance abuse records), although they may choose to do so.

In nontestimonial contexts, courts have found limitations on permissible disclosure based on the implied promise of confidentiality in the professional–patient relationship, violation of the right of privacy, and violation of professional licensing standards. For example, in a 1977 New York case, the court permanently enjoined a psychoanalyst from circulating a book that included detailed information concerning a patient.[140] The patient was identifiable to friends despite the psychoanalyst's efforts to disguise her identity. The court ruled that the book violated the implied covenant of confidentiality and the right of privacy. The court awarded $20,000 to the plaintiff for the 220 copies that had been sold before the injunction.

Courts have ruled in favor of physicians in cases in which the disclosure was intended to prevent the spread of contagious disease.[141] As discussed in the section on common-law duty to disclose information, there could be liability in some circumstances for failing to disclose a contagious disease.

Disclosures to a patient's employer or insurance company have resulted in several suits. In one case, the court ruled that disclosures to the employer without authorization violated the implied promise of confidentiality and could result in liability.[142] However, in another case the court held that when a patient authorized incomplete disclosure to his employer, the physician was not liable for giving a complete disclosure.[143] It is questionable whether other courts would rule this way, so the prudent practice for the nurse is to refuse to release any information when only a misleading partial release is authorized.

Some courts have found implied authorization to release information to an insurance company based on actions of the patient. In a Colorado case, submission to a health examination at an insurance company's request was considered implied authorization.[144] However, it is prudent practice to obtain written authorization from the patient. Most insurance companies do so. There have been cases in which courts have ruled that insurance companies may be sued for inducing a physician to divulge confidential information.[145]

Discipline of Staff Members

Hospital staff members including nurses have been discharged for unauthorized disclosure of health care records. However, courts and arbitration panels tend to reinstate them unless there has been a consistent pattern of enforcement. For example, a Royal Commission that investigated the confidentiality of medical records in Ontario found many unauthorized disclosures. One of the persons responsible for these was a nurse who had given records to her husband, who was an attorney representing patients' opponents in legal proceedings. She was fired, but the arbitration board ordered her reinstatement with the sanction of suspension without pay up to the time of the ruling.[146] The board accepted her position that, because no one else had been disciplined, she was the scapegoat for the hospital's embarrassment concerning the Royal Commission's findings.

Thus, a consistent pattern of enforcement is important both to communicate the importance of confidentiality to the staff and to increase the likelihood that disciplinary actions will be sustained if challenged.

CONCLUSION

Effective and accurate recording of the treatment given to patients is necessary for both the delivery of quality care to patients and malpractice defense should a lawsuit arise. The need to protect patient privacy in the health care setting has been put under significant stress. Nurses, as gatekeepers to the patient and to patient information, can have a significate impact in this area. Effective efforts to protect patient privacy require nurses to be aware of the rules for access to patient information as well as a knowledge of statutes and regulations that require protection of information in certain situations and mandatory disclosure in others.

FOOTNOTES

1. The videotape of an operation performed on a patient, which was made for the physician's use in teaching other physicians, is not a medical record under New York legislation. *See* Hill v. Springer, No. 14186/86 (N.Y. Sup. Ct. July 29, 1986).

2. *See, generally,* Foley v. Flushing Hosp. & Med. Ctr., 341 N.Y.S.2d 917 (N.Y. App. Div. 1973), *rev'd on other grounds,* 359 N.Y.S.2d 113 (N.Y. App. Div. 1974).

3. 42 C.F.R. § 405.1026(g).

4. *E.g.,* CHICAGO MUN. CODE § 137-14.

5. JOINT COMMISSION, ACCREDITATION MANUAL FOR HOSPITALS (1994).

6. *See, e.g.,* N.J. STAT. ANN. § 26:8-5; WASH. REV. CODE ANN. § 70.58.270.

7. JOINT COMMISSION, *supra* note 5.

8. Hiatt v. Groce, 215 Kan. 14, 523 P.2d 320 (1974).

9. 312 N.E.2d 614 (Ill. 1974). *See also* Larrimore v. Homeopathic Hosp. Ass'n, 181 A.2d 573 (Del. 1963); Hansch v. Hackett, 66 P.2d 1129 (Wash. 1937).

10. Engle v. Clarke, 346 S.W.2d 13 (Ky. 1961).

11. 42 C.F.R. § 405.1026(j).

12. Board of Trustees of Mem'l Hosp. v. Pratt, 72 Wyo. 120, 262 P.2d 682 (1953).

13. University of Tex. Med. Branch at Galveston v. York, 808 S.W.2d 106 (Tex. App. 1991).

14. People v. Smithtown Gen. Hosp., 93 Misc. 2d 736, 402 N.Y.S.2d 318 (N.Y. Sup. Ct. 1978).

15. JOINT COMMISSION, *supra* note 5.

16. *Id.*

17. *Id.;* ILL. ADMIN. CODE tit. 77, §§ 250.1510(b)(2) and 250.330.

18. JOINT COMMISSION, *supra* note 5.

19. Kaplan v. Central Med. Group, 419 N.Y.S.2d 750 (N.Y. App. Div. 1979).

20. Pisel v. Stamford Hosp., 41 C.L.J. 43 (1980).

21. AHA & AMRA, STATEMENT ON PRESERVATION OF PATIENT MEDICAL RECORDS IN HEALTH CARE INSTITUTIONS (1977).

22. *E.g.,* Pyramid Life Ins. Co. v. Masonic Hosp. Ass'n, 191 F. Supp. 51 (W.D. Okla. 1961).

23. Connell v. Medical & Surgical Clinic, 21 Ill. App. 3d 383, 315 N.E.2d 278 (1974).

24. McGarry v. J. A. Mercier Co., 272 Mich. 501, 262 N.W. 296 (Mich. 1935).

25. *See, e.g.,* Hernandex v. Lutheran Med. Ctr., 478 N.Y.S.2d 697 (N.Y. App. Div. 1984) ($1 per-page charge for copies of medical record, plus $15 search and retrieval fee is reasonable). *But see* Mauer v. Mount Sinai Hosp., N.Y.L.J., Feb. 1, 1985 (N.Y. Sup. Ct. 1985) ($15 retrieval and assembly fee is reasonable, but $1 per-page copying fee is arbitrary and capricious).

26. REISER, DECK, AND CURRAN, ETHICS IN MEDICINE (1977).

27. AMERICAN MEDICAL ASSOCIATION, PRINCIPLES OF MEDICAL ETHICS (August 1980).

28. AMERICAN NURSES' ASSOCIATION, CODE FOR NURSES, § 2.5 (1976).

29. *See, e.g.,* R.I. GEN. LAWS § 5-37.3-4.

30. *See, e.g.,* S.C. Minimum Standards for Licensing of Hospitals 61-16 § 601.3; Rules and Regulations for Licensure of Hospitals in Virginia § 208.61.

31. *See* Cassingham v. Lutheran Sunburst Health Serv., 748 S.W.2d 593 (Tex. App. 1988), in which the court ruled that a patient could sue a hospital for allowing a professional counselor to read the patient's medical chart, because the hospital failed to prove that the counselor was providing medical treatment within the meaning of the state's confidential communications statute.

32. JOINT COMMISSION, *supra* note 5.

33. Behringer v. Medical Ctr. at Princeton, 592 A.2d 1251 (N.J. Super Ct. App. Div., April 25, 1991).

34. Hyman v. Jewish Chronic Disease Hosp., 15 N.Y.2d 317, 258 N.Y.S.2d 397 (1965).

35. *Id.* at 399.

36. Klinge v. Lutheran Med. Ctr., 518 S.W.2d 157 (Mo. Ct. App. 1975).

37. *Re* General Accident Assurance Co. of Canada and Sunnybrook Hosp. (1979) 23 O.R.(2d) 513 (Ont. High Ct. of Justice).

38. *See generally* 45 C.F.R. Part 46.

39. *See* 45 C.F.R. § 46.102, § 46.111.

40. *See* 42 C.F.R. § 2.52. Although this recognition appears in an interpretive provision of federal regulations that establishes restrictive rules for the release of alcohol and drug abuse patient records, it is broadly stated and demonstrates an awareness of the difficulty of obtaining patient authorizations for disclosure in retrospective studies. *See generally* the regulations governing protection of human research subjects, 45 C.F.R. Part 46.

41. *See* Melum, *Balancing Information and Privacy,* 58 HOSP. PROG. 68–69, 79 (1977); Medical Research Council, *Responsibility in the Use of Medical Information for Research,* BRIT. MED. J. 213–216 (1973).

42. *E.g.,* Wallace v. University Hosps., 170 N.E.2d 261 (Ohio Ct. App. 1960) and Hutchins v. Texas Rehabilitation Comm'n, 544 S.W.2d 802 (Tex. Civ. App. 1976).

43. Rabens v. Jackson Park Hosp. Found., 40 Ill. App. 3d 113, 351 N.E.2d 276 (1976).

44. *See, e.g.,* ILL. COMP. STAT. ANN. ch. 110, § 8-2001; FLA. STAT. ANN. § 395.017.

45. Ehredt v. Forest Hosp., Inc., 492 N.E.2d 532 (Ill. App. Ct. 1986).

46. *See, e.g.,* Colo. Rev. Stat. § 25-1-801(b); Ill. Comp. Stat. Ann. ch. 110, § 8-2001; S.D. Codified Laws § 34-12-15.

47. *See, e.g.,* Okla. Stat. Ann. tit. 76, § 19.

48. Pyramid Life Ins. Co. v. Masonic Hosp. Ass'n, 191 F. Supp. 51 (W.D. Okla. 1961).

49. Pennison v. Provident Life & Accident Ins. Co., 154 So. 2d 617 (La. Ct. App. 1963), *writ refused,* 156 So. 2d 226 (La. 1963).

50. McDonald v. Clinger, 84 A.D.2d 482, 446 N.Y.S.2d 801 (1982).

51. *E.g.,* Iowa Code § 229.25.

52. Yaretsky v. Blum, 592 F.2d 65 (2d Cir. 1979).

53. Bishop Clarkson Mem'l Hosp. v. Reserve Life Ins. Co., 350 F.2d 1006 (8th Cir. 1965).

54. American Hospital Association, *Statement on a Patient's Bill of Rights,* Affirmed by the Board of Trustees, November 17, 1972.

55. Altman, *Patients Who Read Their Hospital Charts,* 302 New Eng. J. Med. 169 (January 17, 1980).

56. *E.g.,* Emmett v. Eastern Dispensary & Casualty Hosp., 396 F.2d 931 (D.C. Cir. 1967).

57. Gaertner v. State, 385 Mich. 49, 187 N.W.2d 429 (1971).

58. *In re* Daniel C.H., 269 Cal. Rptr. 624 (Cal. Ct. App. 1990).

59. H.L. v. Matheson, 450 U.S. 398 (1981).

60. Claim of Gurkin, 434 N.Y.S.2d 607 (N.Y. Sup. Ct. 1980).

61. Emmett, 396 F.2d at 931.

62. *In re* Search Warrant, 810 F.2d 67 (3d Cir. 1987). *See also* Chidnester v. Needles, 353 N.W.2d 849 (Iowa 1984). In this case, the state supreme court granted a county's request for certain medical records needed to complete an investigation of alleged fraudulent Medicaid practices, holding that society's interest in investigating criminal activities outweighs the patient's privacy interest. *See also* Commonwealth v. Cobrin, 479 N.E.2d 674 (Mass. 1985).

63. 42 C.F.R. § 431.107.

64. Gabor v. Hyland, 399 A.2d 993 (N.J. Super. Ct. App. Div. 1979).

65. Md. Code Ann. Health—Gen. I § 4-301(c)(8).

66. Nev. Rev. Stat. § 629.061.

67. N.Y. Mental Hyg. Law § 31.09.

68. *See, e.g.,* Cook County Medical Examiner Ordinance.

69. Miss. Code Ann. § 41-9-79.

70. Community Hosp. Ass'n v. District Court, 570 P.2d 243 (Colo. 1977).

71. *E.g.,* Teperson v. Donato, 371 So. 2d 703 (Fla. Dist. Ct. App. 1979).

72. Schechet v. Kesten, 126 N.W.2d 718 (Mich. 1964).

73. Banta v. Superior Court, 544 P.2d 653 (Ariz. 1976).

74. S.C. Code Ann. § 44-23-1090.

75. Child abuse legislation may specifically authorize such access (*see, e.g.,* Ariz. Rev. Stat. § 36-2281) or simply require that some instances of abuse be reported to law enforcement officials (*see, e.g.,* La. Rev. Stat. Ann. § 14.403(D)).

76. *See* Nev. Rev. Stat. ch. 629, § 1, *as enacted by* A.B. No. 229 (New Laws 1989).

77. *E.g.,* Robinson v. Hamilton, 60 Iowa 134, 14 N.W. 202 (1882).

78. Planned Parenthood v. Danforth, 428 U.S. 52 (1976).

79. *See, e.g.,* CONN. GEN. STAT. § 19a-215; N.Y. PUB. HEALTH LAW § 2101.

80. *See, e.g.,* CAL. HEALTH & SAFETY CODE §§ 199.20, 199.221; ILL. COMP. ANN. STAT. ch. 111½ § 7309; TEX. HEALTH & SAFETY CODE ANN. § 81.103.

81. *See, e.g.,* TEX. HEALTH & SAFETY CODE ANN. § 81.041; COLO. REV. STAT. § 25-4-1403.

82. *See* TEX. HEALTH & SAFETY CODE ANN. § 81.048; WIS. STAT. ANN. § 146.025(5).

83. *See, e.g.,* CONN. GEN. STAT. ANN., Act concerning AIDS-related testing, medical information, and confidentiality, S.B. No. 812 (New Laws 1989); CAL. HEALTH & SAFETY CODE § 199.24; TEX. HEALTH & SAFETY CODE § 81.103(5).

84. *See* CAL. HEALTH & SAFETY CODE § 199.25; ARIZ. REV. STAT. ANN. § 32-1457; KAN. STAT. ANN. § 65-6004(a).

85. WIS. STAT. ANN. § 146.025(14).

86. TEX. HEALTH & SAFETY CODE ANN. § 81.103(7).142.8. *See also* Doe v. Prime Health/ Kansas City, No. 88C (Dist. Ct. of Johnson County Oct. 20, 1988). In this case, a trial court enjoined the health care provider from revealing the results to the man's ex-wife, because the infinitesimal risk of transmission that existed in this case did not justify breaching the duty of confidentiality. Note that Kansas legislation has been amended to allow providers to notify the spouse or partner of a patient who has tested positive for AIDS without court intervention.

87. *In re* Application of Milton S. Hershey Med. Ctr., No. C01001/91 (Pa. Super. Ct. July 30, 1991).

88. *See, e.g.,* MINN. STAT. ANN. § 145.413.

89. *See. e.g.,* ILL. COMP. STAT. ANN. ch. 38, § 81-30.1.

90. *See, e.g.,* N.Y. PUB. HEALTH LAW § 4160.

91. *See, e.g.,* Schulman v. New York City Health & Hosp. Corp., 342 N.E.2d 501 (N.Y. 1975).

92. *See, e.g.,* MINN. STAT. ANN. § 144.68.

93. Ferraro v. Chadwick, No. D009025 (Cal. Ct. App. June 11, 1990).

94. *E.g.,* IOWA CODE § 232.75.

95. Landeros v. Flood, 17 Cal. 3d 399, 551P.2d 389 (1976).

96. 42 U.S.C. § 300aa-25.

97. 42 U.S.C. § 300aa-14.

98. 42. U.S.C. § 300aa-14(b).

99. N.Y. PENAL LAW § 266.25.

100. IOWA CODE § 147.111.

101. 21 C.F.R. § 606.170(b).

102. 21 C.F.R. § 812.150(b).

103. *E.g.,* IOWA CODE § 85.27.

104. *E.g.,* Acosta v. Cary, 365 So. 2d 4 (La. Ct. App. 1978).

105. 5 U.S.C. § 552.

106. *E.g.,* IOWA CODE § 68A.7(2).

107. Eugene Cervi & Co. v. Russell, 184 Colo. 282, 519 P.2d 1189 (1974).

108. Wooster Republican Printing Co. v. City of Wooster, 56 Ohio St. 2d 126, 383 N.W.2d 124 (1978).

109. 42 C.F.R. § 466.70.

110. Tax Equity and Fiscal Responsibility Act of 1982 § 1160(b), Pub. L. No. 97-248, 1982 U.S.C.C. A. N. 7.

111. Jones v. Stanko, 118 Ohio St. 147, 160 N.E. 456 (1928).

112. Derrick v. Ontario Community Hosp., 47 Cal. App. 3d 154, 120 Cal. Rptr. 566 (1975).

113. Estate of Urbaniak v. Newton, 277 Cal. Rptr. 354 (Cal. Ct. App. 1991).

114. Tarasoff v. Board of Regents, 17 Cal. 3d 425, 551 P.2d 334 (1976).

115. Thompson v. County of Alameda, 27 Cal. 3d 741, 614 P.2d 728 (1980).

116. Shaw v. Glickman, 45 Md. App. 718, 415 A.2d 625 (1980).

117. Thornburg v. Long, 178 N.C. 589, 101 S.E. 99 (1919).

118. Allred v. State, 554 P.2d 411 (Alaska 1976).

119. PA. STAT. ANN. tit. 42 § 5929.

120. KAN. STAT. ANN. § 60-427.

121. MICH. COMP. LAWS § 27A.2157.

122. N.Y. C.P.L.R. § 4504.

123. New York City Council v. Goldwater, 284 N.Y. 296, 31 N.E.2d 31 (1940).

124. Cartwright v. Macabees Mutual Life Ins. Co., 65 Mich. App. 670, 238 N.W.2d 368 (1975).

125. *See, e.g.,* Willis v. Order of R.R. Telegraphers, 139 Neb. 46, 296 N.W. 443 (1941).

126. Wenninger v. Muesing, 307 Minn. 405, 240 N.W.2d 333 (1976).

127. Transworld Invs. v. Drobny, 554 P.2d 1148 (Alaska 1976).

128. 42 U.S.C. § 290 dd-3.

129. 42 U.S.C. § 290 ee-3.

130. 42 C.F.R. Part 2.

131. 42 C.F.R. § 2.11.

132. 42 C.F.R. § 2.14.

133. Heng v. Foster, 379 N.E.2d 688 (Ill. App. 1978).

134. *E.g.,* IOWA ADMIN. CODE §§ 590-1.2(d)(6) [nurses] and 470-135.401(10) [physicians].

135. *E.g.,* KAN. ADMIN. REGS. § 28-34-9(b).

136. *E.g.,* CAL. CIV. CODE §§ 56–56.32.

137. IOWA CODE § 140.3 (1983).

138. JOINT COMMISSION, *supra* note 5.

139. *E.g.,* Boyd v. Wynn, 150 S.W.2d 648 (Ky. 1941).

140. Doe v. Roe, 400 N.Y.S.2d 668 (N.Y. Sup. Ct. 1977).

141. *E.g.,* Simonsen v. Swenson, 104 Neb. 224, 177 N.W. 831 (1920).

142. Horne v. Patton, 291 Ala. 701, 287 So. 2d 824 (1973).

143. Clark v. Geraci, 208 N.Y.S.2d 564 (N.Y. Sup. Ct. 1960).

144. Conyers v. Massa, 512 P.2d 283 (Colo. Ct. App. 1973).

145. Hammonds v. Aetna Casualty & Surety Co., 243 F. Supp. 793 (N.D. Ohio 1965).

146. *In re* Metropolitan Gen. Hosp. and Ontario Nurses' Ass'n, 22 L.A.C.2d 243 (Ontario Labor Arbitration 1979).

CHAPTER 9

Authorization for Treatment

Chapter Objectives

1. To outline requirements of consent and informed consent
2. To determine responsibility for obtaining consent
3. To review documentation
4. To determine the decision maker
5. To recognize the right to refuse
6. To consider research

Public consciousness concerning patients' rights has grown significantly over the years. Whereas people previously had been willing to rely heavily on the skill and judgment of their health care providers, it is much more common now for patients to seek active involvement in the decision-making processes affecting their care. The aura of infallibility that surrounded physicians and other health care professionals in the past has diminished, and lay persons seem unwilling to accept on faith the decisions made by others. This is the context in which the present discussion of patient consent must be viewed. Public attitudes have changed, and the law is adapting to these changes. The approaches of health care providers will inevitably have to change as well. Nurses have always involved patients in decisions concerning their care; hence, nursing care may be enhanced in the changing environment in which the patient is more often approached as a "partner" in health care therapies. Although many of the newly emerging consent requirements have arisen in cases involving individual physicians and hospitals, nurses must also be cognizant of their obligations with regard to obtaining and documenting patient consents, particularly advanced nurse practitioners who commonly perform more invasive procedures than staff nurses. In addition, as nurses move into the expanded practice role, their responsibilities for obtaining and documenting patient consent broaden, as in the nurse anesthetist role, in which the nurse must obtain explicit and informed consent from the patient before the nurse anesthetist provides anesthesia.

Health care providers must obtain appropriate authorization before examining a patient or performing diagnostic or therapeutic procedures. In most circumstances, the express or implied consent of the patient or the patient's representative constitutes the authorization. The law requires that the patient (or representative) be given sufficient information concerning the available choices so that the consent is an informed consent. If the decision is not to consent, the examination or procedure usually cannot be performed. However, in several circumstances the law overrides the decision and provides authorization for involuntary treatment, such as for some mental illness and for substance abuse.

The foundation for the consent requirement applicable to practitioners is the tort law of assault and battery—the legal doctrine protecting the right of each individual to be touched only when and in the way authorized by that individual. A landmark case on consent cites as the "root premise" of consent law the oft-quoted statement of Justice Cardias that

> Every human being of adult years and sound mind has a right to determine what shall be done with his own body, and a surgeon who performs an operation without his patient's consent commits an assault for which he is liable in damages.[1]

Medical and surgical procedures that involve touching a patient's person, even the simplest manipulation of a limb, must be properly authorized or the person performing the procedure will be subject to an action for battery. The obvious corollary is that, absent special circumstances, a competent individual has a right to refuse to authorize a procedure, whether the refusal is grounded on doubt that the contemplated procedure will be successful, concern about probable risks or consequences, lack of confidence in the physician recommending the procedure, religious belief, or mere whim.

Physicians and other independent practitioners have the primary responsibility for obtaining informed consent or other authorization for treatment. Nurses are not responsible for obtaining consent unless they are in independent practice or are assigned responsibilities associated with obtaining consent by their employer. If nurses happen to become aware of a lack of informed consent or other authorization, they generally have a responsibility to inform the responsible physician or other independent practitioners and, in some circumstances, inform institutional officials.

Hospitals and other health care institutions generally are not liable for the physician's failure to obtain authorization, unless (1) the physician is an employee or agent of the hospital or (2) the hospital happens to be aware of the lack of consent and fails to take appropriate action. Thus, nurses need to be familiar with the principles discussed in this chapter.

When it is alleged that a patient did not authorize a procedure, the practitioner and/or health care institution involved will be required to prove that a valid consent was obtained. Much of the difficulty of dealing with the consent requirement lies in developing and implementing procedures that satisfy this need for documentation without imposing an undue burden on the therapeutic process. Further, the patient's sensibilities also must be regarded; the health care provider must not subject the patient to needless distress simply to avoid a potential lawsuit. Balancing these three objectives cannot be accomplished by a simple formula. A full understanding of the relevant principles and a high degree of tact are essential.

The requirements of consent and informed consent, the decision-making roles of patients and their representatives, and the exceptions to the consent requirement are discussed in this chapter.

REQUIREMENTS OF CONSENT AND INFORMED CONSENT

Distinction Between Consent and Informed Consent

The common law has long recognized the right of persons to be free from harmful or offensive touching. The requirement that a health care provider obtain the patient's consent for care has its roots in the sanctity that Anglo-American common law accords to the human body. With limited exceptions, every person has a right not to be touched or treated medically. The intentional harmful or offensive touching of another person without authorization is called battery. A threatening approach that puts a person in fear of a battery is an "assault." Although the semantic distinction between the two terms is clear, in common parlance they are often used interchangeably or in combination. When there is no consent or other authorization, the physician or other practitioner doing a medical procedure can be liable for battery, even if the procedure is properly performed and beneficial and has no negative effects. The touching alone leads to liability.

The physician or other practitioner responsible for the procedure has a separate legal duty to disclose sufficient information so that the consent is based on an informed decision. Failure to disclose the necessary information does not invalidate the consent, so the procedure is not a battery. However, failure to disclose is a separate wrong for which there can be liability based on principles applicable to negligent torts. Thus, uninformed consent protects from liability for battery but informed consent is necessary to protect the health care provider from liability for negligence.

In California, the courts have extended the informed consent doctrine to require informed refusal. In 1980, the California Supreme Court ruled that a physician could be liable for a patient's death from cancer of the cervix based on failure to inform the woman of the risks of not consenting to a recommended Pap smear.[2] The Pap smear probably would have discovered her cancer in time to begin treatment that would have extended her life.

Expressed or Implied Consent

Express consent is consent that a patient gives by direct words. These words may be spoken or written; in theory, there is no difference. Practically, however, the problems involved in proving an effective oral consent may be substantial.[3] When possible, the health care provider should always secure a written consent from the patient (or, in certain cases, from another person authorized to act on behalf of the patient). However, a formal written consent is not always sufficient; numerous cases can be found in which it was claimed that extenuating circumstances invalidated the consent formally given by the patient.[4] Moreover, although written documentation is preferable, it is a two-edged sword that is only as good as the documented transaction or occurrence. In cases in which insufficient information has been provided to the patient, documentation of this fact obviously can be detrimental to the provider's legal position. For this reason, standardized consent forms must be treated with great caution, lest they be used in situations for which they are inappropriate.

Implied consent is consent that arises by reasonable inference from the conduct of the patient. Its underlying basis is the reliance of the health care provider on the actions of the patient to conclude that the procedure is authorized. If a patient voluntarily submits to a procedure with actual or apparent knowledge of what is about to transpire, for instance, when a nurse takes the blood pressure of a patient, this submission will constitute implied consent even though there was no explicit oral or written expression of consent.

O'Brien v. Cunard Steamship Co.[5] is a classic case illustrating this principle. A passenger who joined a line of people receiving injections on a ship was held to have given implied consent to a vaccination. The decision's rationale is that an individual who observes and joins a line of people receiving injections apparently knows that he or she will also receive an injection. Thus, the person administering the injection may reasonably infer that the individual's voluntary submission indicates consent to the procedure.

A crucial limitation is that this inference can be drawn only if the patient is aware—or, as a reasonable person, should be aware—of what the act means in the particular context. The scope of the consent implied from a voluntary submission to treatment is limited to the particular treatment contemplated by the parties and, thus, by the knowledge of the patient before the submission. When the nature of the procedure is not obvious or when the patient is unaware of other information material to the treatment decision, for instance, when a nurse submits blood for human immunodeficiency virus (HIV) testing from a general blood screening sample, no implication of consent arises and the fact of consent requires specific proof.

Obviously, the risk in relying on voluntary submission to show consent is that the jury may not believe the testimony of the provider regarding the circumstances of the patient's submission or may not interpret those circumstances as allowing the provider to reasonably infer consent. Where an express consent can be obtained, this is much preferred.

When Consent Is Not Required

In certain situations, the law relaxes the general rule requiring patient consent for medical and surgical treatment. These situations include emergencies. Essential to the presumption of consent to emergency care is a finding that the patient's condition was so serious that the initiation of treatment could not be delayed until consent was obtained.[6] In cases in which delay would not materially increase the hazards, even though it is clear that the medical treatment in question will be needed in the near term, failure to obtain consent cannot be excused on the ground that an emergency existed. Moreover, it should be clear that it is the patient's condition, not the surrounding circumstances, that determines the existence of an emergency. Thus, the fact that an injury occurred during a severe storm would not necessarily create a presumption of consent, even though the weather might loosely be termed an emergency. Of course, if the patient whose condition required rapid treatment was unable to give consent for treatment, the storm might have supplied a necessary element of emergency consent by having made it impracticable to contact the patient's next of kin. Thus surrounding conditions may contribute to a finding of emergency without being determinative of it; the essential focus is on the patient's needs for immediate care.

The requirement that the threat to life or health be immediate is demonstrated by the following case. In *Chambers v. Nottingham,*[7] the administration of a spinal anesthetic to a patient about to undergo an appendectomy was held actionable despite the physician's claim of emergency. The jury determined that there was no acute attack of appendicitis, and thus, the physician's discovery that the plaintiff was unable to take a general anesthetic could have been communicated to the patient and his consent sought for the use of another type of anesthesia. Some courts have applied a much more liberal standard by recognizing the existence of an emergency when treatment is needed immediately to alleviate great pain and suffering, even though the threat of irreversible harm is not present. As one case put it,

> if a physician or surgeon is confronted with an emergency which endangers the life or health of the patient, or that suffering and pain may be alleviated, it is his duty to do that which the occasion demands within the usual and customary practice among physicians and surgeons in the same locality.[8]

However, such a willingness to allow physician intervention without consent beyond the minimum needed may not be in line with the current sentiment toward restricting physician autonomy in favor of greater patient self-determination.

Determining whether the degree of urgency is sufficient to constitute an emergency for consent purposes is a factual question of the type left to the jury in cases in which either party has demanded a jury trial.[9] As with all questions of fact, it is important that the need for haste in rendering treatment be documented fully and carefully. Thus, whenever possible, the health care provider should seek confirmation of a determination that an immediate threat to life or health exists. Where a hospital is involved, it should insist that its staff engage in such consultation as time and circumstances permit. Findings supporting the existence of an emergency should be noted on the patient's record, with particular emphasis on the nature of the threat, its immediacy, and its magnitude. The initialing of such notations by consultant physicians is advisable from an evidentiary standpoint; at the least, their names should be recorded. The nurse practitioner should be wary of proceeding when a difference of opinion surfaces as to the need for immediate treatment. Unfortunately, such disagreements do arise from time to time, forcing providers to choose between a conservative course safeguarding their legal position and the professional and ethical imperative to attempt to preserve life and health.

The emergency doctrine contemplates not only a medical situation requiring immediate treatment but also the provider's inability to consult with the next of kin or others, recognized by the law as capable of giving consent on the patient's behalf. Thus, the search for such a proxy authorization must extend as far as available time reasonably allows.

When the circumstances clearly dictate immediate action on the part of a provider and the person empowered to speak for the patient forbids such action, this prohibition is not absolutely binding on the provider. Assuming the need for the action can be proved, if challenged, the provider will likely not be held liable for proceeding. Such an approach is risky, however; it is much safer for the provider to secure a court order authorizing the treatment if that is practicable under the circumstances.

Consent Must Be "Informed"

The difficulty of obtaining the patient's consent to treatment has been substantially increased by court rulings that consent that is not fully "informed" is not legally valid. As noted in the previous section, earlier cases treated the existence of consent as a relatively straightforward yes/no question. The securing of a consent document signed by the patient or by the patient's proper representative largely determined the issue, although there were exceptions for special situations such as misrepresentation, patient incompetence, and variance of the procedure from that originally authorized.

In 1957, a California court proclaimed that unless the patient understands the procedure to which he or she is consenting and the risks inherent in it, the consent is without legal effect.[10] This decision began a process of judicial deliberation and lawmaking that has gone on for more than two decades without yielding hard and fast rules that can easily be understood and applied. Since 1976 or so, the legislatures of several states have joined the courts in attempting to define what is required for a legally acceptable informed consent, but without great success in reducing the uncertainty inherent in the concept. Because of the almost limitless range of diseases, patients' conditions, patients' personality types, and other relevant factors, simple rules or formulas are not possible. However, some key principles can be enunciated, and no health care practitioner can afford to practice without at least a basic familiarity with them.

The Old Rule: The "Professional Community" Standard

As soon as courts began to hold that a consent could not be legally effective unless it was informed, they were forced to devise a formula for delineating the specific information that had to be provided. Obviously, it would be impractical, if not impossible, to require that the physician disclose all information relevant to the proposed treatment. Much of it might be beyond the patient's ability to comprehend or deal with psychologically; the sheer volume of information could overwhelm the physician–patient interaction and undermine the very communication that the rule was intended to promote. Searching for a principle by which to identify information requiring disclosure, the courts began to judge it as they would other aspects of medical practice by professional custom.

This reliance on the standard of the professional community was dictated by the complexity of the medical questions involved and the need to use the experience and judgment of highly trained, well-intentioned persons who regularly deal with such matters. The policy underlying the rule was consistent with the high esteem in which physicians were generally held and, perhaps more important to the judicial decision, was consistent with the way other medical malpractice questions were decided. The physician's duty of disclosure was defined by the standard of professional colleagues. Thus, a patient seeking to prove that the duty had been violated was required to produce expert medical testimony as to what the standard practice would be in such a case and then to prove the way(s) in which the defendant physician had deviated from such practice. Inability to secure the necessary expert testimony would keep the patient-plaintiff from even getting the case before a jury, where, despite technical deficiencies, it might yet result in a favorable verdict and damage award. The strategic importance of many legal principles and rules of evidence is the way they constrain the jury from hearing the case and applying its own rough sense of justice.

Despite the difficulties with a legal standard based on a doubtful consensus of professional opinion, this older, physician-based rule is still followed in many states.[11] In fact, some few states still adhere to an even more restrictive variant, the so-called locality rule, which ties the disclosure standard to the practices of physicians within the same geographic community as the defendant. Such a rule severely limits the pool from which a patient-plaintiff can draw needed expert medical testimony on disclosure. Most of these states, however, will accept evidence on disclosure practices in either the defendant's community or a similar community.

The New Rule: The "Reasonable Patient" Standard

The more modern rule on informed consent focuses on the informational needs of an average, reasonable patient rather than on professional established standards of disclosure. Under this "new rule," a physician can be held liable if the court finds that a patient did not receive the information material to the decision to accept the proposed treatment. As stated in the landmark case of *Canterbury v. Spence,* the touchstone for the law on informed consent is the patient's right of individual self-determination.

> The root premise is the concept, fundamental in American jurisprudence, that "[e]very human being of adult years and sound mind has a right to determine what shall be done with his own body . . . ." True consent to what happens to one's self is the informed exercise of a choice, and that entails an opportunity to evaluate knowledgeably the options available and the risks attendant upon each.[12]

The *Canterbury* case is the most widely cited example of the newer approach, which measures the physician's disclosure by a patient-based rather than a physician-based standard.

The change in philosophic approach revealed by the *Canterbury* opinion is significant; there is a clear movement away from reliance on the self-regulation and the restraint of professionals. The consumer movement symbolizes the growing distrust of long-respected institutions and has brought about a public insistence on individuals being given relevant information to make important decisions for themselves. In the health care field, the label *patient's rights* is an outgrowth of this type of thinking.

The philosophic shift expressed in the *Canterbury* opinion, although dramatic, is not the most significant aspect of the decision. Rather, the major practical change is that the new rule relieves the patient-plaintiff of the burden of introducing expert testimony as to the professional community standard of disclosure. As previously indicated, the difficulty of securing such testimony constitutes a major obstacle to the prosecution of informed consent claims. By the *Canterbury* rationale, the determinative factor is what a reasonable patient would have considered material, a matter that a lay jury can decide without resort to expert testimony. Freed from the initial evidentiary obstacle, a plaintiff can get the case before a jury much more readily. This, in turn, will increase the number of informed consent complaints filed with the courts, either as separate actions or, more commonly, as additional counts added to suits charging negligent performance of medical procedures. It may also have significant effect on defendants' and insurers' willingness to settle consent claims when they arise.

To be sure, there is still a substantial role for expert testimony in informed consent cases under the patient-based rule. It may be needed, for instance, to establish what the risks of the subject procedure were, as well as the availability and relative merits of alternative treatments. It is relevant also to the question of whether these risks or alternatives were generally recognized in the health care community and, thus, should have been known to the professional-defendant. The law obviously cannot require a provider to disclose things that he or she did not know and could not reasonably have been expected to know.

Because the law is in transition, it cannot be determined which rule represents the majority view of the states. Many states have adopted hybrid laws that defy categorization; others appear to have conflicts between their statute and case law. To generalize, however, it can be said that the approach followed in the *Canterbury* case seems to reflect the trend of judicial thought.

What Information Must the Practitioner Provide?

Under either the old or new approach, the law on disclosure must be brought down to a set of operational rules, specifying the items of information that a physician is required to disclose to a patient. A physician is not required to disclose material risks and alternative forms of treatment to third persons, however.[13] Over the 25-odd years since the term *informed consent* came into usage in the medicolegal context, courts have been developing, on a case-by-case basis, a list of items requiring disclosure. Stated in simple generic terms, the list includes:

- diagnosis (i.e., the patient's condition or problem)
- nature and purpose of the proposed treatment
- risks and consequences of the proposed treatment
- probability that the proposed treatment will be successful
- feasible treatment alternatives
- prognosis if the proposed treatment is not given

The applicability of each of the items on the list may shift from case to case, depending on the particular facts. Nevertheless, the list has value as a disclosure checklist for the practitioner.

Some nurses have suggested that the elements be expanded to include an explanation of the postoperative treatments that they and therapists will provide. Although it is beneficial for patients to have this information to avoid surprises, courts have not required proof that this information was provided unless the patient can prove it was requested. Courts have attempted to focus on disclosure of the more permanent effects of procedures, rather than the accompanying transitory experiences, in recognition of the practical limits on what may be disclosed and understood in a reasonable period of time. Nevertheless, nurses have the same responsibility as physicians to obtain informed consent for the procedures they authorize or perform in independent practice roles.

The Diagnosis

Failure to disclose the diagnosis is rarely the basis for a lawsuit, because it is commonly discussed as a natural part of a physician–patient interchange.[14] However, significant reservations that the physician may have about the diagnosis should be candidly stated, lest the patient perceive certainty where it does not exist.

Nature and Purpose of Proposed Treatment

The nature and purpose of the proposed treatment must be explained in nontechnical terms that a patient can reasonably be expected to understand. Although highly important, this disclosure item has generated little litigation, perhaps because the proposed treatment, like the diagnosis, is an item about which the patient is generally curious and the provider of care is more likely to volunteer information.

Risks and Consequences

Most informed consent cases to date have arisen from the provider's failure to reveal sufficient information about the risks and consequences of the proposed treatment. The *Canterbury* case, for example, involved a neurosurgeon's failure to disclose to his 19-year-old patient that the lumbar laminectomy that he was proposing as a remedy for the boy's debilitating back problems carried with it a risk of paralysis, estimated at trial by the physician-defendant to be about 1 percent. The patient did suffer paralysis after the operation—although whether this was a consequence of the surgery or of a fall sustained during the immediate postoperative recovery period was never determined—and sued. The suit alleged both negligent performance of the operation and nondisclosure of a known risk.

Obviously, not all risks need to be disclosed. Risks that are very remote and improbable can generally be omitted from the disclosure as not material to the patient's decision.[15] Although the courts have not attempted to set a specific probability figure to trigger the requirement of disclosure, this threshold is determined for a given case as the product of the probability and the severity of the risk in question. Thus, a physician might be excused for not mentioning a 5 percent, or even greater, risk of complications that could lengthen the patient's recuperative period, whereas a 1 percent risk of paralysis, as involved in the *Canterbury* case, would be a mandatory item for disclosure. A key California decision has held that any risk of death, however slight, must be disclosed.[16]

At the other end of the probability spectrum, some risks with a high probability may be deemed so commonly known that the physician is not required to speak of them.[17] For instance, the risk of a hematoma resulting from the simple drawing of a blood sample would not likely be part of the required disclosure in any state. Likewise, risks of which the particular patient is proved to have been aware cannot be the basis for a claim of nondisclosure.

A risk is distinguished from a consequence by having a much lower probability. A risk is something that might occur; a consequence is something that can generally be expected to occur. To illustrate: paralysis is a risk of a laminectomy; sterility is the consequence of a hysterectomy. Both risks and consequences must be disclosed to the patient before the performance of a procedure.[18]

Although many cases speak of the physician's duty of disclosure, the essence of informed consent is that the patient know the relevant facts, regardless of the source of that knowledge. Naturally, it may be easier to prove the patient's knowledge if it has been documented that the physician or an associate provided the information in question. But if it can be shown by some other means that the patient's consent was knowledgeable, or informed, that is sufficient.[19]

It should be emphasized that the disclosure obligation extends only to risks that the provider knows, or reasonably should know, are inherent in the proposed procedure. When the risks attending a particular form of treatment cannot be fully quantified—as in the case of an investigational new drug—it is sufficient that this fact be communicated to the patient.[20] Further, there is no obligation to speak of risks that might attend a procedure if it were improperly executed.

Probability of Successful Treatment

Closely related to the disclosure of risks and consequences is a physician's truthful assessment of the likelihood that the proposed procedure will accomplish the intended result. Even if a given treatment did no physical harm, a patient who was induced to submit to it by an intentional or negligent misrepresentation as to its expectable beneficial effects has a legitimate informed consent claim. This principle places a significant constraint on a physician whose modus operandi might be to emphasize positive projections to try to foster a positive optimistic outlook in a patient before and during the proposed treatment. Although building confidence is not to be discouraged, realistic assessment is essential to informed consent.

A provider who makes too straightforward and explicit a projection of the results that can be expected from a proposed procedure can be sued for a breach of warranty for failing to produce the promised result. Damages in such cases are not based on the harm the patient suffers from the treatment; rather, they are computed as the difference between the result promised and that actually delivered.

In the well-known case of *Hawkins v. McGee*,[21] a surgeon promised a minor patient and his father that a skin graft to remove scar tissue on the boy's palm would leave him with "a 100 percent good hand." The skin for the graft was taken from the boy's chest, and a short time after the operation the palm began to grow hair. At trial, the patient-plaintiff was denied a recovery because he was unable to show that the physician had been negligent in his performance of the operation or that having hair on his palm was any worse than having scar tissue there. The appeals court reversed, explaining that the proper question was whether the physician had made good his preoperative promise. Moreover, the proper measure of damages was the difference in value between a "perfect" hand, as promised, and one with hair.

The key to *Hawkins v. McGee* lies in the clear and unequivocal way in which the physician-defendant described the result to be expected. Few providers are imprudent enough to make such a bold commitment.

Feasible Treatment Alternatives

An essential element in a reasonable patient's determination whether to approve the proposed treatment is knowledge of what alternatives are available. Several courts have held that consent is not informed unless the physician discloses to the patient at least those alternatives that would be generally acknowledged within the medical community as feasible in the patient's case.

A key element in any informed consent suit is the patient's claim that he or she would have acted differently had the undisclosed information been provided. *Poulin v. Zartman*[22] was a suit by a parent whose baby suffered retrolental fibroplasia and total blindness as a consequence of excessive oxygen administered after a premature birth. The plaintiff alleged that the attending pediatrician administered the oxygen without informing him of an alternative, more conservative method of oxygenation by titration. Furthermore, the plaintiff asserted that he would have opted for the titration procedure had he known of the risk of blindness inherent in oxygen administered to newborns. Despite this claim, the court held that proximate causation was not established, because "it was conceivable" that the parent would have consented to both alternatives, leaving the final decision to the physician's discretion.[23] It appears that, although the titration method was more in favor with the medical community at the time of the baby's birth, there was some support for the technique used by the physician-defendant, and the defendant had a seemingly well-considered rationale for applying it in this case. It is understandable, given the particular facts, that the court was unwilling to let the plaintiff, with the benefit of hindsight, second-guess the physician's judgment.

Prognosis If Proposed Treatment Is Not Given

Another informational element essential to a patient's informed consent is a projection of what will happen without the proposed treatment. Cases involving this element are rare, perhaps because physicians often use this information in guiding the patient toward acceptance of the proposed treatment.

If a physician fails to disclose to his or her patients all material risks of refusing to undergo a diagnostic test, however, that physician may be held liable for untoward consequences—particularly if a reasonable patient would not have refused the test if adequately informed of all the significant perils. At least one state high court has so ruled when it established the "informed refusal" doctrine in a case involving a 30-year-old woman who for several years before her death from cervical cancer had been advised by her family practitioner to undergo a Pap smear but who was not informed of the potentially fatal consequences of failing to consent to the test.[24] Expert testimony indicated that if the patient had earlier submitted to the diagnostic test, the tumor would have been discovered in time to save her life. Consequently, the court refused to impose on uniformed patients who innocently forego their physicians' advice the responsibility for inquiring as to the possible consequences of their decision and, instead, imposed that burden on the physicians.[25]

Although it is presently acknowledged that a physician must disclose the six previously discussed items to a patient, the list is not necessarily closed. Under the new rule, it includes all information that the physician knows, or reasonably should know, would be material to the patient's decision-making process. Future cases conceivably might expand the list to include such things as the impact of the proposed procedure on the patient's family or job situation, the likely cost of the proposed treatment, or the probability that the treatment would be covered by the patient's insurance. Although there may be sound arguments for not expanding the physician's advisory role to include matters not strictly medical, there is no assurance that this will not happen. Courts may believe that it is the physician's duty to disclose—or at least disclaim consideration of—matters related to the patient's treatment that the patient might reasonably assume the physician is taking into account in making treatment recommendations.

RESPONSIBILITY FOR OBTAINING CONSENT

It is the physician's responsibility, not the nurse's or hospital's, to provide the necessary information and to obtain informed consent. Other independent practitioners, including nurses in independent practice, who order procedures have the same responsibility concerning the procedures they order. A hospital or other health care institution generally is not liable for the failure of the physician or other independent practitioner to get informed consent unless the professional is an employee or agent of the institution.

Under the doctrine of "respondeat superior,"[26] the hospital is liable for any battery or other tort committed by its employees (e.g., staff nurses, servants, and agents) within the scope of their employment. This form of vicarious liability reflects the responsibility that the law places on those who employ others to act for them, even when there has been no wrongful conduct on the part of the employers.

Two elements are necessary for the imposition of respondant superior liability. First, there must be an employer–employee, or master–servant, relationship. Second, the employee's tortious conduct must occur within the scope of the employment. Although the myriad of contractual relationships possible sometimes clouds the distinction between an employee and an independent contractor, it can generally be said that the principal's ability to control the conduct of the one working for him or her determines the legal relationship of employer–employee.[27] The higher the degree of control, the more likely it is that such a characterization will be applied.

In the hospital setting, most persons engaged in patient care are hospital employees. Exceptions are private duty nurses and physicians on the medical staff, who are independent practitioners. Graduation from medical school or the possession of a professional's license do not, however, prevent one from being regarded as an employee. Interns, residents, fellows, and other house staff are employees of the hospital. So are certain radiologists, pathologists, some anesthesiologists, and other hospital-based specialists, depending on the terms of their contracts with the hospital and the ways in which the hospital can regulate their practices. The label that they place on their relationship with the hospital is significant to, but not determinative of, the legal characterization.[28]

If it is determined that a given nurse was acting within the scope of employment as a hospital employee, the hospital will be liable derivatively for any torts committed by that individual. The liability of the nurse and the hospital are "joint and several," meaning that an injured party may sue one or the other, or both. The fact that the hospital is liable does not provide the nurse wrongdoer with immunity against liability. Moreover, an employer has the right, although it is rarely asserted, to recover from a nurse any amounts that the employer is compelled to pay to third parties as a result of the employee's torts.

Respondeat superior liability can be imposed on the hospital for batteries committed by its nurses, just as it is for acts of negligence. Where the act alleged to be a battery was done at the direction of the patient's physician, the hospital may be protected by the so-called borrowed servant doctrine.

Where a procedure is performed on a patient by hospital employees, it is the hospital's responsibility to ensure that the consent obtained from the patient is adequately informed. No court has yet held, however, that the hospital has an affirmative obligation to monitor the content of disclosures given by nonemployed health care practitioners to patients being treated within the hospital's facilities to ensure that consent is "informed."[29] An appeals court in North Carolina did rule, however, that a hospital had an affirmative duty to make a reasonable effort to ensure that the physician had obtained the patient's informed consent.[30] It determined that the hospital nurses should have made sure, when obtaining the patient's signature to the surgical consent form, that the patient received an explanation of the procedure from the physician.

Absent special circumstances, hospitals have no duty to obtain informed consent for a procedure ordered by a nonemployee physician and performed by hospital employees, a New Mexico appeals court has ruled in *Johson v. Sears Roebuck & Co.*[31] After surgery, the nonemployee physician ordered that the patient receive one unit of packed red cells because she showed signs of developing septic shock. The blood was transfused by hospital nurses. The physician had not obtained the patient's consent, and the nurses did not obtain consent or determine if the physician had done so. The patient developed hepatitis and eventually died from complications connected with this disease. The patient's family sued the hospital for failing to obtain consent to the blood transfusion.

The court held that the hospital had no duty to obtain consent or to determine whether the physician had done so. The patient's family had argued that the nurses who transfused the patient had the knowledge to discuss the procedure with the patient and should have obtained her consent. The court, however, pointed out that the nurses did not know the patient's medical history, diagnosis, or other circumstances that would have allowed them to obtain fully informed consent. Imposing such a duty on hospital personnel would interfere with the patient–physician relationship, according to the court. The patient's family contended that the applicable standard of care, as reflected in the policies of similar hospitals in similar circumstances, is for hospitals to ensure that informed consent has been obtained before performing a procedure on a patient. The court concluded, however, that the majority rule remains intact, which is that absent special circumstances, a hospital has no duty to obtain informed consent for a procedure ordered by a nonemployee physician and performed by hospital employees.[32]

Nurses can potentially be involved in obtaining patient consent to four types of procedures: (1) procedures offered by nurses in independent practice roles; (2) nursing procedures not directly related to medical procedures; (3) nursing aspects of medical procedures in which the primary procedure is being provided by another practitioner; and (4) medical procedures being provided by another practitioner. Nurses have the same responsibility as physicians to obtain informed consent for the first type—the procedures they authorize or perform in independent practice roles.

Moreover, the modern team approach to medical care can create problems of informed consent when two or more practitioners are working with the same patient. Which practitioner has the responsibility for making an adequate disclosure of material information and documenting that a valid consent was obtained? The applicable principle is simpler to state than to apply: each practitioner should obtain consent for the particular procedure, or part thereof, that he or she will perform. Where two practitioners have discrete functions—for example, a surgeon and a nurse anesthetist—the division is relatively clear-cut and follows common-sense reasoning. The surgeon should disclose the relevant facts concerning the operative procedure, mentioning anesthesia risks in passing but leaving elaboration of the details to the anesthesia specialist. The nurse anesthetist should separately discuss the risks of anesthesia, alternative types, methods for administration, etc., and obtain the patient's consent to be anesthetized. A single consent form could be used to document both disclosures, but it is generally simpler and safer to use two separate forms. Obviously, some degree of overlap is preferable to an omission at the interface between the two areas of information. Moreover, the timing of the two disclosures may be separated, as when a surgeon discusses a procedure with the patient before the admission to the hospital and the nurse anesthetist speaks with the patient only shortly before the operation.

In a situation involving a primary physician, a surgeon, and a pathologist, a California appeals court ruled that the duty of disclosure of tissue test results to the patient is shared by the primary physician and the surgeon but that the pathologist who performs the test has a duty to disclose results only to the physician who requests the tissue analysis.[33] Because a pathologist analyzes a vast amount of tissue samples, the court reasoned that to impose a duty on the pathologist to communicate with the patient would create an undue burden.

Nurses, regardless of their position, clearly should provide information to patients concerning nursing procedures not directly related to medical procedures. This does not mean that formal informed consent must be obtained. Only in the most unusual circumstances would a signed consent form be appropriate. However, it does mean that nurses should explain what to expect from nursing procedures that the patient will be experiencing. The patient's acquiescence is implied consent. If the patient withdraws consent by objecting, the procedure should be discontinued as expeditiously as possible without endangering the individual. When the patient is unable to understand, implied consent is derived from the person's admission to the institution by the family or guardian or from the emergency doctrine in cases in which such others are not involved.

There is disagreement over the appropriate role of nurses within the third type of procedure (i.e., the nursing aspects of medical procedures in which the primary procedure is being provided by another practitioner). Good patient education includes explaining many postoperative procedures before they are begun. The disagreement concerns whether they should be disclosed before consent is obtained for the operation and, if so, by whom—the nurse or the physician. There is no general legal duty to explain postoperative nursing procedures as part of the disclosure before consent to operative procedures. Some nurses advocate that nurses actively explain postoperative procedures before consent to the operation is obtained. The other position is to place the disclosure responsibility on the physician and give additional nursing explanations only with the physician's authorization or after consent to the operation is obtained. The latter probably is the better approach because it avoids conflicting explanations that could confuse the patient and because it minimizes the nurse's exposure to liability. Nurses should encourage physicians to orient patients to postoperative procedures or to authorize the nurse to do so. One approach is for nurses to contribute to the development of booklets and other educational aids such as audio and visual recordings that orient the patient to the full course of the procedure.

There is disagreement concerning extent of the nurse's involvement in obtaining consent for the fourth type of procedures, which are primarily medical procedures and the responsibility of other health care professionals, especially physicians.[34] Some hospitals permit nurses to obtain the signature of the patient or the patient's representative on the consent form. Some hospitals permit nurses to provide some of or all the information necessary for an informed consent. Both of these practices may affect the physician–patient relationship by reducing the opportunity for adequate communication and negotiation. These practices could shift the liability for disclosure inadequacies to the nurse and to the hospital as the employer of the nurse. One attempt to shift responsibility was a 1979 Missouri case that arose when a nurse gave a patient a consent form authorizing a vaginal hysterectomy. The nurse did not know the physician had failed to explain the procedure to the patient. The patient asked questions about what the form authorized. The nurse replied that the physician knew what the patient wanted. The patient later experienced complications from the surgery (a vesicovaginal fistula) and sued the physician and the hospital employer of the nurse, alleging lack of informed consent. After the physician settled, the court ruled that the nurse and hospital were not liable because they were not responsible for obtaining the informed consent.[35] Some states might have imposed liability because the nurse failed to notify the physician of the patient's questions.

To avoid these adverse consequences, some hospitals do not permit nurses to obtain signatures on consent forms. In hospitals where this rule is not practical, nurses who get the forms signed should not attempt to answer patient questions concerning the procedure unless authorized to do so by the hospital and physician. The physician may legally delegate the obtaining of an informed consent to a nurse or other appropriate person but will be liable if such is not obtained. The nurse and the nurse's employer also will be potentially liable, so a nurse should not accept this delegation unless authorized to do so by the employer. However, when the nurse is placed in a position to obtain the signature of the patient, he or she must ensure that the patient received an adequate explanation of the procedure from the physician. Absent authorization from the employer and physician, if the patient seeks additional information or expresses reluctance, the nurse should contact the physician instead of attempting to convince the patient to sign the form.

To help protect the hospital or health care facility from the risk of liability for lack of consent, most institutions require the use of a standard form before major procedures. The battery consent form described in the next section will fulfill this purpose. The role of nurses and other staff members usually should be limited to

(1) screening for completion of the form or alternative authorization and (2) conveying information to the physician.

For procedures for which the hospital requires consents, nurses and other staff members should be assigned the responsibility of ascertaining whether the consent is appropriately documented or that there is another type of authorization before permitting the procedure to be performed. A staff member who becomes aware of a patient's confusion or change of opinion regarding a procedure should notify the responsible physician. If the physician does not respond, appropriate supervisors, medical staff, or institutional officials should be notified so they can determine whether intervention is necessary.

DOCUMENTATION

Whenever developing or applying a policy involving consent forms, it is essential to remember that the actual process of providing information to the person giving consent and of determining that individuals' decision is more important than the form itself. The form is evidence of the consent process, not a substitute for it. Existence of the form is vital evidence that consent was given. When it is missing, problems of proving consent are considerable and the risk of liability for failing to obtain informed consent increases considerably. There should be someone who has the authority to determine that there is actual consent even when the form has been lost or inadvertently not signed before sedation of the patient or when other circumstances make it difficult to obtain the signature. In those circumstances, a note in the medical record describing the circumstances and the consent can be substituted for the missing form as the best that can be done in the situation to reduce potential liability. Use of a signed consent form is by far the best approach, however.

Consent Forms

There are two basic types of consent forms: (1) the admission consent and (2) the special consent.

Admission Consent Forms

For medical and surgical care rendered in a hospital, the most satisfactory way to prove that the patient has consented is by the integrated use of two consent forms. A general admission consent form should be signed when the patient is admitted to the hospital. Such a form is presently used by many hospitals. It provides a record of consent to routine hospital services, diagnostic procedures, and medical treatment. The only significant danger regarding its use it the possible reliance on it as authorization for specific procedures such as surgery, for which it is not designed and is largely ineffective.

A signed special consent form should be procured before every substantial medical or surgical procedure beyond routine treatment. Proper use of such a form should satisfy the requirements of an informed consent. The special and admission consent forms, used together, will protect the hospital, its employees, and members of the medical staff by reducing the likelihood that a court will find a particular medical or surgical procedure not to have been authorized.

Special Consent Form

The special consent form should not be completed in the admitting office of the hospital. It is meant to serve as a record of a full and complete discussion between the patient and physician, or in some cases between the patient and another member of the health care team, and should not be completed in advance of such discussion.

Generally, the attending physician will take responsibility for completing the special consent form and having it executed by the patient. However, some hospitals have adopted administrative procedures to ensure that such a form is completed and placed on file before any significant medical or surgical procedure may be performed.

Use of the special consent form presupposes a process for disclosure of information by which the physician covers all necessary matters with the patient. Without a disclosure process that provides the patient with the required information (i.e., all information material to the patient's decision to undergo or to refuse the proposed therapy), the form offers few benefits. A disservice may be done if the fact that the form has been completed causes a physician to believe that his or her duty of disclosure has been satisfied when, in fact, it has not.

A special consent form should be executed by the patient or a representative of the patient before any of the following types of procedures are performed:

- major or minor surgery that involves an entry into the body, through an incision or through a natural body opening
- all procedures in which anesthesia is used, regardless of whether an entry into the body is involved
- nonsurgical procedures, including the administration of medicines, that involve more than a slight risk of harm to the patient or that may cause a change in the patient's body structure. Such procedures would include, but are not limited to, chemotherapy for cancer, hormone treatments, and diagnostic procedures such as myelograms, arteriograms, and pyelograms
- all forms of radiologic therapy
- electroconvulsive therapy
- all experimental procedures
- all other procedures that the medical staff determines require a specific explanation to the patient. Any doubts as to the necessity of obtaining a special

consent from the patient for a procedure should be resolved in favor of procuring the consent

Increasingly, states are enacting statutory provisions concerning blood testing for HIV. For instance, North Dakota requires an informed consent to be obtained before performing a blood test for HIV. The subject must sign a consent form that indicates to whom the results may be disclosed. The law specifies who may have access to the results. Written consent to disclose test results must be maintained by the provider. Similarly, New Mexico requires an informed consent to be obtained before performing a blood test for HIV. The test must be explained, including its purpose, potential uses and limitations, and the meaning of the results. Consent need not be in writing if there is documentation in the medical record that the test has been explained and consent has been obtained.

Impact of Statutes

Many states have adopted statutes concerning consent forms. Several of these provide that if the form contains certain information and is signed by the appropriate person, it is conclusive evidence of, or creates a presumption of, informed consent.[36] Such statutes address how the courts shall consider forms that contain certain information. They do not address forms that do not contain the information. Thus, it is not a violation of these statutes to use a form that contains different information or to forego the use of a form. However, especially in states that make certain forms conclusive evidence, health care professionals should give serious consideration to using forms that qualify.

THE DECISION MAKER

The person who makes the decision concerning the treatment or procedure must be legally and actually competent to do so and must be informed, unless one of the exceptions applies. Competent adults and some mature minors make decisions regarding their own care; someone else must make the decisions for incompetent adults and other minors.

Competent Adults

The age of majority is established by the legislature of each state. In most states it now is 18, but there still is some variation. In some states, a person can become adult before the established age by certain actions such as marriage.

Adults are competent if (1) a court has not declared them incompetent and (2) they generally are capable of understanding the consequences of alternatives, weighing them by the degree they promote their desires, and choosing and acting accordingly. There is a strong legal presumption of continued competence.

Incompetent Adults

Lack of competence to consent to treatment may result from a patient's unconsciousness, the influence of drugs or intoxicants, mental illness, or other permanent or temporary impairment of reasoning power. The essential determination to be made is whether the patient has sufficient mental ability to understand the situation and make a rational decision as to treatment.

In terms of mental capacity to consent, the test may be stated as:

> Does the patient have sufficient mind to reasonably understand the condition, the nature and effect of the proposed treatment, attendant risks in pursuing the treatment, and not pursuing the treatment?[37]

Whenever possible, a hospital or other provider of health care services contemplating treatment of a person arguably incompetent should try to obtain "substituted consent" from the person's next of kin or a court order authorizing the proposed treatment.[38]

Consent to Treatment of Minors

The need for a consent to a minor's treatment underlies two separate legal questions. The first relates to the practitioner's liability for battery if valid consent is not obtained. The second concerns the practitioner's right to compensation for services that have not been authorized by someone with legal capacity to make a binding contract.

As a general proposition, the consent of a minor to treatment is ineffective. Thus, the health care provider must secure the consent of the minor's parent or other person standing in loco parentis or risk liability to the minor and/or the parent.[39] The general proposition is rarely applied in a rigid manner, however. There are numerous judicial decisions that respond to a variety of special factual situations by declining to impose liability despite the lack of parental consent. Emergencies requiring immediate treatment to preserve the life of or prevent serious impairment to the health of a minor are the most common such situations. If the parents cannot be located within the time available, the courts usually have held that the existence of an emergency obviates the need for consent.

Parental or guardian consent should be obtained before treatment is given to a minor unless it is (1) an emergency, (2) one of the situations in which the consent of the minor is sufficient, or (3) a court order or other legal authorization is obtained.

Emergency Care

As with adults, consent is implied in medical emergencies when there is an immediate threat to life or health unless the provider has reason to believe that consent would be refused by the parent or guardian. When there is reason to so believe, the procedures for seeking court authorization should be followed whenever treatment is necessary.

Emancipated Minors

Emancipated minors may consent to their own medical care. Minors are emancipated when they no longer are subject to parental control or regulation and are not supported by their parents. The specific factors necessary to establish emancipation vary from state to state. Some states require that the parent and child agree on the emancipation, so a minor cannot become emancipated in those states simply by running away from home.

It is advisable that, whenever possible, the health care provider obtain the consent of an adult parent in addition to that of a minor patient. In this way, the issues of the minor's emancipation and mental capacity will not have to be tested in court. The burden of proving emancipation is always on the person asserting it. Moreover, because emancipation may be either complete or partial, a jury could find a minor emancipated for certain purposes but not for the purpose of authorizing medical care. Thus, excessive reliance should not be put on the concept of emancipation.

Mature Minors

Mature minors may consent to some medical care under common-law and constitutional principles and under the statutes of some states. Many states have statutes empowering older minors to consent to medical treatment. The age limits and scope of treatments vary from state to state. Even in the absence of such factors, however, some courts have rejected chronological age as the sole criterion for determining whether a minor can effectively consent to treatment. The child's maturity, the nature of the procedure, and the benefit, if any, to the child are also considered. In states that do not have an applicable minor consent statute, the risk associated with providing necessary treatment to mature minors with only their consent is minimal. The requirement of parental consent has been adhered to strictly when there was no emergency and the child was of tender years, but it has been relaxed when the minor was older than 15 and the procedure was for the minor's benefit.

When treating any minor, it is prudent to urge that the minor involve the parents. When a mature minor refuses to do so, necessary care can be provided without substantial risk unless (1) institutional policy requires parental involvement or

(2) there is likelihood of harm to the minor or others that requires parental involvement to avoid. When there is likelihood of such harm, parents usually should be involved unless state law or institutional policy forbids their being notified.

Parental or Guardian Consent

Either parent can give legally effective consent except when there is legal separation or divorce. Although it is not necessary to determine the wishes of the other parent, when it is known that the other parent objects, either the procedure should not be done or other legal authorization should be obtained. For example, in 1941 a New York court authorized surgical correction of a child's deformity when the parents disagreed.[40] When the parents are legally separated or divorced, the consent of the custodial parent usually must be obtained.

Consents for Special Problems of Minors

Recognizing that there are certain conditions such as pregnancy, venereal disease, or dependence on alcohol or illegal drugs for which a minor may wish to seek treatment without the knowledge of his or her parents, several states have enacted special provisions dealing with such situations. Because requiring parental consent in these cases might cause minors to delay to forego necessary treatment to prevent their parents from learning of their problems, these states have passed statutes providing that a minor can give an effective consent to treatment and ensuring the minor's confidentiality.

A key consideration regarding minors seeking medical assistance for sex-related problems and needs is the preservation of the minor's confidentiality. In general, the law has respected minors' wishes to keep certain sensitive information from their parents. This attitude is not universal, however. In one case,[41] a 15-year-old single girl attempted to challenge a county health department's refusal to supply contraceptives to minors without parental consent. The federal district court would not even consider her claim without first notifying her parents and appointing a guardian ad litem to ensure that she would know the risks and side effects of birth control pills. On appeal, the Eighth Circuit ruled that such a procedure would violate the very right of privacy that the girl was seeking to protect. The district court's order was vacated, and the case was remanded for consideration of its merits.

THE RIGHT TO REFUSE

An adult patient who is conscious and mentally competent has the right to refuse to permit any medical or surgical procedure. A competent patient's refusal must be honored whether the refusal is grounded on a doubt that the contemplated procedure will be successful, a concern about the probable or possible results of the procedure, a lack of confidence in the surgeon who recommends it, a religious belief, or a mere whim.[42]

The attempt to save a patient's life in the face of the patient's express prohibition is a humanitarian gesture that may not be supported by law. Even if the procedure is skillfully performed, the patient's right to be secure in his or her person has been violated, and damages may be sought for the unauthorized treatment. A sizable award seems unlikely, however, in a case in which the patient's life was saved by treatment rendered in disregard of his or her rights.

The right to refuse continues to apply even after consent is given. Patients or their representatives generally can withdraw their consent by, for example, objecting to continuation of treatment. When nurses become aware that consent has been withdrawn, they should discontinue the procedure as expeditiously as possible without endangering the patient and promptly inform the physician or other responsible practitioner of the situation. A reasonable effort to convince the patient to continue to accept treatment is appropriate before discontinuing it. In some situations, withdrawal in the middle of a sequence of procedures poses too great a danger to the patient to permit consent to be withdraw. For example, after an operation the immediate postoperative procedures necessary to ensure a safe transition from an anesthetized state cannot be refused. However, when oriented and readapted to room air, most patients can refuse continued care unless other factors are present.

Most courts have found that because a competent adult has the right to refuse, those making decisions on behalf of incompetent adults and minors must have a right to refuse on their behalf in appropriate situations. However, in certain situations courts have found that the state's interest outweigh those of the patient and have ordered treatment. When the patient's right to refuse is honored, the patient may have to forego other benefits.

There are three legal bases for the right to refuse treatment: (1) the common law right to freedom from nonconsensual invasion of bodily integrity, embodied in the informed consent doctrine and the law of battery; (2) the constitutional right of privacy; and (3) the constitutional right to freedom of religion.

Minors and Incompetent Adults

The courts have tended to find that because a competent adult has the right to refuse, those making decisions on behalf of minors and incompetent adults have a right to refuse on their behalf in some situations. However, because the decision makers have an obligation to act in the best interests of the minor or incompetent adult, they must provide necessary treatment. Their discretion to decline treatment is limited to situations in which the treatment is elective or not likely to be beneficial. The duty to provide necessary treatment to minors is reinforced in all states by legislation concerning abused or neglected minors that facilitates state inter-vention to provide needed assistance. Legislation concerning abused or neglected adults has been enacted in a few states.

Courts generally have permitted the refusal of extraordinary care for terminally ill or irreversibly comatose minors and incompetent adults. For example, the New Jersey Supreme Court permitted the father of an adult daughter in an irreversible coma to authorize the withdrawal of respiratory support.[43] The Massachusetts Su-preme Judicial Court agreed that no resuscitative efforts need be attempted in the event of cardiac or respiratory arrest of a child younger than one year of age who was terminally ill.[44]

The state may order medical treatment of seriously ill children over the reli-gious objections of their parents, the Massachusetts' high court has ruled.[45] Physi-cians treating an eight-year-old patient suffering from leukemia wanted to give her a blood transfusion before instituting additional treatment. The child's parents were Jehovah's Witnesses, however, and refused to provide their consent. The hospital sought and obtained a lower court order authorizing it to administer the transfusion. The lower court found that without chemotherapy and blood transfu-sions, the child faced certain death, and ordered the hospital to provide all reason-able medical care necessary including transfusion. The lower court noted that there were five factors in support of a transfusion: (1) the child's age, (2) the risk to the child's health and life if the transfusion was not ordered, (3) the real probabil-ity that the child's illness would be in remission if given a transfusion, (4) the substantial chance for a cure and normal life if the transfusion was administered, and (5) the minimal risks associated with a transfusion. The factors weighing against the transfusion were the religious beliefs of the parents and the child. Mas-sachusetts' highest court also noted that the state had three interests in allowing a sick child to receive treatment over the parents' religious objections: (1) to protect the welfare of children, (2) to preserve life, and (3) to maintain the integrity of the medical profession. Because the court concluded that the child's best interest and the state's interests outweighed those of the parents, it upheld the order that the hospital provide a transfusion.

Obtaining Legally Valid Consent

Persons or institutions providing health care to incompetents should be aware of their state's procedural requirements for obtaining and documenting consent. Some states have statutes dictating the procedure to be followed in obtaining the consent of institutionalized patients to treatment. The consent of a close relative or a legally appointed guardian is often sought to authorize treatment of incompetents.

The order of preference among next of kin for obtaining a substituted consent is spouse, parent, adult child, sister or brother, uncle, aunt, and grandparent.[46] When no next of kin is available to give substituted consent for the care of an incompetent, the health care provider may have to seek consent from the patient's guardian or a court order before proceeding.

The problem for a health care provider is more difficult when two or more relatives of the same order of affinity to the patient disagree on whether the proposed treatment should be rendered. In such case, the legal situation may be sufficiently unclear to induce the provider to turn to the courts for resolution. Most likely, courts would rule that, when relatives of equal status disagree as to the patient's treatment, the consent of one of them would insulate the hospital and/or health professional from liability if the care rendered was such as the provider deemed best under the circumstances. It is understandable, however, that providers may be unwilling to act in such situations without specific authorization by a court.

Protecting the Provider from Liability

It is recommended that no medical or surgical procedures be performed within the hospital if a patient refuses treatment. To avoid liability for not providing appropriate treatment, however, the hospital should first ascertain that the patient is competent at the time of the refusal. Any question regarding competence should be considered by the attending physician in consultation with at least one other physician, and their determination should be documented. The refusal should be noted in the medical record, and the physician should render the best care possible within the limits imposed by the patient's refusal. If possible, a written release should be secured from the patient so that the record will reflect that appropriate treatment would have been rendered if the patient had not refused. Whether the treatment was offered and refused is a question of fact for the jury to decide. Thus, it is just as necessary to be able to prove the refusal if treatment is not rendered as it is to prove consent when treatment is rendered.

RESEARCH

Ordinarily, a patient who accepts treatment expects the use of the drugs and procedures customarily used for the condition. When experimental methods are used or established procedures are used for purposes of research, the investigator must disclose this to the subject and obtain the consent of the subject or the subject's representative. This relatively simple approach of applying to experimentation general principles of informed consent has been substantially influenced in recent years by governmental provisions for the protection of human subjects of biomedical research. The field has thus become complex and deserving of special consideration. Moreover, staff nurses may be involved in collecting research data for clinical research; an understanding of patients' rights within the context is necessary.

Federal Regulations

Federal guidelines for experimentation involving human subjects were first issued in 1971[47] and later in 1981 in response to the recommendations of the National Commission for the Protection of Human Subjects of Biomedical and Behavioral Research and of a similar presidential commission concerning institutional review boards (IRB), the Department of Health and Human Services (HHS) issued final regulations clarifying its policy for the protection of human research subjects.[48] According to these regulations, HHS regulatory coverage is substantially reduced by exempting broad categories of research that normally present little or no risk of harm to the subjects. Specifically, the final regulations exempt from coverage most social, economic, and educational research in which the only involvement of human subjects will be in one or more of the following categories: (1) the use of survey and interview procedures; (2) the observation of public behavior; or (3) the study of data, documents, records, and specimens. In addition, the regulations require IRB review and approval of research involving human subjects if supported by HHS funds and not exempt from coverage. Finally, although institutions engaged in research involving human subjects must provide assurances to HHS that the regulations are being complied with, no such research may ever be initiated unless the legally effective informed consent of the subject or the subject's legally authorized representative has been obtained. Participation as an institutional provider under the Medicare or Medicaid programs does not, of itself, obligate an institution to observe these protocols, although protection of patients' rights, including a requirement for informed consent, is indirectly made a part of the conditions of participation.[49]

Institutional Review Boards

HHS regulations require each institution to have an IRB, composed of no less than five persons whose background and experience enable them to assess research applications and proposals in terms of institutional commitments and regulations, applicable law, standards of professional conduct and practice, and community attitudes. No IRB may consist entirely of persons employed by or affiliated with the institution, nor may it consist entirely of members of a single professional group. No IRB member may participate in the review of an activity in which he or she has a conflicting interest.

The function of the IRB is to review in advance all proposed research activities that involve the institution or its patients to determine whether any research subjects will be placed at risk and, if risk is involved, whether

1. Risks to subjects are reasonable in relation to anticipated benefits, if any, to subjects, and the importance of the knowledge that may reasonably be expected to result.

2. In evaluating risks and benefits, the IRB should not consider possible long-range effects of applying knowledge gained in the research (e.g., the possible effects of the research on public policy) as among those research risks that fall within the purview of its responsibility.
3. Informed consent will be sought from each prospective subject.[50]

The benefit–risk analysis required by item 1 is the key element of the review. It is clear that research procedures or studies that promise some therapeutic benefit to the research subject will be viewed much more favorably than those that might simply add to scientific knowledge or yield benefit to others or to society at large.

No application to HHS for funding of research involving human subjects will be considered unless the individual submitting it is affiliated with or sponsored by an institution that not only can and does assume responsibility for the subjects involved but also submits a certification of its review and approval of the proposed research. Proposals involving investigational new drugs and devices must also satisfy the requirements imposed by the Food and Drug Administration under the Federal Food, Drug and Cosmetic Act.[51]

Obtaining and Documenting Informed Consent to Research

Assuming that the proposed research is deemed justifiable by the IRB, approval still cannot be given unless the research protocol provides for the securing of adequate informed consent from all subjects. The HHS regulations mandate that in seeking informed consent the following information shall be provided to each subject:

1. a statement that the study involves research, an explanation of the purposes of the research and the expected duration of the subject's participation, a description of the procedures to be followed, and identification of any procedures that are experimental
2. description of any attendant discomforts and risks reasonably to be expected
3. description of any benefits reasonably to be expected
4. disclosure of any appropriate alternative procedures that might be advantageous for the subject
5. a statement describing the extent to which confidentiality of records identifying the subject will be maintained
6. for research involving more than minimal risk, an explanation as to whether any medical treatments are available if injury occurs
7. offer to answer any inquiries concerning the procedures
8. instruction that the person is free to withdraw his or her consent and to discontinue participation in the project or activity at any time without prejudice to the subject[52]

Under this definition, it is essential to legally effective consent that the person consenting, either the subject or someone legally authorized to act on the subject's behalf, be competent to do so and that the consent be wholly voluntary. Because consent cannot be voluntary if there is duress or undue inducement, it must be made clear to the person from whom consent is sought that the care of the subject will in no way be compromised by an initial refusal to cooperate in the study or a decision at some later time to withdraw from it. Promises of compensation or special favors in return for participation must be carefully scrutinized to see that they do not overbear the will of the proposed subject.

A particularly troublesome problem is presented by research protocols that involve deception or the withholding of certain information from the subject, as, for example, when subjects in a control group are to be treated with a placebo instead of an active drug agent. To satisfy HHS requirements, this fact would have to be disclosed as part of the consent process, although a given subject would not have to be told whether he or she was to receive the placebo or the actual drug. Disclosure of this information might compromise the scientific validity of the research, but this is unavoidable under the HHS regulations.

CONCLUSION

In general, consent to treatment is required before any health care diagnosis or treatment can be rendered to patients. Informed consent requires patients to receive information about the risks, benefits, and alternatives of treatment. Although competent adults have a right to refuse treatment, minors and incompetent adults whose decisions are made by others also have this basic right to bodily integrity, although these decisions receive more scrutiny. Nurses are not responsible for obtaining consent unless they are in independent practice or are assigned responsibilities associated with obtaining consent by their employers. However, nurses practicing independently in the expanded role have primary responsibilities for obtaining informed consent or other authorization for treatment.

FOOTNOTES

1. Canterbury v. Spence, 464 F.2d 772 (D.C. Cir. 1972), quoting Schloendorff v. Society of New York Hosp., 211 N.Y. 125, 105 N.E. 92, 93 (1914).

2. Truman v. Thomas, 27 Cal. 3d 285, 611 P.2d 902 (1980).

3. *See, e.g.,* Kelly v. Gershkoff, 112 R.I. 507, 312 A.2d 211 (1973); Grannum v. Berard, 422 P.2d 812 (Wash. 1967); Arballo v. Nielson, 166 P.2d 621 (Cal. 1946).

4. *See, e.g.,* Demers v. Gerety, 92 N.M. 396, 589 P.2d 180 (1978), where the patient alleged the administration of anesthesia had rendered him incapable of giving a voluntary and intelligent con-

sent. At one stage in this lengthy case, the jury accepted this contention and entered a verdict against the defendant physician.

5. 154 Mass. 272, 28 N.E. 266 (1891).

6. *See, e.g.,* Stafford v. Louisiana State Univ., 448 So. 2d 852 (La. Ct. App. 1984), in which a physician who amputated a patient's gangrenous lower leg without obtaining a valid informed consent was not liable for performing unauthorized surgery because the patient's condition constituted a life-threatening emergency, which vitiated the need for consent.

7. 96 So. 2d 716 (Fla. Dist. Ct. App. 1957); *see also* Perry v. Hodgson, 168 Ga. 678, 148 S.E. 659 (1929); Hively v. Higgs, 120 Or. 588, 523 P. 363 (1927); Rolater v. Strain, 39 Okla. 572, 137 P.2d 96 (1913).

8. Sullivan v. Montgomery, 155 Misc. 448, 449, 279 N.Y.S. 575, 577 (1935) (anesthesia applied and suspected ankle fracture of 20-year-old man set in cast without consulting the parents or telling the man about the fracture); Wells v. McGehee, 39 So. 2d 196 (La. Ct. App. 1949) (11-year-old child died when physician administered chloroform before setting her broken wrist; the wrist injury apparently was not life-threatening). *See also* ARK. STAT. ANN. § 82-364, which recognizes an emergency when the person's safety would be affected or disfigurement or impairment of faculties might be expected to result.

9. Moore v. London, 29 App. Div. 2d 666, 286 N.Y.S.2d 319 (1968).

10. Salgo v. Stanford Univ. Bd. of Trustees, 154 Cal. App. 2d 560, 317 P.2d 170 (1957).

11. *See, e.g.,* Ficklin v. MacFarlane, 550 P.2d 1295 (Utah 1976); Bly v. Rhoads, 22 S.E.2d 783 (Va. 1976).

12. 464 F.2d 772, 780 (D.C. Cir. 1972), quoting Schloendorff v. Society of N.Y. Hosp., 105 N.E. 92, 93 (N.Y. 1914).

13. *See* Crawford v. Wojnas, 754 P.2d 1302 (Wash. Ct. App. 1988), in which the court ruled that a physician who inoculated an infant with a live polio vaccine had no duty to disclose alternative types of vaccines that would be less contagious to the infant's mother, who contracted polio from the vaccine.

14. *But see* Eisbrenner v. Stanley, 308 N.W.2d 209 (Mich. App. Ct. 1981), in which a physician's failure to disclose a diagnosis of rubella to a pregnant woman provided sufficient grounds for suit by the parents of a baby born with severe rubella-caused birth defects.

15. *See, e.g.,* Henderson v. Milobsky, 595 F.2d 654 (D.C. Cir. 1978); Parker v. St. Paul Fire & Marine Ins. Co., 355 So. 2d 725 (La. Ct. App. 1976); Sard v. Hardy, 367 A.2d 525 (Md. Ct. Spec. App. 1976); Longmire v. Hoey, 512 S.W.2d 307 (Tenn. Ct. App. 1974).

16. Cobbs v. Grant, 502 P.2d 1, 11 (Cal. 1972).

17. See Canterbury v. Spence, 464 F.2d 772, 788 (1972).

18. See Nisenholtz v. Mt. Sinai Hosp., 483 N.Y.S.2d 568 (N.Y. Sup. Ct. 1985), in which a New York trial court ruled that physicians discussing the possible risks and consequences of a procedure may be also required to describe the various ways in which undesirable results can occur.

19. *See, e.g.,* Fleishman v. Richardson-Merrell, Inc., 226 A.2d 843 (N.J. Super. Ct. 1967).

20. Drug experimentation and certain other biomedical research activities are subject to federal regulation.

21. 146 A. 641 (N.H. 1929).

22. 542 P.2d 251 (Alaska 1975).

23. *Id.* at 275.

24. Truman v. Thomas, 611 P.2d 902 (Cal. 1980). *See also* Madsen v. Park Nicollet Med. Ctr., 419 N.W.2d 511 (Minn. Ct. App. 1988), in which the court ruled that a physician had a duty to inform a pregnant patient who was leaking amniotic fluid of the risks of not being hospitalized.

25. *See also* Stager v. Schneider, 494 A.2d 1307 (D.C. 1985), in which the D.C. Court of Appeals ruled that a woman who had chest radiographs taken as part of a standard preoperative examination, which revealed a suspicious spot on her lungs, had no duty to call and seek her test results.

26. (Literally translated: "Let the master answer.") *See* Hohenthal v. Smith, 114 F.2d 494 (D.C. Cir. 1940), for an extensive citation of authorities for this rule.

27. *See* RESTATEMENT (SECOND) OF AGENCY 2d § 220 (1958), which sets forth suggested criteria for determining the existence of the relationship. Although the terms *master* and *servant* are frequently used to describe the relationship, for simplicity herein, the terms *employer* and *employee* will be used.

28. Nor is it determinative that house staff may not be regarded as employees entitled to collective bargaining protection under the 1974 Health Care Amendments to the National Labor Relations Act. *See* Cedars-Sinai Med. Ctr., 223 N.L.R.B. 57 (1976), and subsequent cases.

29. *But see* Magana v. Elie, 439 N.E.2d 1319 (Ill. App. Ct.1982), in which an Illinois appeals court ruled that a hospital may have a duty to its patients to ensure that independent medical staff physicians inform them of the risks of and alternatives to surgery.

30. Campbell v. Pitt County Mem'l Hosp., 352 S.E.2d 902 (N.C. Ct. App. 1987).

31. 832 P.2d 797 (N.M. Ct. App. 1992).

32. *See also* Howell v. Spokane & Inland Empire Blood Bank, 1785 P.2d 815 (1990); Pauscher v. Iowa Methodist Med. Ctr., 408 N.W.2d 355 (Iowa 1987); Kershaw v. Reichert, 445 N.W.2d 16 (N.D. 1989).

33. Mahannah v. Hirsch, 237 Cal. Rptr. 140 (Cal. Ct. App. 1987).

34. For an article advocating increased nurse and hospital responsibility for informed consent, see Greenlaw, Jane, *Should hospitals be responsible for informed consent?* 11 L. MED. & HEALTH CARE 174 (1983); for an article advocating maintaining the physician's responsibility, see Chushing, *Informed Consent: An MD Responsibility?* 84 AM. J. NURSING 437 (April 1984).

35. Roberson v. Menorah Med. Ctr., 588 S.W.2d 134 (Mo. Ct. App. 1979); *see also* Cooper v. Curry, 92 N.M. 417, 589 P.2d 201 (N.M. Ct. App. 1978) (hospital not liable for admission clerk's failure to obtain informed consent).

36. *E.g.,* NEV.REV.STAT. § 41A.110 (1981) (conclusive evidence); IOWA CODE § 147.137 (1983) (presumption).

37. In the Matter of William Schiller, 372 A.2d 360, 367 (1977). *See also* In the Matter of Edith Armstrong, 573 S.W.2d 141 (Mo. Ct. App. 1978).

38. If the next of kin refuses to consent, it may still be possible to obtain a court order allowing the treatment. *See, e.g.,* MISS. CODE ANN. § 41-41-9. *But see* Eis v. Chestnut, 627 P.2d 1244 (N.M. Ct. App. 1981), in which *temporary* incapacity was not considered a valid reason for a physician to initiate nonemergency treatment on the consent of someone other than the patient.

39. *In re* Hudson, 126 P.2d 765 (Wash. 1941); Bonner v. Moran, 126 F.2d 121 (D.C. Cir. 1941); Rogers v. Selb, 61 P.2d 1018 (Okla.1936); Sullivan v. Montgomery, 279 N.Y.S. 575 (1935); Zoski v. Gaines, 260 N.W. 99 (Mich. 1935); Zaman v. Schultz, 19 Pa. D. & C. 309 (1933); Bishop v. Shurly, 211 N.W. 75 (Mich. 1926); Browning v. Hoffman, 111 S.E. 492, 497 (W.Va. 1922); Moss v. Rishworth, 222 S.W. 225 (Tex. Comm'n App. 1920).

40. *In re* Rotkowitz, 25 N.Y.S.2d 624 (N.Y. Fam. Ct. 1941).

41. M.S. v. Wermers, 409 F. Supp. 312 (D.S.D.1976), *vacated and remanded,* 557 F.2d 170 (8th Cir. 1977).

42. Note, however, that a refusal based on religious belief partakes of direct First Amendment protection, whereas the right of privacy that would otherwise be the main support for the patient's position is not expressly stated in the Constitution. Because an implicit right of privacy has been widely recognized by the courts, *e.g.,* Roe v. Wade, 410 U.S. 113 (1973), this distinction may have little legal significance.

43. *In re* Quinlan, 70 N.J. 10, 355 A.2d 647 (1976).

44. Custody of a Minor, 434 N.E.2d 601 (Mass. 1982).

45. Matter of McCauley, 565 N.E.2d 411 (Mass. 1991).

46. *See also* Aponte v. United States, 582 F. Supp. 65 (D.P.R. 1984), in which a federal trial court ruled that a Veterans Administration hospital that declared a patient mentally incompetent and appointed the patient's wife to act in his behalf must obtain surgical consent from the wife notwithstanding that she had not been named as her husband's official guardian.

47. The Institutional Guide to DHEW Policy on Protection of Human Subjects, DHEW Publication No. 72-102, December, 1971 (U.S. Gov't Printing Office No. 1740-0326).

48. 45 C.F.R. Part 46.

49. Under § 1865 of the Social Security Act, 42 U.S.C. § 1395 bb, a hospital is deemed to meet Medicare's Conditions of Participation if it is accredited by the Joint Commission on Accreditation of Healthcare Organizations. Most Medicare providers are qualified through this "deemer" mechanism, and thus, most comply with Joint Commission standards on informed consent.

50. 45 C.F.R. § 46.111(2) and (4).

51. 21 U.S.C. § 355(i), as further defined by FDA regulations, 21 C.F.R. § 312.1.

52. 45 C.F.R. § 46.116(a).

CHAPTER 10

Reproductive Issues

Chapter Objectives
1. To discuss contraception
2. To discuss assisted conception
3. To review the legal aspects of abortion
4. To examine postbirth liability

The desire to have—or not to have—children arises from deeply felt personal, philosophic, moral, religious, and political beliefs. Indeed, except for death and dying, no other aspect of health care so intimately involves personal values and emotions as does human reproduction. Advances in medical technology have made it increasingly possible to create and sustain life outside the womb; to identify fetal characteristics, including birth defects; and to correct in utero conditions that in the past may have caused fetal death or damage. These medical possibilities may conflict with the wishes of the individual.

The constitutional principle of the right of individual privacy has frequently been applied in cases involving reproductive issues. Questions relating to contraception, conception, sterilization, pregnancy termination, and genetic counseling go to the heart of individual and societal value systems, inevitably raising such issues as the point at which life begins, the value of an impaired life, the quality of life, and the relative roles of the individual and the society in answering these questions. Because of sharply differing moral or religious views about the propriety of medical interference in the reproductive process, these issues have engendered intense levels of social and political controversy.

This chapter discusses these issues, as well as prenatal testing, genetic screening, and liability for the birth of children after negligent sterilizations or failure to inform of genetic risks. Nurses working in a variety of settings such as women's health care clinics, infertility practices, teen pregnancy centers, or obstetric units in the traditional or expanded role need to be aware of the status of the law on these reproductive issues, because of the far-reaching implications they have on nursing practice and patient counseling in this rapidly developing area of health care.

CONTRACEPTION

Contraception includes the various drugs, devices, and procedures, both prescription and nonprescription, designed to avoid pregnancy.

Contraceptive Drugs and Devices

Numerous drugs and devices are available to reduce the probability of pregnancy. In the first case to address the constitutionality of such provisions, the U.S. Supreme Court in 1965 declared a Connecticut law forbidding the use of contraceptives by married persons to be an unconstitutional violation of the right of privacy.[1] In a 1972 case, the Court voided a Massachusetts law forbidding the sale or use of contraceptives by unmarried persons.[2] The Court ruled that whatever the rights of adults may be to have access to contraceptives, they are the same for married and unmarried persons. The Court said: "If the right to privacy means anything, it is the right of the individual, married or single, to be free from unwarranted governmental intrusion into matters so fundamentally affecting a person as the decision whether to bear or beget a child."[3]

It is clear from these two cases that a state may not prohibit the use of contraceptives by its adult population. Many states, however, have continued to regulate the sale and distribution of contraceptives to some extent. In a 1977 case, the Supreme Court limited the extent to which a state may restrict the sale and distribution of contraceptives by holding that a provision in a New York statute prohibiting the distribution of nonprescription contraceptives to persons older than 16 by anyone other than licensed pharmacists was an undue burden on an individual's right to decide whether to bear a child.[4] The Court invalidated the prohibition on advertising and display of prescription as well as nonprescription contraceptives, at least when the advertising is done by persons licensed to sell such products.

Thus, few legal barriers confront adults who seek to obtain contraceptives. For presumed safety reasons, prescription contraceptives or those requiring fitted insertion must be obtained through a physician or nurse practitioner. Nonprescription birth control devices can be purchased legally in drug stores, vending machines, or through mail-order services.

Minors

Although it now is relatively easy for adults to obtain contraceptives, minors still face many obstacles. The Supreme Court's first comment on a minor's right of access to birth control came in the New York case. Four members of the Court agreed that "the right to privacy in connection with decisions affecting procreation extends to minors as well as to adults . . . and since a state may not impose a blanket prohibition or even a blanket requirement of parental consent on the choice of a minor to terminate her pregnancy, the constitutionality of a blanket prohibition on the distribution of contraceptives is foreclosed."[5] The four justices also held that allowing a minor to obtain contraceptives only from a physician gave the physician absolute and possibly arbitrary discretion over the privacy rights of a minor and that such power was impermissible. Three other members of the Court concurred in the result of the case but for other reasons. These three and the two dissenting justices did not agree that the right of privacy in decisions affecting procreation extends to minors.

In a 1980 case, a court ruled that minors have a right to contraceptive devices from a county-run family planning center without parental notification or consent.[6] In another case, a court ruled that federally funded family planning centers could not require parental notice or consent as a condition to the providing of services.[7] The court based its ruling on its interpretation of the federal statute authorizing the program, not on constitutional principles.

State laws cannot restrict the use of federal funds for family planning services offered to minors. In *Planned Parenthood Association v. Dandoy,* the state of Utah refused to distribute Medicaid funds to family planning programs that rendered services to minors, relying on a state law that prohibits the use of state funds for such purposes unless parental consent is obtained.[8] The U.S. Court of Appeals for the Tenth Circuit declared that Utah cannot place restrictions on federal Medicaid law, which requires states to fund family planning programs, including those that serve minors acting without parental advice. The court concluded that Utah can choose to remain in the Medicaid family planning program and continue to receive federal funding or can withdraw from the federal program and use its own funds to provide family planning services in harmony with state law.

Although the most prudent practice is to encourage minors to involve their parents in the decision making, it must be recognized that many minors cannot or will not do so. Physicians and nurse practitioners then must decide whether to prescribe contraceptives in the absence of parental involvement. Health care providers who choose to prescribe contraceptives to unemancipated minors face a theoretical possibility of civil liability for battery or malpractice in some states. Several states explicitly authorize minors to consent to these services.

In actuality, even in states without a minor consent statute, the legal risk is small, especially when the minor is mature. The most likely difficulty for the care providers will be in collecting payment because the parents probably will not be responsible. The nurse has an important role in ensuring that minors have adequate information on which to base their decisions and that they are aware of their rights and the availability of information on contraception.

Liability for Side Effects

Both oral contraceptives and intrauterine devices are known to have harmful side effects in a few instances. Litigation has resulted in the most serious of these situations, much of it against the manufacturer and based on product liability or inadequate warnings of the risks involved in taking birth control pills or using certain devices. It appears that health care providers will not be held liable in the absence of negligence or intentional misconduct.

Liability of health care providers and hospitals can result from negligent prescription of an oral contraceptive, negligent insertion of a contraceptive device, failure to advise a patient adequately of possible risks, and failure to monitor a patient who is at risk of or who develops adverse reactions.[9] Therefore, documentation that risks, benefits, and alternatives have been discussed with the patient and that any package insert materials provided by the manufacturer have been discussed with and given to the patient is desirable.

Voluntary Sterilization

Sterilization involves termination of the ability to produce offspring. Sterilization may be the desired result of a surgical operation or may be the incidental consequence of an operation to remove a diseased reproductive organ or to cure a particular malfunction of such an organ. When the reproductive organs are not diseased, most sterilizations are effected by vasectomy in males and tubal ligation in females.

In the past, there were concerns about the legality of voluntary sterilizations of competent adults. States recognized a distinction between therapeutic sterilizations to protect a woman who was at risk of impairment of life or health if she became pregnant and contraceptive sterilizations for which there was no therapeutic reason. Some states permitted therapeutic but not contraceptive sterilizations. However, these restrictions have been eliminated so that no state now prohibits voluntary consensual sterilization of a competent adult regardless of the purpose.

Federal regulations require the signing of a special consent form at least 30 days before sterilizations funded by Medicaid.[10] Exceptions are made for some therapeutic cases. Some states impose similar requirements on all sterilizations performed in the state. A California court upheld the constitutionality of that state's requirements in a 1981 case.[11]

The specific wording of the federal consent forms and the 30-day wait requirement do not apply to other patients unless required by state law. However, the consent of the person who is to be sterilized or subjected to an operation that may incidentally destroy the reproductive function should be obtained first. In the absence of consent, even if an operation is medically necessary, a sterilization almost always constitutes a battery. Courts are less likely to find that there is implied consent to a sterilization than to other extensions of surgical procedures.

When it may be predicted that an operation necessary to cure a condition will incidentally destroy the ability to procreate, the consequences to the reproductive function should be clearly brought to the attention of the patient. When sterilization is to be performed in conjunction with another procedure, specific reference should be made to the sterilization. The use of a specific consent form that clearly indicates the effect on the reproductive process is recommended. It is important that the risk that the sterilization could be unsuccessful also be disclosed in addition to the disclosure that reproduction probably will not be possible. Failure to inform of the small risk of future reproductive ability can expose the provider to liability (as discussed later in this chapter).

Ordinarily, the consent of the patient alone is sufficient authorization for any operation. But because sterilization affects the legally sensitive procreative function, some hospitals and physicians have a policy of requiring that the consent of the spouse also be obtained when the patient is married. It is doubtful whether public hospitals can enforce such policies. In several cases, courts have declared such a public hospital policy to be an unconstitutional violation of the right of privacy.[12]

In a 1973 case, a court ruled that a governmental hospital may not impose greater restrictions on sterilization procedures than on other procedures that are medically indistinguishable from sterilization with regard to risk to the patient or demand on staff or facilities. The hospital was enjoined from enforcing its policy against all contraceptive sterilization procedures.[13] However, private hospitals can forbid contraceptive sterilizations or require spousal consent, but if so, the policy should be applied equally to both male and female patients. For example, a 1976 case held that federal courts do not have jurisdiction to order a private hospital to end its policy of requiring spousal consent to sterilization because state action was involved.[14]

In the past, several states had laws requiring spousal consent to sterilization, but when these laws have been challenged, federal courts consistently have declared them unconstitutional and enjoined their enforcement.

It is prudent to encourage spousal involvement in the decision, especially when the two are not estranged. Individual physicians may have a personal practice of not performing sterilizations without spousal consent in any hospital if the practice is not required by institutional policy. In one case, the court found no violation of the Constitution in a physician's personal policy to condition treatment of pregnant indigent patients on their involuntary submission to sterilization after the delivery of their third living child.[15] The fact that the doctor served Medicaid patients did not make his actions "state action." He applied his policy to all his patients and notified them of his practice early in their relationship so they were free to go elsewhere for care.

There is little legal risk from performing a sterilization procedure without spousal consent. In Oklahoma, the court dismissed the suit because the husband had no right to a child-bearing wife as an incident to marriage so he had not been legally harmed by the procedure.[16]

Parental Consent or Notification

It is unclear whether parental consent can be required for sterilization of minors. Some states have legislation specifying a minimum age (usually 18) for consent to such procedures.[17] Because sterilization is expected to end the patient's reproductive capability permanently, a requirement for parental concurrence in the request of an unemancipated but otherwise competent minor might well be upheld as consistent with the desirability of involving parents in major decisions related to the growth and well-being of their offspring.[18]

Performance of Voluntary Sterilization Procedures

Some states have enacted legislation stating that hospitals are not required to permit the performance of sterilization procedures. Whether a hospital must permit elective sterilization procedures depends on whether it is a private or a public hospital. A private hospital may prohibit voluntary sterilization procedures in its facilities.[19] It appears, however, that public hospitals may not prohibit elective sterilizations.[20]

Just as private hospitals may refuse to permit voluntary sterilization procedures, so individual practitioners may refuse to participate in them. Many states have "conscience clauses" that specifically allow physicians or nurses to refuse to participate in procedures that violate their moral or religious beliefs (e.g., abortions or sterilizations) without fear of reprisals.[21] When a nurse anesthetist who had been discharged from her employment because she refused to participate in a sterilization procedure filed suit against the hospital, asserting her rights under a Montana conscience clause, the Supreme Court of Montana determined not only that the nurse had a statutory right to refuse to participate in the sterilization procedure but also that her refusal could not be a basis for disciplinary, discriminatory, or recriminatory action.[22] Because the statutory right was unqualified, her right to refuse could not be outweighed by any considerations or discomfitures that resulted from its exercise. Even in the absence of such a statute, the refusal of a practitioner to participate in these procedures has been upheld.[23]

ASSISTED CONCEPTION

Couples or individuals who wish to have a child but are unable to conceive a child naturally have a variety of alternatives. Fewer children are available for adoption than in the past because of the increased use of contraceptives and the availability of abortion, but current techniques such as artificial insemination, in vitro fertilization (IVF), and surrogate motherhood offer the hope of producing a child. These techniques have become increasingly important as a way of providing offspring to prospective parents.

Artificial Insemination

For numerous couples who are unable to produce children because of physical or psychological barriers or because of genetic incompatibility and, more recently, for unmarried women who simply wish to have a child, artificial insemination has become quite widely available. Artificial insemination is the introduction of semen of the husband (AIH) or another donor (AID), or a combination of the two (AIC), into the vagina through a syringe.[24] As the number of women who have been artificially inseminated has increased, there has been a concomitant rise in the number of legal issues and problems associated with it, particularly with respect to the use of donor semen. Many states have responded to those practices by enacting legislation that governs the use of artificial insemination.[25]

Most states that have statutes governing artificial insemination require that it be performed by a licensed physician.[26] This could change as nurse practitioners become more specialized and trained in this area. Under such a statute, self-insemination or insemination by a nonphysician would constitute the unauthorized practice of medicine and would be subject to the penalties applicable to that offense. Even in the absence of such a statute, insemination by nonphysicians could still be considered unauthorized practice under a generalized statute prohibiting the practice of medicine by lay persons.[27]

The Single Woman

Increasingly, physicians and hospitals associated with fertility programs are being faced with requests for AID from single women. Many physicians refuse to perform artificial insemination on single women, and many states prohibit it by statute. These statues raise serious constitutional questions in the light of the Supreme Court's decisions that an individual's decision to procreate is a fundamental interest encompassed within the constitutional right to privacy and that this privacy right extends to unmarried as well as married persons.[28] It is unlikely, however, that a private institution could be compelled to offer artificial insemination to single women.

Confidentiality

For the most part, the identity of the semen donor is kept confidential, although occasionally an AID recipient requests that semen from a particular donor be used. The confidentiality of AID records, particularly with respect to the donor's identity, presents a problem that may be litigated in the future.[29] Like the adopted children who seek to learn the identity of their biologic parents, an AID child (if aware that the actual father is not the biologic father) may claim the right to know the identity of the semen donor.

Although an AID child may have a strong emotional interest and, in some cases, a strong medical interest in learning the identity of the AID-father, the donor may have an equally strong interest in keeping his identity confidential. Generally, the donor expects that his identity will not be disclosed to anyone except the physician and has no intention of taking on any of the responsibilities of parenthood.[30] It seems unfair to the donor to reveal his identity or to impose the emotional and financial obligations of parenthood on him when those were not his reasonable expectations. The mother of an AID child, as well as her husband, may also want the donor's identity to remain anonymous to protect the unity of their family. To date, no jurisdiction has enacted legislation requiring that the identity of AIDs be disclosed under any circumstances.

In Vitro Fertilization

IVF involves withdrawal of sperm from a man and an ovum from a woman, joinder of the sperm and ovum outside the woman's body, and implantation of the fertilized ovum in the woman's womb. The process of IVF and embryo transfer, once highly experimental, is now actively used as a clinical procedure to treat fertility problems.[31]

Some states, such as Louisiana, have enacted laws to protect ova fertilized in vitro.[32] The Louisiana statute forbids the culture or farming of an in vitro fertilized human ovum solely for research or for any other purpose except for implantation in a human womb. The law confers on the ovum the status of a person created by the law. Regarding ownership of the ovum, the law states:

> An in vitro fertilized human ovum is a biological human being which is not the property of the physician which acts as an agent of fertilization. . . . If the in vitro fertilization patients express their identity, then their rights as parents . . . will be preserved. If the in vitro fertilization patients fail to express their identity, then the physician shall be deemed to be temporary guardian of the in vitro fertilized ovum until adoptive implantation can occur.[33]

Problem Areas

Many of the potential legal problems associated with IVF are similar to those associated with artificial insemination. When the husband provides the sperm and the wife the ovum, the legal situation is analogous to that of AIH, and the child is the biologic offspring of both husband and wife.[34] When a donor provides the sperm used in IVF, the legal situation is similar to that of AID.

If the ovum comes from a donor, the problem becomes more complex. Motherhood has never been subject to question in the past—the identity of the woman who physically bore a child has been conclusive proof of motherhood. When the ovum comes from one woman, is fertilized, and then is transferred into another woman's uterus, the question becomes whether contributing the germ cell or carrying and giving birth to the child entitles a woman to claim motherhood.

The availability of IVF originally generated concern among those who fear that the process would be abused, as indicated in the report of the Ethics Advisory Board:

> A number of fears have been expressed with regard to adverse effects of the technological intervention in the reproductive process: fears that such intervention might lead to genetic manipulation or encourage casual experimentation with human embryos, or bring with it the use of surrogate mothers, cloning, or the creation of genetic hybrids. Some have suggested that such research might also have a dehumanizing effect on investigators, the families involved, and society generally.[35]

More recently, several cases have highlighted, but by no means resolved, some actual legal issues that IVF has generated. In one Tennessee divorce case,[36] the wife sued for custody of seven frozen embryos she had created with her husband through an IVF program, declaring that she wanted to use them for implantation purposes. The husband objected to the use of the embryos for reproduction purposes, arguing that because they were joint property, neither he nor the wife should use them in any manner without the consent of the other. The court granted the couple joint control of the embryos, making it necessary for both husband and wife to consent to their use for reproductive purposes.

As with artificial insemination, special consent forms should be used by any provider using IVF. These forms should set forth, as precisely as possible, the procedures to be followed, the responsibility of the would-be parents for any child born as a result of the procedure, and any potential risks to the mother or the child. It is important to make clear to the potential parents that it has not yet been firmly established that this procedure poses no special risks to either the mother or the developing fetus.[37]

Surrogate Parenthood

When the wife is incapable of bearing a child, a couple wishing to become parents may take a rather new approach, the use of the surrogate mother. The husband and wife enter into a contractual relationship with the surrogate mother, who agrees to be artificially inseminated with the husband's sperm, to bear a child, and to relinquish all her rights to the child, to the husband, the biologic father of the child, and his wife. In exchange for her services, the surrogate mother usually receives a fee and payment of all her maternity expenses, such as medical care, lost wages, special clothing, and hospitalization. Such a contractual arrangement relating to the creation of human life raises unique legal issues that the courts and legislatures are just beginning to address.[38]

The Surrogate Parent Contract

Although it is not clear that a surrogate mother contract would be enforceable in any state, such arrangements are generally based on a written agreement between the couple who wish to have a child and the woman who is going to bear the child. The contract may be entered into directly by the three parties, or, when anonymity is desired, an agent may act as intermediary and enter into separate agreements with the surrogate mother and the couple desiring the child.

Under a typical contract, the surrogate agrees (1) to undergo artificial insemination with the semen provided, (2) to carry the pregnancy to term, and (3) to relinquish all rights to the child. If the surrogate is married, her husband should also consent to the agreement and agree to relinquish all parental rights. The written agreement should contain the payment terms and schedules for any fees and expenses involved, a statement on whether insurance policies will be purchased for the surrogate mother or the child, specific language indicating that the money is paid for the service of bearing a child, and any provisions desired to protect the anonymity of the surrogate mother and her husband.

The couple who desire a child are also parties to the agreement. The husband agrees (1) to provide sperm to inseminate the surrogate, (2) to be identified as the natural father of the child, (3) to pay all expenses relating to the pregnancy, (4) to accept custody of and financial responsibility for the child, and (5) to adopt the child legally if necessary. His wife should also be a party to the agreement and should agree to adopt the child (if state law requires) and to care for the child as if the child were her own.

Establishing Legal Parenthood

Under state paternity laws, the birthing mother is generally considered the legal mother. The wife of the biologic father would have to adopt the child to become his or her legal mother.

State legislation governing surrogacy has in some cases provided guidance in determining paternity rights. Arkansas law provides that the intended parents, rather than the surrogate and her husband, are the legal parents.[39] In other states, the surrogate and her husband are deemed the legal parents of the child, and the biologic father must adopt to become the legal parent.

When surrogate parenting legislation does not regulate paternity, state paternity laws presume that if the surrogate is married, her husband is presumed to be the child's legal father. In some states, the presumption cannot be rebutted, and the biologic father in a surrogacy arrangement could not assert his paternity except through adoption procedures.[40]

Legislation governing artificial insemination in nearly half the states further complicates paternity issues in surrogacy arrangements. These statutes provide that a man who donates sperm to a woman who is not his wife is not the legal father of the child.[41] The existence of a contract between the man and the mother of a child providing that the donor will be the legal father can, in some cases, defeat this presumption.

Husband and Wife: Sanctions Preventing Adoption

Criminal sanctions against the sale of babies may pose problems for a couple entering into a contract with a surrogate mother. Legislatures in almost one-half the states have enacted statutes to address such an abuse by prohibiting private adoptions or restricting independent placement for adoption and requiring the use of an adoption agency unless the placement involves a blood relative.[42] Other laws proscribe paying or offering to pay to obtain a parent's consent for adoption or to gain custody of another person.[43] Courts have been inclined to apply adoption legislation prohibiting the adoption of a baby for money to surrogate agreements.

Contract Enforcement and Breach

Whether surrogate contracts fall within the purview of state adoption legislation has become a lesser issue within the broader and more significant issue of whether the contract can be enforced. State legislatures have been active in regulating this issue more than any other aspect of surrogate parenting. Arizona has simply banned surrogacy arrangements,[44] and in Louisiana, legislation states that surrogate motherhood contracts are null, void, and unenforceable as contrary to public policy.[45] Other legislatures have adopted statutes specifically prohibiting surrogate parenting arrangements for profit or gain.

ABORTION

Medically, an abortion may be defined as the premature expulsion from the uterus of the products of conception. An abortion may be classified as spontaneous or induced. An induced abortion can be for the purpose of saving the life of the fetus, saving the life or health of the mother, or terminating the pregnancy to preclude the birth of a child. The attention of the law has focused on the induced abortions that are intended to prevent the birth of a live child.

Historically, the common law did not prohibit induced abortions before the first fetal movements. Many states by statute made induced abortions a crime, whether before or after fetal movements began, unless performed to preserve the life of the mother. These laws were amended in the 1960s and early 1970s to permit induced abortions when there were threats to the physical or mental health of the mother, the child was at risk of severe congenital defects, or the pregnancy resulted from rape or incest. A few states such as New York permitted induced abortions on request up to a designated stage of pregnancy if performed by a licensed physician in a licensed hospital.

The Legal Status of Abortion

In 1973, the U.S. Supreme Court ruled that a state must show a "compelling interest" to support restrictions on the right of a woman to terminate her pregnancy. In *Roe v. Wade,*[46] and its companion case, *Doe v. Bolton,*[47] the Court ruled unconstitutional both a Texas statute that prohibited any abortion not necessary to save the life of the mother and most aspects of a Georgia statute that imposed a variety of stringent procedural restrictions on abortions. The Court said that it was necessary to reach a balance between the woman's right to privacy and the state's interest in protecting maternal health or preserving the life of the fetus.

In the late 1980s, state legislatures forced the Supreme Court to revisit and clarify the precedent created by the *Roe v. Wade* decision. The court responded by ruling in two cases that will no doubt acquire the same importance in judicial history as the case that spawned them. The first of these cases, *Webster v. Reproductive Health Services,*[48] involved a Missouri statute declaring in its preamble that human life begins at conception. The law prohibits public employees from performing or assisting with abortions not necessary to save the life of the mother, stipulates that no public funds may be used for the purpose of encouraging or counseling a woman to have an abortion, and requires a physician to conduct tests to determine the viability of the fetus when planning to perform an abortion on a woman whom the physician suspects or knows is 20 weeks or more pregnant. The Supreme Court swept aside the lower court rulings in a decision that broadens state authority to restrict abortions at any stage of pregnancy while stopping short of formally reversing *Roe v. Wade.*

In a sharply divided opinion, the U.S. Supreme Court ruled that neither the factual basis nor the legal principles underlying the *Roe v. Wade* decision had changed, and it therefore reaffirmed that decision. In accordance with *Roe,* the Court asserted, a woman has the right before the fetus is viable to obtain an abortion without undue state interference. After viability, a state can restrict and even prohibit abortions except when the patient's health is endangered. The Court rejected, however, the rigid trimester framework to determine the point of viability as enunciated in *Roe.* Medical advancements that change the point of viability do not affect the notion of viability as a critical starting point to determine the constitutional validity of state intervention, the Court declared. The state also has legitimate interests throughout pregnancy in protecting the woman's health and the fetus' potential life. To protect the central right to an abortion while at the same time accommodating state interests, the Court ruled that the undue burden standard should be used. Legislation places an undue burden on a woman's right to an abortion if its purpose or effect is to place substantial obstacles to her seeking an abortion before the fetus attains viability.

Although the precise significance of the *Webster* decision is not yet determined, this decision does contain some guidelines on the constitutional validity of state abortion regulations. Notably, the Supreme Court has swept aside the trimester framework that had served to determine the permissible degree of state interference at various stages of pregnancy. Rather, the point of viability determines whether a woman has a constitutionally protected right to an abortion. After viability, a woman's constitutional liberty to terminate a pregnancy is extinguished. Accordingly, states may prohibit abortions after viability, as long as the prohibition contains exceptions for pregnancies that endanger a woman's life or health.

Before viability, however, a woman's right to choose to terminate or continue a pregnancy is constitutionally protected against undue state interference. A state's interest in potential life is not strong enough at this stage of pregnancy to support a prohibition on abortion. Accordingly, states are "free to enact laws to provide a reasonable framework for a woman to make a decision that has such profound and lasting meaning, as long as their regulations do not impose an 'undue burden' on a woman's right to an abortion."[49]

Status of State and Local Regulation

Under the *Roe* decision, the standard for review of state legislation was one of strict scrutiny within the trimester framework. During the first trimester of pregnancy, the state had almost no power to restrict or regulate abortion, because neither the state's interest in protecting maternal health nor that in protecting the fetus outweighed the woman's right of privacy in procreative decision making.

During the second trimester, the state was deemed to have a compelling interest in the health of the mother and could regulate the abortion procedure, provided that the regulation was reasonably related to the preservation and protection of maternal health.

The state's compelling interest in the protection of potential life was considered dominant as of the third trimester because the fetus becomes viable. The Supreme Court recognized, however, that viability is ultimately a matter of medical judgment, skill, and technical ability.[50] Accordingly, a statute defining viability based strictly on the duration of pregnancy was invalidated.[51] In addition, to protect fetal life, a state could proscribe abortion in the third trimester except when necessary to preserve the life or health of the mother.[52]

In short, the trimester framework allowed the state to place increasingly stringent restrictions on abortion as the pregnancy progressed, provided they were justified by the compelling state interest to be served by the restriction. Many state legislatures enacted statutes in which they attempted to regulate abortion in accordance with the principles of the trimester framework, in such areas as informed consent, spousal and parental notification and consent, permissible medical procedures, zoning, mandatory reporting requirements, and funding limitations.

The U.S. Supreme Court significantly altered its position on the validity of state regulations, however, in the *Casey* decision.[53] By rejecting the trimester framework and adopting viability as the reference point for establishing the degree to which states can regulate abortion, the Court has generated uncertainty about what restrictions are now permissible.

State Regulations

The ultimate test of various state efforts to regulate abortion is the undue burden standard. Accordingly, a state has legitimate interests in protecting a woman's health and a fetus' potential life throughout pregnancy. State regulations, however, may not unduly interfere with a woman's right to obtain an abortion before the fetus is viable. After viability, a state may ban abortions, as long as the regulations provide exceptions if the patient's health is endangered. The following sections will examine specific types of state regulations.

Parental and Spousal Consent. Generally, statutes requiring parental or spousal consent as a precondition to an abortion have been struck down. In *Planned Parenthood of Central Missouri v. Danforth,*[54] in which a statute requiring parental consent to abortions for unmarried women younger than 18 years of age and spousal consent to abortion for a married woman was challenged, the Supreme Court struck down both requirements, stating that "clearly, since the State cannot regulate or proscribe abortion during the first stage, when the physician and his patient make that decision, the State cannot delegate authority to any particular person, even the spouse, to prevent abortion during that same period."[55] Other courts have used the same reasoning to disapprove an absolute requirement for parental approval.[56] Even under the Supreme Court's more recent use of viability as a starting point for measuring the legitimacy of state regulations, parental and spousal consent requirements would likely be struck down.

Parental and Spousal Consultation/Notification. The U.S. Supreme Court ruling in *Casey* clearly holds that spousal notification requirements unduly burden a woman's right to seek an abortion. In this case, a Pennsylvania statute prohibited physicians from performing abortions unless the patients had provided signed statements indicating that they had notified their husbands of their intent. The Court rejected the argument that a father's interest in a fetus' welfare is equal to the mother's protected right to an abortion, because state regulation with respect to the fetus will have a far greater impact on a pregnant woman's bodily integrity than it will on the father.

Parental notification statutes have frequently been upheld, especially when they provide a judicial alternative to notification before a physician performs an abortion. In *H.L. v. Matheson,*[57] for example, the U.S. Supreme Court upheld a Utah statute that required physicians to "notify if possible" the parents or guardian of an unmarried minor who sought an abortion.

Some parental notification statutes have been struck down, however, when more than simple notification is required. For example, a Georgia parental notification law was ruled unconstitutional by a federal trial court because it required the minor to verify that she notified a parent or guardian of her decision to obtain an abortion by having the parent or other adult accompany the minor to the abortion clinic to furnish an affidavit that the parent was notified.[58]

In *Hodgson v. Minnesota,*[59] the Supreme Court allowed a 48-hour two-parent notice requirement if it coexisted with a judicial bypass procedure. The 48-hour waiting period provides a parent the opportunity to consult with a spouse or family physician and inquire into the competence of the physician performing the procedure. Therefore, the Court declared, the delay imposes only a minimal burden on the right of a pregnant minor to decide whether to terminate her pregnancy. The Court found, however, that not only does the two-parent notification requirement not further any legitimate state interest, it disserves the state's interest in protecting minors in dysfunctional families.

Judicial Consent. The presence of a judicial bypass mechanism, creating an exemption to parental consent or notification requirements if a minor obtains court authorization to proceed with an abortion, has often been a factor in courts' decisions to uphold or strike down such requirements. In *Belloti v. Baird,*[60] the Court ruled that the state must provide the pregnant minor with a timely and confidential opportunity to show that she is mature enough and well enough informed to make her own abortion decision, in consultation with her physician.[61] If the court or other responsible agency finds the minor not sufficiently mature to give consent, it must authorize an abortion if this is found to be in the girl's best interests.[62] If the legislation contains these provisions, then requiring parental consent would not constitute the "absolute, and possibly arbitrary veto"[63] that was found impermissible in *Danforth.*

In the 1992 *Casey* decision, the Court applied its 1983 ruling in *Akron,* that state regulations requiring parental consent are constitutional as long as the statute provides for an adequate judicial bypass procedure.

Informed Consent. The two issues that courts have struggled with perhaps the most since the *Roe v. Wade* decision concern state attempts to regulate informed consent requirements and mandatory waiting periods for abortion procedures. In *Danforth*,[64] the Supreme Court ruled that a state may require written consent before an abortion. In that case, the Court construed informed consent to mean simply telling the woman "just what would be done and . . . its consequences."

Subsequently, many states enacted legislation setting forth in great detail the information that a woman seeking an abortion must be given.[65] The Supreme Court had the opportunity to review this type of restriction in *City of Akron v. Akron Center for Reproductive Health.*[66] The Supreme Court held that the state had an interest in protecting the health of a pregnant woman, by ensuring that the "important and stressful" decision to abort is made with full knowledge of its nature and consequences.[67] The Court ruled, however, that the government could not decide what specific information the woman must be given. Rather, the Court concluded, it is the responsibility of the physician "to ensure that appropriate information is conveyed to the patient depending on her particular circumstances."[68]

Counseling Requirements. The issue of state-mandated counseling requirements overlaps to some extent with state requirements that physicians or nurse-midwives provide specific information to patients seeking abortions. As is discussed above in the section dealing with informed consent, under the Supreme Court's holding in *Casey,* states may require that women seeking abortions obtain specific information drafted to discourage them from pursuing this course of action. States have not attempted to impose other types of "counseling" requirements, and the *Casey* opinion is therefore the current authority on this issue.

In *Casey,* the Court explicitly overruled its holding in *Akron* regarding mandatory waiting periods. The Court simply stated that its previous ruling on this issue was wrong in theory and found that in practice, waiting periods do not pose a substantial obstacle to obtaining an abortion.

Reporting Requirements. In the *Casey* decision,[69] the Court once again addressed reporting provisions requiring facilities to file reports identifying the physician, the facility, the woman's age, number of prior pregnancies and abortions, fetal gestational age, the type of abortion procedure, the basis for determining that the abortion was medically necessary, the weight of the aborted fetus, whether the woman was married, and if so whether notice had been given her husband. The Court ruled that these requirements met the standards enunciated in *Danforth,* with the exception of the spousal notification provisions.

Another type of reporting requirement in abortion legislation requires victims of rape and incest to report the crimes to the police or child protective agency before the state will subsidize their abortions. A Pennsylvania trial court upheld such a provision, finding that the state's interests in prosecuting criminals outweighs the abortion patients' right to privacy.[70] A patient's constitutionally protected privacy right to withhold personal information when obtaining a subsidized abortion is not absolute, the court concluded, and the individual's privacy right in this case must be balanced against the state's interest in deterring crime.

Conduct Surrounding Abortion Clinics

Recently, another issue regarding access to abortion clinics and what is permissible conduct in the areas surrounding clinics has emerged. In particular, protests that block access to abortion clinics by pro-life groups have generated a substantial amount of litigation. Protestors have been successfully sued on state grounds of trespass, public and private nuisance, interference with business relations,[71] and intentional infliction of emotional distress. Courts have in some instances enjoined protestors from harassing and intimidating patients,[72] entering clinics,[73] or limiting the number of protestors allowed to demonstrate in one geographic area at any given time.[74]

The litigation has also raised the issue about whether such conduct violates federal civil rights law. The issue reached the U.S. Supreme Court in the early 1990s in a suit by abortion clinics to enjoin protesters from demonstrating in front of facilities.[75] Opposition to abortion is not analogous to race discrimination, the Court declared, because the protests do not reflect animosity against women in general. Although the demonstrations are directed at women, they are intended to protect the victims of abortion, stop its practice, and make it illegal, the Court concluded.

Conscience Clauses

Because the performance of abortions conflicts with the moral or ethical codes of certain organized religions and of many individuals, many states have enacted laws that allow institutions to choose whether they will provide abortion services and practitioners to choose whether they will participate in abortion procedures.[76] Several courts have ruled that private hospitals may refuse to perform abortions.[77] Although private hospitals may refuse to permit abortions, public hospitals may not.[78]

Some courts have held that only private hospitals acting in accord with formalized institutional beliefs may prohibit abortions in their facilities.[79] In *Doe v. Bridgeton Hospital Association,* the court held that, unlike a private Catholic or denominational hospital, a private, nonsectarian eleemosynary institution presenting its facilities to the general public for use cannot use moral concepts to rationalize a prohibition against the performance of abortions.

When a hospital does permit abortions, state law may make it unlawful to fire an employee, such as a nurse, who refuses to participate in abortion procedures. It appears that such a nurse may be transferred to another comparable position,[80] however, so long as the transfer does not cause the nurse to suffer any detriment in pay, benefits, seniority, or working conditions.

Funding for Abortions

Although access to abortions may not be restricted, neither federal nor state governments are required to pay for abortions for indigent women. In 1976, Congress limited the federal government's participation in the funding of abortions for indigent women by enacting the Hyde Amendment as a rider to an appropriations bill. The Hyde Amendment—which has been reenacted each year since 1976—prohibits the use of federal Medicaid funds for abortions, except when "the life of the mother would be endangered if the fetus were carried to term."[81]

POSTBIRTH LIABILITY

In conjunction with the growing availability of contraceptive devices and agents, sterilization, and abortion, the advances in medical science that have made it possible to identify, either preconception or early in pregnancy, the existence of genetically transmitted or transmissible abnormalities have led many potential parents to expect that the birth of a child can be a planned event. If either the birth itself or the condition of the child is unexpected, parents are inclined to initiate litigation. These suits often claim that the child was injured as a result of acts or omissions occurring before conception, that the defective child was born because of a failure to provide genetic counseling or adequate testing, or that the child was born because an abortion or sterilization was negligently performed.

Whatever the factual basis for them, such complaints are generally couched in terms of negligence, and the elements of the cause of action are those necessary to sustain any negligence action: a legal duty, a breach of that duty, damages, and a causal relationship between the breach of duty and the damages sustained. Because the tort actions arising from birth-related claims seek to prove these elements based on facts and circumstances that raise profound moral, philosophic, and religious questions, it is not surprising that the courts had difficulty in resolving many of these matters.

Preconception and Prenatal Negligence

Today, there is legal recognition that a fetus who is injured or killed before birth as a result of a tort committed against his or her mother has a cause of action.[82] A Michigan appeals court has held that a health care provider who fails to test for or immunize a woman against rubella may be liable for injuries to a child not yet conceived.[83] The court found the health care providers liable for preconception negligence, emphasizing that the specific purpose of rubella immunizations is to alleviate the type of injury the child had sustained in this case.

Genetic Counseling

Advances in both genetic knowledge and medical technology have now made it possible for a physician to predict the likelihood that prospective parents will give birth to children with certain genetically transmitted defects. Tests of amniotic fluid are now commonly available to detect the presence of many genetic abnormalities, including Down's syndrome, Tay-Sachs disease, sickle cell disorder, and neural tube defects. The sex of the fetus can also be determined. Amniocentesis or chorionic villa sampling (CVS) is now generally recommended for pregnant women older than age 35, those with a history of multiple miscarriages, or those with certain genetic histories.

Because amniocentesis and CVS involve some potential risk to the fetus, it is important that this risk be disclosed and that the informed consent of the mother (or both parents)[84] to the procedure be obtained and documented. If the mother decides not to undergo the procedure, even though it is indicated because of her age or family history, the record should include documentation that the test was offered and discussed. When amniocentesis or CVS is performed, it should be determined whether the parents wish to learn the child's sex in advance of birth; if state law permits, parental wishes in this regard should be followed.[85]

The purpose of preconception or in utero genetic screening, counseling, or testing is to provide the potential parents with information so they may exercise their right to choose contraception or abortion. The health care provider has an obligation—under certain circumstances—to provide access to available genetic information, but the choice of contraception, sterilization, or abortion, however, is that of the potential parents.

Blood tests can be performed shortly after birth to detect certain genetically based treatable disorders, such as phenylketonuria (PKU), a condition producing severe mental retardation. Such testing may be mandated by state or local law.[86] Even if such testing is not required by law, it should be offered and its importance explained to avoid liability for failure to identify this condition while it is still treatable.

In any claim alleging a failure of genetic testing or counseling, the critical issue is the fact that the alleged negligence deprived the parents of their constitutionally protected right to procreative choice or, with PKU children, treatment. The claim does not allege that the negligence caused the genetic defect. In addition, failure to disclose to parents the risk of children being born with a genetic abnormality has been held to constitute negligent nondisclosure by a Minnesota appeals court under the informed consent theory of liability because genetic counseling is "treatment," which must be disclosed to the parents so that they can make a major informed health care decision.[87]

Wrongful Birth/Wrongful Life Lawsuits

The increase in the availability of birth control, including sterilization, the greater knowledge of human genetics, and the liberalized access to abortion have created situations in which traditional tort law analysis is applied to the birth of children. The basic allegation in such cases is that negligence by a physician, nurse-midwife, or some other provider resulted in the birth of a child who is unwanted for socioeconomic reasons or because of deformities that could have been detected. Lawsuits based on these facts are generally referred to as wrongful birth, wrongful conception, or wrongful life claims. Although the claims all spring from the same event, the birth of an undesired child, the causes of action are quite different.

Wrongful birth (or wrongful conception) is a cause of action brought by a parent or parents who claim that, but for a breach of duty on the part of a physician, nurse practitioner, genetic counselor, or laboratory, the child would not have been born. Although most of the cases in this category involve the birth of an abnormal child, allegedly because of a failure to advise or to test the potential parents for genetically based problems, similar suits are being filed when a healthy child is born after an attempted abortion or sterilization.

Wrongful life, however, is a cause of action brought by a child who claims harm by virtue of being born abnormal. To date, such claims have been brought only by children who were born with a diagnosable genetically linked condition (e.g., Down's syndrome or Tay-Sachs disease) or those who were born with a defect because of their mother's exposure to an improperly diagnosed illness, often rubella, during the early stages of pregnancy.

In each of these causes of action, it is necessary to determine whether liability should be imposed as a result of the alleged negligence and, if there is liability, how damages are to be measured. Because application of tort principles to claims arising from the birth of children raises ethical and religious issues, the courts have had some difficulty in dealing with these cases and have arrived at a variety of results.

Wrongful Birth/Conception

Wrongful birth litigation has traditionally followed the birth of a child with an impairment that could have been predicted or identified by reasonably available procedures such as amniocentesis. Such a claim alleges the negligent failure by a physician or other provider either to detect the impairment or to advise the parents that an impairment was possible. The basis for the parents' action is that they were denied their right to choose to prevent or abort the pregnancy because of this failure. The most difficult issue in such cases is damages. Some states have enacted laws prohibiting suits for wrongful birth and wrongful life.[88]

Failure to Diagnose. Failure to diagnose a pregnancy or a disease (such as rubella) that threatens the well-being of the fetus in sufficient time to permit a safe abortion may result in a wrongful birth claim.

Rubella during early pregnancy creates a serious risk of birth defects, and the failure to diagnose the disease carries a significant potential for liability. In one such case, the parents of a severely retarded child sued both the hospital and the physician for failing to diagnose the mother's rubella when she went to the emergency department one month into her pregnancy. The court allowed the claim, concluding that damages should equal the excess cost required to raise the impaired child over that which it would otherwise cost to raise a normal, healthy child.[89]

As long as abortion remains an option allowed by law, a physician owes a duty to provide prospective parents with adequate information to enable them to decide whether to choose that course of action. In Kansas, the parents of a child born with severe and permanent birth defects were allowed to sue based on the claim that had they been properly advised of the risks or existence of birth defects, they would have terminated the pregnancy.[90]

Failure to Test. In many states, a cause of action has been recognized on behalf of parents who give birth to an abnormal child because a physician has negligently failed to test for genetic problems, where indicated, and to identify parental genetic traits that may lead to impaired children. Liability may also attach if an abnormal child is born after negligent performance of genetic screening.

A finding of liability in cases involving genetic testing or screening involves the application of negligence principles to a recently developed medical procedure. Although the damages awarded differ, the prevailing rule in such cases appears to be that, if negligence is established, the parents are entitled to compensation for direct economic losses, for those costs of raising the impaired child that exceed the costs of raising a healthy child, and for emotional suffering.[91]

Wrongful Life

Wrongful life is a cause of action that has been brought only by children who were born with an impairment that, it is alleged, could and should have been recognized in time to prevent conception or terminate the pregnancy. For the most part, such actions have been rejected by the courts on the ground that there is no recognized legal right not to be born and that, therefore, there is no basis for awarding damages because of existence.[92]

Courts in some states have, however, departed from the majority rule and recognized a cause of action for wrongful life. In *Curlender v. Bio-Science Laboratories*,[93] a California appeals court became the first to recognize the concept of wrongful life and awarded damages to an infant plaintiff against a laboratory that had performed genetic screening tests and failed to tell the parents of potential genetic defects in the then-unborn fetus. The Supreme Court of California ruled that the damaged infant could not recover general damages but could recover any special expenses for teaching, training, or equipment if the parents did not claim such damages in their cause of action.

The Washington Supreme Court has also allowed damaged infants to recover the costs of medical expenses, therapy, training, and other special costs but disallowed their claim for pain and suffering.[94]

In reviewing children's claims that they should not have been born, the courts have struggled with the metaphysical question of life in an impaired state versus nonexistence.[95] One issue that has disturbed the courts is the potential—if the wrongful life cause of action were recognized against physicians, it might be expanded by the child to include a cause of action against the parent for permitting an abnormal child to be born. California has enacted a statute that precludes children from suing their parents for bearing them.[96]

CONCLUSION

Reproductive issues present special challenges to nurses and nurse practitioners given the emotional issues surrounding the beginning of life and the various perspectives that are present in this area. Contraception and sterilization issues raise patients' rights issues. Abortion remains recognized as legal in the United States, but the procedure is subject to an increasing variety of restrictions at both the federal and state level. Postbirth liability remains an area of potential litigation. Nurses who work in this area are faced with a number of challenges—personally, emotionally, ethically, professionally, and legally—in the care they provide to their patients.

FOOTNOTES

1. Griswold v. Connecticut, 381 U.S. 479 (1965).
2. Eisenstadt v. Baird, 405 U.S. 438 (1972).
3. *Id.* at 453.
4. Carey v. Population Servs. Int'l, 431 U.S. 678 (1977).
5. *Id.* at 693–694.
6. Doe v. Irving, 615 F.2d 1162 (6th Cir. 1980).

7. Doe v. Pickett, 480 F. Supp. 1218 (S.D.W.Va. 1979).

8. 810 F.2d 984 (10th Cir. 1987).

9. *E.g.,* Godard v. Ridgway, 445 P.2d 757 (Wyo.1968); Doyle v. Planned Parenthood, 639 P.2d 240 (Wash. 1982); McKee v. Moore, 648 P.2d 21 (Okla. 1982); Sciacca v. Polizzi, 403 So. 2d 728 (La. 1981).

10. 42 C.F.R. §§ 441.250–441.259.

11. California Med. Ass'n v. Lachner, 124 Cal. App. 3d 28, 177 Cal. Rptr. 188 (1981).

12. *See, e.g.,* Sims v. University of Ark. Med. Ctr., No. LR 76-C-67 (E.D. Ark. March 4, 1977).

13. Hathaway v. Worcester City Hosp., 475 F.2d 701 (1st Cir. 1973).

14. Taylor v. St. Vincent Hosp., 523 F.2d 75 (9th Cir. 1975), *cert. denied,* 434 U.S. 948 (1976).

15. Walker v. Pierce, 522 P.2d 302 (4th Cir. 1977).

16. Murray v. Vandevander, 522 P.2d 302 (Okla. Ct. App. 1974).

17. *E.g.,* GA. CODE ANN. § 25-6-102; N.C. GEN. STAT. § 90-271. *But see* Bellotti v. Baird, 443 U.S. 622, 99 S. Ct. 3035 (1979), in which the requirement of parental consent, in the context of abortions, was construed as unconstitutionally burdensome.

18. H.L. v. Matheson, 450 U.S. 298, 101 S. Ct. 1164 (1981).

19. Doe v. Bellin Mem'l Hosp., 479 F.2d 756 (7th Cir. 1973).

20. Hathaway v. Worcester City Hosp., 475 F.2d 701 (1st Cir. 1973).

21. *E.g.,* ILL. COMP. STAT. ch. 111½, §§ 5301–5314; MASS. GEN. LAWS ANN. ch. 112, § 121; MONT. CODE ANN. § 50-5-502; OR. REV. STAT. § 435.485.

22. Swanson v. St. John's Lutheran Hosp., 597 P.2d 702 (Mont. 1979).

23. Padin v. Fordham Hosp., 392 F. Supp. 447 (S.D.N.Y. 1975).

24. STEDMAN'S MEDICAL DICTIONARY 714 (5th Lawyer's Ed. 1983).

25. CAL. CIV. CODE § 7005; COLO. REV. STAT. § 19-4-106; GA. CODE ANN. § 43-34-42; KAN. STAT. ANN. § 23-128 to 129; N.C. GEN. STAT. § 49A-1; OR. REV. STAT. §§ 109.239–109.247.

26. *E.g.,* OR. REV. STAT. § 677.360; GA. CODE ANN. § 43-34-42(a); OKLA. STAT. ANN. tit. 10, §§ 551–553.

27. Wadlington, Walter. *Artificial Insemination: The Dangers of a Poorly Kept Secret,* 64 Nw. U. L. REV. 777, 796 (1970).

28. Carey v. Population Serv. Int'l, 431 U.S. 678, (1977); Planned Parenthood v. Danforth, 428 U.S. 52 (1976); Roe v. Wade, 410 U.S. 113 (1973); Eisenstadt v. Baird, 405 U.S. 438 (1972); Griswold v. Connecticut, 381 U.S. 479 (1965).

29. Greenbert & Hirsh, *Surrogate Motherhood and Artificial Insemination: Contractual Implications,* MED. TRIAL TECH. Q. 165 (Fall 1982).

30. For a rare case in which an AID did intend to take on the responsibilities of parenthood, *see* McIntyre v. Crouch. No. CA A44574 (Or. Ct. App. 1989), *cert. denied,* 100 S. Ct. 1924 (1990). *See also* In the Interest of R.C., 775 P.2d 27 (Colo. 1989).

31. Edwards & Steptoe, *Biological Aspects of Embryo Transfer,* Symposium on Legal and Other Aspects of Artificial Insemination by Donor (A.I.D.) and Embryo Transfer, CIBA Foundation, 11 (1972). Comment, *The Use of In Vitro Fertilization: Is There a Right to Bear or Beget a Child by Any Available Medical Means?* 12 PEPP. L. REV. 1033 (1985).

32. LA. REV. STAT. ANN. §§ 9:121–9:133.

33. LA. REV. STAT. ANN. § 9:126.

34. Edwards & Steptoe, *supra* note 31, emphasizing that "embryo transfer will be used almost exclusively for many years to come to alleviate infertility within a marriage, by giving husbands and wives a chance to have their own children. Relatively few women need an oocyte or embryo from a donor to alleviate their infertility; such treatment will be limited to only a small number of patients."

35. 44 Fed. Reg. 35,056 (June 18, 1979); *see also* Lorio, *In Vitro Fertilization and Embryo Transfer: Fertile Areas for Litigations,* SPECIALTY L. DIG.: HEALTH CARE, Feb. 1983, at 5. Note, *Tempest in the Laboratory: Medical Research on Spare Embryos from In Vitro Fertilization,* 37 HASTINGS L.J. 977 (May 1987).

36. Davis v. Davis, No. 180 (Tenn. Ct. App. Sept. 13, 1990). Note that the Tennessee Supreme Court affirmed the appeals court ruling, specifically stating that the embryos cannot be used for implantation in the biologic mother or any other woman without the father's consent and that they are not entitled to protection as persons under federal law. Davis v. Davis, 842 S.W.2d 588 (Tenn. 1992).

37. For a discussion of legal risks in the in vitro fertilization process, *see* Hubble, *Liability of the Physician for the Defects of a Child Caused by In-Vitro Fertilization,* J. LEGAL MED. 501 (1981); Flannery et al., *Test Tube Babies: Legal Issues Raised by In-Vitro Fertilization,* 67 GEO. L.J. 1295 (1979); Lorio, *supra* note 35; Comment, *In Vitro Fertilization: Third Party Motherhood and the Changing Definition of Legal Parent,* 17 PAC. L.J. 231 (Oct. 1985).

38. For a discussion of the issues involved in a surrogate arrangement, *see Surrogate Mothers: The Legal Issues,* 7 AM. J.L. & MED. 323 (Fall 1981); Brophy, *A Surrogate Mother's Contract to Bear a Child,* 20 J. FAM. L. 263 (1981–82).

39. ARK. CODE ANN. § 9-10-201 (1991). Note that this provision only applies to uncompensated surrogacy.

40. ALA. CODE § 26-17-6(c) (1986); COLO. REV. STAT. § 19-6-1107(3) (1986); W. VA. CODE § 48-A-6-1(7) (1989). These statues provide that a man claiming to be the biologic father can only make such a claim if there is no presumed father.

41. *See, e.g.,* ALA. CODE § 26-17-21(b) (1986); CAL. CIV. CODE § 7005(b); MO. ANN. STAT. § 210.824 (1989).

42. *See* ARIZ. REV. STAT. ANN. § 8-105; COLO. REV. STAT. § 19-5-206; CONN. GEN. STAT. ANN. § 17a-149; KY. REV. STAT. ANN. § 199.473; N.H. STAT. ANN. § 170-B:8.

43. *See, e.g.,* CAL. PENAL CODE § 181.

44. ARIZ. REV. STAT. ANN. § 25-218(4).

45. LA. REV. STAT. ANN. § 9:2713.

46. 410 U.S. 113, 93 S. Ct. 705 (1973).

47. 410 U.S. at 179, 93 S. Ct. at 739.

48. 109 S. Ct. 3040 (1989).

49. Planned Parenthood v. Casey, 744 F. Supp. 1323 (E.D. Pa. 1990); 947 F.2d 682 (3d Cir. 1990).

50. Planned Parenthood v. Danforth, *supra* note 28, at 2836 fn.110.

51. Hodgson v. Anderson, 378 F. Supp. 1008 (D. Minn. 1974), *appeal dismissed,* 420 U.S. 903 (1975).

52. Roe v. Wade, 93 S. Ct. 705 (1973).

53. 112 S. Ct. 2791 (1992).

54. 428 U.S. 52, 96 S. Ct. 2831 (1976).

55. 428 U.S. at 69, 96 S. Ct. at 2841; Doe v. Doe, 314 N.E.2d 128 (Mass. 1974).

56. State v. Koome, 530 P.2d 260 (1975).

57. 450 U.S. 398, 1101 S. Ct. 1164 (1981).

58. Planned Parenthood Ass'n v. Harris, 670 F. Supp. 971 (N.D. Ga. 1987).

59. 110 S. Ct. 2926 (1990).

60. 443 U.S. 662, 99 S. Ct. 3035 (1979).

61. 443 U.S. at 643, 99 S. Ct. at 3048.

62. *Id.*

63. *Id.*

64. Planned Parenthood v. Danforth, 428 U.S. 52 (1976).

65. *See, e.g.,* ILL. REV. STAT. ch 38 §§ 81-23.2, 81-23.5.

66. 103 S. Ct. 2481.

67. *Id.* at 2499.

68. *Id.* at 2500.

69. 112 S. Ct. 2792 (1992).

70. Fischer v. Department of Public Welfare, 543 A.2d 177 (Pa. Commw. Ct. 1988).

71. Women's Health Care Servs. v. Operation Rescue-National, 733 F. Supp. 258 (D. Kan. 1991).

72. Parkland Co. v. Pro-Life Counseling Inc., 88 A.2d 534 (1982) and Bering v. Share, 721 P.2d 918 (1986).

73. Northern Va. Women's Med. Ctr. v. Balch, 617 F.2d 1045 (4th Cir. 1980).

74. Bachelier v. Hamilton County, Ohio, 931 F.2d 893 (6th Cir. 1991).

75. Bray v. Alexandria Women's Health Clinic, 113 S. Ct. 753 (U.S. 1993).

76. *E.g.,* ILL. COMP. STAT. ch. 111 , §§ 5301–5314.

77. *See, e.g.,* Doe v. Berlin Mem'l Hosp., 479 F.2d 756 (7th Cir. 1973); Watkins v. Mercy Med. Ctr, 364 F. Supp. 799 (D. Idaho 1973).

78. Nyberg v. City of Virginia, 667 F.2d 754 (8th Cir. 1982).

79. Doe v. Charleston Area Med. Ctr., 529 F.2d 638 (4th Cir. 1975).

80. Swanson v. St. John's Lutheran Hosp., 597 P.2d 702 (Mont. 1979); Jeczalik v. Valley Hosp., 434 A.2d 90 (N.J. Super. 1980).

81. Department of Labor and Health, Education, and Welfare Appropriations Act of 1977, Pub. L. No. 94-439, § 209, 90 Stat. 1418, 1434 (1976).

82. Peters, *Wrongful Life: Recognizing the Defective Child's Right to a Cause of Action,* 18 DUQ. L. REV. 857, 862 (1980). *But see* Walker v. Rinck, 566 N.E.2d 1088 (Ind. Ct. App. 1991), in which the court refused to recognize a tort for children born with disabilities caused by negligent prenatal care to their mothers.

83. Monusko v. Postle, No. 95314 (Mich. Ct. App. Feb. 23, 1989).

84. *See* Reiser v. Lohner, 641 P.2d 93 (Utah 1982), in which it was ruled that the consent of the mother alone is sufficient.

85. Some physicians and geneticists are reluctant to reveal fetal sex because of a fear that parents whose child is the "wrong" sex may choose abortion. *See* Solens & Swazey, *Sex and the Single Chromosome,* GENETICS AND THE LAW 259 (1980).

86. *E.g.,* ILL REV. STAT. ch. 111½, § 4903.

87. Pratt v. University of Minn. Affiliated Hosps. & Clinics, 403 N.W.2d 865 (Minn. Ct. App. 1987).

88. *See, e.g.,* ME. REV. STAT. ANN. tit. 24 § 2931. *See also* PA. CONS. STAT. tit. 42 §§ 8305–8306.

89. Dumer v. St. Michael's Hosp., 233 N.W.2d 372 (Wis. 1975).

90. Arche v. United States, 798 P.2d 447 (Kan. 1990).

91. Surrogate Parenting v. Commissioner *ex. rel.* Armstrong, 704 S.W.2d 209 (Ky. 1986).

92. Becker v. Schwartz, 386 N.E.2d 807, 812 (N.Y. 1978); Azzolino v. Dingfelder, 337 S.E.2d 528 (N.C. 1985); Ellis v. Sherman, 515 A.2d 1327 (Pa. 1986); Bruggeman v. Schimke, 718 P.2d 635 (Kan. 1986); Smith v. Cote, 513 A.2d 341 (N.H. 1986). *See also* Atlanta Obstetrics & Gynecology Group v. Abelson, 398 S.E.2d 557 (Ga. 1990).

93. 165 Cal. Rptr. 477 (1980), *rev'd on other grounds.*

94. Harbeson v. Parke-Davis, Inc., 656 P.2d 483 (Wash. 1983).

95. Many commentators have also addressed the issue. *See* Waters, *Wrongful Life: The Implications of Suits in Wrongful Life Brought by Children against Their Parents,* 31 DRAKE L. REV. 411 (1981–82); Brown, *Wrongful Life: A Misconceived Tort—An Introduction,* HEALTH CARE L. DIG. 5 (Dec. 1982); Peters, *Wrongful Life: Recognizing the Defective Child's Right to a Cause of Action,* 18 DUQ. L. REV. 857 (1980); Pace, *The Treatment of Injury in Wrongful Life Claims,* 20 COLUM. J.L. & SOC. PROBS. 145 (1986).

96. CAL. CIV. CODE § 43.6.

Chapter 11

AIDS in Health Care

Chapter Objectives

1. To discuss access to care
2. To outline confidentiality issues
3. To examine exposure or infection by health care workers or patients
4. To review employment laws that protect HIV-positive individuals
5. To consider HIV issues specific to health care workers

As the acquired immune deficiency syndrome (AIDS) epidemic has grown, so too have the legal issues that have arisen because of this disease. Although every aspect of society has been affected by the spread of the human immunodeficiency virus (HIV), nurses, physicians, and other health care personnel must face legal issues that do not arise in other contexts. Nurses and other health care providers are confronted with issues such as providing nursing and medical treatment, patient testing, and confidentiality of medical information. In addition, AIDS presents areas of potential liability arising from patient care treatment. Nurses and other health care employees must be aware of the legal issues regarding AIDS in the workplace. Because of the uniqueness of health care facilities, however, nurses and other health care providers face employment issues that do not arise in other contexts.

ACCESS TO CARE

The question may arise as to whether providers must accept HIV-positive patients for treatment. Both private and public hospitals are subject to state and federal laws designed to ensure access to health care for various groups. Several of these laws appear to apply to HIV-positive patients.

Nonemergency

Hill-Burton Act regulations contain a community service provision that requires a facility constructed with federal assistance to provide services to those residing in the facility service area "without discrimination on the ground of race, color, national origin, creed, or any other ground unrelated to an individual's need for the service or the availability of the needed service in the facility."[1]

According to the Rehabilitation Act of 1973, hospitals receiving Medicare or Medicaid funds or a Hill-Burton grant cannot deny hospitalization or treatment to a person merely because that person is handicapped. In one case, a hospital was found liable under the Rehabilitation Act for the refusal of one of its medical staff members to perform elective surgery on an HIV-infected patient.[2] Several courts have specifically ruled that AIDS is a protected handicap under the Rehabilitation Act.[3]

Other statutes are applicable to AIDS patients. The Americans with Disabilities Act of 1990 (ADA) prohibits places of public accommodation from discriminating against the handicapped in the provision of goods and services[4] and has been specifically held applicable to AIDS. In addition, many states have public accommodation laws that cover hospital services and prohibit discrimination on the basis of handicap or disability.

Emergency

The Emergency Medical Treatment and Active Labor Act sets forth parameters regarding the treatment and transfer of all patients.[5] Individuals who come to the emergency department seeking treatment must be examined to determine if an "emergency medical condition" exists. An *emergency medical condition* is defined as an illness so severe that lack of treatment will put the health of the patient in serious jeopardy or will seriously impair bodily functions or organs. If the patient does have an emergency medical condition, the patient must be treated until the condition is stabilized.

Patient Testing

HIV blood testing for the purpose of diagnosis and treatment is considered medically appropriate. Most states with HIV-specific laws (e.g., California and New York) require written informed consent before HIV testing.[6] In other states, special consent may not be required for routine blood testing. Because of the far-reaching consequences, both medical and social, of a positive HIV test, however, specific consent for HIV blood testing is highly recommended.

In Tennessee, for example, a new law allows hospitals to test blood of a patient for HIV or hepatitis B (HBV) if a nurse or other health care provider at the facility is exposed to the blood or other body fluid of the patient. The testing must be confidential and at no charge to the patient.[7]

Counseling

Counseling, both pretest and posttest, should be considered a part of HIV testing. Pretest counseling may be considered part of the informed consent process, during which the individual is informed of the test procedure itself as well as the implications of a positive test. Posttest counseling may include an explanation of the medical and social implications of a positive test result. The individual will need to know what to do to avoid spreading the disease, what medical care is available, and what support services, such as psychological counseling, are available. Many state laws require counseling of persons with positive test results.[8]

CONFIDENTIALITY ISSUES

The confidentiality issues surrounding the AIDS virus are wide ranging and are a significant area of potential liability for nurses and other health care providers. Many states have enacted laws specifically addressing the confidentiality of medical information concerning the AIDS virus. These laws prohibit disclosure of HIV status without patient consent, although all the laws contain statutory exceptions to this blanket prohibition.[9] Several states also have general medical record confidentiality statutes. In addition to statutory protections, if confidential information is improperly revealed, the person could sue for invasion of privacy, defamation, or intentional infliction of emotional distress. In *Anderson v. Strong Memorial Hospital,* for example, a hospital and physician were found liable for defamation when a newspaper printed the picture of an HIV-positive patient who was being treated at the hospital.[10]

Reporting Requirements

All states must report AIDS cases to the federal Centers for Disease Control (CDC). HIV is specifically reportable in 38 states[11] and is reportable under the general disease reporting laws in those states that do not have HIV-specific legislation. Most states require HIV test results to be reported to the state health department, but a few require reporting to local health departments, and several others require results to be reported to either or both state or local health departments.[12]

The states are beginning to enact laws requiring reporting of health care providers with HIV infection to licensure boards. In Louisiana, for example, licensed health care providers and licensure applicants must report their HIV status to the appropriate licensure board.[13]

The laws vary widely as to who has the duty to report, what information must be reported, and what form of the disease must be reported (AIDS, HIV-positive, AIDS-related complex).

For example, in Minnesota, there is a self-reporting law that requires health care workers diagnosed with HIV to report that information to the Commissioner of Health no more than 30 days after learning of the diagnosis or 30 days after becoming licensed or registered by the state.[14]

Disclosure of Confidential Medical Information

Disclosure can be made with the consent of a patient to anyone the person indicates. This will usually be a health care provider or an insurance company. Consent to disclose confidential information should be carefully documented, and care should be taken to ensure that the disclosure is limited to only those authorized to receive the information.

Disclosure to Health Care Workers

Many state HIV laws have provisions permitting disclosure of the HIV status of a patient to health care workers for purposes of diagnosis or treatment. California law, for example, states that

> [t]he information may be disclosed to providers of health care or other health care professionals or facilities for purposes of diagnosis or treatment of the patient. This includes, in an emergency situation, the communication of patient information by radio transmission between emergency medical personnel at the scene of an emergency or in an emergency medical transport vehicle, and emergency medical personnel at a health facility.[15]

Another reason for disclosing patient HIV status to health care workers is concern for the safety of those who may be at risk of contracting the virus while rendering care. Kansas law permits physicians to disclose the HIV status of a patient to nurses and other health care workers if they will be in contact with the bodily fluids of a patient during a medical or surgical procedure.[16]

When health care workers or emergency personnel have been significantly exposed to a patient's blood, several states authorize HIV testing without consent, including, for example, Arizona, Colorado, Delaware, Florida, Hawaii, Idaho, Illinois, Michigan, Missouri, Nebraska, New Mexico, Texas, West Virginia, and Wisconsin.[17] When a sample of the blood of the patient already exists for testing, other states allow testing without consent after significant exposure, including, for example, Connecticut, Louisiana, Montana, Pennsylvania, Rhode Island, and Wyoming.[18] If a patient refuses consent for HIV testing after significant exposure, still others, for example, permit court ordered testing (Maine, Ohio, Oregon, and Washington).[19]

Disclosure of Health Care Provider's HIV Status to Patients

The CDC guidelines recommend that HIV-positive health care workers and nurses notify prospective patients of their HIV status before the patients undergo exposure-prone invasive procedures.

In *Behringer v. The Medical Center at Princeton,* a New Jersey court upheld the requirement of a hospital that an HIV-positive surgeon disclose his HIV status to prospective patients as part of the informed consent procedure.[20]

A few states (e.g., Texas) require HIV-positive nurses and other health care workers who perform exposure-prone procedures to notify prospective patients of their seropositive status and obtain written consent from patients before patients undergo exposure-prone procedures.[21]

A hospital may make the decision to inform patients that a provider who treated them is HIV-positive. Some states (e.g., Illinois) require notification of an individual who may have been exposed to HIV through contact with an HIV-infected provider.[22]

The CDC guidelines recommend a case-by-case approach to deciding whether patients should be notified of possible exposure.[23] The guidelines state:

> The public health benefit of notification of patients who have had exposure-prone procedures performed by health care workers infected with HIV . . . should be considered on a case-by-case basis, taking into consideration an assessment of specific risks, confidentiality issues, and available resources. Decisions regarding notification and follow-up studies should be made in consultation with state and local public health officials.

Disclosure to Sexual Partner or Needle Partner

Some state laws, such as those in California and Hawaii, permit disclosure of HIV status to the spouse, sexual partner, or needle partner of an HIV-positive individual.[24]

Disclosure to Other Third Parties

State laws provide for disclosure of medical information to various groups and professionals. For example, states permit disclosure of medical information to quality assurance committees, accreditation committees, and oversight review organizations[25]; funeral directors or coroners[26]; facilities or providers that procure, process, distribute, or use human body parts for transplant, semen for artificial insemination, or blood products for transfusion or injection[27]; epidemiologists[28];

victims of sexual offenses[29]; authorized agencies in connection with foster care or adoption of a child[30]; and researchers.[31]

The Illinois Confidentiality Act contains a provision addressing positive test results for minors.[32] Under the statute, the health care provider who ordered the test is required to make a reasonable effort to notify the parent or legal guardian of a minor if notification would be in the best interest of the child and the provider has first tried unsuccessfully to persuade the minor to notify the parent, or a reasonable time after the minor has agreed to notify the parent, the provider has reason to believe that the minor has not made the notification. The law states that there will be no civil or criminal liability of a provider acting in good faith for either notification or nonnotification of the test results of a minor.

EXPOSURE AND INFECTION

Patient Exposed to HIV or Infected by Health Care Worker

Patients who have been exposed to the AIDS virus by a nurse or other health care worker may sue the facility for negligence on the basis of failing to institute or failing to enforce proper infection control procedures.[33] A Maryland court has ruled, however, that a patient cannot sue a hospital or the estate of a physician who died of AIDS because she feared contracting the disease as a result of surgery the physician had performed on her.[34] Although the patient was seronegative, she claimed she had sustained injury because of her fear of having been exposed to the disease. The court, however, held that without proof of exposure (i.e., without a positive HIV test), the patient did not suffer any compensable injury and could not recover for the year that something that did not happen could have happened.

Another court has viewed this liability for exposure issue differently. A patient who reasonably fears she has contracted AIDS as a result of undergoing surgery by an AIDS-infected surgeon may recover for emotional distress, even if she later tests negative for the disease, a California appeals court has ruled.[35] The patient learned from a television story that a surgeon who had performed uterine surgery on her two years earlier had AIDS. The patient underwent testing for AIDS within a day of the broadcast and received her negative results two weeks later. In her suit, she argued that, in addition to compensation for the emotional distress she suffered, she should recover for battery, as she had consented to surgery after receiving assurance from the surgeon that he was in good health.

A patient cannot sue a hospital for fear of contracting AIDS after hospital personnel told her that she had been injected with blood that had tested positive for HIV, a Pennsylvania appeals court has ruled.[36] The patient sued the hospital after the hospital erroneously told her that donated placental blood she received during an in vitro fertilization procedure tested HIV-positive. The court noted that both the donor and the patient subsequently tested negative and that the patient offered no evidence, other than the first incorrect test, that the placental blood was infected.

A patient who was exposed to poorly sterilized or unsterilized surgical instruments may sue the hospital where the surgery was performed, even if she does not develop any infectious disease as a result, the highest court in Virginia has ruled.[37] The patient, who immediately feared she had contracted HIV, was treated by the hospital's infectious disease specialist with antibiotics to prevent a variety of infections. During her hospitalization, she received intravenous medication, as well as injections. Her blood was drawn frequently, and she experienced side effects as a result of the antibiotic treatment (e.g., vomiting, fever, sweating, chills, "raw" mouth, nose, and sinuses, and vaginal discharge). She continued to fear infection for six months after the surgery, although she did not contract any virus. The court ruled that the intravenous tubes and needles used to administer the medication and withdraw the blood of the patient, as well as the side effects she experienced as a result of the treatment, constituted physical pain and discomfort sufficient to support a suit for medical malpractice.

Employee Exposed to HIV or Infected by Patient

A hospital or other facility has a duty to maintain a safe workplace for its nurses and other employees. If the facility does not institute and enforce proper infection control procedures, it could be exposed to liability for negligence.

In a 1992 case, a court upheld the conclusion of a jury that the HIV infection of a blood bank technician was due to her own conduct rather than the negligence of a blood bank director.[38] Because a patient needed an immediate platelet transfusion, a blood donor was scheduled for an apheresis procedure without pretesting for HIV. During the procedure, the equipment malfunctioned and the technician was covered in blood, which she did not wash off until the procedure was complete. She also cleaned the equipment and work area without wearing gloves. The technician later died, and her husband sued, claiming that the director improperly scheduled the apheresis procedure without knowing the HIV status of the donor, did not tell the technician that the test results were unknown, and did not require the technicians to wear gloves. The court held that there was sufficient evidence supporting the conclusion of the jury that the negligence of the director was irrelevant and that the conduct of the technician was the cause of her HIV infection.

EMPLOYMENT LAWS THAT PROTECT HIV-POSITIVE INDIVIDUALS

There are several laws that protect employees who are HIV-positive. These include the Rehabilitation Act of 1973, the ADA, state antidiscrimination laws, and municipal ordinances. The following sections briefly introduce these laws and discuss the central issues that arise under these laws: whether HIV-positive nurses or other employees are handicapped, what makes a handicapped employee "otherwise qualified," and what constitutes reasonable accommodation of an otherwise qualified handicapped employee.

Who Is a "Qualified Handicapped Individual"?

Although both federal and state laws recognize HIV-positive individuals as handicapped, the laws protect the employment status only of "qualified" handicapped persons. Under regulations implementing the Rehabilitation Act, for example, a qualified handicapped person is defined as one who "with reasonable accommodation, can perform the essential functions of the job in question."[39]

In *Leckelt v. Board of Commissioners of Hospital District No. 1,* the court ruled that a nurse who was discharged after refusing to disclose the results of his HIV test was not "otherwise qualified" to perform his job.[40] The court found that the hospital had a legitimate interest in monitoring the health status of employees and that requiring disclosure of HIV status was a legitimate part of the infection control policy. There was also evidence that the nurse had refused to follow the infection control policies of the hospital in the past. The court concluded that the failure of the nurse to adhere to the infection control policy rendered him "not otherwise qualified" to perform his job.

Because AIDS is a progressive disease, a person who at one point may be qualified to do a job may not remain qualified. For example, persons with AIDS are particularly susceptible to various opportunistic infections including tuberculosis (TB), which is highly contagious. An HIV-positive health care worker who may be initially qualified to perform a job may not remain so if that worker contracts TB or another contagious or disabling disease.

Reasonable Accommodation

Both the Rehabilitation Act and the ADA require reasonable accommodation or modification for otherwise qualified individuals unless it would pose an undue hardship. Accommodation may require adaptation of facilities, modification of equipment, or job restructuring to provide a more flexible schedule. What is reasonable accommodation will depend on the specific situation. An employer will not be required, however, to enter into an accommodation that would alter the fundamental nature of the business or would be extraordinarily costly.

At least two states have passed legislation addressing the status of infected health care workers. In New Hampshire, health care workers who know they carry the HIV or HBV may not perform exposure-prone invasive procedures unless an expert review panel has approved a special application. The panel must make its determination based solely on the risk of infecting patients and may place conditions on approval, such as notifying patients, or limiting invasive procedures.[41] Alabama has adopted a similar statute.

HIV ISSUES SPECIFIC TO HEALTH CARE WORKERS

The states are beginning to enact laws designating various bodies—advisory panels, expert review panels, licensure boards, or hospital-created panels—to establish protocols for health care workers who perform exposure-prone procedures.[42] Under such laws, the appointed body decides on a case-by-case basis what restrictions are appropriate. Some laws provide that health care workers who refuse or fail to abide by the recommendations are subject to professional discipline.[43]

Whether hospitals have a duty to inform patients of the HIV status of a physician is an area of liability that is evolving. In some states, confidentiality laws prohibit release of this information. In addition, releasing such information without the permission of a physician may subject a hospital to liability for invasion of privacy and defamation.

The issue of whether to inform patients after they have been exposed to an HIV-positive nurse or other worker during an exposure-prone procedure is another matter. The CDC states that this should be determined on a case-by-case basis. Individual hospitals must make the determination of whether to do a so-called look-back based on the seriousness of the exposure as well as other relevant factors.

Health Care Employee Testing

Both the CDC and the American Hospital Association advocate the use of universal precautions rather than mandatory testing of health care workers to protect the health of both health care employees and patients. There are practical as well as legal problems with mandatory HIV testing. Because of the nature of the disease, a person could have been recently exposed to the virus, yet have a negative test result. Because exposure could occur at anytime, constant retesting would be necessary, which would be both costly and intrusive.

Mandatory testing of nurses or other employees may be subject to constitutional challenge on grounds of invasion of privacy and illegal search and seizure under the Fourth Amendment.

In *Leckelt v. Board of Commissioners of Hospital District No. 1*, a Louisiana court held that a nurse was properly terminated for failing to reveal the results of his HIV test.[44] The nurse challenged his termination on constitutional grounds. The court concluded, however, that the interest of the hospital in learning of the test results outweighed the privacy interests of the nurse. The hospital contended that it needed to know the information because the nurse engaged in invasive procedures (starting IVs) and therefore could present a risk to patients. This case seems to indicate that a hospital has a right to know the HIV status of an employee, at least when the hospital has a need to know that is related to patient safety.

Under the ADA of 1990, medical testing or examination of existing employees is permitted only if it is job related and consistent with business necessity.[45]

Several states have enacted laws prohibiting employers from requiring employee HIV testing except when based on bona fide occupational qualifications. Some state laws require that health care workers submit to HIV testing if there has been patient exposure to the blood or body fluid of a worker.

Refusal of Nurse Employee to Care for AIDS Patients or to Work with HIV-Positive Coworkers

The refusal of a nurse to care for HIV-infected patients may be based on the failure of the hospital to follow proper infection control procedures. If this is true, the employee may be protected under the Occupational Safety and Health Act (OSH Act).[46] If nurses have a reasonable good-faith belief that the workplace poses an immediate and grave danger to their health and safety, OSH Act regulations allow employees to refuse to work and state that they cannot be discharged for such refusal.[47] In addition, nurse employees may be protected under the National Labor Relations Act (NLRA).[48] It is often an unfair labor practice for an employer to discharge or discipline an employee for exercising NLRA rights.

If the hospital is enforcing proper infection control procedures and an employee refuses to care for an HIV-positive patient or work with an HIV-positive coworkers, the employer should ensure that the nurse is properly educated about how the virus is transmitted and how employees can protect themselves using universal precautions. The nurse could have legitimate reasons for his or her refusal. For example, a nurse who is on steroids or undergoing chemotherapy may have a diminished immune system that would make the nurse more susceptible to the secondary infections that an HIV-positive individual may be experiencing. This should be evaluated on a case-by-case basis in the light of the most current medical information. If the health concern is legitimate, the employer should try to reasonably accommodate the health care worker.

In most cases, if a hospital is following proper infection control techniques and properly educates the nurse but the nurse continues to refuse to care for an HIV-positive patient or to work with an HIV-positive coworker, the hospital can impose discipline, including termination.[49] If there is a collective bargaining agreement, the hospital must follow any contract procedures and requirements for discipline.

A pregnant home care nurse who was fired because she refused to treat an AIDS-infected patient cannot sue for pregnancy discrimination, a federal trial court in Alabama ruled.[50] The nurse declined to care for the patient, even with universal precautions, because she feared the accompanying opportunistic infections often present in AIDS patients, (in this case, cryptococcal meningitis) would harm the fetus. The policy of the hospital requiring all nurses to treat AIDS patients or be subject to termination applies to nonpregnant as well as pregnant nurses, the court observed. Because the nurse could not establish that the standard of the hospital impacts on pregnant women more harshly than other classifications of employees, the court dismissed the suit.

Health Care Employee Safety Issues

The CDC issued recommendations in July 1991 for preventing the transmission of HIV and HBV during invasive procedures in health care settings.[51] The recommendations emphasize adherence to universal precautions that require blood and other bodily fluids of all patients to be handled as if they contain blood-borne pathogens. The recommendations also stress that infected nurses or other health care workers who adhere to universal precautions and who do not perform invasive procedures pose no risk for transmitting HIV or HBV to patients. Infected nurses and health care workers who adhere to universal precautions and perform certain exposure-prone procedures, however, pose a small risk for transmitting HBV to patients.

To minimize the risk of HIV or HBV transmission, the CDC recommends that all nurses and health care workers adhere to universal precautions. Workers who have exudative lesions or weeping dermatitis should refrain from all direct patient care and from handling patient care equipment in performing invasive procedures. The CDC does not recommend restricting the practice of infected nurses and health care workers who perform invasive procedures that are not exposure-prone, however, as long as they comply with recognized standards of performance and universal precautions. Nurses and health care workers who perform exposure-prone procedures should know their HIV antibody status and their hepatitis B surface (antigen) status unless they have serologic evidence of immunity to HBV. Nurses and health care workers who are infected with HIV or HBV should not perform exposure-prone procedures unless they have obtained counsel from an expert review panel and have been advised under what circumstances, if any, they may continue to perform such procedures. Nurses and health care workers whose practices are modified because of their HIV or HBV infection status should, whenever possible, have the opportunity to continue patient care activities.

In October 1991, a law was enacted that gave states until October 1992 to certify that they have instituted the CDC or equivalent guidelines.[52] Texas was the first state to adopt the CDC guidelines by legislation.[53] In addition, the CDC has issued modified HIV testing and counseling recommendations for acute care hospital patients.[54] The CDC recommends that hospitals encourage nurses and other health care providers to routinely ask patients whom they admit or treat in emergency departments about their risks for HIV infection. Patients at risk should be offered HIV counseling and testing services with informed consent obtained in accordance with local laws. In addition, the CDC recommends that hospitals with an HIV-seroprevalence rate of at least 1 percent or an AIDS diagnosis rate greater than or equal to 1.0 per 1,000 discharges should consider adopting a policy of routinely offering these services to patients aged 15 to 54.

The Occupational Safety and Health Administration (OSHA) issued a final bloodborne pathogens standard on December 2, 1991, to protect more than 5.6 million workers from bloodborne infections.[55] The standard applies to all nurses and employees who could be "reasonably anticipated" to face contact with blood or other potentially infectious bodily fluids as the result of performing their job duties. It requires employers to identify in writing tasks and procedures, as well as job classifications, in which occupational exposure to blood occurs, without regard to use of personal protective clothing and equipment. The OSHA regulations make universal precautions (treating bodily fluids as if they are infectious) mandatory. The standard stresses hand washing and requires employers to provide facilities and ensure that employees use them after exposure to blood. Employers must also provide, require employees to use, and replace as necessary personal protective equipment such as gloves, gowns, masks, and mouthpieces. Postexposure evaluations and follow-ups, including laboratory tests, must be available at no cost to all employees who have had an exposure incident.

CONCLUSION

AIDS remains a major problem for society in general and health care workers, including nurses, in particular who often face providing nursing care on a daily basis to those patients. Patient confidentiality remains a major issue that often conflicts with the government reporting requirements. Although hospitals and other facilities have a duty to maintain a safe workplace for its employees, nurses and other health care providers working with HIV-exposed or HIV-infected patients face a daily threat of contamination by HIV-infected body fluids. Infected health care workers have protection from a variety of statutes. The number of cases involving transmission continues to grow, given the increase in AIDS cases and the devastating implications of infection. OSHA and CDC guidelines on health care worker protection are now well established.

FOOTNOTES

1. 42 C.F.R. § 124.603.
2. Glanz v. Vernick, 756 F. Supp. 632 (Mass. 1991).

3. *See, e.g.,* Chalk v. United States Dist. Ct. Cent. Dist., 832 F.2d 1158 (9th Cir. 1987); Doe v. Centinela Hosp., 57 U.S.L.W. 2034 (C.D. Cal. 1988).

4. Pub. L. No. 101-336 § 302.

5. 42 U.S.C.A. § 1395(dd).

6. CAL. HEALTH & SAFETY CODE § 199.22; N.Y. PUB. HEALTH LAW § 2781.

7. TENN. CODE ANN. § 68-11-122(d).

8. *See, e.g.,* WIS. STAT. § 146.025(2)(b); ILL. REV. STAT. ch. 111 1/2, para. 7305.

9. *See, e.g.,* FLA. STAT. § 381.609; VA. CODE ANN. § 16-3C-1.

10. 531 N.Y.S.2d 735 (N.Y. Sup. Ct. 1988).

11. AIDS Policy Center, Intergovernmental Health Policy Project, October 1992.

12. *Id.*

13. La. H.B. 1526 (New Laws 1991).

14. Minn. S.B. 2732, (New Laws 1992).

15. CAL. CIVIL CODE § 56 as amended by Ch. 911 and Ch. 1363, L. 1990, effective January 1, 1991. *See also* N.C. GEN. STAT. § 130A-143.

16. KAN. STAT. ANN. § 65-004(a).

17. AIDS Policy Center, Intergovernmental Health Policy Project, October 1992.

18. *Id.*

19. *Id.*

20. No. L88-2550 (N.J. Super. Ct. April 25, 1991).

21. TEX. HEALTH & SAFETY CODE ANN. § 85.201.

22. Ill. S.B. 999 (New Laws 1991).

23. MORBIDITY & MORTALITY WKLY. REP., July 12, 1991.

24. CAL. HEALTH & SAFETY CODE § 199-24(c); Hawaii S.B. No. 3306 (New Laws 1992).

25. *See, e.g.,* DEL. CODE ANN. § 1203(a)(7).

26. *See, e.g.,* WIS. STAT. ANN. § 146.025.

27. *See, e.g.,* W. VA. CODE § 16-3C-3(a)(1).

28. *See, e.g.,* WIS. STAT. ANN. § 146.025(2)(a)(5m).

29. *See, e.g.,* TEX. HEALTH & SAFETY CODE ANN. § 81.103(b).

30. *See, e.g.,* N.Y. PUB. HEALTH LAW § 2782.

31. *See, e.g.,* N.J. REV. STAT. § 26:5C-8.

32. 410 ILL. COMP. STAT. ANN. 305/9.

33. *See* Thompson v. Methodist Hosp., 367 S.W.2d 134 (1962) as an example of a hospital infection case (non-HIV).

34. Rossi v. Estate of Rudolph Almaraz & Johns Hopkins Hosp., No. 90344028/CLI 23396 (Md. Cir. Ct. May 23, 1991).

35. Kerins v. Hartley, 21 Cal. Rptr. 2d 621 (Cal. Ct. App. 1993), *rev. granted,* 860 P.2d 1182 (Cal. 1993).

36. Lubowitz v. Albert Einstein Med. Ctr., 623 A.2d 3 (Pa. Super. Ct. 1993).

37. Howard v. Alexandria Hosp., 429 S.E.2d 22 (Va. 1993).

38. James v. Nolan, No. 1944 (Pa. Super. Ct. Sept. 9, 1992).

39. 45 C.F.R. § 84.3(k).

40. 909 F.2d 820 (5th Cir. 1990).

41. N.H. Rev. Stat. Ann. §§ 141-F:9-a through 141-F:9-d.

42. *See, e.g.,* N.Y. SI 8179-A, ch. 786 (1992); Iowa S.B. 2323 (New Laws 1992).

43. *See, e.g.,* Minn. S.B. 2732 (New Laws 1992).

44. *Leckelt, supra* note 40.

45. § 102[c][3].

46. 29 U.S.C. §§ 102, 157.

47. 29 C.F.R. § 1977.12

48. 29 U.S.C. §§ 102, 157.

49. *See, e.g.,* Stepp v. Review Bd. of Ind. Employment Sec. Div., 521 N.E.2d 350 (Ind. Ct. App. 1988).

50. Armstrong v. Flowers Hosp., Inc., No. CV-92-A-101 (M.D. Ala. Feb. 9, 1993).

51. *Recommendations for Preventing Transmission of Human Immunodeficiency Virus and Hepatitis B Virus to Patients during Exposure-Prone Invasive Procedures,* Morbidity & Mortality Wkly. Rep., July 12, 1991.

52. Pub. L. No. 102-141.

53. Tex. Health & Safety Code Ann. § 85.201.

54. Centers for Disease Control, *Recommendations for HIV-Testing Services for Inpatients and Outpatients in Acute-Care Hospital Settings,* Morbidity & Mortality Wkly. Rep., March 5, 1993.

55. Occupational Exposure to Bloodborne Pathogens, 56 Fed. Reg. 64,004 (1991).

CHAPTER 12

Withholding and Withdrawing Treatment from the Dying

Chapter Objectives

1. To discuss refusal of treatment
2. To consider incompetent individuals and medical decisions
3. To review civil statutes and regulations concerning treatment decisions
4. To determine civil and criminal liability
5. To address the dying patient and the limits to the patient's choices

Nurses regularly become involved in situations involving withholding or withdrawing treatment from dying patients. More attention is being focused on the dying process because of achievements in modern medical care that make it possible to sustain life, several widely publicized legal cases, and the increasing openness of discussions concerning death. More and more, both state and federal legislators are enacting laws recognizing the rights of patients to determine the course of their treatment should the need for life-sustaining measures ever arise and establishing decision-making procedures in the absence of advance directives. A clear understanding of the legal aspects of the dying process is essential for nurses so that they may deal humanely with this crisis in the lives of patients and their family and friends, while complying with the law.

Nurses, physicians, other involved professionals, and health care institutions have legally recognized duties to all patients. These legal duties have always been shaped by (1) the needs and wishes of patients and their representatives, (2) professional practices, (3) the capacities of medical science and the individual professionals and hospital involved, and (4) societal expectations and norms. Professional practice has long reflected the different needs of terminally ill and irreversibly comatose patients. The famous New Jersey Supreme Court decision concerning the care of Karen Ann Quinlan, who was irreversibly comatose, states the difference as follows:

> We glean from the record here that physicians distinguish between curing the ill and comforting and easing the dying; that they refuse to treat the curable as if they were dying or ought to be; and that they have sometimes refused to treat the hopeless and dying as if they were curable.[1]

The law also has recognized this difference.

There is no widely accepted definition of terminal illness; it remains a diagnosis based on medical judgment. Clearly, one element is that no available course of therapy offers a reasonable expectation of remission or cure of the condition. Another element is that death is imminent, but there is no consensus on the time period; this results largely from the fact that it is not possible to predict a time of death precisely. Some courts have accepted patients as terminally ill with predicted lives of one and five years.[2] In most jurisdictions, a definition that includes a period of one year appears to be acceptable, with the possibility that longer periods would be acceptable in some jurisdictions.

All classification systems must take into account the role of the involved professionals, the patient, and the family and/or guardian of the patient. The initial medical decision concerning diagnosis and prognosis must be made by the physician. The patient and the family of the patient have no role in this judgment, which establishes the range of medically appropriate classifications of the patient. The patient then has the important role of deciding whether to accept the elements of care that are associated with the classification by the physician or to seek the treatment associated with another classification by insisting on additional elements of care or by refusing certain elements of care. When the patient either is unable to participate or desires family participation, then the family and/or guardian of the patient become involved. When there are irresolvable disagreements concerning the elements of care, courts may have to become involved.

Professional decisions can be made either by the attending physician or by a committee, which may be established either formally or informally. Standards of the Joint Commission on Accreditation of Healthcare Organizations (Joint Commission) now require hospital-wide policies on the withholding of resuscitative services and the foregoing or withdrawing of life-sustaining medical treatment. These policies must describe the roles of physicians, nurses, other appropriate staff, and family members in making such decisions.[3]

Generally, ethics committees have a role in the creation of hospital policies, in their implementation through staff education, and in prospective treatment conferences. Although they are not usually routinely involved in treatment decisions, some hospitals require that ethics committees become involved in controversial or disputed decisions or as a safeguard for vulnerable patients.

The patient and the family or guardian of the patient usually have an important role in the decision making; ultimately, the patient has the final authority regarding these fundamental decisions concerning life. In recognition of the emotional strain on patient and family in this situation and the potential for family guilt feelings in the future, many physicians present their decision regarding treatment for patient and family concurrence, rather than placing the entire decision-making burden on them. This avoids many potential problems while giving family members an opportunity to veto the decision of the physician if it does not comport with their wishes.

The courts have tended to become involved only when the professionals, the patient, and the family or guardian disagree on treatment. In such cases, courts have reiterated the right of the family to make the final decision. In Minnesota, for example, a probate judge ruled that a family should decide not to terminate life support for an incompetent patient despite recommendations by the patient's physicians that support be withdrawn.[4] In Georgia, a court denied a request of a hospital to deescalate artificial support or enter a do-not-resuscitate (DNR) order without the consent of both of the parents of a 13-year-old patient in an almost complete state of unconsciousness.[5]

REFUSAL OF TREATMENT

"Do-Not-Resuscitate" Orders

The term *cardiopulmonary resuscitation* (CPR) describes a series of steps developed over the past two decades to reestablish breathing and heartbeat after cardiac or respiratory arrest. The most basic form of CPR, which is being taught to large numbers of the public, involves recognizing the indications for intervention, opening an airway, initiating mouth-to-mouth breathing, and compressing the chest externally to establish artificial circulation. In hospitals and in some emergency transport vehicles, CPR also can include the administration of oxygen under pressure to the lungs, the use of intravenous medications, the injection of stimulants into the heart through catheters or long needles, electric shocks to the heart, insertion of a pacemaker, artificial ventilation, and open heart massage. Some of these procedures are highly intrusive and even violent in nature. They all are medically justified and indicated for patients whose condition is not yet diagnosed or for those who have a hopeful prognosis. The purpose of CPR is the prevention of sudden unexpected death. However, it is not indicated in certain situations, such as in cases of terminal irreversible illness in which death is expected.

To ensure that CPR is not initiated when it is not indicated, it is important for the physician to write "Do Not Resuscitate" or "No CPR" in the orders concerning the treatment of the patient. Many institutions call the CPR team by announcing "Code Blue," so the order might read "No Code Blue." A written DNR order documents the fact that a decision has been made and by whom; it ensures that the decision is communicated to nurses and other staff so inappropriate CPR is not initiated. When CPR clearly is not part of the planned care, nurses can act in accordance with the decisions without concern that they misunderstood them or later will be thought to have neglected the patient. Written orders reflect that these decisions are an appropriate part of health care practice and have been made after careful deliberation.

The patient or the representative of the patient should be involved in the decision and concur in the DNR order. The nature of the care to be withheld should be explained by the physician before obtaining the concurrence. A DNR order was challenged in a 1981 Minnesota case, and the court was not convinced that the parents of the patient knew what they were declining. Therefore, the court ordered that the DNR order be canceled until the parents of the patient gave "knowledgeable approval" to reinstate it.[6]

No Extraordinary Care

Theologians and ethicists have long recognized a distinction between ordinary and extraordinary medical care. They have maintained that humans have a moral and ethical responsibility to seek and accept ordinary medical care to save their lives but that extraordinary medical care may be declined. However, the law generally has recognized a legal right to refuse even ordinary care. Most physicians and nurses, although often deeply troubled by refusals of ordinary care by nonterminal patients, have accepted this legal principle. They find it easier to accede to the wishes of the terminally ill patients and their families who decline extraordinary care, however, and may even recommend that such treatment not be pursued in some instances.

A precise definition of which care is ordinary and which is extraordinary is not possible. One of the most widely quoted definitions is by a Roman Catholic ethicist, Gerald Kelly:

> Ordinary means all medicines, treatments, and operations which offer a reasonable hope of benefit and which can be obtained and used without excessive pain, or other inconvenience. Extraordinary means are all medicines, treatments, and operations which cannot be obtained or used without excessive expense, pain, or other inconvenience, or if used, would not offer a reasonable hope of benefit.[7]

It is clear that it is not possible to create a list of "extraordinary" procedures. The circumstances of the individual situation and the judgment of those involved determine whether a procedure is extraordinary.

Since 1988, the Joint Commission has required all hospitals to have a resuscitation policy in place. Joint Commission standards require that the policy describe the mechanisms for reaching the DNR decision and the mechanisms for resolving conflicts in decision making. The policy must also include the requirement that the order be written by the physician who is primarily responsible for the care of the patient and inscribed in the medical record of the patient.[8]

The fear of legal liability for physicians who write DNR orders have virtually disappeared in the light of numerous court decisions that endorse such practices, provided that the principles of informed consent are respected, and in the light of the recognition of this practice by the Joint Commission.

Maintenance of Supportive Care

Even when terminally ill patients are not receiving extraordinary care, physicians, nurses, and hospitals have duties to them. Although some patients, such as Karen Ann Quinlan, appropriately can be transferred to nursing homes, others require continued hospitalization. Ordinary supportive care must be continued— the "comforting and easing the dying" to which the *Quinlan* decision referred. It is clear that this includes appropriate medications for pain.

Indeed, because the distinction between ordinary and extraordinary has become so confused, the President's Commission for the Study of Ethical Problems in Medicine has recommended that the phrases no longer be used in the interest of encouraging clarity.[9] The Commission instead preferred that laws and medical policies speak in terms of "the proportionate benefit and burdens of treatment as viewed by particular patients."

The American Medical Association (AMA) has also questioned the appropriateness of the distinction between ordinary and extraordinary medical treatment to determine whether life-sustaining treatment can be refused by a patient. If "ordinary care" is defined as treatment that provides a basic requirement of life regardless of the underlying condition, ventilators that provide oxygen to patients would also be ordinary care, the AMA has indicated. Moreover, the standard of extraordinary versus ordinary treatment implies that ordinary, unlike extraordinary life-sustaining treatment, is not burdensome to the patient. The AMA points out that artificial nutrition and hydration immobilizes the patient to a large degree and can be extremely uncomfortable.[10] The AMA does, however, refer to extraordinary life-sustaining measure in its official opinion on withholding or withdrawing life-prolonging medical treatment.[11]

Earlier court cases arrived at decisions to withhold or withdraw treatment by distinguishing between ordinary and extraordinary care. Most of those decisions addressed the use of respirators. The court in *Quinlan,* for example, discussed the distinction between ordinary and extraordinary care, at length, citing religious and medical sources; it concluded that it was extraordinary care to use a respirator for a comatose young woman in a chronic, persistent vegetative state with no reasonable possibility of emerging to a cognitive, sapient state and authorized discontinuance of the respiratory assistance. [12] The intermediate court in *Eichner v. Dillion* also discussed the distinction and concluded that the use of a respirator was extraordinary care for a comatose elderly man with a similar prognosis. [13] Other, unpublished decisions in California,[14] Ohio,[15] and Tennessee[16] have reached the same conclusion regarding the use of respirators for the irreversibly comatose. Although not using the extraordinary–ordinary terminology, the Florida courts authorized a competent adult with amyotrophic lateral sclerosis (Lou Gehrig's disease) to discontinue use of a respirator.[17]

Other cases have addressed several other treatments. In *Superintendent of Belchertown v. Saikewicz,*[18] the court discussed the distinction between extraordinary and ordinary care and stated its decision was intended to be consistent with this "medical ethos." It implicitly concluded that chemotherapy could be extraordinary care when it approved withholding chemotherapy from a profoundly mentally retarded 67-year-old man with leukemia. The court in *Spring* did not use the extraordinary–ordinary terminology but reached a similar differentiation based on the "magnitude of the invasion." It concluded that it is appropriate to discontinue dialysis for a 78-year-old man with irreversible kidney failure and chronic organic brain syndrome, but it was not appropriate to discontinue "supportive oral or intravenous medications."[19]

As more and more states adopt living will legislation and as hospitals have implemented the Patient Self-Determination Act, the distinction between ordinary and extraordinary medical care will become increasingly theoretical. Through a living will, a person can specifically dictate the kinds of life supports that should be used and under what conditions. For example, a person might decline a ventilator but not medications if terminally ill or refuse a feeding tube if permanently unconscious but not if terminally ill. In addition, living will legislation in many states applies not only to patients who are terminally ill but also to permanently unconscious patients. Because numerous legislatures have recognized the right to withdraw or withhold specific types of medical treatment under specific circumstances, the issue of ordinary and extraordinary medical measures is less and less relevant.

Whether feeding may be withheld or withdrawn from a patient is not a settled issue. In *Barber v. Superior Court,*[20] a California appeals court determined that using medical procedures to provide nutrition and hydration is no different from using respirators or any other life support equipment that can legally be discontinued. Therefore, the court reasoned, two physicians who had removed a respirator and had withdrawn intravenous nourishment from a comatose, brain-damaged patient should not be charged with murder for their actions.

Increasingly, the withdrawal or withholding of artificial feeding is equated with the use of a respirator when it is necessary to determine the right of a patient to determine the course of medical treatment.[21] The AMA had endorsed this view in an official opinion from its Council on Ethical and Judicial Affairs, stating that

> [l]ife-prolonging medical treatment includes medication and artificially or technologically supplied respiration, nutrition or hydration. In treating a terminally ill or permanently unconscious patient, the dignity of the patient should be maintained at all times.[22]

Some courts, however, have distinguished between termination of food and water and termination of mechanical respiration. One court in New York likened the termination of feeding to the withholding of life-saving blood transfusions.[23] The court noted that removal of a respirator results in death in a short time, whereas death from the removal of food and nutrition can take a week or more. The court was also hesitant to order the discontinuance of supportive care for the 33-year-old patient because he was not terminally ill or brain-dead but rather in a chronic vegative state. Refusing to sanction a broad-scale judicial policy of euthanasia, the court denied the family's petition to remove the patient's feeding tube and stop all nutrition and hydration.

Courts that have authorized the withdrawal of artificial feeding have done so based on similar but varying principles. One of the first major rulings in this area was *In re Conroy,* in which the New Jersey Supreme Court enumerated three standards governing the withholding or withdrawal of life support.[24] The first standard involves the *subjective test,* in which withholding or withdrawal of support is permitted because of clear evidence that the patient would have refused treatment if mentally competent. The second test, the *limited objective test,* is also based on evidence that the patient would have refused treatment, but it requires, in addition, consideration of objective evidence that the patient's life would be burdened more with treatment than without it. The third standard, the *pure objective test,* should be used when there is no evidence of the patient's wishes and the burdens of treatment markedly outweigh the benefits. There also must be an assessment of whether treatment would be inhumane if the patient is in severe pain. The court limited this decision to nursing home patients with life expectancies of less than one year.

Hospitals are allowed some discretion in formulating policies and procedures on the withdrawal of supportive care, but those policies must not conflict with the patient's constitutional right to refuse treatment, with state legislation, or with the requirements of the Patient Self-Determination Act, which is described later in this chapter.

The New Jersey Supreme Court has held that a nursing home could not refuse to participate in the withdrawal of a feeding tube from a young, mentally incompetent patient or force the patient to transfer to another facility that does not have a policy prohibiting such a practice.[25] In this case, the court declared, the nursing home had not informed the family of its policy against withdrawal of nutritional support until the patient had been a resident there for several years; to force the patient to transfer to another facility would frustrate her right of self-determination.

A federal trial court in Colorado has ruled, however, that a hospital and a physician did not violate section 504 of the Rehabilitation Act by refusing to remove a physically handicapped patient's feeding tube after the patient asked that it be disconnected.[26] The court found that the Act does not apply to a request to terminate medical treatment made by a physically handicapped individual of questionable mental competency.

Common Law and Constitutional Right to Refuse Treatment

Competent adults have the right to refuse treatment, unless state interests outweigh that right. The right to refuse is based on (1) the common-law right to freedom from nonconsensual invasion of bodily integrity, reflected in the informed consent doctrine and the law of battery; (2) the constitutional right of privacy; and (3) the constitutional freedom of religion.

Common-Law Bodily Integrity

The right of every individual to be free from nonconsensual invasion of bodily integrity has been well established under common law. One element of this is the right of competent adults to make their own decisions regarding medical care.[27] Without the patient's express or implied consent, medical care is a battery. The common-law doctrine of informed consent has evolved to ensure that the patient is given adequate information for a knowledgeable decision.

Courts have long recognized that a patient's right to make decisions concerning medical care necessarily includes the right to decline medical care.[28] This was restated by the highest court of New York in *In re Storar* (sometimes known as the *Eichner* case, by virtue of a companion case bearing that name),[29] when it based the right of Brother Fox through his guardian Eichner to decline respiratory support on these common-law principles. It observed that, under existing common-law principles, civil liability could be imposed on those who perform treatment without consent. The highest court of Massachusetts has also stated that common-law principles established that "a competent person has a general right to refuse medical treatment in appropriate circumstances."[30]

Right of Privacy

The second basis for the right to refuse medical treatment is the constitutional right of privacy. Infringements of bodily integrity have been recognized to violate the right of privacy, unless state interests outweigh the right. In *Satz v. Perlmutter*,[31] the Florida courts recognized the right of a competent 73-year-old man with amyotrophic lateral sclerosis to discontinue the use of a respirator. They based this right primarily on the constitutional right of privacy. This right was also recognized as a basis for refusal of care in the *Quinlan* and *Saikewicz* decisions,[32] even though the patients in both cases were unable to express their wishes. The California Supreme Court also refused to review the ruling in *Bouvia v. Superior Court,* in which an appeals court, based on the right of privacy, ordered a hospital to remove a feeding tube from a nonterminal, mentally competent young woman with cerebral palsy.[33]

Following the U.S. Supreme Court decision in *Cruzan,* described below, a court may be inclined to recognize a competent patient's constitutional right to die based on his or her constitutionally protected liberty interest rather than the patient's right to privacy. This was illustrated in a Nevada Supreme Court decision allowing a 31-year-old mentally competent quadriplegic to disconnect the respirator that kept him alive for 21 years.[34] The evidence in this case revealed that the patient's quadriplegia was irreversible but nonterminal as long as he remained on the respirator. The court observed that numerous other decisions have allowed termination of life support based on the patient's constitutional right to privacy, but the court preferred to endorse the U.S. Supreme Court's finding in the *Cruzan* case that the fundamental constitutional right implicated in such cases is the patient's liberty interest.

Freedom of Religion

In several recent decisions, the constitutional freedom of religion has been discussed as a potential basis for the right to refuse medical care. In the *Quinlan* decision, the court pointed out the long-recognized distinction between religious beliefs and actions, when it observed that "the right to religious beliefs is absolute but conduct in pursuance thereof is not wholly immune from government restraint." It declined to use freedom of religion as a basis for its decision.[35] The New York appellate court in the *Eichner* case also pointed out the difficulties in using freedom of religion as a legal basis for refusal of medical care.[36] Another reason that freedom of religion did not have an important role in these cases is that the patients' religions did not command that they refuse the treatment; they merely permitted refusal.

State Interests

The possible state interests that have been advanced include (1) preserving life; (2) protecting third parties especially minor dependents; (3) preventing irrational self-destruction; and (4) maintaining the ethical integrity of health care professionals and institutions.

Preserving Life

The preservation of life is the most basic of the state interests that have been presented as outweighing the right to refuse medical care. Courts have uniformly ruled that this interest does not outweigh the right of the terminally ill to refuse treatment. The *Quinlan* decision expressed this consensus as follows:

> We think that the State's interest *contra* weakens and the individual's right to privacy grows as the degree of bodily invasion increases and the prognosis dims.[37]

In Georgia, the Supreme Court allowed a competent 33-year-old patient to turn off the ventilator upon which he was dependent, because the state had conceded that its interest in preserving life did not outweigh the patient's right to refuse medical treatment.[38] In Nevada, the state did not vigorously contest an application from a 31-year-old mentally competent quadriplegic to disconnect his respirator.[39] These later cases indicate a growing acknowledgment that a competent patient's right to terminate medical treatment outweighs a state's interest in preserving life and that states are increasingly less inclined to actively intervene in such instances.

Protecting Third Parties

As noted in the *Saikewicz* decision:

> [a] second interest of considerable magnitude, which the State may have some interest in asserting, is that of protecting third parties, particularly minor children, from the emotional and financial damage which may occur as a result of the decision of a competent adult to refuse life-saving or life-prolonging treatment.[40]

This state interest has been recognized in cases in which Jehovah's Witnesses refused blood transfusions. Usually, the patient was an otherwise healthy parent who could be restored to normal functioning by the blood transfusion. The cases regarding terminally ill patients have not involved minor dependents, so the courts have not had an opportunity to discuss the weight to be given this interest under such circumstances. In many such cases, especially when the patient is comatose, there may be greater emotional and financial damage from continued treatment; therefore, it is doubtful that this state interest would be determinative in many situations involving the terminally ill.

Preventing Irrational Self-Destruction

Courts have recognized a state interest in preventing suicide. However, in the *Saikewicz* decision, the court observed:

> Furthermore, the underlying State interest in this area lies in the prevention of irrational self-destruction. What we consider here is a competent,

rational decision to refuse treatment when death is inevitable and the treatment offers no hope of cure or preservation of life. There is no connection between the conduct here in issue and any State concern to prevent suicide.[41]

The other courts that have addressed this question have similarly found that refusal of medical care by a terminally ill person is not suicide.[42]

Maintaining Ethical Integrity of the Medical and Nursing Professions

Several courts, while recognizing that the state has an interest in maintaining the ethical integrity of the medical and nursing professions and allowing hospitals the opportunity to care for patients who have been admitted, have also recognized that participating in withholding or withdrawing care from the terminally ill pursuant to their wishes is consistent with existing medical and nursing ethics.[43] In withdrawal of artificial feeding cases, a few courts, acknowledging the disagreement within the medical profession regarding the ethical and moral correctness of such actions, have allowed objecting hospitals to transfer a patient who is refusing treatment to the patient's home or to other hospitals where the patient's desire to stop nutritional support can be carried out. [44]

The medical profession has obviously had to respond to the rapid evolution of judicial opinion, legislation, and social beliefs in this area. In particular, recent cases involving physician-assisted suicide have made it necessary for the AMA to clarify its position on the participation of physicians in patients' decisions to end their lives.

The AMA Council on Ethical and Judicial Affairs notes that there is an ethical distinction between euthanasia, defined as the "medical administration of a lethal agent to a patient to relieve intolerable and untreatable suffering,"[45] and physician-assisted suicide. Physician-assisted suicide, the Council notes, affords patients a more autonomous way of ending their lives because the patients perform the life-ending act themselves. Both practices are similar, however, because they are essentially interventions intended to cause death. The Council concluded that physician-assisted suicide, like euthanasia, violates the traditional prohibition against using the tools of medicine to cause a patient's death and stated that physicians must not participate in either procedure.

INCOMPETENT INDIVIDUALS AND MEDICAL DECISIONS

Effect of Loss of Competence

In virtually all adults, those who were competent when they first expressed their desire to have certain treatments withheld or withdrawn generally become incompetent before they die. The refusal of medical care must apply through the period of incompetence, or the right of these patients to make decisions regarding their own care is vitiated. Many states have attempted to address this situation through statutes, and state legislatures have been very active in this area since the U.S. Supreme Court's ruling in *Cruzan,* described below. When there is no applicable statute, however, or the statutory procedures have not been followed, it is necessary to act according to the underlying common law and constitutional principles.

A distinction is often made between (1) a decision made when the person knows of the terminal condition and (2) a decision made when the person is considering future care without reference to a specific known condition. The first is generally respected, whereas the second may be subjected to more scrutiny because less information was available at the time the decision was made. When the circumstances are substantially different from those the person anticipated in reaching the decision, there must be more latitude to act contrary to the patient's stated wishes.

Courts are by no means in agreement, however, about what evidence is sufficient to determine the wishes of an incompetent patient with respect to life-sustaining medical treatment. Many courts have adopted the "clear and convincing evidence standard" but have interpreted this standard in various ways. The case of Nancy Cruzan was ultimately decided on the basis of the clear and convincing evidence standard. After the U.S. Supreme Court upheld the Missouri Supreme Court's use of the standard, the parents applied for a second hearing, claiming that they had new evidence that their daughter would not want to be sustained artificially. Three acquaintances testified about conversations regarding life-sustaining measures they had with Nancy Cruzan before her accident. Finding that this new evidence met the clear and convincing standard, a Missouri probate court approved removal of the feeding tube.[46]

Documentary evidence of the patient's wishes will obviously be given even greater weight. Written advance directives are becoming more and more frequent as state legislatures enact laws that govern living wills. A living will is a written patient directive expressing in advance the patient's wishes regarding the use or withholding of extraordinary life-sustaining measures in the event he or she is incapacitated or terminally ill.

Common Law and Constitutional Right to Refuse for Incompetents

Some patients who have never expressed their wishes regarding treatment become irreversibly incompetent and unable to communicate. Others have never had an opportunity to express their wishes because of youth or mental retardation. The courts that have been confronted with such cases have concluded that, because adults have the right to refuse treatment, there must be a means for the same right to be exercised on behalf of incompetent patients.

In the *Quinlan* decision, it was stated that all patients have a right of choice in this situation, but for the incompetent:

> The only practical way to prevent destruction of the right is to permit the guardian and family of Karen to render their best judgment, subject to the qualifications hereinafter stated, as to whether she would exercise it in these circumstances.[47]

The qualifications were concurrence by the attending physicians and concurrence by a hospital ethics committee or like body regarding the hopelessness of the prognosis.

Clearly, the most significant decision in this area is the U.S. Supreme Court ruling in *Cruzan v. Director, Missouri Department of Health*.[48] The parents of a young woman in a persistent vegetative state since her injury in an automobile accident in 1983 requested a court order to remove the gastrostomy tube through which their daughter received life-sustaining nutrition and hydration. A trial court granted the request, ruling that the patient had a state and federal constitutional right to withdraw the treatment, and that while competent, she had expressed the wish that she not be medically sustained in this manner. The Missouri Supreme Court found, however, that a patient has no absolute state or federal constitutional right to refuse medical treatment. In addition, because the Missouri living will statute embodies a state policy strongly favoring the preservation of life, the court ruled that the parents could not request that their daughter's treatment be terminated, unless there was clear and convincing evidence that she would make the same decision if she were competent.

The U.S. Supreme Court agreed, holding that the patient did not have a federal constitutional right to withdraw life-sustaining nutrition. Although the court assumed that, under the federal constitution, a competent person has a general liberty interest in refusing medical treatment, it emphasized that an incompetent patient is unable to exercise such a right. Such a right must be exercised for the patient by a surrogate, the Court observed, noting that the Missouri Supreme Court has recognized that a surrogate may act on behalf of an incompetent patient in making this type of decision. To safeguard the state's interest in the protection and preservation of human life, the court requires clear and convincing evidence of the patient's intent to ensure that the surrogate respects as much as possible the wishes expressed by the patient while competent. Imposing a higher standard of proof than is required in most civil suits is a legitimate way to protect state interests, the court declared, because the decision to withdraw life-sustaining treatment is so significant and irreversible. In addition, the court found that the federal constitution does not require states to accept the "substituted judgment" of close family members and only recognizes a personal right to make such decisions.

Severely Deformed or Impaired Newborns

An especially perplexing case for nurses and physicians concerns the newborn infant with severe deformities that are inconsistent with prolonged or sapient life. Traditionally, it had been accepted practice in many medical centers, on the concurrence of the parents and the treatment team, to provide only ordinary care to these infants so that their suffering was not prolonged through extraordinary efforts.[49]

In 1984, Congress amended the Child Abuse Prevention and Treatment Act[50] that governs the provision of care to disabled infants.

> [T]he term "withholding of medically indicated treatment" means the failure to respond to the infant's life-threatening conditions by providing treatment (including appropriate nutrition, hydration, and medication) which, in the treating physician's or physicians' reasonable medical judgment, will be most likely to be effective in ameliorating or correcting all such conditions, except that the term does not include the failure to provide treatment (other than appropriate nutrition, hydration or medication) to an infant, when, in the treating physician's or physicians' reasonable medical judgement—
>
> (A) the infant is chronically and irreversibly comatose;
> (B) the provision of such treatment would—
>   (i)   merely prolong dying;
>   (ii) not be effective in ameliorating or correcting all of the infant's life-threatening conditions; or
>   (iii) otherwise be futile in terms of the survival of the infant and the treatment itself under such circumstances would be in humane.[51]

Not uncommonly, health care professionals disagree as to which conditions are sufficiently severe that treatment offers no reasonable likelihood of benefit. Although there is general acceptance of withholding treatment when the condition is anencephaly (the absence of the higher brain) or another condition that precludes the development of sapient life or is inconsistent with prolonged life, there is no such agreement in regard to the surgical repair of problems associated with spina bifida.

Neither mental retardation if it is a sapient level nor physical deformities if they are consistent with prolonged survival are considered to justify withholding treatment from newborns. Only extraordinary treatments may be withheld in these cases. Ordinary care, such as feeding, must be continued according to the Child Abuse Amendments of 1984, which prohibits the withholding of appropriate nutrition and hydration from disabled infants.

Other Minors

Minors are generally treated as incompetents for purposes of medical care decisions. When the minor is able to participate in the decision, however, the minor's wishes should be given substantial weight. This presents no difficulty when the minor and the parents or guardian agree, such as when the minor initiates the idea of withholding treatment and the parents agree. The case is more complex when there is irreconcilable disagreement. If the minor is immature and either the minor or a parent or a guardian want to treat, treatment should be pursued, even though court authorization is required if only the minor wants the treatment. If the minor is mature, court resolution of the conflict should be pursued.

For example, the Maine Supreme Court ruled that a gastrostomy tube should not be reinserted into a 17-year-old patient in a persistent vegetative state because the patient had, while competent, expressed the desire not to be maintained in such a manner.[52] In this case, a trial court had found that the patient, while competent, had expressed in a serious and deliberative manner his desire not be sustained by artificial means if ever he were medically incompetent. The supreme court agreed that the patient should be allowed to die, finding that the fact the patient was a minor when he made these statements did not reduce their legal significance.

Role of the Courts

The necessity of involving the courts to determine whether to withdraw or withhold treatment from incompetent patients is not yet clearly established and varies from state to state. As a general rule, however, courts will intervene if there is disagreement among those involved in the decision making. Usually, the disagreement that leads to court involvement is between a health care provider and the patient's family. Health care providers have intervened in such cases to oppose termination of life-sustaining treatment, as in the *Cruzan* case, and have also become involved if they question a family member's decision to prolong treatment.

Courts have not only had to determine whether they should become involved in these cases, but also the type of evidence required for an appropriate order concerning incompetent patients who have not executed advance medical directives indicating how they would want to be treated under such circumstances. As a result, the central issue is the evidentiary standard that must be met to determine if the patient, when competent, indicated whether he or she would want to be kept alive by artificial means.

Numerous courts have adopted the clear and convincing evidence standard and have authorized the termination of life-sustaining treatment because patients, while competent, clearly and convincingly expressed the desire not to be maintained by artificial treatment if ill with no hope of recovery. In *Cruzan*,[53] the U.S. Supreme Court validated the clear and convincing evidence standard, ruling that states are not required to accept the "substituted judgment" of close family members and may impose a higher standard of proof with respect to the patient's personal choice.

Courts have given extensive consideration to what constitutes clear and convincing evidence of an incompetent patient's intent with respect to life-sustaining medical treatment. Some courts, for instance, have applied the standard quite liberally. In one case, a New York appeals court found that a patient, while commenting on artificial means of survival, had extracted promises from her family that she not be maintained in such a manner.[54]

Other courts, however, have applied the clear and convincing standard in a more rigorous manner by requiring that a patient's prior rejection of life-sustaining procedures be highly specific. One of the more significant cases to adopt this line of reasoning is the New York high court ruling in *In the Matter of Mary O'Connor*.[55] In this case, the court allowed a hospital to insert a nasogastric tube into an elderly patient who had suffered substantial and permanent brain damage. Although the court insisted that it is not necessary for a patient to have specifically rejected a particular treatment for a precise condition, it ruled that it is important to ascertain if the patient's statements were made in response to situations and procedures that were qualitatively different from the patient's own current situation.

Who May Decide in Absence of Court Involvement?

When patients have not expressed their wishes and are unable to do so, some individual or group must be able to make decisions for them. Obviously, the nurses, physicians, and other professionals involved in the care of the patient have an important role and are relatively easy to identify. It is sometimes more difficult to identify the proper person to represent the patient in the decision making. When there is a guardian, there is usually no problem because the guardian can make the required decisions on behalf of the patient. Occasionally, however, close family members disagree with the guardian; in this instance, guidance from the court may be needed.

When there is no guardian, it is generally accepted that the spouse or next of kin of the incompetent patient may make decisions that cannot be deferred until the patient is competent. The decision-making role of the family is limited by the physician's diagnostic role and responsibility to the patient. The family can decide to withhold or withdraw treatment without court involvement only when the physician determines that the patient is terminally ill or irreversibly comatose and the physician accepts the family's treatment decision. When the physician and family concur in withholding treatment from an incompetent patient who is terminally ill or irreversibly comatose, the risk associated with carrying out the decision is minimal.[56]

CIVIL STATUTES AND REGULATIONS CONCERNING TREATMENT DECISIONS

Before the evolution of the judicial consensus regarding the rights of the terminally ill, many physicians and hospitals were reluctant to respect the wishes of terminally ill patients and their families that treatments be limited. A substantial minority of physicians still do not accept refusals of care because of either their personal ethics or their concerns regarding legal risks. To facilitate carrying out the wishes of the patient and others and to relieve the concerns of the physicians, several laws or regulations that explicitly authorize health care personnel to honor these wishes have been enacted.[57]

Legislation requiring that all federally funded facilities inform patients of their rights under state law to accept or refuse medical treatment was enacted in 1990 and is commonly referred to as the Patient Self-Determination Act (PSDA).[58] The PSDA requires health care providers and institutions that receive Medicare or Medicaid funding to advise patients of their legal rights to accept or refuse medical or surgical treatment and of the right of the patient to formulate advance directives. "Advance directive" is defined as a written instruction, such a living will or durable power of attorney for health care, recognized under state law and relating to the provision of medical care when the individual is incapacitated. The PSDA applies to hospitals, long-term care facilities, home health care agencies, hospice programs, and health maintenance organizations (HMO). Under the PSDA, each state must prepare a written description of the law in that state regarding advance directives and distribute this information to any individual admitted as an inpatient at a hospital or a resident at a skilled nursing facility, to HMO enrollees, and to recipients of home health care, personal care services, or hospice program services.

In accordance with the law, health care facilities must develop written policies requiring that patients receive legal information regarding the exercise of their rights as well as information about the policy itself. The policies must require that a patient's medical record indicate whether the patient has an advance directive. In addition, health care providers must ensure that a patient will not be discriminated against on the basis of the existence or absence of an advance directive and provide community and staff education about advance directives. Nurses and physicians also must educate their staffs and the community on issues concerning advance directives but recognize the validity of state legislation that allows employees to refuse to implement advance directives as a matter of conscience. The PSDA also requires the Department of Health and Human Services to develop and implement a national campaign to inform the public of their option to execute advance directives and to develop nationwide informational materials on this subject to be distributed by providers.

The Joint Commission has also incorporated in its *Accreditation Manual* many of the duties imposed on hospitals by the PSDA. A standard addresses the issues of patients' rights and requires that hospitals' policies describe the means by which those rights are protected and exercised.[59] A patient's right as defined in the standard includes the opportunity to create advance directives, access to information necessary to make informed decisions about medical treatment, and the right to participate in discussions of the ethical issues that may arise during the patient's care. Hospitals must also adopt a policy on the use of DNR orders and the withholding or withdrawal of life-sustaining treatment and institute a mechanism to ascertain the existence of advance directives at the time of a patient's admission. Advance directives must appear in the patient's medical record and be reviewed periodically with the patient or the surrogate decision maker.

Living Will Legislation

The most widely available instrument for recording future health care–related decisions is the living will. The vast majority of states have enacted legislation recognizing the right of a competent adult to prepare a document providing direction as to medical care if the adult becomes incapacitated or otherwise unable to make decisions personally. Historically, living will legislation, often embodied in natural death acts, was limited to directives regarding the treatment of terminal illness. In addition, there was some doubt as to whether a patient could use a living will as an instrument to request withholding or withdrawing of artificial nutrition. More recently, however, several states have amended their living will laws so this form of advance directive can be specifically applied if the patient is suffering from a terminal condition *or* is irreversibly unconscious.

Living will legislation covers a variety of topics, including how to execute such a document, physician certification of terminal illness or irreversible coma, immunity from civil and criminal liability for providers who implement the decisions, and the right to transfer a patient to another facility if a provider cannot follow the directive for reasons of conscience. Most living will statutes authorize only competent adults to sign directives. Although there is a common-law presumption that each adult is competent, several of the natural death acts restate this presumption.[60]

Although some state laws used to contain statutorily dictated wording for written directives, the trend has been away from mandating the contents of living wills toward requiring that these documents contain "substantially" or "essentially" the same information as in the statutory model. State legislation also specifies the formality with which the directive must be executed. All the acts require witnesses, and some disqualify certain people from being witnesses (e.g., relatives, those who will inherit the estate, those who have claims against the estate, the attending physician, nurses, and employees of the physician or hospital).

State laws also specify the means to revoke a directive. Written revocations generally must meet requirements (i.e., they must be signed, dated, and communicated to the attending physician). In most states, however, any verbal revocation is effective on communication to the attending physician.[61] Regardless of the technicalities of statutory interpretation, it is best not to carry out a directive if there is any reason to believe the patient has had a change of mind.

The effect of the directive is also defined in state law. Most statutes specify that any physician may decline to follow the directive but must make an effort to transfer the patient to a physician who will follow it.[62]

Several states specify other limits on the effectiveness of a directive. Many of the statutes provide that a directive shall not apply while the patient is pregnant.[63] In states that do not specify whether a directive is effective if the patient is pregnant at the time of implementation, the legal ramifications of withholding or terminating life-sustaining treatment for a pregnant patient are by no means clear. The right of a pregnant patient to refuse care for herself and consequently for her unborn child is a much-debated issue and hinges to a large extent on the evolving legal status of abortion.

All the statutes provide some immunity for those who act or refrain from acting in accordance with a directive that complies with the act. Typically, the laws state that death that results from the withholding or withdrawal of life-sustaining treatment is not a suicide. Nurses, physicians, or other providers are not subject to civil or criminal liability or any other sanction if they implement a declaration in good faith.[64] However, because the diagnosis of terminal illness or permanent unconscious condition is a professional responsibility for which physicians should be accountable, none of the statutes provide any protection from liability that arises from negligent diagnosis. Accordingly, some states limit the statutory immunity by excepting actions that are not in "good faith,"[65] are not in accord with "reasonable professional care or judgment,"[66] or are "negligent."[67]

Durable Power of Attorney

A *power of attorney* is a written document that authorizes an individual, as an agent, to perform certain acts on behalf of and according to the written directives of another, the person executing the document, from whom the agent obtains authority. The agent is called the *attorney-in-fact*; the person executing the document is called the *principal*. Usually an agent's powers cease with the disability of the principal. If a state statute provides for a *durable* power of attorney, however, such as the Uniform Durable Power of Attorney Act (UDPAA), adopted by the vast majority of states, the subsequent disability of incompetence of the principal does not affect the attorney-in-fact's authority. Indeed, a "springing" durable power of attorney does not even become effective until the principal becomes disabled. Most durable power of attorney legislation is general in nature and is not tailored to health care decision making. For this reason, the vast majority of states have gone further to provide for durable powers of attorney specifically for health care decisions. Under this type of legislation, the state authorizes the appointment of an individual who is specifically empowered to make personal health care–related decisions for another person in the event that he or she becomes incapacitated. Many state legislatures have provided model forms in the statutes, which include specific choices for the conditions under which life-sustaining treatment may be withdrawn. For the power of attorney to have any legal effect, the principal must be mentally competent when executing it.[68]

Because the attorney-in-fact will be making significant decisions affecting the principal's life, the principal must choose as attorney-in-fact someone he or she trusts. The attorney-in-fact's interests should not be adverse to those of the principal, and the attorney-in-fact should not be the same person who is to determine the principal's incapacity.

The exact working of durable powers of attorney varies from state to state and like living wills is largely dictated by models contained in the statutes. In general, these documents grant agents full power and authority to make health care decisions for principals to the same extent as principals would themselves if they were competent. In exercising this authority, the agent must, to the extent possible, make decisions that are consistent with the principal's desires by using the substituted judgment doctrine or make decisions based on what the agent believes to be the principal's best interests. The power of attorney can also enumerate specifically the principal's desires regarding different types of life-sustaining measures, admission or discharge from facilities, pain relief medication and anatomic gifts. It should also allow the agent to gain access to the principal's medical records to be able to make informed decisions.

Of paramount importance is the actual determination of the principal's disability or incompetence. The durable power of attorney should state who will determine the principal's incompetence and set forth the standards to be used in making that determination. It is best for one or more physicians, named in the document or chosen according to a procedure set forth in the writing, to establish incompetence. Disability and incompetence should be defined in the durable power of attorney and should be mutually acceptable to the principal and physicians involved. Copies of the durable power of attorney should be given to the attorney-in-fact, the principal's physician, and close family members. Extra copies should be kept for inclusion in hospital medical records.

A competent principal can revoke the durable power of attorney at any time. The instrument also may be terminated if it contains an expiration clause. Under the UDPAA, a revocation is not effective until the attorney-in-fact has received notice of the revocation.[69] In fact, if the attorney-in-fact states in an affidavit that he or she does not have actual knowledge of the revocation of the writing at the time of acting, the affidavit serves as conclusive proof of the nontermination or nonrevocation of the power of attorney.[70]

Health care providers view the durable power of attorney for health care as a more flexible instrument than a living will. The scope of a living will is generally limited to situations in which the patient is either terminally ill or permanently unconscious. The power of attorney, however, can apply to a wide range of situations in which the patient is unable to communicate a choice regarding a health care decision. In addition, the power of attorney allows the agent to make any decision regarding an incapacitated patient's health care and is not limited to specific life-sustaining measures.

CIVIL AND CRIMINAL LIABILITY

Because of a fear of civil or criminal liability, nurses, physicians, and hospitals have sometimes been reluctant to honor the wishes of terminally ill or persistent vegetative state patients or their families. Although there is theoretically a possibility of liability, it is no more likely that nurses, physicians, and other health care providers will be held liable for withholding or withdrawing treatment in these cases than for the many other decisions and actions they must make every day. The U.S. Supreme Court ruling in *Cruzan* confirming that the provision of artificial nutrition is medical treatment has clarified this issue.

Civil liability for withholding or withdrawing medical treatment would have to be based on negligent or deliberate failure to act in accordance with some duty to the patient. The duty to the patient is shaped by the patient's condition, and there is no duty to treat the terminally ill as if they are curable.

The best indication of the limited exposure to civil liability is the apparent absence of lawsuits brought against physicians for withholding or withdrawing medical treatment from terminally ill patients with the concurrence of the patient or the family. The greatest exposure to liability appears to be from misdiagnosis of terminal illness or unjustifiable failure to secure the concurrence of the patient or the family, but there are no reported liability cases addressing those issues. The unlikelihood of criminal liability in cases involving the withdrawal or withholding of treatment seems clear. It would appear, however, that in cases of physician-assisted suicide, the risk of criminal prosecution is becoming more likely. Living will legislation generally grants statutory immunity from criminal liability for actions in accordance with valid directives.

THE DYING PATIENT: LIMITS TO THE PATIENT'S CHOICES

Occasionally, terminally ill patients or their families seek therapies that are outside the accepted range or seek hospitalization beyond the time necessary. These are normal responses to an extremely stressful situation. Reliance must be placed primarily on patience and tactful communications to give these patients and their families the time, information, and support to accept the limitations of medical science. Sometimes, they are not able to accept the limitations, however, and other approaches become necessary.

The duty of a nurse, physician, and other health care staff to a patient is shaped by many forces. The duty to a dying patient is somewhat different from the duty to other patients. Although terminally ill patients can refuse treatment, they can alternatively seek the entire range of accepted appropriate therapies for their conditions.

Patients do not have a right to insist on treatment outside the accepted range of therapies. Physicians have the responsibility and authority to refuse to provide illegal or inappropriate therapies. The U.S. Supreme Court has ruled that the terminally ill have no special right to treatment that the government has declared illegal.[71] A physician who provided a legal, but inappropriate, treatment might be liable for malpractice notwithstanding the patient's consent to such treatment.[72] If there is a difference of opinion among reputable physicians regarding the appropriateness of a legal treatment, reasonable efforts should be made to transfer the care of the patient to a physician who concurs with the patient. Sometimes, if the inappropriate treatment desired by the patient is neither illegal nor dangerous, the most prudent course may be to acquiesce, as long as the patient is willing to continue accepted therapy simultaneously.

CONCLUSION

The right of competent patients to refuse treatment is now well established. Patients can make their wishes known through living wills and durable powers of attorney. Advanced care directives, such as living wills, continue to be ways in which patients and their families can make their wishes known at the end of life. The nurse, by understanding these legal aspects of death and dying, can continue being an effective patient advocate and caregiver to the patient and his or her family in this crisis situation.

FOOTNOTES

1. *In re* Quinlan, 70 N.J. 10, 355 A.2d 647, 677 (1976).
2. *E.g.,* Matter of Dinnerstein, 6 Mass. App. 466, 380 N.E. 2d 134, 135 (1978) (one year); Satz v. Perlmutter, 362 So. 2d 160, 161 (Fla. Dist. Ct. App. 1978), *aff'd,* 379 So. 2d 359 (Fla. 1980); Matter of Spring, 405 N.E. 2d 115, 118 (Mass. 1980) (five years).
3. JOINT COMMISSION ON ACCREDITATION OF HEALTHCARE ORGANIZATIONS, ACCREDITATION MANUAL FOR HOSPITALS, Patient Rights (1994).
4. *In re* Wanglie, No PX-91-283 (Minn. P. Ct., May 13, 1991).

5. *In re* Doe, No. D-93064 (Ga. Super. Ct., Oct. 17, 1991).

6. Hoyt v. St. Mary's Rehabilitation Ctr., No. 774555 (Minn. Dist. Ct., Hennepin County, February 13, 1981).

7. Eichner v, Dillon, 73 A.D.2d 431, 426 N.Y.S.2d 517, 527 (1980).

8. JOINT COMMISSION, *supra* note 3.

9. PRESIDENT'S COMMISSION FOR THE STUDY OF ETHICAL PROBLEMS IN MEDICINE AND BIOMEDICAL AND BEHAVORIAL RESEARCH, DECIDING TO FOREGO LIFE-SUSTAINING TREATMENT (1983), at 82–89.

10. *Decisions Near the End of Life,* Report of the Council on Ethical and Judicial Affairs, American Medical Association (AMA), adopted by the House of Delegates, June 25, 1991.

11. *Withholding or Withdrawing Life-Prolonging Medical Treatment,* Current Opinions of the Council on Ethical and Judicial Affairs, AMA, Nos. 2.20 and 2.21 (1989).

12. Matter of Quinlan, 355 A.2d 647, 658–659, 671 (1976).

13. 426 N.Y.S.2d 517, 527 (1980).

14. *In re* Benjamin C, No. J914419 (Cal. Super. Ct., Los Angeles County, Feb. 15, 1979) (3-year-old); *In re* Young, 48 U.S.L.W: 2238 (Cal. Super. Ct., Orange County, Sept. 11, 1979).

15. Leach v. Akron Gen. Med. Ctr., No. C80-10-20 (Ohio C.P. Ct., Summit County, Dec. 18, 1980).

16. Dockery v. Dockery, No. 51439 (Tenn. Ch. Ct., Hamilton County, Feb. 11, 1977), *appeal dismissed as moot,* 559 S.W.2d 952 (Tenn. Ct. App. 1977), *cert. denied,* (Tenn. 1977).

17. Satz v. Perlmutter, 379 So. 2d 359 (Fla. 1980), *approved,* 362 So. 2d 160 (Fla. Dist. Ct. App. 1978).

18. 370 N.E.2d 417, 423–429 (1977).

19. Matter of Spring, 405 N.E.2d 115, 122–123 (Mass. 1980).

20. 195 Cal. Rptr. 484 (Cal. Ct. App. 1983).

21. *See, e.g., In re* Conroy, 486 A.2d 1209 (N.J. 1985); Brophy v. New England Sinai Hosp., Inc., 497 N.E.2d 626 (Mass. 1986); Corbett v. D'Alessandro, 487 So. 2d 368 (Fla. Dist. Ct. App. 1986); *In re* Jobes, No. C-4-971-85E (N.J. Super. Ct. Ch. Div. Apr. 23, 1986); Bouvia v. Superior Ct., 225 Cal. Rptr. 297 (Cal. Ct. App. 1986), *cert. denied,* No. B019134 (Cal. July 22, 1986). For commentary, *see* Gostin, *A Right to Choose Death, The Judicial Trilogy of Brophy, Bouvia, and Conroy,* 14 L. MED. & HEALTH CARE 198 (1986); Meyers, *Legal Aspects of Withdrawing Nourishment from an Incurably Ill Patient,* 145 ARCHIVES INTERNAL MED. 125 (1985); Rothenburg, *Foregoing Life-Sustaining Treatment; What Are the Legal Limits in an Aging Society?,* SPECIALTY L. DIG.; HEALTH CARE, January 1991.

22. *Withholding or Withdrawing Life-Prolonging Medical Treatment, supra* note 11.

23. Delio v. Westchester County Med. Ctr., 510 N.Y.S.2d 415 (N.Y. Sup. Ct. 1986); *see also* Vogel v. Foreman, 512 N.Y.S.2d 622 (N.Y. Sup. Ct. 1986).

24. 486 A.2d 1209 (N.J. 1985).

25. *In re* Jobes, 529 A.2d 434 (N.J. 1987).

26. Ross v. Hilltop Rehabilitation Hosp., 676 F. Supp. 1528 (D. Colo. 1987).

27. Schloenfordd v. Society of N.Y. Hosp., 105 N.E. 91 (1914).

28. *See, e.g.,* White v. Chicago & N.W. Ry. Co., 124 N.W. 309, 311 (1910).

29. 438 N.Y.S.2d 266, 420 N.E.2d 64 (1981).

30. Matter of Spring, *supra* note 19.

31. Satz v. Perlmutter, 362 So. 2d 160, 162 (Fla. Dist. Ct. App. 1978), *approved,* 379 So. 2d 359 (Fla. 1980).

32. Matter of Quinlan, *supra* note 12 at 662–663; Superintendent of Belchertown v. Saikewicz, 370 N.E.2d 417, 426 (1977).

33. 225 Cal. Reptr. 297 (Cal. Ct. App. 1986), *cert. denied,* No. B01934 (Cal. July 23, 1986).

34. McKay v. Bergstedt, No. 21207 (Nev. Nov. 30, 1990).

35. Matter of Quinlan, *supra* note 12 at 661–662.

36. Eichner v. Dillon, 426 N.Y.S.2d 517, 537 (1980), *aff'd sub. nom. In re* Storar, 438 N.Y.S.2d 266, 420 N.E.2d 64 (1981).

37. Matter of Quinlan, 355 A.2d 647, 664 (1976).

38. Georgia v. McAfree, 385 S.E.2d 651 (Ga. 1989).

39. McKay v. Bergstedt, No. 21207 (Nev. Nov. 30, 1990).

40. Superintendent of Belchertown v. Saikewicz, 370 N.E.2d 417, 426 (1977); *see also* Satz v. Perlmutter, 362 So. 2d 160, 162 (Fla. Dist. Ct. App. 1978), *approved,* 379 So. 2d 359 (Fla. 1980); Eichner v. Dillon, 426 N.Y.S.2d 517, 544 (1980), *aff'd sub nom. In re* Storar, 438 N.Y.S.2d 266, 420 N.E.2d 64 (1981).

41. *Superintendent of Belchertown, supra* note 40, at 426.

42. *Satz, supra* note 17, at 162–163; *Eichner, supra* note 7.

43. *Eichner, supra* note 7.

44. *See, e.g.,* Brophy v. New England Sinai Hosp, Inc., 497 N.E.2d 626 (Mass. 1986); Matter of Requena, 517 A.2d 869 (N.J. Super. Ct. App. Div. 1986).

45. *Decisions Near the End of Life,* Report of the Council on Ethical and Judicial Affairs of the American Medical Association, *adopted by* AMA House of Delegates, June 25, 1991.

46. Cruzan v. Mouton, No. CV384-9P (Mo. Probate Ct. Dec. 14, 1990). Note that in this instance, the Missouri Attorney General declared that the state no longer had a recognizable legal interest in the case.

47. Matter of Quinlan, *supra* note 12 at 664.

48. 110 S. Ct. 2841 (June 25, 1990).

49. Duff, *Counseling Families and Deciding Care of Severely Defective Children,* 67 PEDIATRICS 315 (1981); Victoroff, *The Ballad of Baby Doe: Parental Discretion or Medical Neglect?* 13 PRIMARY CARE 171 (1986); McLone, *The Diagnosis, Prognosis, and Outcome for the Handicapped Newborn: A Neonatal View,* 2 ISSUES L. & MED. 15 (1986); Rhoden & Arras, *Withholding Treatment from Baby Doe: From Discrimination to Child Abuse,* 63 MILBANK MEMORIAL FUND Q. 18 (1985).

50. 42 U.S.C. §§ 5101–5106.

51. 42 U.S.C. § 510g (10).

52. *In re* Swan, No. 5341 (Me. Feb. 15, 1990).

53. 110 S. Ct. 2841 (June 25, 1990).

54. Elbaum v. Grace Plaza, 544 N.Y.2d 840 (N.Y. App. Div. 1989).

55. No. 312 (N.Y. Oct. 14, 1988).

56. *See* Areen, *The Legal Status of Consent Obtained from Families of Adult Patients to Withhold or Withdraw Treatment,* 258 JAMA 229 (1987), for a discussion of the legality of treatment decisions made by families without involvement of the court system.

57. *See generally* Miskkin, *Planning Ahead for Difficult Health Care Decisions,* HEALTH-SPAN 3, Apr. 1987.

58. Pub. L. No. 101-508, 104 Stat. 291 (1990).

59. JOINT COMMISSION, *supra* note 3.

60. *See, e.g.,* KAN. STAT. ANN. § 65-28, 106.

61. *See, e.g.,* CAL. HEALTH & SAFETY CODE § 7189(a); W. VA. CODE § 70.122.040.

62. *See, e.g.,* TEX. REV. CIV. STAT. ANN. § 672.016; W. VA. CODE § 70,122.070(2); OR. REV. STAT. § 127.625.

63. *See, e.g.,* CAL. HEALTH & SAFETY CODE § 7189.5 and KAN. REV. STAT § 65-28, 103. Texas includes a provision in its model form relating to the nonapplicability of a declaration if the patient is pregnant. *See* TEX. REV. CIV. STAT. ANN. § 672.004.

64. *See, e.g.,* TEX. REV. CIV. STAT. ANN. art 672.015; W. VA. CODE § 70.122.050; OR. REV. STAT. § 127.635; ARK. CODE ANN. § 20-17-208; N.M. STAT. ANN. § 24-7-7.

65. KAN. STAT. ANN. § 65-28, 106; OR. REV. STAT. § 127.645(2); WASH. REV. CODE ANN. § 70.122.050.

66. N.M. STAT. ANN. § 24-7-7 (1991).

67. TEX. REV. CIV. STAT. ANN. art. 672.015.

68. 3 AM. JUR. 2D, at 532.

69. Uniform Durable Power of Attorney Act § 4(a).

70. *Id.* at § 5.

71. United States v. Rutherford, 442 U.S. 544, S. Ct. 2470 (1979).

72. King v. Solomon, 323 Mass. 326, 81 N.E.2d 838 (1948).

CHAPTER 13

Legal Aspects of Death

Chapter Objectives

1. To define death
2. To discuss the handling of dead bodies

The definition of death is relatively settled, but its application requires great care. The law regarding handling dead bodies also is settled and must be followed strictly because of the important societal and individual interests affected. It is important for nurses to be familiar with the law concerning the determination of death and the handling of bodies so that nurses can fulfill their responsibilities both professionally and to the patient and his or her family and not inadvertently interfere with other staff members who are carrying out other duties.

DEFINITION OF DEATH

The question of the definition of death is distinct from the questions concerning treatment of the living. Once the patient is legally dead, there no longer is a patient. Patient care should be discontinued. The institution becomes the custodian of a dead body with the responsibilities discussed later in this chapter.

Modern technology is able to sustain vegetative functions of persons with irreversible cessation of brain function. Because of this development, irreversible cessation of brain function has become accepted as the definition of death when vital signs of a patient are being maintained artificially. The traditional definition still is applicable in all other situations.

Medical Definition of Death

For more than a century, the traditional definition of death has been the cessation of respiration, heartbeat, and certain indications of central nervous system activity (e.g., responsiveness to pain and reaction of pupils to light). Advances in technology in the 1950s and 1960s produced cardiac pumps and respirators that can maintain the first two traditional indicators of life for indefinite periods, well beyond the irreversible cessation of all detectable brain activity; thus, medical science was forced to decide whether such an individual was alive or dead when the first two traditional life indicators were being maintained artificially.

It was concluded that such individuals were dead and that the use of machines should be discontinued. In 1974, the House of Delegates of the American Medical Association recognized that "permanent and irreversible cessation of function of the brain constitutes one of the various criteria which can be used in the medical diagnosis of death."

It is accepted in the medical profession that death occurs when there is irreversible cessation of all brain functions, including the brain stem. Although it may be appropriate to discontinue certain treatments for patients with only brain stem functioning, it is not appropriate to declare them dead until the brain stem also irreversibly ceases to function.

There still is some debate regarding optimal diagnostic criteria. The first widely publicized criteria were announced in 1968 by the Ad Hoc Committee of the Harvard Medical School to Examine the Definition of Brain Death. The lack of consensus at that time is reflected in the cautiously worded title of its report, *A Definition of Irreversible Coma.*[1] This title is unfortunate because it had led some to believe that the criteria can be used to assess only higher brain function, when in fact they can also be used to assess brainstem activity. Thus, despite the title, the Harvard criteria do apply to irreversible cessation of total brain function.

The report set forth the following criteria:

1. "unreceptivity and unresponsivity" to "externally applied stimuli and inner need"
2. absence of spontaneous muscular movements or spontaneous respiration
3. absence of any elicitable reflexes

A flat (isoelectric) electroencephalogram (EEG) was mentioned as having "great confirmatory value" in the diagnosis. There also was a warning that either hypothermia (low body temperature) or central nervous system depressants could cause the criteria to be met, so an assessment in the presence of either would not be valid. The report also specified that all the criteria had to be met again at least 24 hours later.

The EEG is not a mandatory adjunct to the diagnosis, but it is helpful. If appropriate EEG machines, trained operators, and trained interpreters are available in the hospital, it may be difficult to explain a failure to use them because some of the public unfortunately has identified brain death with the flat line on the EEG tracing. However, if all the listed criteria are present, it is permissible to diagnose brain death without the EEG.

Although the Harvard criteria still are widely used, various organizations have proposed modifications. In addition, the President's Commission for the Study of Ethical Problems in Medicine and Biomedical and Behavioral Research released in 1981 a set of guidelines developed by its medical consultants on the diagnosis of death.[2] Although the commission presented these solely as advisory guidelines, they can be expected to receive increasing recognition.

Some of the modifications include (1) focus on the importance of the cause of the condition, (2) changes in the length of time for the diagnosis, (3) use of other tests, and (4) other matters. The Harvard criteria focused not on cause but entirely on the present condition of the patient. The only reference to cause in the Harvard criteria is the statement that if there is evidence of drug intoxication, time should be allowed for elimination of the intoxicating agent before the diagnosis is made.

The commission guidelines emphasize the importance of determining cause but recognize that it is not necessary in all cases. The commission urged caution when (1) diseases or drugs that may cause total paralysis are involved, (2) metabolic abnormalities may be present, or (3) the patient is in shock. The Harvard criteria addressed the length of time for diagnosis by specifying that all tests must be repeated after at least 24 hours. It now is recognized that, in some cases (e.g., when the cause clearly is massive head trauma), a much shorter period may be appropriate. There is some acceptance of a 12-hour or even 6-hour period in cases in which drug intoxication is not suspected.

Legal Definition of Death

The common-law definition of death includes brain death as determined in accordance with usual medical standards. In the first years that followed the medical recognition of brain death, some lower courts had difficulty accepting brain death in suits involving organ donations for heart transplants. One California trial court refused to accept brain death as death, acquitting the person who had been charged with manslaughter in the death of the donor. Such trial court cases now are historical anomalies.

The statutory recognition of brain death not only has superseded these decisions in their jurisdictions but also has resolved the question in more than half of the states. The common-law definition now also clearly includes brain death. Every appellate court that has ruled on the question has recognized brain death as legal death. Since 1977, the highest courts of Arizona, Colorado, Indiana, Massachusetts, and Washington, among others, all have adopted the brain death standard.[3]

Laws that include brain death in the definition were passed in an effort to avoid the case-by-case approach of the common law. The early contradictory trial court decisions added impetus to the statutory trend. Many of these cases involved organs removed from victims of apparent homicides. Some persons accused of homicide argued that they were not responsible for the death of the victim whose organs were transplants.

To avoid this issue, many centers did not accept organ donations from victims of apparent homicide. An important factor in the passage of the statutes was that they facilitated organ donations from such victims, increasing the number of organs available to treat others and frequently helping the bereaved family to find some solace in helping others.

The details in the brain death laws vary from state to state, so physicians and nurses must be familiar with local law to ensure compliance, especially with consultation and documentation requirements. Several groups have developed model legislation in an effort to achieve more uniformity. In 1980, several of the major groups involved in this effort agreed on the following model: "An individual who has sustained either (1) irreversible cessation of circulatory and respiratory functions, or (2) irreversible cessation of all functions of the entire brain, including the brain stem, is dead. A determination of death must be made in accordance with accepted medical standards."[4] Since agreement was reached on a single model, numerous states have responded by adopting the definition contained in the model legislation. More than two-thirds of the states have adopted the Uniform Brain Death Act.

An anencephalic infant cannot be considered legally dead for purposes of organ donation, the Florida Supreme Court has ruled. Anencephalic children are born with only a brainstem and generally have only limited capacity to maintain autonomous bodily functions such as breathing and heartbeat.[5] For this reason, anencephaly is a fatal birth defect, and infants who are so afflicted generally survive only a few days after birth, if at all. In this case, the parents learned during the eighth month of pregnancy that their child would be born anencephalic. They chose to deliver the child by Caesarean section so that her organs would be less damaged and could be used for transplant in other sick children. Because anencephalic children usually cease to be suitable donors by the time there is a complete absence of brainstem function, the parents applied for a court determination that the child was legally dead while her brainstem continued to function. At the time of trial, the child was breathing unaided, but she died soon after. The trial court ruled that under Florida law, the child could not be declared legally dead as long as her brainstem functioned. The state supreme court upheld the lower court's ruling. The Florida law defining death states that irreversible cessation of brainstem function may determine the occurrence of death when the artificial support of respiratory and circulatory function makes it impossible to determine if these functions have ceased. The statute does not resolve this issue in this case, however, because it only provides a way of defining death if an individual is artificially sustained. Accordingly, the court reasoned, the common-law cardiopulmonary definition of death, which states that death occurs when breathing and heartbeat have stopped entirely, applies to this case. Under the common-law definition, the infant would not be considered legally dead, because she was breathing on her own, the court declared. Although the court acknowledged that some lives might be saved by extending the definition of death to anencephaly, it concluded that public policy does not justify such an extension because of the total lack of consensus about the issue and questions about the overall use of these donations.

DEAD BODIES

This section discusses the duties of institutions and health care professionals in handling dead bodies and communicating with the family and legal authorities. Autopsies and anatomic donations are discussed in the following sections.

Communications with the Family

The health care facility in which a patient dies has a duty to inform an appropriate member of the family of a death. This is necessary not only ethically but also legally to permit arrangements to be made for disposition of the body. Information regarding deaths should be confirmed before being communicated. Erroneous notification will be upsetting to the family and may cause them to make expenditures for funeral arrangements—or even file a lawsuit. The health care facility could be liable for the emotional harm and expenses.

Failure to make reasonable efforts to notify the appropriate member of the family within a reasonable time also can result in liability. In most institutions, it is the responsibility of the physician to make the notification. However, in some institutions or circumstances, nurses may be expected to assist. Nurses should be familiar with their responsibilities so they can make appropriate communications—and refrain from them when others are doing so.

The method by which the family is informed also is important. In 1977, a New Jersey court ruled that a hospital could be sued for the method in which a mother had been informed of the death of her baby.[6] While still in the hospital where the birth occurred, the mother had been telephoned by a person from the hospital to which her baby had been transferred for specialized care. The caller, who was otherwise unidentified, told her the baby was dead, and the mother became hysterical. In addition to the potential liability issues, this case illustrates the humanitarian reasons for thoughtful communications with the family. If it can be avoided, members should not be informed of unexpected deaths by telephone unless someone is with them to provide support. Obviously, when death is anticipated, there may be less need for immediate support.

Release of the Body

On the death of a patient, the health care facility in which the person dies becomes the temporary custodian of the body. The institution is responsible for releasing the body to the proper recipient in the proper condition in accordance with state law. Thus, nurses and other institutional staff members should be familiar with the laws in their state that apply to handling and releasing dead bodies.

In general, the proper recipient of the body has a right to its prompt release in the condition at death unless the deceased has directed otherwise or the body is being retained or examined in accordance with law. Thus, the major issues are (1) scope of the deceased's authority, (2) the authority of others to act in the absence of binding directions by the decedent, (3) the timing of the release of the body, and (4) the condition of the body when it is released.

Some statutes give individuals broad authority to direct the disposition of their remains. All states now have enacted a version of the Uniform Anatomical Gift Act[7] so that individuals can donate their body or certain organs for various purposes. When the situation is not covered by statute and the person entitled to dispose of the body is not willing to carry out the wishes of the deceased, the common law determines whether the wishes of the individual can be enforced. In general, however, organ donation will not occur against the wishes of the family.

In the absence of binding directions by the deceased, the surviving spouse is recognized as the person who controls the disposition of the remains. However, in some states, if the surviving spouse has abandoned and is living apart from the deceased, the right is waived. If there is no surviving spouse or if that person fails to act or waives the right, then control passes to the next of kin. Unless statute or common-law precedent in the jurisdiction establishes a different order of kinship, the priority generally is recognized to be adult child, parent, and adult sibling. If the person with the highest priority either fails to act or waives the right, the next priority level becomes the highest priority level and has control. The interests of nontraditional significant others, however, are best protected by directions of the deceased, usually through a will.

The person who is entitled to control of the body is entitled to have it in the condition at the time of death. The change in condition that most frequently has led to litigation has resulted from an autopsy. An autopsy that is done without proper consent or other lawful authority can result in liability for violation of the right to the body in the condition at the time of death.

When a person dies of a transmittable disease, the person to whom the body is actually released should be informed so appropriate precautions can be taken for the public health and the health of nurses or others involved in preparing the body.

When the disease is an unusual one, such as the slow virus of the Creutzfeldt-Jakob disease,[8] it is important that the mortician be advised that additional precautions are necessary. If the appropriate precautions are not known locally, then the mortician should be referred to expert pathologic consultation. There are no court decisions involving transmission of disease from a body to a mortician's staff, perhaps because of the precautions taken. However, this is not just a theoretical problem, because disease has been transmitted through donated organs.

Some states require by law that hospitals notify the individual or organization to which it releases the body if the patient was infected with a communicable disease. In Virginia, for example, hospitals must notify funeral homes if a dead patient was infected with a disease that can be transmitted through exposure to bodily fluids.[9] In Rhode Island, if a patient dies with a communicable disease, including acquired immune deficiency syndrome, a written notification must accompany the body when it is picked up for disposition.[10]

Autopsies

Autopsies are the most frequent cause of litigation involving dead bodies and health care providers. This section outlines the legal prerequisites to autopsies and the potential sources of liability involving them.

Autopsies are performed primarily to determine the cause of death. This finding can be crucial in detecting crime or ruling out transmittable diseases that may be a threat to the public health. More frequently, the cause of death can affect whether death benefits are payable under insurance policies, workers' compensation laws, and other programs. Autopsies help to advance medical science by permitting the correlation of anatomical changes with other signs and symptoms of disease. At the same time, they can be educational for those involved in them.

Community mores and religious beliefs have long dictated respectful handling of dead bodies. Societal views now have evolved to the point that a substantial portion of the population recognizes the benefit of autopsies. Out of respect to those who continue to find autopsies unacceptable, the law requires appropriate consent before one can be performed, except when it is needed to determine the cause of death for public policy purposes.

Authorization by Decedent

The statutes of many states permit people to authorize an autopsy to be performed on their bodies after death. In states that do not explicitly address authorization before death, the Anatomical Gift Act can be used. The person can donate the body for the purpose of autopsy, with such conditions as are desired, by following the rules for executing an anatomic gift. Even when there clearly is valid authorization for the decedent, hospitals and physicians may decide in some cases to decline to perform an autopsy—for example, when it is contrary to the strongly held wishes of the family.

Authorization by Family or Others

When the patient has not given legal authorization for an autopsy, authorization must be obtained from someone else. Many states have statutes that specify who may authorize an autopsy. Some specify a priority ordering; the available person with the highest priority may give the authorization.[11] Others specify that the person assuming responsibility for disposal of the body may consent to the autopsy.[12] This second type of statute does not specify a priority, so common-law principles must be followed to determine that point. In a few states, autopsy authorization statutes do not establish priority but rather specify the priority of the duty to assume custody for disposal.[13] In such cases, the courts look to the duty of disposal statutes to establish the priority. In the absence of either an autopsy authorization or duty-of-disposal statute, the common-law priority is followed.

The general common-law rule is that the surviving spouse has the highest priority and duty to arrange for disposal and, thus, is the proper person to authorize an autopsy. If there is no surviving spouse or the right of the spouse is waived, the next of kin has the responsibility. The most common order is child, parent, sibling, then other next of kin. Most statutes disqualify any on the list who are not adults.

Under most of the statutes, the authorization of the highest priority person who can be located with reasonable efforts is sufficient unless there is actual knowledge of the objections of a person of the same or a higher priority or of the deceased. In these states, objections by persons of lower priority have no legal effect. However, a few states permit persons of lower priority to veto an authorization, so familiarity with state law is essential.

Most of the authorization statutes specify others who may authorize an autopsy when there is no spouse or next of kin available. In most states, the final priority rests with whoever assumes responsibility for disposal of the remains. A few states permit a physician to perform an autopsy without authorization when there is neither knowledge of any objection nor anyone assuming responsibility for disposal after due inquiry.

Scope of Authorization

The general rule is that whoever authorizes the autopsy may limit its scope by imposing conditions. If these conditions are not met, then the autopsy is not authorized. If the conditions are unacceptable, however, the physician who is to perform the autopsy may decline to do so. Examples of conditions include limits on the areas to be examined, restrictions on retention of parts of the body, and requirements that certain observers be present. Unless the authorization specifically includes permission to retain parts of the body, an autopsy authorization usually is interpreted not to permit retention.

Form of Authorization

A few states require that an autopsy be authorized in writing. Many states include telegrams and recorded telephone permissions as acceptable forms of authorization. Common law does not require that the authorization be documented in a particular way. A written authorization or recorded telephone authorization obviously is easier to prove.

Medical Examiner or Other Legal Officials

There are many circumstances in which authorization of the deceased, a family member, or friend is not required. Determination of the cause of death is so important in some cases that statutory authority has been granted to certain public officials to order an autopsy. In addition, courts have the authority to issue an order.

All states have a state or county officer, usually called a medical examiner or coroner, who is authorized to investigate certain deaths. In most states, the medical examiner has the authority to perform an autopsy when it is necessary for the investigation. In some of the states, other officials also are given the power.

Liability for Unauthorized Autopsies

Under general principles of liability, a health care facility can be liable for unauthorized autopsies by its employees and agents. Health care facilities are not the insurers of the safety of dead bodies, so they are not generally liable for unauthorized autopsies by persons not acting on behalf of the institution, but they must take reasonable steps to protect the body from an unauthorized autopsy.[14]

Donation of Bodies

Prior to 1969, the uncertainty surrounding the authority of persons to make binding anatomic donations before death and of others to make such donations after death limited the availability of organs for transplantation. The Uniform Anatomical Gift Act was developed as a model to resolve the uncertainty.[15] It was approved by the National Conference of Commissioners on Uniform State Laws and the American Bar Association in August 1968. Laws substantially equivalent to the model were enacted in all the states by the end of 1971. Every state now has statutory authority and procedures for anatomic gifts, so the uncertainty has been removed.

The Uniform Anatomical Gift Act specifies who may donate and who may receive anatomic gifts. It specifies the documentation required, the permitted uses of the anatomic gift, and how a gift may be revoked. It also provides some limitations on liability.[16] Many of the states modified the act before enactment or by subsequent amendment. For example, the age requirements for donation and the liability limitation provisions vary. The act is subject to all laws regarding autopsies. It gives the responsibilities and duties of the medical examiner a higher public priority than anatomic donations. Nurses who are involved in communication with patients and families concerning organ donation should be aware of these requirements.

CONCLUSION

The definition of death is now well established. Brain death has become widely accepted criteria. Nurses must be certain that dead bodies are treated with respect and turned over to the appropriate persons as soon as possible.

FOOTNOTES

1. 205 J.A.M.A. 337 (1968).
2. President's Commission for the Study of Ethical Problems in Medicine and Biomedical and Behavioral Research, Defining Death (July 1981).
3. State v. Fierro, 603 P.2d 74 (Ariz. 1979); Lovato v. District Court, 601 P.2d 1072 (Colo. 1979); Swafford v. State, 421 N.E.2d 596 (Ind. 1981); Commonwealth v. Golston, 366 N.E.2d 744 (Mass. 1977), *cert. denied,* 434 U.S. 1039 (1978); *In re* Welfare of Bowman, 617 P.2d 731 (Wash. 1980).
4. Horan, "Definition of Death: An Emerging Consensus," 12 Trial 22, 25–26 (1980).
5. *In re* T.A.C.P., No. 79,582 (Fla. Nov. 12, 1992).
6. Muniz v. United Hosps. Med. Ctr. Presbyterian Hosp., 153 N.J. Super. 72, 379 A.2d 57 (N.J. Super. Ct. App. Div. 1977).
7. 8 U.L.A. 15 (1972).
8. Gajdusek, *Precautions in Medical Care of, and in Handling Materials from, Patients with Transmissible Virus Dementia (Creutzfeldt-Jakob Disease),* 297 New Eng. J. Med. 1253 (1977).
9. Va. Code Ann. § 32-1.37.1.
10. R.I. Gen. Laws § 23-5-9.
11. *E.g.,* Iowa Code § 144.56.
12. *E.g.,* Colo. Rev. Stat. Ann. § 12-36-133.
13. *E.g.,* Ariz. Rev. Stat. Ann. § 36-831.
14. *E.g.,* Grawunder v. Beth Israel Hosp. Ass'n., 272 N.Y.S. 171 (1934), *aff'd,* 195 N.E. 221 (1935).
15. 8 U.L.A. 15 (1972).
16. Williams v. Hoffman, 223 N.W.2d 844 (Wis. 1974) (liability limitation constitutional but not applicable to treatment of donor before death).

CHAPTER 14

General Principles of Civil Liability

Chapter Objectives

1. To discuss contracts
2. To present the general principles of tort liability
3. To review defenses
4. To address breach of implied warranties and strict liability
5. To determine who is liable
6. To study tort reform/responses to the malpractice crisis
7. To outline risk management
8. To discuss insurance

Everyone involved in the delivery of heath care is acutely aware of the potential for patients or their families to make legal claims seeking money because of injuries they believed were caused by malpractice or other wrongful conduct. Much of this concern on the part of nurses is caused by the mystery and uncertainty surrounding the legal process and principles of liability. This chapter is designed to take away some of that mystery. By developing a basic understanding of liability principles, nurses can help minimize claims and facilitate proper handling of claims that are made.

Civil liability is the liability, or legal responsibility, imposed through mechanisms other than criminal law. Civil liability can be divided into liability that is based on contract and liability that is based on tort. A tort is a private or civil wrong committed by a person or persons against the person or property of another. It generally is based on a violation of a duty owed to the injured party, for instance, the act of the nurse who dispenses an incorrect medication to a patient. The review of tort law includes (1) the three basic types of tort liability: strict liability, liability for intentional torts, and liability for negligent torts; (2) the basis for personal and institutional liability; and (3) recent attempts to reform tort law. (Specific cases illustrating the tort liability of nurses are surveyed in Chapter 15.)

CONTRACTS

A contract is a legally enforceable agreement. Nurses may work under a contract of employment and, in all likelihood, will provide care to patients who are being cared for under a contract between a hospital or agency and a governmental agency or third-party provider. Nurses also work under numerous agreements between the hospital and business or labor organizations, including contracts for rental of equipment and labor contracts specifying terms of employment. These contracts may be written or verbal.

The primary purpose of a written contract is to describe clearly the elements of the agreement. It is important that the agreement be clear among all parties to facilitate compliance, not to prepare for litigation. It is essential that all elements of contracts be carefully thought through and clearly articulated. This section outlines just some of the problems associated with contracts, for the law of contracts is complex.

Enforcement and Nonenforcement

To be enforceable, every contract must specify certain things, including the participants in the agreement, the terms (what each participant agrees to do or not do), and dates within which it is effective. Generally, the signature of a person on a contract binds only that person to the terms of the agreement, but some persons, known as agents, are authorized to act for others, and the signatures of agents are binding on the people or organizations they represent.

Some agreements are not enforceable, including those to agree in the future. In most situations, the courts require all participants in the agreement, called parties, to promise to do something (e.g., to perform or to pay money) or not to do something for there to be a contract. This is called consideration for the contract. In some situations, when one party has not promised or provided any consideration, the courts will not enforce the contract.

There are many other contracts that the courts will not enforce: illegal contracts, those viewed by the courts as being against public policy, oral contracts of the type that the law requires to be written, and unconscionable contracts. Unconscionable contracts are those that shock the conscience of the court, usually because they are so one-sided. Generally, courts apply the unconscionability doctrine only to consumer contracts. Some hospital contracts with patients (e.g., exculpatory contracts purporting to limit the right of a patient to sue) could be found to be unconscionable and thus unenforceable.

Courts tend to limit their review of contracts to what is stated in the written document by applying the "parol evidence rule" under which prior oral agreements are assumed to be incorporated into the written contract. Under this rule, which applies only to certain types of contracts, an oral promise made during negotiations that is not included in the final written agreement is assumed to have been negotiated away. The court will not hear evidence on an oral promise that is not reflected in the final document. Hence if oral statements or agreements between a nurse and his or her employer are important to the understanding of the employment contract, those provisions should be in the written contract; the nurse should not depend on oral agreements with his or her employer.

Litigation and Damage Awards

The purpose of a contract is to document careful planning for completion of an agreement and for dealing with contingencies that preclude performance of the contract. As a last resort, litigation can be required to deal with breach of contract. In a few situations, the court will compel performance of a contract that has been breached by one of the parties. Courts sometimes will issue an injunction prohibiting another party from violating a restrictive covenant, such as an agreement not to compete against an employer after the employment contract is terminated.

In most situations, however, the only remedy the court will award is money, called damages. When it will be difficult to calculate the damages resulting from a breach of contract, the parties sometimes agree in advance what the amount will be; this agreed amount is called liquidated damages. Although courts usually will not enforce contract provisions that are considered penalties, they frequently do enforce liquidated damages provisions as long as the amounts are reasonable.

Contracts can address other issues concerning dispute resolution. They can specify the law of a particular state to govern the contract and will specify where litigation can be brought. Some contracts specify that disputes will be resolved by arbitration rather than court litigation.

There are several defenses to contract suits, including waiver and default. Sometimes courts interpret conduct of the parties, such as regular acceptance of late performance without complaint, to imply a modification to the agreement and thus a waiver of rights. Under a default defense, the law recognizes that some promises are dependent on others and that a sequence of events is either express or implied. If one party fails to perform an earlier step in the sequence, it can be found to be in default, excusing the other parties from carrying out subsequent steps.

Promise to Cure or to Use a Certain Procedure

Most malpractice suits against nurses and hospitals are based on tort law, not on contract law. However, a few suits against health care professionals and hospitals are based on contract principles. One type is the allegation that the physician promised a certain outcome that was not achieved. Absent a specific promise to cure, the law does not consider the physician to be an insurer of a particular outcome. However, if the health care provider is incautious enough to make a promise, the law will enforce it. Nurses, physicians, and others should be careful what they say to patients so they do not go beyond reassurance to promising an outcome that may not be possible.

GENERAL PRINCIPLES OF TORT LIABILITY

A tort is a civil wrong that is not based on a violation of contract. Tort liability almost always is based on fault (i.e., something was done incorrectly, or something that should have been done was omitted). This act or omission can be intentional or can result from negligence. There are some exceptions to the requirement of fault in which there is strict liability for all consequences of certain activities regardless of fault.

The Negligence Factor

Most cases involving nurses are based in negligence, and it is interesting to note the development of causes of action over the years. The earliest malpractice litigation involving nurses generally was based on patient injury sustained as a result of a nurse improperly carrying out an order of a physician. Most of these early cases involved patients being burned by hot water bottles. Another common action was based on postoperative patients who were discovered to have a sponge or surgical instruments left in the incisional site.

The legal issues in the above cases usually involved the extent of the liability of a physician for the actions of the nurse. However, more recently, a third common case involved improperly administered injections that led to the patient sustaining nerve damage. Reflecting the increasingly autonomous role of the professional nurse, the focus of current malpractice suits have shifted away from the liability of the physician for the inappropriate action of the nurse and toward the duties of nurses to observe the patient, report to the physician, and make independent judgment.[1]

Intentional Torts

Although most incidents involving the issue of the liability of a nurse for harm to a patient result from negligence, a nurse also may be liable for intentional wrongs. An intentional tort always involves a willful act that violates the rights of a patient. Intentional torts include assault and battery, defamation, false imprisonment, invasion of privacy, and the intentional infliction of emotional distress.

Assault and Battery

An assault is an action that puts another person in apprehension of being touched in a manner that is offensive, insulting, provoking, or physically injurious without lawful authority or consent. No actual touching is required; the assault is simply the credible threat of being touched in this manner. If actual touching occurs, then it is called battery. Liability for these wrongs is based on the right of individuals to be free from unconsented invasions of their persons.

Assault or battery can occur (1) when medical treatment is attempted or performed without lawful authority or consent and (2) in other circumstances, such as in attempts to restrain patients who are competent and oriented without lawful authority.

When an assault and/or a battery has occurred, the law provides the injured person with the right to recover payment, called damages, for the interference. Thus, the injured person can sue the wrongdoer for the injury suffered. Even if no actual harm occurs, the law presumes a compensable injury to the person from the assault and/or battery.

In the health care context, the legal principles related to assault and battery are closely related to the requirement for consent to medical and surgical procedures. Procedures performed on the patient without consent can give rise to a suit for assault and/or battery. Even if a procedure has improved the health of a patient, an individual who did not consent to the touching may be entitled to damages.

For example, in an early Minnesota case, the patient had consented to surgery to remove a polyp from her right ear. When the patient was anesthetized and the physician could examine her ears, he discovered that the left ear was more seriously involved than the right ear. The physician operated on the left ear, although the patient had consented to surgery on her right ear. The court concluded that this was a battery because surgery was performed on the left ear without a consent.[2] The legal principle established by this case—that a procedure performed without the consent of a patient can give rise to civil liability—should serve as a warning to health care practitioners to act within the scope of the patient's consent.

Assault and battery cases also have been brought on behalf of nurses who were injured by patients. For example, a private duty nurse in Hawaii was hit on the head by a patient who was having delirium tremens. The court held that, in accepting employment with the patient, the nurse did not "assume the risk" of injury unless she could have, in the exercise of due care, prevented the injury. Thus, she could sue the patient.[3]

Defamation

Defamation is the wrongful injury to the reputation of another person. Written defamation is called libel and spoken defamation is called slander. The defamatory statement must be communicated to a third person; defamatory statements made only to the injured party are not grounds for an action. A claim of defamation can arise from the inappropriate or inaccurate release of medical information or from untruthful statements about other members of the hospital or medical staff.

Essentially, there are two defenses to a defamation action: truth and privilege. A statement that is damaging to the reputation of another person will not be the basis for liability if it can be shown that the statement is true. A privileged communication is a disclosure that might be defamatory under different circumstances but is not because of a legally recognized higher duty that the person making the communication must honor.

Courts have recognized the importance of communications concerning the performance of a staff member to supervisory staff and on up through the organizational structure. Such communications are protected by a "qualified privilege" when they are made in good faith to the persons who need to know. This means that liability will not be imposed for defamation even if the communication is false as long as it was made without malice. For example, one federal court held that a report submitted to a nursing supervisor concerning a disagreement over the order of a physician could not be the basis for a libel suit.[4] For a communication to be privileged, it must be made within appropriate channels to a person who has a legitimate reason to receive the information. Discussions with others will not be protected by the qualified privilege.

Many courts have recognized a qualified privilege for assessments provided by a former employer to a prospective employer. This is illustrated by a Michigan case in which the director of a department of health that had employed a nurse was found not liable for providing a prospective employer with information concerning the abilities of a nurse. The court ruled that the qualified privilege applied, and no malice had been shown.[5] Many employers do not release information regarding former employees unless a written request from the former employee is received, so they do not need to rely on the court to decide that the qualified privilege applies. Of course, liability still could be imposed for untruthful information released with malice.

False Imprisonment

False imprisonment is the unlawful restriction of the freedom of a person, including physical restraint or unlawful detention. Holding a person against his or her will by physical restraint, barriers, or even threats of harm can constitute false imprisonment if not legally justified. Claims of false imprisonment have often arisen from patients being detained inappropriately in hospitals or from patients challenging their commitments for being mentally ill. In *Stowers v. Wolodszko,* a psychiatrist was held liable for damages of $40,000 when he prevented a patient who had been involuntarily committed to a mental institution from contacting any relatives or friends. Although state statue permitted her commitment, the court held that his actions constituted false imprisonment arising from the unlawful restraint on her freedom.[6]

Hospitals do have the common-law authority to detain patients who are disoriented. All states also have a legal procedure to obtain authorization to detain some categories of persons who are mentally ill, are substance abusers, or have contagious diseases, sometimes through the use of physical and chemical restraints. When a patient is oriented, competent, and not legally committed, nurses should avoid detaining the person unless authorized by an explicit hospital policy or by a hospital administrator.

Mentally ill patients may be detained in the hospital if there is a danger that they will take their own life or jeopardize the lives and property of others. Patients who are mentally ill or insane can be restrained only if they present a danger to themselves or others. Only as much force as is reasonably necessary under the circumstances may be used. The use of excessive force in restraining a patient may produce liability for battery for the hospital and the nurse. If a mentally ill patient is detained in the hospital, commitment procedures should be begun expeditiously.

Invasion of Privacy

The legal right of privacy is the right to be free from unwarranted publicity and exposure to public scrutiny, as well as the right to avoid having his or her name, likeness, or private affairs made public against his or her will. Hospitals, physicians, and nurses may become liable for invasion of privacy if they divulge information from a medical record to improper sources or if they commit unwarranted intrusions into the personal affairs of a patient. Examples of unwarranted intrusion include some uses of a photograph of a patient without permission.

Information concerning a patient is confidential and should not be disclosed without authorization. Claims for invasion of privacy can arise from the unauthorized release of information concerning a patient. However, not all releases of information violate the right to privacy. For example, the Minnesota Supreme Court found that, even though a patient had explicitly requested that the information not be released, it was not an invasion of privacy to disclose orally the fact that she had been discharged from the hospital and that she had given birth, as long as the information was given in response to a direct inquiry concerning the patient and at a time reasonably near the time of her stay in the hospital.[7] The case involved an inquiry by the sister of the patient whether the patient had been discharged. The sister was told that the patient had gone home but that the baby was still hospitalized. The court stated that the oral disclosure of the information did not involve "medical records" and was not covered by the state statute governing confidentiality of medical records. However, state law and regulations in some states may not permit this disclosure. Most hospitals also prohibit such disclosure by policy. The better and recommended practice is to avoid the release of discharge and birth information.

Obviously, institutional policies concerning confidentiality must be followed because some courts will impose liability for failure to do so. Occasionally, a nurse may be required to disclose certain information. The reporting of communicable diseases, wounds of violence, child abuse, and other matters are required by law in most states, and the disclosure of such information to the appropriate officials (but not necessarily to the general public or the press) is justified by public policy.

Intentional Infliction of Emotional Distress

Intentional infliction of emotional distress is another intentional tort. It includes several types of outrageous conduct that cause emotional trauma. It should be easy to avoid this tort by remembering to treat patients and their families in a civilized fashion. This apparently was forgotten in the following two examples involving actions after the deaths of patients.

In a Tennessee case, a mother sought the body of her baby who had died in the hospital. A hospital staff member gave the body to her preserved in a jar of formaldehyde.[8] Another example, in Ohio, dealt with communications after death. A woman died and a month later the office of her family physician sent a notice for her to come in for a periodic checkup. The court said that this first notice was an excusable error. Her husband sent the physician a letter explaining that the patient had died. The husband later sued the physician for malpractice in her death. After the suit was filed, the office of the physician sent two more reminders for the dead woman to come in for a checkup, one of which was addressed to the youngest daughter of the deceased. The court said that the second and third reminders could be the basis for liability.[9]

Negligent Torts

The most frequent basis for liability of nurses, physicians, and hospitals is the negligent tort. Fortunately, negligence by itself is not enough to establish liability; there must also be an injury caused by the negligence. Four elements must be proved to establish liability for negligence: (1) duty (what should have been done), (2) breach of duty (deviation from what should have been done), (3) injury, and (4) causation (the injury was the direct and legal cause of the deviation from what should have been done). These elements are discussed in more detail next.

There is a "fifth element" that courts do not discuss but that nurses should remember: there must be someone willing to make a claim. Health care providers who maintain good relationships with their patients before and after incidents are less likely to be sued. If a hospital staff member suspects that an incident has occurred, the persons responsible for risk management in the institution should be notified promptly so that steps can be taken to minimize the chance of a claim. In addition, after an incident has occurred, nurses and other staff members, whether in institutional or independent practice, should try to maintain a good relationship with the patient and the family.

Duty

The first element that must be proved in any action for negligence is the duty. Duty has two aspects: (1) it must be proved that a duty was owed to the person harmed; and (2) the scope of that duty, sometimes called the standard of care, must be proved.

In general, common law does not impose a duty on individuals to come to the rescue of persons for whom they have no other responsibility, although some states recently have attempted to impose such a duty by statute. Under the common-law rule, an individual walking down the street has no legal obligation to come to the aid of a heart attack victim, unless (1) the victim is the individual's dependent; (2) the individual contributed to the cause of the heart attack; (3) the individual owns or operates the premises where the heart attack occurred; or (4) the individual has a contractual obligation to come to the aid of the person (e.g., by being on duty as a member of a public emergency care team). In most situations involving potential liability for incidents in hospitals or other institutions, it is not difficult to establish a duty based on the admission of the patient.

After the existence of a duty is established, the second aspect, the scope of the duty, must be established. This sometimes is called the obligation to conform to the standard of care. The standard of care for nurses is the degree of care that would be exercised by a "reasonably prudent nurse" acting under similar circumstances. A judge or jury will make this determination based on one or more of the following: (1) expert testimony, (2) common sense, or (3) published standards.

The technical aspects of care must be proved through expert testimony, usually by other health professionals engaged in similar practice. Several court decisions have addressed the issue of who is the appropriate expert in nursing practice cases. In early malpractice actions, physicians frequently testified as to the standard of care for nurses. In more recent cases, nurses have been used as experts.

With regard to expert testimony, another court has also recognized the greater and more critical role nurses now have in the diagnosis and treatment of patients. Finding that a nurse was qualified as an expert in the field of intravenous therapy, with expertise "no less exalted" than a physician's, the court in *Maloney v. Wake Hospital Systems, Inc.*[10] held that the trial court's exclusion, based on lack of the nurse's licensure as a physician, of the nurse's expert opinion as to the cause of the plaintiff's injury was a reversible error.

Based on the standard of care requiring a nurse to exercise that degree of learning, skill, and care possessed by a prudent and competent nurse, nurses may be held negligent for a failure to follow a physician's orders. In *Cline v. Lund,*[11] the nurse's failure to check the patient's vital signs every 30 minutes as ordered by the attending physician and to notify the physician promptly when the patient's condition became serious was held to constitute negligence. Similarly, a nurse who ignored the dietary restrictions ordered by the attending physician for a tonsillectomy patient was found to have acted negligently in *Striano v. Deepdale General Hospital.*[12]

A case of nursing negligence was found to exist in the case of *Toth v. Community Hospital at Glen Cove,*[13] in which there was evidence from which the jury could have concluded that the nurses administered 6 L of oxygen per minute to the infant plaintiffs rather than 4 L per minute as ordered by the attending pediatrician. Arguing that the dismissal in favor of the hospital was proper, the hospital contended that the treatment actually given by its nurses conformed to the then accepted standard of care relating to the administration of concentrated oxygen. The court rejected this contention, stating:

> Insofar as the hospital is concerned, whether the administration of oxygen was proper or not is completely immaterial. We are not here dealing with a matter usually left by a physician to the discretion of the hospital staff. Rather involved here is a situation where the attending physician gives direct and explicit orders to the hospital staff. In such cases, nurses are not authorized to determine for themselves what is a proper course of medical treatment. They may not invade the area of the physician's competence and authority to overrule his orders.[14]

Accordingly, the court reversed and remanded for a jury determination of whether the nurses' negligence was the proximate cause of the infants' blindness.

Nontechnical aspects of care can be proved by nonexperts. Some courts will permit juries to use their own knowledge and common sense when the duty is considered common knowledge. For example, many courts consider one of the nontechnical aspects to be how a disoriented patient should be protected from falling out of bed. Another issue many courts consider nontechnical is how to protect patients from burns.

Some courts will look to published standards such as licensure regulations, institutional rules, standards promulgated by professional and specialty organizations, and accreditation standards. Courts have permitted published standards to be used in two ways. In many cases, published standards are used in place of expert testimony; the jury may consider them along with all other evidence to determine the standard of care. In other cases, published standards are presumed to establish the standard of care unless the defendant can prove otherwise. In most cases, published standards are used in addition to expert testimony and do not create a presumption of the standard of care.

Violations of statutes or government regulations can be used to establish the standard of care when the plaintiff is a member of the class of people that the rule is designed to protect and the injury suffered is of the general type that it is designed to prevent. For example, a Maryland court found a hospital liable for injuries because of failure to comply with a licensing regulation requiring segregation of sterile and nonsterile needles.[15] The patient had a liver biopsy with a needle that was suspected of being nonsterile, requiring postponement of other therapy and requiring immediate treatment with a series of painful gamma-globulin injections to prevent infection from the needle. This clearly was the type of patient that the regulation was designed to protect and the kind of harm it was intended to prevent.

Hospital policies and procedures also can be used to establish the standard of care. Although individual rules and regulations of the hospital do not alone establish the standard of care the facility owes a patient, failure to follow such rules can be evidence of negligence. For example, the highest court of New York ruled that a hospital could be liable for injuries because of failure to raise the bed rails for a patient when the institution had a rule requiring bed rails to be raised for all patients older than the age of 50.[16]

It is important for nurses to be familiar with and act in compliance with the rules and policies of their institution applicable to nursing practice. If the rules are impossible to follow, steps should be taken to modify them instead of ignoring them. Eliminating all rules, however, is not a solution, as the failure to adopt necessary regulations can be a violation of the standard of care for hospitals. In Michigan, a hospital was found liable for the transmission of infection by a transplanted cornea because it did not have a procedure to ensure that the relevant medical records of the proposed donor were reviewed before the transplant.[17]

The violation of a hospital policy can be the basis for a finding of nursing liability for negligence. In a West Virginia case, a patient who was being treated for a broken wrist developed signs of severe infection. The nurse reported the symptoms of the patient to his physician, who took no action, nor did the nurse. Later, the arm of the patient was amputated. The court ruled that liability could be based on the failure of the nurse to comply with a hospital policy that required any nurse who had reason to doubt or question the care of a patient to report it first to the attending physician, then to the department head if the problem was not resolved.[18]

The proof of duty can become confused when there are two or more accepted approaches to a situation. This is particularly true in nursing practice, in which there may be several different, equally safe and effective ways to perform a procedure. The courts have attempted to resolve this through the "respected minority" rule. If a health professional follows the approach used by a respected minority of the profession, then the duty is to follow that approach properly. The courts will not permit liability to be based simply on the decision not to follow the majority approach. In a case involving a physician who used one of two procedures to perform a thyroidectomy, the laryngeal nerve of the patient was cut. The patient claimed that the physician should have used the alternative procedure rather than claiming that the procedure was not performed carefully. The court rejected the argument stating that both procedures were acceptable.[19]

In the past, some courts limited the standards of hospitals and health care professionals to the practice in the same or similar communities. This meant that experts testifying on the standard of care had to be from the same community or, in states that allowed the standards of similar communities to be considered, from a similar setting.

This rule was designed to avoid finding rural hospitals and physicians liable for not following the practices of urban medical centers. In practice, the rule made it very difficult to obtain expert testimony. The rule has been abandoned in nearly every state for hospitals and physicians, so that experts from anywhere generally can testify if they are familiar with the relevant standard of care. However, the applicability of the locality rule to nursing practice still is an open issue in many states.

Courts occasionally will impose a new duty not previously recognized by the profession. A court may find that the whole profession is lagging in its standards, so it imposes a more stringent legal standard. In a 1974 case, the Washington Supreme Court determined that an ophthalmologist was negligent in failing to administer a simple glaucoma test to a patient, although there was uncontradicted expert testimony that it was the universal practice for ophthalmologists not to administer glaucoma tests to patients younger than age 40. The courts said the reasonable precaution of giving the test to the patient was so important as well as simple, inexpensive, and painless that the fact that it was not the standard of the ophthalmology profession was not excuse for negligent behavior.[20] In another case, the California Supreme Court found liability for the failure of a psychiatrist to warn a woman that his patient had threatened to kill her, even though other psychiatrists would have acted in the same manner.[21]

Breach of Duty

After the duty is proved, the second element that must be proved is the breach of this duty (i.e., there must be a deviation in some manner from this standard, which is established on showing that something was done that should not have been done or something was not done that should have been done). The proof of breach of duty hinges on a showing that the care of the patient was substandard. This can be shown through the nursing record or the expert testimony of witnesses.

Injury

The third element that must be shown to prove negligence is injury. The person making the claim must demonstrate physical, financial, or emotional injury. In many malpractice cases, the existence of the injury is very clear by the time the suit is brought, although there still may be disagreement concerning the dollar value of the injuries.

With some exceptions, most courts will not allow suits based solely on negligently inflicted emotional injuries; generally, the emotional injuries are compensated only when they accompany physical injuries. Intentional infliction of emotional injury is compensated without proof of physical injury. In some states, negligently inflicted emotional injuries are compensable without accompanying physical injuries in some circumstances.

The most widely accepted circumstance is when the plaintiff was in the "zone of risk" created by the negligence of the defendant (i.e., when the plaintiff has been exposed to risk of injury). This rule allows recovery to a plaintiff who is in the zone of physical danger created by a defendant's negligence. In New York, for example, the parents of a child with a contagious disease claimed that they were placed within the zone of danger because of their prolonged exposure to their child's disease, which had not been properly diagnosed.[22] The court held that the claim was valid to the extent that the parents' psychic trauma from being in increased danger of physical harm from the disease was attributable to the negligence of the hospital and physicians in failing to diagnose bacterial meningitis.

A few states have extended this rule to when the plaintiff is not in the zone of risk but witnesses injury of a close relative. A California court permitted a father to sue for his emotional injuries when he was present in the delivery room when his wife died, and he placed his hands on her body after her death and felt the unborn child die.[23] There is a trend toward compensating more negligently inflicted emotional injuries without requiring physical harm.

Causation

The fourth element is causation: the breach of duty must be proved to have legally caused the injury. This means showing that the injury would not have occurred "but for" the defendant's act. Often, however, interning forces increase the injury, therefore the courts require the negligence to be the "cause in law" or the proximate cause of the injury. Moreover, on occasions, the courts have decided that some of but not all the injuries of the patient resulted from negligence. For instance, in *Mehigan vs. Sheehan,* a woman who suffered a miscarriage charged her obstetrician with negligence in failing to treat her. The obstetrician lived close to the house of the patient but failed to personally check in on her. The court held that the negligence of the obstetrician did not cause the miscarriage, but he was held liable for the pain and suffering of the patient that occurred from her being left alone in her house.[24] For example, a treatment may be negligently administered (which is a breach of duty) and the patient may die (which is an injury), but the person suing still must prove that there was substantial likelihood that the person would have lived if the treatment had been administered appropriately. Thus, causation can be the most difficult element to prove.

There have been several cases involving the negligence of nurses in which causation of the injury was a key issue. An Illinois case addressed a child in an incubator who became overheated, had febrile seizures, and eventually was found to be brain damaged. There was no thermometer in the incubator, and the practice was to check the temperatures of infants once daily. There was conflicting expert testimony on the cause of the brain damage to the baby. The court was critical of the nursing care given to the baby but said that causation was not proved.[25]

Another example is a Texas case concerning a nurse who gave a patient solid food immediately after colon surgery (which is a breach of duty), and eight days later the ends of the sutured colon came apart (which is an injury). Because of the time lag, the patient was not able to prove causation.[26] Causation can be proved in many cases, however, as illustrated in a Colorado case in which a nurse had put a 3-year-old in an adult-sized bed. The child slipped through the side-rail and strangled. The court held that the nurse violated her duty to furnish adequate attention to the patient and that her acts were the direct cause of the death of the child.[27]

Res Ipsa Loquitur

The doctrine of res ipsa loquitur is an exception to the general principle that a plaintiff must present proof of actual negligence to establish the defendant's liability. Instead, the doctrine, which translates as "the thing speaks for itself," is applied when the court determines, as a matter of law, that "the occurrence is such as in the ordinary course of things would not have happened if the party exercising control or management had exercised proper care."[28] Thus, when the doctrine applies, the trier of fact can infer, based on common knowledge and experience, that the conduct of the nurse was negligent.[29]

In England, in the 19th century, the courts were confronted with a case arising from a barrel of flour that had rolled out of an upper story window, hitting a pedestrian on the head. The pedestrian tried to sue the owner of the building, who claimed that the four elements of negligence had to be proved. Of course, the person suing could not find out the specifics of what went wrong in the upper story room, so the case would have been lost. However, the court said the owner could not take advantage of the rules to escape liability in cases like this in which barrels do not normally fall out of windows and someone clearly had done something wrong. There, the court developed the doctrine of res ipsa loquitur.

For the doctrine to apply, several elements must be established. First, the defendant must have exclusive control over the injury-producing instrumentality, as would be the case, for example, when an injury results from the misapplication of a cast (instrumentality) by a nurse (control). Although this element is typically easy to prove, the patient is frequently unable to prove control and the specific instrumentality, because the injury often occurs while the patient is anesthetized or otherwise unconscious. The courts have reached varying results in interpreting this requirement.

The second element of the doctrine requires that the injurious occurrence ordinarily does not happen unless the defendant is negligent.[30] The determination of what "ordinarily does and does not happen must be within the common knowledge and experience of a layperson."[31] Proof of this element often depends on a determination of whether the resulting injury was unusual in the light of the procedures and risks involved in treatment. In *ZeBarth v. Swedish Hospital Medical Center,*[32] the court held that application of the doctrine was appropriate, because paralysis would not ordinarily result from radiation treatment unless such treatment was administered improperly.

A third element of the res ipsa loquitur doctrine is the requirement that the injury could not have resulted from any voluntary action on the part of the plaintiff. The unconscious hospital patient certainly fulfills this criterion. Other hospital-related injuries should be examined for the possibility of contributory behavior by the patient.

A final requirement applied in some states is that the defendant enjoy superior knowledge of the cause of the accident. The plaintiff's inability to discover the cause of an injury is a major policy reason supporting use of the doctrine. This element is aimed at the preservation of this policy. It typically will be satisfied in claims alleging hospital negligence in which the patient is either unconscious at the time of the injury or is unable to understand its medical cause.

Courts frequently have applied this rule to two types of malpractice cases: (1) sponges and other foreign objects left unintentionally in the body and (2) injuries to parts of the body distant from the site of treatment (e.g., a leg laceration during eye surgery). Some courts have extended the applicability of the rule to other types of malpractice cases. An example is a California case in which a patient had a cardiac arrest and subsequently died as a result of the nurses' failure to observe, monitor, exercise appropriate care in performing procedures, and institute emergency resuscitation. The court applied the doctrine of res ipsa loquitur.[33]

The applicability of res ipsa loquitur to various types of injuries may be defined by statute. In Delaware, for example, a statute restricts the use of res ipsa loquitur to instances in which (1) a foreign object was unintentionally left in a patient's body during surgery; (2) an explosion or fire originating in a substance used in treatment occurred during treatment; or (3) surgery was performed on the wrong patient or the wrong organ, limb, or body part.[34]

Liability is not automatic in res ipsa loquitur cases. The persons being sued may attempt to explain why the injury was not the result of negligence. This can be done successfully in some circumstances. For example, a physician could establish the absence of negligence by proving the sponge was left in the body because the patient had to be closed quickly on an emergency basis to save the person's life and there was no time for a sponge count, as in cases of sudden life-threatening deterioration of the patient. The evidence necessary to avoid liability varies among states because there is variation to the degree to which the burden of proof shifts to the defendant in res ipsa loquitur cases.

DEFENSES

Several defenses are available in a negligence action, including time limits within which suits must be started, releases, contributory or comparative negligence, and immunity statutes.

The statute of limitations specifies the time limit within which a lawsuit must be filed, with suits barred after the period has expired. The time varies depending on the nature of the suit; in many states, for malpractice suits it is one or two years. In most states, the time for a malpractice suit begins when the patient discovers that the injury may have been caused by negligence. Actual knowledge is not required. If the patient through reasonable diligence should have known the injury was due to negligence, discovery is legally considered to have occurred, starting the time period.

For example, in a Utah case a patient who was a nurse began to have pain and numbness in her jaw immediately after receiving two injections from a dentist. She did not determine that the cause of her pain was the negligence of the dentist until more than two years after the injection—and two years was the time limit for malpractice suits in the state. She claimed that she had not discovered that her injury was due to negligence until she actually had determined the cause. The court ruled she should have known the cause sooner, so her suit was barred.[35]

Some states have enacted absolute time limits for most malpractice suits. For example, in Iowa, a malpractice suit must be commenced within two years of discovery of the potential suit, but no longer than four years after the occurrence of the injury, unless a special exception applies.[36] In other circumstances, however, the actions of a party in covering up a potential wrong-doing may extend the statute of limitations.

Many states have special exceptions for cases involving minors, foreign objects unintentionally left in the body, and other situations. In many states, a suit involving a minor patient may be commenced at any time before the minor's 19th birthday if the time period would otherwise expire before that date.[37] A few states have adopted shorter time limits for malpractice suits involving minors.[38]

In some states that have enacted absolute time limits for most malpractice suits, a special exception is retained for cases involving foreign objects unintentionally left in the body, so that these have no absolute time limit. However, these suits still are subject to a time limit that begins with the discovery of the foreign object.[39] When there is no statutory exception for foreign object suits, some courts have created similar exceptions by judicial interpretation. For example, an Ohio court ruled that leaving a surgical needle in an incision was not "malpractice" for purposes of the statute of limitations, so that the longer time period for "personal injuries" applied. Thus, the suit against the responsible nurse and her hospital employer was not barred.[40]

Some lawsuits, especially those involving care of newborns, can be started many years after the care is provided. Because few people have memories that long, it is important to document thoroughly the care given to patients. Accurate and legible records will be the only way to prove what was done. Most courts assume that if it was not written down, it was not done.

Another defense is a release. As a part of the process of settling a claim, the claimant is usually asked to sign a release of all future claims arising from the same incident. In most cases, if such a release has been signed, it will bar a future suit based on the same incident. An exculpatory contract is different from a release because it is signed before the care is provided and generally will not be a successful defense. For example, some providers has asked patients to sign an exculpatory contract agreeing not to sue or agreeing to limit the amount of any suit, but courts have refused to enforce such contracts on the ground that they are against public policy.[41]

Contributory negligence and comparative negligence operate to reduce or eliminate a defendant's ultimate liability to a plaintiff who has established the negligence of the defendant. The two doctrines are similar only in their potential for limiting the scope of a defendant's liability.

Contributory negligence is an absolute defense to a plaintiff's tort-based cause of action. Specifically, the doctrine allows a defendant whose negligence has been established to plead and prove that the plaintiff's conduct breached the duty of self-protection and contributed as a legal cause of the injury. In a jurisdiction that adheres to this doctrine, a defendant who can establish the plaintiff's breach is relieved of all liability.

The elements that a defendant must establish to support a finding of contributory negligence are similar to those that the plaintiff must establish to prove the defendant's negligence. It must be shown that the plaintiff failed to exercise the care that a reasonably prudent person would have taken to avoid the injury.

Cases in which contributory negligence has occurred include (1) the patient fails to follow clear orders and does not return for follow-up,[42] (2) the patient walks on a broken leg,[43] (3) the patient gets out of bed and falls,[44] (4) the patient lights a cigarette in bed when unattended,[45] or (5) the patient deliberately gives false information that leads to the wrong antidote being given for a drug overdose.[46]

The success of this defense depends on the intelligence and degree of orientation of the patient. Obviously, a patient who does not appear to be able to follow orders cannot be relied on to follow orders, so contributory negligence would not be a successful defense against a claim by such a person.

The doctrine of contributory negligence has been criticized almost from the time of its inception. As it has been applied by the most restrictive courts, the doctrine has operated to deny recovery to any plaintiff whose negligence has contributed in the slightest degree to the injury. Even under the more widely accepted rule that the contributory negligence must be the proximate cause of the injury, defendants are often relieved of all liability for their negligent actions. Courts and legislatures have responded to these perceived inequities in various ways, the most significant being the adoption of a comparative negligence standard for determining the extent of a defendant's liability.

Most states have abandoned the all-or-nothing contributory negligence rule; instead, they apply comparative negligence, which means the award is decreased by the percentage of the responsibility of the patient for the injury.[47] For instance, a jury may decide a nurse was 60 percent negligent and the patient was 40 percent negligent and as a result, the patient would be awarded a reduced amount of damages.

Courts and legislatures have adopted varying forms of comparative negligence. In a jurisdiction that applies the pure form of comparative negligence, the plaintiff is entitled to recover for the portion of the injury attributable to the defendant's negligence, regardless of which party was at greater fault.[48] Under the majority approach, a modified comparative negligence analysis is applied, and the plaintiff whose negligence is found to have exceeded that of the defendant is barred from recovery.[49]

In a case involving a patient's injury caused by the negligence of both the patient and the hospital, the scope of the liability of the nurse depends on which of these doctrines is applied. In practice, a nurse situated in a contributory negligence state enjoys a narrower exposure to liability than does his or her counterpart in a state that applies a modified or pure form of comparative negligence.

Some states have statues that extend some degree of immunity from some types of suits. These statutes are another source of defense. A suit still may be filed, but an attorney can win dismissal if the statute applies. The most widely adopted type of immunity statute is the Good Samaritan Law, which applies to care provided gratuitously in an emergency situation. In most states, persons who provide care in emergencies are protected if their actions are in good faith and not reckless, but it is helpful to be familiar with the details of the applicable statute because there are variations in the protection afforded by the statute. For example, in Florida, the Good Samaritan Law does not apply if the patient objects to the care provided.[50] As a practical matter, negligence actions against persons who attempt to provide aid at the scene of an accident are rare.

BREACH OF IMPLIED WARRANTIES AND STRICT LIABILITY

The major exception to the requirement that liability be based on fault involves breach of implied warranties and strict liability in tort. This is an area of the law in which liability based on contract and liability based on tort overlap. The implied warranties of merchantability and fitness for a particular use are based on contract. These warranties form the basis for finding liability without fault for many of the injuries caused by use of goods and products. Normally, the seller is liable for the breach of the warranties, but in some situations persons who lease products to others have been found liable.

Strict liability applies to injuries caused by the use of a product that is unreasonably dangerous to a consumer or user and that reaches the user without substantial change from the condition in which it was sold. Usually it is the manufacturer or seller of the product who is liable. Strict liability in tort does not require a contractual relationship between the seller and the person injured to establish the liability of the seller. Some courts have extended strict liability to persons who furnish goods or products without a sale.

Hospitals almost always are considered to be providing services, not selling or furnishing products, so they seldom have been found liable for breach of warranties or strict liability. However, plaintiffs and their attorneys have made numerous efforts to convince courts to apply these principles to make it easier to establish liability. These efforts have been based on services involving blood transfusions, drugs, radiation, and hospital equipment.

A hospital's liability for negligence in transferring a disease to a patient by way of a blood transfusion depends on whether the disease is discoverable. Serum hepatitis, syphilis, and acquired immune deficiency syndrome (AIDS) are the major diseases that can be transferred to a patient by a blood transfusion. Because adequate tests are available to detect the presence of syphilis, the failure to do so results in liability.[51] At present, tests that have been developed to detect the presence of serum hepatitis are imperfect. Consequently, this disease may be transferred to a patient without any negligence on the part of a hospital, blood bank, or other testing agency.[52]

A test has also been developed to detect antibodies to the virus that causes AIDS. This test is used to screen blood, plasma, and other blood products to prevent the transmission of AIDS in blood transfusions or in the use of blood products. Consequently, a hospital that fails to test, or conducts defective testing of, donated blood for human immunodeficiency virus (HIV) will be guilty of negligence. This is particularly true in the light of recent legislation in some states that requires all facilities collecting blood from individual donors to test the blood for the potential presence of HIV. In Tennessee, for example, any person who contracts AIDS from contaminated blood, except in emergency situations in which a physician determines that failure to transfuse will be life-threatening to a patient, may bring a cause of action against any facility providing the blood if the blood received was not tested.[53]

The difficulty of proving negligence has led some courts to apply products liability principles to injuries sustained through a blood transfusion. Although most courts have characterized supplying blood as a service, a few notable decisions have held that a blood transfusion constitutes a sale to which the products liability theories apply.[54] In *Cunningham v. MacNeal Memorial Hospital,*[55] the Illinois Supreme Court found the provision of blood constituted the sale of a product. The presence of a serum hepatitis virus was found to be a defect rendering the blood unreasonably dangerous to the consumer; the court found the hospital liable despite its inability to detect the presence of the virus.[56] The Colorado Supreme Court has ruled that blood banks cannot be held strictly liable for the transmittal of serum hepatitis through blood transfusions, because such a vitally important, although contaminated, product remains unavoidably unsafe even after "state of the art preparation."[57]

At least one decision has allowed a cause of action under a theory of breach of implied warranty in the transfusion of impure blood.[58] Most decisions, however, have denied liability under a warranty theory.[59]

Apparently responding to the possibility that hospitals and blood banks could be liable under warranty or strict liability theories, despite the lack of a test for determining the presence of the serum hepatitis virus, almost every state has enacted legislation denying liability in the absence of negligence. The legislatures were motivated by the public interest in access to often necessary blood transfusions. The Illinois statute is typical.[60] It provides that transfusing blood or blood products is not a sale and that no warranties attach. Liability will only lie for negligence or willful misconduct. Negligence is then defined as the failure to exercise due care or to follow professional standards determined by the current state of the medical arts. In a Washington case, a hospital's failure to maintain duplicate blood donor records, as required by statute, did not strip the hospital of immunity in an action brought by a patient who allegedly contracted hepatitis from blood he received during surgery.[61]

The adoption of these blood shield statutes has met with various types of legal challenges. In response to constitutional attacks, courts have found that they do not violate equal protection guarantees, nor are they unconstitutional as special legislation.[62]

The responsibility for ensuring the proper administration of blood rests primarily on the physician attending the transfusion. The physician is responsible for the correct insertion of the needle, for protecting against air embolism, and for setting the flow rate. In *Powell v. Fidelity & Casualty Co. of New York,*[63] the physician determined the rate at which blood would be transfused into the patient. The Louisiana court noted that a nurse had neither the right nor the duty to change the prescribed rate and was therefore not negligent in not doing so. Monitoring the patient for adverse reaction, however, is usually the responsibility of the hospital nursing staff. Although a hospital may not be held strictly liable for the adverse reaction produced by transfusion of wholesome but incompatible blood,[64] the hospital will be liable for the negligence of its employees if they fail to monitor the patient adequately for such reaction.[65] When the transfusion needle slipped and filled a patient's arm tissue with blood, the hospital was liable for the negligence of its nurse and orderly who failed to observe the conditions causing the injury.[66]

Efforts to use implied warranties or strict liability to impose liability on hospitals for the administration of drugs generally have been unsuccessful. For example, a Texas court refused to apply these product liability principles to the administration of a contaminated drug.[67]

Hospital Equipment

Courts also have declined to apply implied warranties or strict liability in tort to hospital equipment. For example, a California court ruled that the hospital was the user, not the supplier, of a surgical needle that broke during an operation.[68] Of course, the hospital still may be liable based on negligence, and the manufacturer may be liable based on implied warranties or strict liability in tort.

WHO IS LIABLE?

Liability can be divided into personal liability, liability for employees and agents, and institutional liability.

Individual Liability

Individual staff members are liable for the consequences of their own acts. Individual liability almost always is based on the principle of fault. To be liable, the person must have done something wrong or failed to do something that should have been done.

Employer Liability

There are several situations in which the negligent act of an individual or group of individuals is imputed to the hospital. In these situations, the hospital is held vicariously liable, even though it is otherwise without fault. The most common doctrine imposing vicarious liability is known as respondeat superior, in which the wrongful acts of an employee resulting in injury to a third party are imputed to the employer, who is otherwise without fault, simply because of the existence of the employment relationship. For this theory to apply, however, the employee must have been acting within the scope of employment.[69]

This doctrine is based on the theory that an employer has the right to control and direct the conduct of its employee. Therefore, the hospital is said to be responsible, along with the employee who negligently performs an act. The employee is not relieved of liability, nor is the employer held liable for any direct act of negligence; rather, both have liability for the employee's negligent conduct.[70]

There are times, however, when a hospital is said to have relinquished its rights to direct and control the activities of its employees and to have transferred these rights to another person such as a staff physician. In such circumstances, the employee is said to be a "borrowed servant" of the physician, and the doctrine of respondeat superior does not apply to the hospital (although it may apply to the physician).

Further, there are several situations in which the hospital can be held liable for the acts of an independent contractor. In such situations, hospital liability is based on an apparent agency relationship with a particular physician, owing to the position held by that physician.

Respondeat Superior

Like graduate medical trainees and residents, nurses are generally considered to be employees of a hospital. Therefore, the negligence of nurses, whether registered or practical, may be imputed to the hospital for acts or omissions within the scope of employment.[71] If the nurse is acting under the direct control of an independent staff physician, however, the hospital may avoid liability under the "borrowed servant" doctrine.[72]

The conduct of nursing personnel is to be measured against the standard of care generally observed by other members of the nursing profession in the community.[73] Conduct by a nurse that exceeds the scope of nursing licensure prerogatives may, however, result in the use of a higher standard of care. Thus, in *Barber v. Reinking,*[74] the court held that a practical nurse was to be judged by the standard of care required of a registered nurse, when the patient alleged injury resulting from the practical nurse's administration of an inoculation, an act that should be performed only by a registered nurse, under the state licensing statute. Similarly, in *Thompson v. Brent,*[75] the performance of a task deemed to be medical in nature, the removal of a cast with a Stryker saw, required use of a standard of care applicable to physicians.

In a 1979 case, however, the court recognized that, under certain circumstances, a nurse may exercise independent judgment in the administration of medication pursuant to a physician's order and is entitled to a certain amount of discretion in carrying out that order. Appealing from an adverse jury verdict, the plaintiff in

Fraijo v. Hartland Hospital[76] challenged the following jury instruction as inappropriate in determining nursing negligence, as opposed to physician negligence:

> Where there is more than one recognized method of diagnosis or treatment, and no one of them is used exclusively and uniformly by all practitioners of good standing, a physician *or nurse* is not negligent if, in exercising their best judgment they select one of the approved methods, which later turns out to be a wrong selection, or one not favored by certain other practitioners. [emphasis added][77]

The court rejected the plaintiff's contention and held that the instruction was proper. In so holding, the court noted that current standards for nursing provide for delegations of responsibility that nurses with superior education and experience often exercise independent judgment as to the care of patients in a hospital setting. The court concluded that nurses making such judgments must be accorded the same benefits derived from jury instructions that have traditionally been reserved for physician malpractice cases.

A special nurse, one hired by the patient or the patient's agent to perform nursing services, is not generally regarded as a servant of the hospital. The hospital, therefore, is usually held not liable for the wrongful conduct of such a special nurse. In some respects, the position of a special nurse might be likened to that of a staff physician. Thus, it has been held that a hospital may exclude a special nurse from practicing within the institution.[78] As with staff physicians, the hospital may require a special nurse to observe its rules as a precondition to working in the hospital. The fact that the special nurse must observe hospital rules is typically insufficient, however, to raise a master–servant relationship between the hospital and the nurse. Under ordinary circumstances, a special nurse is an employee of the patient. The hospital ordinarily has no authority to hire or fire the nurse or control her conduct on the case[79] but retains responsibility to protect patients from incompetent and unqualified special nurses.

Even though a special nurse is employed by the patient, there are certain circumstances in which the hospital may be held liable when a special nurse is negligent in the performance of administrative duties required by the hospital.[80] Moreover, use of the designation *special nurse* does not preclude the nurse from being held an employee or agent of the hospital under certain circumstances. When the facts of the situation indicate that a master–servant relationship exists between the hospital and the special nurse, the usual doctrine of respondeat superior may impose liability on the hospital for the nurse's wrongful conduct.[81] Thus, in *Emory University v. Shadburn,*[82] the court, emphasizing that the nurse was procured and paid through the hospital, said:

Where an application in behalf of the patient is made to the hospital to furnish to the patient a special nurse, and a special nurse is selected and procured by the hospital and placed in charge of the patient, notwithstanding the services of the nurse may be specially charged for by the hospital and paid for by the patient, but where the hospital itself is paid for the service of the nurse and the hospital afterwards settles with the nurse, the inference is authorized that the special nurse is the agent of the hospital to care for and look after the patient; and where the injuries received by the patient in jumping out of the window of the hospital under the conditions referred to are caused from any negligence of the nurse in leaving the patient alone, such negligence is imputable to the hospital.[83]

The mere fact that a patient pays the special nurse has been held not to be conclusive evidence that the special nurse was not the employee of the hospital.[84] The existence of an employer–employee relationship, which determines the applicability of respondeat superior, is a matter of fact to be determined by the jury under proper instructions.[85]

Finally, the adequacy of nursing care will be judged by what is required under the circumstances of treatment as well as by the status of the individual nurse. Although all nurses must adhere to minimal professional standards, those with certified expertise will be held to a higher standard of care when they are involved in a specialized procedure.[86]

The supervisor is not the employer. Because the supervisor also is an employee, respondeat superior does not impose liability on the supervisor for acts or omissions of persons being supervised. Supervisors are liable only for the consequences of their own acts or omissions, but this liability can be extended to the supervisor for the negligent delegation of supervisors responsibilities to someone unqualified to perform them. Of course, the employer also can be liable for the acts and omissions of both the supervisor and the person being supervised.

The liability of the employer under respondeat superior is for the benefit of the person who is injured, not the employee. The liability of an employer does not mean that the employee must be provided with liability protection. It means that the person who is injured can sue the employer, the employee, or both. If the employee is individually sued and found liable, the employee must pay. If, as usually occurs, the employee is not individually sued, then the employer must pay. Technically, the employer can sue the employee to get the money back. The repayment is called indemnification. However, indemnification is almost never sought because of the negative effects on future recruiting efforts. In addition, many employers provide individual liability protection for their employees (as is discussed in the insurance section at the end of this chapter) through the employer's procurement of professional liability insurance or through a self-insurance program whereby the employer self-funds this liability protection.

Institutional Liability

Institutions can be liable for the consequences of breaches of duties owed directly to the patient. These duties include the maintenance of buildings and grounds, the selection and maintenance of equipment, and the proper selection and supervision of employees. Failing to exercise reasonable care in the discharge of any of these duties can impose liability on the institution for resulting injuries.

In a 1978 Washington case, another form of institutional liability was imposed. The court found the hospital liable for the treatment provided in an emergency department by an independent professional corporation because it considered the emergency services to be an inherent function of the overall enterprise of the hospital for which it bears some responsibility.[87] Other courts have not adopted this position.

Liability of Contracting Agency

A proliferation of agencies that employ nurses and contract with hospitals or other health care centers to provide services on a contract basis has occurred throughout the country. Under these circumstances, the nurse's employer is the personnel agency, and the allocation of liability for a nurse's negligent acts can be complex. Generally, the employing personnel agency will be liable for the negligent acts of the nurse under respondeat superior. The hospital, however, could be liable in whole or in part for a nurse's negligence if it did not exercise due care in the selection of the agency or in the assignment and supervision of the nurse.

The agreement between a personnel agency and health care facility should allocate liability and the responsibility for maintaining insurance. A nurse who is employed by such an agency should understand its scope of liability coverage. This is particularly essential if the nurse works in more than one setting, because there are likely to be differences in institutional liability coverage among various settings and institutions.

TORT REFORM/RESPONSES TO THE MALPRACTICE CRISIS

The cumulative effect of the increasing number of medical malpractice cases and the growing cost of individual cases has led to a surge in the cost of malpractice insurance and, in some areas of the country, a reduction in its availability for some medical specialists. This malpractice insurance crisis led nearly every state to review and revise its laws concerning tort suits. These tort reforms can be grouped into (1) changes in dispute resolution mechanisms, (2) changes in the amount of the award and how it is paid, (3) changes in the time in which the suit must be brought, and (4) various other changes. These tort reforms have received a mixed reception in the courts, which have disagreed on whether they violate various state and federal constitutional provisions.

Dispute Resolution Mechanisms

The two primary changes in mechanisms for dispute resolution have been the introduction of screening panels and the authorization of binding agreements to arbitrate disputes.

Screening Panels

Several states have enacted laws that require all malpractice claims to be screened by a panel before a suit can be filed. These screening panels are designed to promote settlement of meritorious claims and abandonment of frivolous claims.

A few courts have held screening panels to be an unconstitutional infringement of rights under state constitutions to access to the courts.[88] The Florida Supreme Court declared the medical mediation requirement of that state unconstitutional on the ground that it violated due process by being arbitrary and capricious in operation because of its arbitrary 10-month limitation on the mediation process.[89] The process was not completed in more than half the cases because there was no procedure to extend the time, so the court ruled the law unconstitutional in its entirety.

Most courts have upheld the required use of screening panels because the plaintiffs still have the right to sue after the screening process is completed.[90] The federal courts require plaintiffs to complete the screening process, if required by applicable state law, before pursuing a malpractice claim in federal court based on the diversity jurisdiction (i.e., jurisdiction based on the fact that the parties to the suit are from different states).[91]

Arbitration

Several states have authorized binding agreements to arbitrate future malpractice disputes. In many states, agreements to arbitrate were not valid unless signed after the dispute arose, so changes in the law were necessary to make agreements that were signed before the dispute enforceable. When there is a valid agreement to arbitrate, the dispute is submitted to an arbitrator who decides whether there should be any payment and, if so, how much. Many agreements provide for an arbitration panel rather than a single arbitrator. Several states specify that certain elements must be included in agreements to arbitrate, such as a right to withdraw from the agreement within 30 days after signing or 60 days after discharge.[92] The laws vary on which health care providers are eligible to enter arbitration agreements.

Arbitration is favored by some health care providers and patients because it is faster and somewhat less costly than litigation. It is a less formal process, avoiding adverse publicity and the complex rules of litigation that promote adversarial positions. Others are opposed to arbitration because they prefer having their disputes decided by a jury using procedures with which attorneys are more familiar. Some providers believe they have a better chance of avoiding any payment in a jury case, whereas some patients believe that if they win they will be awarded a larger payment from a jury.

Amount and Payment of Award

The amount of the award has been limited in a few states by imposition of a ceiling. Some have abolished the "collateral source" rule, reducing the amount paid. State payment mechanisms that pay part of any malpractice award have been created. Award of periodic payments has been authorized.

Another legislative response to the perceived malpractice crisis has been the enactment of statutes that impose ceilings on the amount recoverable in an action by a patient against a physician or hospital.[93] In some statutes, the cap on recovery applies to the total amount of damages that a plaintiff may seek in a malpractice action, whereas in others, the statutory limit only restricts the amount of noneconomic damages. The approximate range of this maximum figure is from $150,000 to $750,000.

Courts have disagreed on states' statutory limits on recovery. For the most part, however, courts have struck down damages caps because they violate the relevant state constitution. The Kansas Supreme Court invalidated a $1 million cap on total recovery because the statute not only violated the right to a jury trial but also failed to provide an adequate substitute remedy to replace it.[94] More recently, the Texas Supreme Court illustrated how the specific wording of a statute can affect the outcome of such constitutional challenges.[95] In striking down that state's $500,000 limit on nonmedical damages, the court observed that the statute acknowledged the existence of a medical malpractice crisis but also provided that the measures it contained might not resolve the crisis. The court declared that, in the context of persons catastrophically injured by medical negligence, it is unreasonable and arbitrary to limit their recovery in a speculative experiment to determine if liability insurance rates will, in fact, decrease. In addition, the court rejected the statute's purpose of ensuring that awards are rationally related to actual damages, declaring that it was unreasonable and arbitrary to conclude that uniformly applicable damages caps would establish a rational correlation between actual damages and the amount of monetary awards. In Virginia, a federal trial court invalidated a state law that imposed a $750,000 limit on damages,[96] but more recently, the supreme court in that state upheld the statute, ruling that it did not violate either state or federal constitutions.[97]

In most states, the defendant must pay for the entire cost of the injuries even if the plaintiff already has been compensated in part by some other source such as insurance or workers' compensation. This is called the collateral source rule. Several states have abolished the collateral source rule, so the amount of compensation the plaintiff receives from other sources is deducted from the amount the defendant owes. This has been declared constitutional by several courts.[98]

The current trend among the states is to abolish the collateral source rule. The laws, however, are not uniform; some permit the jury to make the deduction, whereas others require the court to do so; some explicitly deny the right of subrogation to providers of collateral benefits, whereas others imply such a denial; some allow introduction of all benefits received, whereas others exclude evidence of life or accident insurance.

Some states have created insurance mechanisms that pay part of any malpractice award. These laws generally have been upheld, including the requirement that all health care providers contribute to the fund.[99]

Under common law, court judgments must be paid in a single lump sum. One of the advantages of settling cases involving large liabilities is that the parties can agree to periodic payments that are more reasonable for the defendant to pay. Some states have passed laws that authorize courts to direct that large judgments be paid by means of periodic payments. The courts have not agreed on whether these laws are constitutional.

Statute of Limitations

One of the most common legislative responses to the malpractice dilemma has been the shortening of the time period for bringing a medical malpractice action. In enacting such laws, legislatures sought to reduce the number of malpractice claims filed. In addition, the shortened time period allows insurance companies to predict their liability more accurately.

The statue of limitations specifies the time period in which suits must be filed or forever barred. Before the malpractice crisis amendments, nearly all statutes of limitations permitted minors to wait to file suits until after they became adults. One type of amendment limits minors to a specific number of years after the right to sue accrues. These special time constraints for initiating medical malpractice actions have been challenged in several states. In some instances, the statutes have been upheld as constitutional.[100] Other courts have ruled that shortened limitation periods for medical malpractice cases are unconstitutional as applied to particular situations.[101] The Ohio Supreme Court has upheld a one-year limit on the time minors have to sue.[102]

Other Tort Reforms

In medical malpractice cases, the plaintiff's attorney generally is reimbursed on a contingency fee basis. Under this arrangement, the attorney is compensated by a percentage of the amount the client recovers, the most common fee rate being 33⅓ percent of the award. Commentators claim that the contingency fee system encourages the filing of frivolous lawsuits by persons who could not otherwise afford to sue. Others argue that many people with legitimate claims would not be able financially to seek a remedy without benefit of the contingency fee arrangement.

States have begun to limit attorneys' fees in medical malpractice cases in various ways. Some simply require that attorneys' fees be reasonable. Others use a sliding-scale contingency fee system. Under this arrangement, an attorney may recover, for example, 30 percent of the first $100,000, and a smaller percentage of any recovery above that amount. Attorney fee limits have been challenged as unconstitutional but have generally been upheld.[103]

Other tort reform amendments include (1) limiting the grounds for suits based on lack of informed consent,[104] (2) prohibiting asking for a certain amount of money in the suit,[105] and (3) restricting who can give expert testimony.

RISK MANAGEMENT

Joint Commission on Accreditation of Healthcare Organizations (Joint Commission) standards mandate a quality assurance program that includes the correction of identified patient care problems.[106] One mechanism used to implement this standard is risk management. The concept of risk management, originated by the insurance industry in the 1950s, focuses on loss prevention by advising clients on how to evaluate potential risks and prevent injuries from them. In hospitals, risk management includes evaluating and controlling environmental hazards that affect the condition of patients or staff members. An effective risk management program not only focuses on prevention but also identifies existing risks and documents actions taken to minimize damage and avoid future injuries from the same cause.

Two factors are critical in the evaluation of risks to patients: accurate date collection and appropriate data analysis. Data collection requires a system that will record all incidents of patient injury or system breakdown in an accurate, complete, and objective manner. Analysis of incidents includes detection of trends or patterns, identification of potentially compensable incidents, and timely action.

In all risk management systems, there is a tension between the desire to collect and analyze needed information and the desire to avoid creating documentation that will increase the liability exposure of the hospitals, nurses, and other staff members. These factors are balanced differently in each institution, depending on state law, risk exposure, insurance policies, and institutional philosophy.

A significant consideration in the design of all systems is a desire to minimize the possibility that the most sensitive documentation can be seen or used by the patient or the lawyer for the patient. State law varies concerning the extent of protection of risk management documents and what must be done to qualify for the protection. It is important for nurses to respect and follow institutional policies, because their defense will be based on the assumption that the policies are being followed. If there are apparent deficiencies in the policies, formal change should be sought rather than making ad hoc, unilateral changes that could jeopardize the nurse and institution.

Hospitals differ in their approaches to the evaluation and minimization of patient injuries. Several of these programs are described next. Frequently, a combination of approaches is used.

Incident Reports

Some type of reporting of incidents is an essential element of any risk management program. Incidents cannot be recorded, analyzed, or responded to unless someone identifies their occurrence and reports them. Nurses have a central role in reporting because they usually are the first to discover incidents and frequently are responsible for follow-up.

All types of unusual occurrences should be reported unless institutional policy expressly provides some other procedure for addressing particular types of events. When there is any doubt, an incident should be reported. Most institutions have adopted broad definitions of "incidents" to encourage reporting. Thus, any unusual occurrence not consistent with the routine operation of the institution or the routine care of a particular patient should be reported, whether it is a potential danger or results in an actual injury and whether it involves a patient, visitor, or staff member. Incidents include patient falls, medication errors, and blood mishaps. It is important to document system breakdowns (e.g., the wrong patient being sent to the operating room) as well as physical hazards and injuries.

Traditionally, incident reports have included a narrative description of what happened and a list of witnesses. The reports are routed through channels specified in institutional policy and are evaluated to determine whether immediate action is required. If not, they are used for statistical analysis of emerging trends or common factors.

Some institutions have adopted notification forms in place of the traditional incident report form. The notification form is designed to quickly notify appropriate administrative personnel of an unusual occurrence and of its type, but not the details or the follow-up. If the administrative personnel believe the event warrants special investigation, it is conducted by a member of the risk management staff or an attorney. This approach has been adopted (1) to avoid delays in initial reporting by making the form easier to complete quickly; (2) to reduce the time of nursing and other patient care staff devoted to the forms; (3) to ensure consistency in how occurrences are investigated and reported; and, (4) in some states, to reduce access of patients and their representatives to detailed reports. The forms also may be designed so that the information can be put into a computer easily for faster and more comprehensive statistical analysis.

A frequent question associated with incident reports is whether they are subject to discovery (i.e., whether they can be obtained for use in a lawsuit). The answer depends on the law of the particular state involved, the procedure used by the institution, and use of the report. Generally, if a report is prepared for the attorney for the hospital for the purpose of obtaining advice on how to handle the incident, the report is protected by the attorney–client privilege. Because discovery applies to nonprivileged information, it does not extend to materials that are privileged. Information obtained by the attorney in anticipation of or in preparation for litigation also is protected. Incident reports prepared primarily for nursing or hospital administration are not protected, however.

Some nurses are reluctant to report incidents, especially ones for which they may share responsibility. Prompt reporting is in the best interest of the involved nurse. It helps to protect the nurse, patient, other staff members, and the institution by facilitating (1) prompt action to minimize injuries from the incident, (2) proper interaction with the patient to decrease the likelihood of a claim, and (3) appropriate action to reduce the likelihood of similar incidents in the future. Incident reporting should lead not to punishment but to positive action. If there is a perception in an institution that incident reporting leads to inappropriate punishment, nursing and institutional officials should be told so that they can foster a better climate for reporting. Nurses should not fear liability for defamation for making reports, as long as they are made through official channels and without malice. There is a risk of liability for defamation if reports are made outside of official channels.[107]

Each institution should have a policy specifying how unusual occurrences should be reported and investigated. Some states mandate certain reporting procedures.[108] Nurses should be familiar with the policies of all institutions in which they practice.

Closed Claims Studies

One method of risk management consists of using information obtained from insurance companies regarding claims against hospitals and health professionals. These data then are analyzed to identify areas of high risk to patients or employees.

Review of Medical Records

Review of medical records addresses only unusual incidents that are documented in the medical record of the patient. It can be a useful adjunct to other approaches if it is remembered that other methods must be used to address incidents not reflected in the medical record. This method allows complete data analysis because of the availability of the information on the subsequent hospital course of the patient.

Role of the Nurse in Risk Management

To establish a basis for analysis, prevention, and follow-up of actual or potential patient injuries, the first important step is the documentation of incidents. This documentation will require the cooperation of all levels of nursing personnel likely to discover incidents. Reports should be completed as soon as possible after the incident is discovered and should be clear, complete, and legible.

When nursing unit administrators are charged with immediate investigation of potentially compensable injuries, they need to focus on three areas: (1) checking the report for clarity and accuracy, (2) interviewing the person reporting and witnesses for additional details, and (3) ensuring that the medical record is complete and accurate, unless these responsibilities are assigned to someone else by hospital policy. Steps must be taken, at all times, to ensure confidentiality. There should be immediate notification of nursing department or hospital administrators when any major event occurs. A serious accident or problem of potential liability should go first to a supervisor or administrator for timely intervention, with retrospective analysis of the report assuming a secondary role.

Safekeeping of the Property of the Patient

At the time of admission, most hospitals direct that patients send home the belongings they will not need. Patients also are encouraged to place valuables such as money and jewelry in the hospital safe to minimize the chances of loss or theft. Nevertheless, many patients keep with them some money and a variety of items of personal property. Some hospitals have patients sign a release of responsibility for loss or breakage of items. This serves to notify them that there will be no reimbursement for loss or damage to property kept against advice. A release form may not excuse the hospital if staff members assume responsibility for patient property or are directly responsible for its loss or damage.

There are some circumstances in which the hospital may accept responsibility for patient property, such as when the person is transferred or goes to the operating room. The nurse who accepts responsibility for patient property but fails to take appropriate steps to safeguard it may incur personal liability for lost articles or cause liability for the hospital.

The basis for this liability is the law of bailments. A bailment is the delivery of property by one party to another party to be held by the latter. When property is held by a hospital or nurse for a patient, a contract of bailment arises and the hospital or nurse has a duty to exercise reasonable care in keeping the property and delivering it to the patient on demand. The law imposes liability on hospitals and staff members for the loss of or damage to property for which they have assumed responsibility.

Many common incidents of damage to property involve patients' dentures. In a New York case involving the liability of a private duty nurse for the loss of the false teeth of a patient, the court found that the evidence was insufficient to establish that the nurse had assumed responsibility for the dentures. However, it assumed that the nurse would have been liable for the loss if responsibility had been accepted.[109]

When a nurse becomes aware that a patient has property of substantial value in a hospital room, institutional officials should be notified promptly so that steps can be taken to (1) remove the property from the hospital, or (2) provide security, or (3) identify and evaluate the property and obtain a release from liability.

INSURANCE

All practitioners should know the extent of insurance coverage for their activities. Many employing agencies provide some level of liability protection for their employees. This does not mean that the employer must buy commercial insurance. Many employers choose to provide individual liability protection through self-insurance. Most who do so cover only job-related activities, so some nurses in such cases elect to purchase coverage for their outside activities, such as volunteer services not covered by the insurance of the organization for which they are providing the volunteer services. Personal malpractice insurance may not cover nurses for some activities outside the scope of nursing practice. Each nurse should be aware of the scope of the state nurse practice act and the institutional policies that define nursing practice for employees. The nurse who is not aware of what protection is provided by the employer should request a statement of clarification to evaluate the need for additional personal liability coverage.

Professional liability policies include the following: the insurance agreement, the amounts payable under the policy, the defense and settling of claims, the period of time during which the policy covers the practitioner, and conditions that must be met to ensure that coverage will be provided. Typically, the nurse must notify the insurance company of claims within a certain period. The company then will select and pay attorneys to defend the nurse for claims made while the policy was in effect. Some policies require the approval of the nurse for any settlement, but many policies do not give the nurse that right.

Most policies limit coverage in some way, such as excluding criminal acts or actions outside the scope of nursing practice. Some policies limit coverage to assigned job responsibilities and exclude actions outside the hospital.

Several suits between practitioners and their insurers have arisen out of situations in which the company refused to pay a claim. In some cases, this is because the nurse did not meet the requirements of the policy (e.g., notification to the company). For example, when a physician failed to notify the company of the claim pending against him, the Tennessee Court of Appeals upheld the denial of benefits.[110]

Other suits have involved questions of whether the alleged negligent acts occurred during the period covered by the insurance. Some insurance policies, called "occurrence" policies, cover all claims arising out of acts or commissions during the period they cover, regardless of when the claim is made. However, many insurance policies, called "claims made" policies, cover only claims made during the time they are in effect so professionals must continue renewing them to maintain coverage for past incidents, unless they purchase a relatively expensive special policy that covers future claims. Generally, the special policy known as "tail" coverage is not purchased until the professional wishes to end active practice or to change insurance companies. The nurse should find out whether the institutional or personal liability policy covers future claims, so that if it does not, arrangements can be made for desired coverage.

In the decision whether to acquire a personal professional policy, nurses should consider several factors, including that if they lose a judgment and they are not covered by insurance, personal assets may be used to satisfy the award. In most states, judgments remain open until satisfied or dropped. Carrying a personal professional liability insurance policy can mean duplication in circumstances in which the employer also has malpractice coverage. However, duplication usually is preferable to having a portion of liability not covered.

CONCLUSION

This chapter provided an overview of the principles of civil liability. Most actions brought against health care providers are civil actions brought to seek damages, usually paid by insurance coverage. Civil actions are usually brought claiming a tort, or civil wrong. Torts are further classified as intentional and unintentional. Unintentional torts form the basis of most professional liability actions. These unintentional torts require that the care given not conform to the standard of care for similar professionals, that the patient was harmed, and that the provider's action was the cause of the harm. Nurses are generally considered to be employees of a hospital; therefore, the negligence of nurses may be imputed to the hospital for acts or omissions within the scope of employment. However, when the hospital's right to direct and control the employee is delegated to an independent staff physician who assumes such a responsibility, the physician may incur liability. Nurses who are not considered employees, who contract with health care organizations independently, or who are in private practice are liable for the consequences of their own acts. Therefore, all nurses, including those who function in the extended role, need to take precautions to conduct their professional practice within the scope of their state nurse practice act, conform their actions to the obligated standard of care, and carry professional liability insurance to cover potential malpractice lawsuits.

FOOTNOTES

1. *E.g.,* Howard v Piver, 279 S.E.2d 876 (N.C. 1981); Baur v. Mesta Machine Co., 176 A.2d 684 (Pa. 1962).
2. Mohr v. Williams, 95 Minn. 261, 104 N.W. 12 (1905).
3. Burrows v. Hawaiian Trust Co., 417 P.2d 816 (Hawaii 1966).
4. Malone v. Longo, 463 F. Supp. 139 (E.D.N.Y. 1979).
5. Wynn v. Cole, 91 Mich. App. 517, 204 N.W.2d 144 (1979).
6. 386 Mich. 119, 191 N.W.2d (1971).
7. Koudski v. Hennepin County Med. Ctr., 317 N.W.2d 705 (Minn. 1982).
8. Johnson v. Women's Hosp., 527 S.W.2d 133 (Tenn. Ct. App. 1975).
9. McCormick v. Haley, 37 Ohio App. 2d 73, 307 N.E.2d 34 (1973).
10. 262 S.E.2d 680 (N.C. App. 1980).
11. 107 Cal. Rptr. 629 (1973).
12. 387 N.Y.S.2d 678 (1976).
13. 239 N.E.2d 368 (1968).
14. *Id.* at 374.
15. Suburban Hosp. Ass'n v. Hadary, 22 Md. App. 186, 322 A.2d 258 (1974).
16. Haber v. Cross County Hosp., 37 N.Y.2d 888, 340 N.E.2d 734 (1975).
17. Ravenis v. Detroit Gen. Hosp., 63 Mich. App. 79, 234 N.W.2d 411 (1975).
18. Utter v. Hospital Ctr., Inc., 236 S.E.2d 213 (W. Va. 1977).
19. Di Fillipo v. Preston, 53 Del. 539, 173 A.2d 333 (1961).
20. Helling v. Carey, 83 Wash. 2d 514, 519 P.2d 981 (1974).
21. Tarasoff v. Board of Regents, 17 Cal. 3d 425, 551 P.2d 334 (Cal. 1976).
22. Landon v. New York Hosp., 189 N.Y.L.J., No. 80, p. 7 (N.Y. Sup. Ct. Apr. 26, 1983).
23. Austin v. Regents of Univ. of Cal., 89 Cal. App. 3d 354, 152 Cal. Rptr. 142 (1979).
24. Mehigan v. Sheehan, 94 N.H. 274, 51 A.2d 632 (1947).
25. Horowitz v. Michael Reese Hosp., 5 Ill. App. 3d 508, 284 N.E.2d 4 (1972).
26. Lenger v. Physician's Gen. Hosp., 455 S.W.2d 703 (Tex. 1970).
27. St. Luke's Hosp. Ass'n v. Long, 125 Colo. 25, 240 P.2d 917 (1952).
28. Walker v. Rumer, 381 N.E.2d 689, 691 (1978).
29. For further discussion dealing with the application of the doctrine of res ipsa loquitur to malpractice and hospital cases, *see generally* 82 A.L.R. 2d 1262.
30. *See, e.g.,* Tice v. Hall, 303 S.E.2d 832 (N.C. Ct. App. 1983).
31. Todd v. Eitel Hosp., 237 N.W.2d 357, 79 A.L.R. 3d 907 (Minn. 1975); Anderson v. Gordon, 334 So. 2d 107 (Fla. Dist. Ct. App. 1976).

32. 499 P.2d 1 (1972).

33. Sanchez v. Bay Gen. Hosp., 116 Cal. 3d 678, 172 Cal. Rptr. 342 (1981).

34. Del. Code Ann. tit. 18, § 6853.

35. Hove v. McMaster, 621 P.2d 694 (Utah 1980).

36. Iowa Code § 614.1(9).

37. *E.g.,* Iowa Code § 614.8.

38. *E.g.,* Fla. Stat. Ann. § 95.11(4)(b).

39. *E.g.,* Iowa Code § 614.1(9).

40. Neilson v. Barberton Citizens Hosp., 446 N.E.2d 209 (Ohio Ct. App. 1982).

41. *E.g.,* Tatham v. Hoke, 469 F. Supp. 914 (W.D.N.C. 1979).

42. *E.g.,* Roberts v. Wood, 206 F. Supp. 579 (D. Ala. 1962).

43. *E.g.,* Shirley v. Schlemmer, 223 N.E.2d 759 (Ind. Ct. App. 1967).

44. *E.g.,* Jenkins v. Bogalusa Community Med. Ctr., 340 So. 2d 1065 (La. Ct. App. 1976).

45. Seymour v. Victory Mem'l Hosp., 60 Ill. App. 3d 366, 376 N.E.2d 754 (1978).

46. *E.g.,* Rochester v. Katalan, 320 A.2d 704 (Del. 1974).

47. *E.g.,* Goetzman v. Wichern, 327 N.W.2d 742 (Iowa 1982).

48. *E.g.,* N.Y. Civ. Prac. Law § 1411; Wash. Rev. Code Ann. §§ 4.22.005–4.22.925.

49. *E.g.,* Ark. Code Ann. ¶ 16-64-122; Wis. Stat. Ann. § 895.045.

50. *E.g.,* Botte v. Pomeroy, 438 So. 2d 544 (Fla. Dist. Ct. App. 1983).

51. *See, e.g.,* Giabozi v. Peters, 16 A.2d 833 (1940).

52. Warvel v. Michigan Community Blood Ctr., 253 N.W.2d 791 (1977); Balkowitsch v. Minneapolis War Mem'l Blood Bank, Inc., 132 N.W.2d 805 (1965).

53. H.B. No. 1142 (New Laws 1986).

54. Shepard v. Alexian Bros. Hosp., Inc., 109 Cal. Rptr. 132 (Cal. Ct. App. 1973).

55. 266 N.E.2d 897 (1970).

56. *Id.; see also* Rostocki v. Southwest Fla. Blood Bank, Inc., 276 So. 2d 475 (Fla. 1973).

57. Belle Bonfils Mem'l Blood Bank v. Hansen, 665 P.2d 118 (Colo. 1983).

58. Hoffman v. Misericordia Hosp., 267 A.2d 867 (1970).

59. Perlmutter v. Beth David Hosp., 123 N.E.2d 792 (1954), *cert. denied,* 125 N.E.2d 869 (1955); Koenig v. Milwaukee Blood Ctr., Inc., 127 N.W.2d 50 (1964); Roberts v. Suburban Hosp. Ass'n, 532 A.2d 1081 (Md. Ct. Spec. App. 1987).

60. Ill. Rev. Stat. ch. 111½, § 5101.

61. Garvey v. St. Elizabeth Hosp., 697 P.2d 248 (Wash. 1985).

62. Bingham v. Lutheran Gen. & Deaconess Hosp., 340 N.E.2d 220 (1975). *See also* Samson v. Greenville Hosp. Sys., No. 22868 (S.C. May 9, 1988); and McKee v. Cutter Laboratories, Inc., 866 F.2d 219 (6th Cir. 1989).

63. 185 So. 2d 324 (La. Ct. App. 1966).

64. Evans v. Northern Ill. Blood Bank, Inc., 298 N.E.2d 732 (1973).

65. Joseph v. W. H. Groves Latter-Day Saints Hosp., 348 P.2d 935 (1960).

66. Sherman v. Hartman, 290 P.2d 894 (1955).

67. Shiver v. Good Shepherd Hosp., 427 S.W.2d 104 (Tex. Civ. App. 1968).

68. Silverhart v. Mount Zion Hosp., 20 Cal. App. 3d 1022, 98 Cal. Rptr. 187 (1971).

69. *See, e.g.,* Evington v. Forbes, 742 F.2d 834 (4th Cir. 1984), in which a hospital was found liable for personal injuries a man sustained in an automobile accident involving a hospital employee who was returning to work in response to a telephone pager message.

70. Ultimately, the employee may bear the entire loss if the employer hospital elects to pursue and successfully prosecutes a claim for indemnification or contribution, when permitted, against its employee.

71. *See, e.g.,* Foster v. Englewood Hosp. Ass'n, 313 N.E.2d 255 (1974).

72. *See, e.g.,* Hudmon v. Martin, 315 So. 2d 516 (Fla. Dist. Ct. App. 1975).

73. *See, e.g.,* Collins v. Westlake Community Hosp., 312 N.E.2d 614 (1974); Norton v. Argonaut Ins. Co., 144 So. 2d 249 (La. Ct. App. 1962).

74. 411 P.2d 861 (1966).

75. 245 So. 2d 751 (La. Ct. App. 1971).

76. 160 Cal. Rptr. 3d 246 (Cal. Ct. App. 1979).

77. *Id.* at 251, n. 8.

78. Ashley v. Nyack Hosp., 412 N.Y.S.2d 388 (N.Y. App. Div. 1979).

79. *See, e.g.,* Kamps v. Crown Heights Hosp., 14 N.E.2d 184 (1938).

80. *See, e.g.,* Roth v. Dade County, 71 So. 2d 169 (Fla. 1954); Ware v. Culp, 74 P.2d 283 (1937).

81. *See, e.g.,* Ware v. Culp, 74 P.2d 283 (1937).

82. 171 S.E. 192 (1933), *aff'd,* 180 S.E. 137 (1935).

83. *Id.* at 193–194.

84. *Id.* at 192.

85. *See, e.g.,* Hawkins v. Laughlin, 236 S.W.2d 375 (Mo. Ct. App. 1951).

86. Webb v. Jorns, 488 S.W.2d 407 (Tex. 1972), *subsequent appeal in same case,* 530 S.W.2d 847 (Tex. Civ. App. 1975).

87. Adamski v. Tacoma Gen. Hosp., 20 Wash. App. 98, 579 P.2d 970 (1978).

88. *E.g.,* State *ex rel.* Cardinal Glennon Mem'l Hosp. v. Gaertner, 583 S.W.2d 107 (Mo. 1979).

89. Aldana v. Holub, 381 So. 2d 231 (Fla. 1980).

90. *E.g.,* Paro v. Longwood Hosp., 373 Mass. 645, 369 N.E.2d 985 (1977); Johnson v. St. Vincent Hosp., Inc., 404 N.E.2d 585 (Ind. 1980).

91. *E.g.,* Feinstein v. Massachusetts Gen. Hosp., 643 F.2d 880 (1st Cir. 1981).

92. *E.g.,* Cal. Civ. Proc. Code § 1295.

93. Ind. Code Ann. § 16-9.5-2-2; La. Rev. Stat. Ann. § 40:1299:42(B).

94. Kansas Malpractice Victims Coalition v. Bell, 757 P.2d 251 (Kan. 1988).

95. Lucas v. United States, 757 S.W.2d 687 (Tex. 1988).

96. Boyd v. Bulala, No. 83-0557-A-C (W.D. Va. Nov. 5, 1986).

97. Etherbridge v. Medical Ctr. Hosp., 376 S.E.2d 525 (Va. 1989).

98. *E.g.,* Rudolph v. Iowa Methodist Med. Ctr., 293 N.W.2d 550 (Iowa 1980).

99. *E.g.,* Johnson v. St. Vincent Hosp., Inc., 404 N.E.2d 585 (Ind. 1980).

100. *See, e.g.,* Brubaker v. Cavanaugh, 741 F.2d 318 (10th Cir. 1984); Roberts v. Durham County Hosp., 289 S.E.2d 875 (N.C. Ct. App. 1982).

101. *See, e.g.,* Austin v. Litvak, 682 P.2d 41 (Colo. 1984); Neagle v. Nelson, 685 S.W.2d 11 (Tex. 1985).

102. Baird v. Loeffler, 434 N.E.2d 194 (Ohio 1982).

103. *See, e.g.,* Roa v. Lodi, 695 P.2d 164 (Cal. 1985), *appeal dismissed,* 106 S. Ct. 421 (1985); DiFillippo v. Beck, 520 F. Supp. 1009 (D. Del. 1981).

104. *E.g.,* FLA. STAT. ANN. § 768.46.

105. *E.g.,* IOWA CODE § 619.18.

106. JOINT COMMISSION ON ACCREDITATION OF HEALTHCARE ORGANIZATIONS, ACCREDITATION MANUAL FOR HOSPITALS.

107. *E.g.,* Malone v. Longo, 463 F. Supp. 139 (E.D.N.Y. 1979).

108. *E.g.,* FLA. STAT. ANN. § 768.41; FLA. ADMIN. CODE ANN. ch. 100-75.

109. Fischer v. Sydenham Hosp., 176 Misc. 7, 26 N.Y.S.2d 389 (1941).

110. Osborne v. Hartford Accident & Indem. Co., 476 S.W.2d 265 (Tenn. 1971).

CHAPTER 15

Tort Liability and Nurses

Chapter Objectives

1. To review assessment
2. To discuss planning
3. To address intervention
4. To present evaluation
5. To consider liabilities of nursing staff

The previous chapter reviewed the general principles of civil liability. This chapter discusses the application of these principles in a variety of specific situations involving nurses, to illustrate the many duties nurses have to patients, clients, and others.

A professional nurse is held to the standard of care generally observed by other competent nurses under similar circumstances. The standard may vary depending on the circumstances. For example, a Texas court ruled that a nurse specialist is held to the standard of care observed by those in the same specialty under similar circumstances.[1] A Louisiana court held that when a person assisting a physician performs a task deemed medical in nature, such as removal of a cast with a Stryker saw, the person is held to the standard of care applicable to physicians.[2] The standard of care applicable to nursing students is the same as that for professional nurses. The standard of care is an essential element that must be proved to establish liability. To establish liability, it must be shown that a patient's injury was caused by the failure to meet the applicable standard of care.

The first half of this chapter reviews areas of potential liability in each step of the nursing process: (1) assessment, (2) planning, (3) intervention, and (4) evaluation. The second half analyzes special problems involving supervisors, students, nursing specialists, and nurses in various nonhospital settings.

ASSESSMENT

The nurse has a responsibility to assess the health status and needs of the patient or client and to communicate that assessment properly. Assessment is a process of gathering information and analyzing it to reach a working decision concerning status and needs. The decision is subject to revision at any time because of subsequent assessments. The steps required will vary, depending on the setting and the degree of involvement of other health professionals in the care of the patient.

Assessment errors can arise from (1) failure to take appropriate steps to gather information, (2) failure to recognize the significance of information gathered, and (3) failure to communicate steps taken or information gathered.

Monitoring and Other Steps to Gather Information

Steps to gather information include asking questions, taking vital signs, making other observations, and taking further actions such as probing wounds. For example, a Mississippi hospital was found liable when an emergency department nurse failed to obtain necessary information from the ambulance personnel who had brought a profusely bleeding patient to the hospital. The nurse transferred the patient, a veteran, to a Veterans Administration hospital without making any effort to assess the extent of the bleeding or to stop it. The patient died because the bleeding was not stopped.[3] In a California industrial accident case, a worker who had received a puncture wound on his forehead went to see the nurse in his employer's first aid room. She swabbed the wound with mercurochrome and bandaged it. The nurse and her employer were found liable for subsequent injuries to the worker because she did not probe the wound before bandaging it.[4]

Generally, nurses do not have to reexamine areas checked by other nurses or physicians if the earlier examination is reliable, properly communicated, and not outdated. If a nurse has reason to suspect that the earlier examination is incomplete, inaccurate, or outdated because of the changing condition of the patient, then reexamination by the nurse or a physician is warranted. If no physician is involved or available, the nurse may be expected to examine areas that normally would be the responsibility of the physician. The probing of the wound in the California case is an example.

When a nurse has the responsibility to monitor a patient over a period of time, information gathering is a continuing responsibility that requires repeated observation. When a patient reaches a condition that could have been avoided by earlier intervention, a question is raised as to whether the responsible nurse should have detected it earlier. This usually becomes a question of whether the nurse observed the patient frequently enough. Most courts recognize that few patients can be observed continuously, so the appropriate frequency for observations is determined by reference to institutional policy, physician orders, and the needs of the patient.

A hospital's internal policies and procedures may establish the requisite degree of patient surveillance. In *Bost v. Riley*,[5] the court stated that the hospital's failure to enforce its own rule requiring physicians to make postoperative progress notes violated the hospital's duty to monitor the condition of a surgical patient who subsequently died of liver failure induced by sepsis. Reinstating a jury verdict against the hospital, the court in *Utter v. United Hospital Center, Inc.*[6] premised the hospital's liability on the failure of its nurses to comply with the hospital's nursing manual and report the patient's deteriorating condition to the department chairman when the attending physician failed to respond adequately to the patient's worsening condition. The court explained its ruling as follows:

> In the dim hours of the night, as well as in the light of day, nurses are frequently charged with the duty to observe the condition of the ill and infirm in their care. If that patient, helpless and wholly dependent, shows signs of worsening, the nurse is charged with the obligation of taking some positive action. . . . One may feel that this places too great a burden on the nurse. In fact, the burden is that of the hospital and if that entity will enforce its requirements, better care will result and perhaps more patients will recover.[7]

In 1982, a District of Columbia court found a hospital liable when an elderly disoriented patient fell out of bed after having not been checked during the hour before the fall.[8] There was a question as to whether the patient had been restrained before the fall. The court concluded that whether or not she had been restrained, she should have been checked more frequently. Expert testimony was not required to establish that duty. A hospital policy requiring restrained patients to be checked at least every half-hour helped to establish the standard. In 1973, a California hospital was found liable for the death of a patient because of the failure of a nurse to follow the orders of the physician concerning observations. The nurse had been ordered to check the patient's vital signs every 30 minutes but did not do so.[9]

Physicians' orders will not protect nurses from liability when reasonable nursing judgment would require more frequent observations. A Massachusetts trial court dismissed a suit against a nurse because of the suicide of a psychiatric patient for whom she was responsible. The court based its decision in part on its belief that the nurse should not be responsible, because three days before the death a psychiatrist had determined that suicide precautions were not necessary. The appellate court overruled the dismissal and ordered a trial.[10] The court ruled that a jury could find the nurse liable because deterioration in the condition of the patient during the three days should have led either to closer supervision or at least to a request for permission to do so. The nurse had not observed the patient for the 40 minutes before the discovery that the patient had drowned in a bathtub. A nurse expert testified that the condition of the patient required observations every 15 minutes.

The duty to monitor a patient's condition can include the duty to question or disagree with a physician's orders, the Supreme Court of South Dakota has ruled.[11] On the day that a patient was discharged in accordance with her physician's orders, the patient's temperature was recorded at 100.2 degrees. The patient was subsequently readmitted to the hospital with severe pain and infection. She died two months later. The court allowed the patient's family to sue the hospital based on the alleged negligent monitoring by its nursing personnel. In particular, the court found that it was possible to conclude that the nurses had a duty to attempt to delay the patient's discharge if her condition warranted continued hospitalization. Because the nursing staff had possibly neglected its advocacy role, the court concluded that the suit should proceed to trial.

Similarly rejecting the hospital's argument that it could not be held liable when its nurse simply carried out the direct order of the physician, the court, in *Variety Children's Hospital v. Osle,*[12] concluded that there was evidence of nursing negligence because of the nurse's failure to segregate the cysts removed from each of the plaintiff's breasts before sending them to the pathologist for a determination of malignancy. The pathologist found that only one of the cysts was malignant, but by that time there was no choice but to remove both the plaintiff's breasts. In the ensuing lawsuit, the court refused to relieve the nurse of responsibility, even though the surgeon who removed the cysts allegedly approved the commingling of the two cysts in one container when the nurse questioned the procedure.

Some patients, especially young children and persons recovering from anesthesia, require virtually continuous observation. A Tennessee court found a nurse and her physician employer liable for the death of a 22-month-old child who the nurse had left unattended on a treatment table. The patient vomited while lying on his back on the table. The court concluded there was sufficient evidence that the nurse could have saved the child if she had been present.[13]

The condition of patients recovering from anesthesia is sufficiently unstable to require virtually minute-by-minute observation. In 1982, a Hawaii court upheld a $400,000 judgment against the state of Hawaii for the death of an eight-year-old boy from cardiac and respiratory arrest during the postoperative period after a tonsillectomy and adenoidectomy. The arrest occurred sometime between the 8:35 AM and 8:45 AM checks on the condition of the patient. Resuscitation restored circulation and respiration, but the patient did not regain consciousness before dying two weeks later. The one registered nurse in the recovery room had been busy with another patient between 8:35 and 8:45. She attempted to convince the court that she had detected the arrest at 8:40 and had initiated intervention then, but all the records indicated discovery at 8:45, and the court did not believe her testimony because of her evasive and inconsistent answers during the trial.[14]

The negligence must be the legal cause of the injury before there can be liability. This is illustrated by a Minnesota case that arose from a cyanotic episode with a newborn who later had severe mental retardation and other injuries.[15] There were no recorded observations of the patient for the half-hour before the discovery of the cyanotic condition. There was testimony that observations every 15 minutes were required, so there was evidence of negligence. However, because there were several other likely causes of the patient's condition, the court ruled that causation of the injury had not been demonstrated, so there was no liability.

The actions of patients can create a duty to observe or assist them more frequently. The Vermont Supreme Court found a hospital liable for the failure to respond to a call light.[16] The sedated patient used the call light to attempt to obtain a bedpan. When there was no response, she attempted to go to the lavatory and fell, causing back injuries. The court concluded that responding to a call light was an element of routine care, so no expert testimony was needed to establish the duty to respond.

Juries often will recognize that nurses cannot be in two places at the same time. In a 1975 Utah case, the jury was asked to decide whether the nurse was negligent for not making a vaginal examination of a pregnant patient (in labor) when the nurse was busy with another complicated emergency delivery.[17] The woman who was not examined had a stillborn baby. The jury found the defendants not liable. This case illustrates the importance of exercising appropriate judgment when confronted with multiple responsibilities. When time and available staffing permit, assistance should be sought to avoid postponing necessary care.

Recognition of Significance of Information

Nurses have a responsibility to understand the significance of the information they gather within the limits of ordinary prudent nursing knowledge. They are not expected to have full medical knowledge. In some situations, the only responsibility of the nurse is to understand that the information should be communicated to a physician. In other situations, the nurse should understand the significance and be able to plan and initiate appropriate intervention.

A 1981 California case illustrates a combination of failure to make timely observations, failure to understand the significance of the observations made, and failure to respond to the observations.[18] The case dealt with a patient who had undergone an elective laminectomy. She received appropriate care until transferred to a postoperative unit. No vital signs, neurologic examinations, or tests for responsiveness were taken on transfer. Her chart was not examined, so the nurses on the unit (1) did not know she had been vomiting, so no suctioning equipment was ordered, and (2) did not know she had an atrial catheter, so they believed it to be a peripheral intravenous line. Ten minutes after transfer to the unit, her blood pressure, pulse, and respiration were measured and reflected a substantial decrease, but the nurses were not aware of this because they did not compare the results to earlier measurements. Because they did not understand the significance of the measurements, no one was informed of the deteriorating condition of the patient. She vomited, which was reported to the nursing team leader, who merely rechecked the vital signs. When the patient's heart arrested 25 minutes after the transfer, the nurse panicked and did nothing to assist her. When an emergency department physician arrived, he was not told that the line was an atrial catheter so he mistook it for a peripheral intravenous line and had all medications administered through it. The patient entered a vegetative state that lasted until death two months later. The court applied the doctrine of res ipsa loquitur and found the hospital liable. This case also illustrates that it is often necessary to compare measurements to previous data to detect changes and understand the significance of the newer ones.

A 1983 Louisiana case arose from the failure of a nurse to recognize and respond properly to the signs of hemorrhage.[19] A heparinized patient in an intensive care unit complained to the nurse concerning pain at 7:30 AM. At 9:30, the nurse charted the complaint of pain and her observation of swelling. She did not call the physician until the patient complained of pain again at 11:50 AM because she did not see evidence of a hematoma. When the physician arrived at noon, he discovered a large hematoma. The patient experienced extended hospitalization and permanent disability to her hand and arm because the physician was not called when the swelling was first observed. The hospital was found liable as the employer of the nurse because she did not understand that she should report the swelling.

Communication

Part of the assessment process is communication of observations and knowledge gained. This communication includes timely oral notification, when necessary, and proper documentation.

Oral communications may include information that (1) was gained during the initial contact with a new patient, (2) was obtained from monitoring a patient, (3) should be shared with others who are working with the patient at the same time, and (4) should be shared with those who are assuming responsibility for care of the patient.

In emergency departments, nurses frequently are given information concerning new patients that they have a responsibility to convey accurately to the responsible physician. Liability can arise when patients are injured by failure to fulfill this duty. In 1977, a Maryland case concerned misdiagnosis of two children taken to an emergency department with rashes.[20] The mother told the nurse that she had removed two ticks from one child several days earlier. The nurse did not tell the physician this. A routine tick search ordered by the physician was fruitless, so he diagnosed measles and prescribed appropriate treatment for that. One child died of Rocky Mountain spotted fever before it was diagnosed accurately. The other child then was treated and cured. The hospital was found liable for the failure of the nurse to report the ticks, delaying the proper diagnosis.

Telephone communications tend to lead to more problems. A 1982 Alaska court decision addressed an early morning emergency department visit by a person who had taken a drug overdose.[21] The court did not criticize the practice in the remote community of having the nurse telephone the on-call physician concerning emergency patients and having the physician decide whether he needed to come to the hospital to see the patient. The content of the telephone conversation was the issue. The patient had told his wife before going to the hospital that he had taken 30 Darvon pills but told the nurse he had taken 10 pills. The nurse reported this to the physician by saying that maybe the patient had taken a few more than 10 pills. The physician concluded it was not an emergency and did not see the patient, so the man was sent home and died that night of a large overdose of Darvon and alcohol. The jury ruled in favor of the physician and hospital. This decision may have been due to the determination by the jury that the communication of the nurse was sufficiently accurate or the suspicion of the jury that the fatal dose was taken after the patient left the emergency department. Even though the defendants won, this illustrates the potential injury to patients and the potential liability from such communications.

In some areas of the country, particularly urban areas, telephone communications never are considered sufficient. A federal court in Pennsylvania found that the standard in Philadelphia was for a licensed physician to examine the patient or the chart of the patient personally before anyone was discharged from an emergency department.[22] The judge found the United States liable for the death of a woman whose subarachnoid hemorrhage was not diagnosed in a Navy hospital emergency department because she was seen by only a nurse and a physician's assistant.

Nurses have a duty to monitor the patient. They are expected to distinguish abnormalities in the condition of the patient and determine whether nursing care is a sufficient response or whether assistance from a physician or others may be required. The nurse also has a responsibility to inform the physician promptly of abnormalities that may require the attention of a physician. A Kansas nurse and hospital were sued because of injuries to a woman during delivery of a baby without the attendance of a physician.[23] The nurse had refused to call the physician despite the clear signs of imminent delivery. The nurse and hospital were found liable for the failure of the nurse to give timely notification to the physician of the impending delivery. A Massachusetts hospital was found liable when a nurse attended seven hours of labor of a patient before calling a physician, despite vomiting by the woman and despite fluctuating fetal heartbeats.[24] The nurse called the physician when she no longer could detect a fetal heartbeat. An emergency Caesarean section was performed, but there was a stillbirth. A West Virginia court ruled that the hospital could be found liable for the death of a patient when the nurse failed to notify the physician of the symptoms of heart failure for six hours.[25]

A 1979 Minnesota decision illustrates both liability for failure to notify the physician and an application of the comparative negligence rule. A patient with a wrist fracture had a cast applied and was admitted to the hospital. Two days later, the nurses observed that his hands and fingers were swollen and bluish. Although they were concerned, they did not call the physician until five days after admission. The physician immediately removed the cast. The patient left the hospital against medical advice 17 days later and engaged in activities he was told to avoid. Two months later, his arm had to be amputated below the elbow. The $350,000 in damages were allocated as follows: (1) 10 percent from the patient for not following advice; (2) 30 percent from the physicians for making the cast too tight and other errors; and (3) 60 percent from the hospital for the nurses' delay in reporting the swollen and bluish hand and fingers.

Nurses do not have to report every patient complaint orally to the physician. For example, a hospital and nurse were found not liable for injuries resulting from grande mal seizures of a patient with a history of epilepsy.[26] The physician had withdrawn all medications on admission to reestablish appropriate levels. The nurse called the physician at 5 AM to report that the patient was restless, coughing, and complaining of pain. The physician ordered a medication. At 5:25 AM, the patient said she thought that she was going to have an unconscious spell. The nurse gave the ordered medication and did not call the physician again. The next morning the patient had six seizures, causing significant damage. The court concluded there was no duty to report the 5:25 AM complaint and no evidence that the lack of a report caused the harm. It was within the range of appropriate nursing judgment to decide whether another report was immediately necessary.

When a nurse has information that should be reported to the physician, failure to report is not excused by the belief of the nurse that the physician is not likely to respond. If the physician does not respond, the nurse has a duty to notify her supervisors or follow other institutional procedures to bring the nonresponse to the attention of those who can provide necessary care for the patient. A California court ruled that two nurses and a hospital could be sued for the death of a woman from severe bleeding from an incision made to assist her to give birth to a child.[27] Although the nurses believed the patient was bleeding heavily, they did not notify the physician until nearly three hours later, when the patient went into shock. One nurse explained that she did not call the physician because she did not believe he would respond. The court concluded that she should have notified the attending physician and taken other steps to safeguard the life of the patient by notifying her superiors in the event the physician did not or could not respond rapidly enough.

A Kansas hospital was exposed to liability by the failure of several nurses to make sufficient efforts to obtain a physician's presence.[28] A patient asked the nurses to call a physician because of pain. A nurse tried to call the physician at 11:01 AM. When she could not reach him, she talked to his partner, who ordered Demerol. The nurse documented 12 more efforts by the patient to convince them to find a physician but made no further efforts to do so. When the physician finally arrived at 9:30 PM, he found the patient suffering from acute gastric dilation.

In the famous case of *Darling v. Charleston Community Memorial Hospital,* one of the reasons for the imposition of liability on the hospital for the amputation of the patient's leg was the failure of the nurses to inform administration of the progressive gangrenous condition of the leg and the inappropriate efforts of the attending physician to address the condition.[29] No effective alternative channel had been established for direct nursing notification of the medical staff and for appropriate medical intervention. The court held that hospital administration should have been notified so that it could provide appropriate medical staff intervention.

Most hospitals today have established direct communication channels between nursing administration and the medical staff leadership, so direct hospital administration involvement is less frequent. These channels must be used when necessary. For example, in *Utter v. United Hospital Center, Inc.,*[30] the evidence showed that the condition of the plaintiff's injured arm began to deteriorate seriously during the day shift of August 27, 1974; that the deterioration continued through August 28, when several nurses observed that the arm was swollen, black, and emitting a foul-smelling drainage; and that the patient was delirious with a high temperature. On August 28, the charge nurse informed the treating physician of the patient's inability to retain oral antibiotics and of other obvious symptoms but did not report the patient's delirium or the drainage from his arm. At the trial of the plaintiff's suit for the ultimate amputation of his arm, the treating physician testified to the critical importance of being advised of the patient's delirium and the serious drainage from the arm, stating that the nurse's failure to provide such information deviated from the normal standard for nursing care.

Nurses have a responsibility to orally communicate information that is needed by those working with the patient at the same time. The United States was found liable when a nurse anesthetist did not inform a nurse who was inserting a catheter that the patient was under light anesthesia.[31] The catheter broke when the patient moved his arm.

When a patient is transferred to another unit or facility, it is necessary to ensure that appropriate information is communicated to those assuming responsibility for the patient. In some circumstances, this communication process is the responsibility of the nurse. A Florida nursing home transferred a patient to a hospital without reporting his senility and need for special supervision.[32] The nursing home was found liable for the death of the patient when he wandered away from the hospital.

In addition to the responsibility to communicate certain information orally, there is a responsibility to document the assessment of the patient. A California nurse, acting pursuant to a telephone order from a physician, gave an injection of Phenergan in the buttock of a woman in labor.[33] The patient reported immediate pain radiating downward from her buttock and later made repeated complaints of a similar nature. The nurse did not record any of the complaints and did not contact the physician. Even though the patient did not include the failure to contact the physician as one of the grounds for her suit, the court ruled that the failure to document the complaints could be the basis for liability of the employer of the nurse.

Sometimes, nurses claim to have observed the patient more frequently than is indicated in their documentation. The jury or judge has to decide whether the error was a failure to make the observation or a failure to document it. Courts tend to conclude that if an observation is not documented, it did not occur. An Illinois hospital was sued for the loss of a leg by a patient.[34] The patient had been admitted for treatment for a broken leg. The admitting physician entered an order to "watch condition of toes" and testified at the trial that routine nursing care required frequent monitoring of the circulation of a seriously injured patient, even in the absence of a physician's orders. The patient developed irreversible ischemia in his leg, requiring its amputation. The nursing notes for the seven-hour period before the discovery of the irreversibility of the ischemia did not reflect any observations of the circulation of the patient. The court ruled that the jury could conclude that absence of entries indicated the absence of observations. Thus, the nurse and hospital could be liable even if the nurse actually had made the observations. In these circumstances, it is as important to document no change as it is to document changes, so that the time when changes occur can be identified.

Deficiencies in charting must contribute to the injuries suffered by a patient before they can lead to liability. In a 1983 Louisiana case, a woman experienced severe hemorrhaging after childbirth.[35] Her physicians performed a series of operations resulting in the removal of her uterus and cervix. The court found that the records concerning her vital signs were incomplete and poorly kept but concluded that these deficiencies played no part in causing her problems.

PLANNING

A nurse must plan appropriate nursing care for each patient based on the information gathered and assessed. A nurse also must plan how to carry out the orders of a physician. Few court decisions focus on this step because planning almost always must result in an act or omission of intervention before liability is likely to be found. The court decisions therefore focus on the act or omission.

One example of poor planning was the decision by a licensed practical nurse in a Veterans Administration hospital to send a patient unaccompanied to a laboratory for a test when the licensed practical nurse was aware the patient had been administered several drugs and had suffered chest pains.[36] The United States was found liable for the amputation of the finger of the patient from injuries received when the individual fainted while standing in line.

Another example of poor planning arose when a woman with a Dalkon Shield, an intrauterine contraceptive device, sought help from a health plan in Massachusetts.[37] The woman was experiencing a foul odor, and a nurse practitioner told her to douche with yogurt. When the woman called again reporting pain, the nurse told her to wait until she had a fever before calling back. When she finally was examined by a physician, multiple abscesses were found, requiring a total hysterectomy.

The court noted that the douche was a substandard lay remedy and that the failure to recommend a prompt examination by a physician was substandard. The nurse practitioner also had a duty to inform the patient of the risks associated with the Dalkon Shield or arrange for a physician to do so. She had a duty to keep herself informed of well-publicized current developments in areas about which she was advising patients. The problems with Dalkon Shields had been well publicized before the first call from the patient. Thus, the court ruled that the health plan that employed the nurse practitioner could be liable for her advice to the patient.

Planning decisions of supervisory nurses concerning allocation of staff time have resulted in liability. Examples are discussed in the Supervisors section of this chapter.

INTERVENTION

Intervention is the carrying out of the plan derived from the assessment. Intervention can involve carrying out nursing care that does not require physician orders as well as implementing physicians' orders. Obtaining physician attention, as necessary, can be viewed as an intervention, but it also can be one of the communication responsibilities that are part of assessment, which is the way it is addressed in this chapter.

Duty to Interpret and Carry Out Orders

Nurses have a duty to interpret and carry out orders properly. They are expected to know basic information concerning the proper use of drugs and procedures that they are likely to be ordered to use. When an order is ambiguous or apparently erroneous, the nurse has a responsibility to seek clarification from the ordering physician. This almost always will result in correction or explanation of the order. In the unusual situations in which that does not occur, the nurse has a responsibility to inform nursing, hospital, or medical staff officials designated by institutional policy who can initiate review of the order and, if necessary, other appropriate action. Pending review, if the drug or procedure appears dangerous to the patient, the nurse should decline to carry out the order but should immediately notify the ordering physician.

Hospitals should have established procedures for nurses to follow when they are not satisfied with the appropriateness of an order. Frequently, this procedure will involve notification of a nursing supervisor, who then will contact appropriate medical staff officials. Hospital administration occasionally may need to become involved to resolve individual issues.

A hospital obviously may incur liability for the negligence of its nursing personnel in failing to follow a physician's orders. Thus, a nurse's failure to notify the attending physician for nearly six hours of the patient's symptoms of heart failure, as requested by the physician, was sufficient to consider in determining the hospital's negligence for the patient's subsequent death.[38] Similarly, in *Cline v. Lund*,[39] a finding that hospital negligence caused the death of a postsurgical patient was based in part on evidence of the nurse's failure to check the vital signs of the patient every 30 minutes, as ordered by the attending physician, and her failure to notify the physician promptly when she discovered a life-threatening situation.

Similarly, a nurse's failure to make hourly examinations of a patient's leg, as ordered by a physician, constitutes negligence on the part of the nursing staff of a hospital.[40] A patient's physician left instructions with the nursing staff to perform certain tests and observations of a patient and to notify him if problems developed. When examining the patient two days later, the physician observed that her foot was white and that there was no discernible pulse. The nurses' chart notes recorded sporadic testing. Despite the hospital's contention that expert medical testimony failed to establish that the nurses' negligence was the cause of injury, the court held that there was a reasonable probability that the change in the condition of the leg became discernible several hours before the physician saw the patient, as the patient's chart clearly indicated that no tests were performed for four and one-half hours before the physician's examination. Therefore, the court ruled that the nursing staff was negligent in its failure to follow the physician's instructions.

If the physician's directions are unclear or unorthodox or if the prescription contravenes the drug manufacturer's instructions, the nurse has an obligation to challenge or demand clarification of the physician's orders. For example, in the case of *Norton v. Argonaut Insurance Co.*,[41] the physician prescribed Lanoxin for an infant patient without indicating whether the medication was to be administered in its oral or injectable form. The evidence established that the dosage prescribed was fatal if the drug was administered in its injectable form but not if the oral form was used. Although recognizing her own uncertainty as to the proper method of administration, the nurse administered the drug in its injectable rather than its oral form without contacting the prescribing physician for clarification. The patient died several hours later as a result of the lethal overdose. On appeal, the court affirmed the judgment against the physician, the nurse, and the hospital. The nurse's liability rested on her failure to contact the prescribing physician for clarification of the admittedly confusing order. The hospital was held vicariously liable for the negligence of its employee, the nurse.

A Louisiana court focused attention on the responsibility of a nurse to obtain clarification of an apparently erroneous order from a physician.[42] The order, as entered in the chart, was incomplete and subject to misinterpretation. Believing the medication order to be incorrect because of the dosage, the nurse asked two physicians whether it should be given as ordered by the physician. They did not interpret the order as the nurse did and therefore did not share the same concern, commenting that the instruction of the attending physician did not appear out of line. The nurse did not contact the attending physician and administered the misinterpreted dosage of the medication, leading to the death of the patient.

The appellate court upheld the finding of the jury that the nurse had been negligent in failing to contact the attending physician before giving the medication, and the nurse and her employer were held liable, as was the physician who wrote the ambiguous order that led to the fatal dose. This case illustrates the way in which the conduct of the nurse is measured against the practice of competent and prudent nurses. There had been testimony at the trial that a prudent nurse, when confronted with an ambiguous or confusing medication order, will obtain clarification from the prescribing physician. However, the nurse who administered the medication did not seek such clarification, and the departure from the standard of competent nursing practice provided the basis for holding the nurse liable for negligence.

Sometimes, an order that is correct when originally given becomes apparently erroneous because of changes in the condition of the patient or because the therapy ordered usually should not be continued for such a long period without reevaluation. An Indiana hospital was found liable because a nurse did not question an excessively long, continuous intubation of a patient.[43] After the endotracheal tube had been in place for five days, the physician ordered the nurse to remove it, but she could not do so. The physician immediately removed it, and injuries to the throat and vocal cords were discovered. Experts testified that the tube should not have been left in continuously for more than four days. The nurse should have brought the problem to the attention of the physician and, if he did not respond, to the attention of her supervisor.

In some situations, nurses are given authority to adjust the amount of some drugs or other substances being given to patients within guidelines established by the physician. In such situations, the nurse has the added responsibility to exercise the appropriate judgment in making those adjustments. In many states, there are legal limits on the discretion that can be delegated concerning some drugs and substances, so familiarity with local law is important. In addition, as with all delegations, the physician should provide guidance and delegate this responsibility only to nurses who are able to make the required judgments.

In 1979, a California court recognized the appropriateness of delegating to a nurse the decision concerning when a prescribed pain medication was needed.[44] The patient suffered cardiopulmonary arrest and died soon after she was given the pain medication. The court ruled that it was appropriate for the trial court to give the jury two special instructions usually used only for physicians because the case involved a nurse who was exercising independent judgment delegated by the physician. One instruction emphasized that perfection was not required, so liability could not be based on a mere error in judgment by a nurse who possessed the necessary learning and skill and exercised the care ordinarily exercised by reputable nurses under similar circumstances. The standard applied was the conduct of nurses, not physicians. The other instruction emphasized that when there is more than one recognized method of treatment, it is not negligent to select one of the approved methods that later turns out to be wrong or to be not favored by certain other practitioners. The appellate court upheld the jury verdict in favor of the nurse and hospital.

Unless an order is ambiguous or apparently erroneous, the nurse has a responsibility to carry it out. For instance, a New York nurse and hospital were held liable for the scalding of a young tonsillectomy patient by water that was served as a part of his meal by a nurse, contrary to the dietary instructions ordered by the attending physician.[45] A Texas hospital was sued because a nurse gave a patient solid food after a colon resection, contrary to orders.[46] The hospital avoided liability because the patient could not prove that the solid food was the cause of the separation of the sutured ends of the colon several days later. In *Doctor's Hospital of Augusta, Inc., v. Poole,* a Georgia hospital was held liable when a patient fell after a nurse instructed the patient to use the bathroom without supervision, contrary to the physician's order requiring an attendant.[47] Last, a New York hospital was sued for the blindness of an infant caused by too much oxygen when a nurse gave 6 L/min instead of the 4 L/min ordered by the physician.[48] The hospital presented evidence that 6 L/min was within the range of permissible dosages. The court found this irrelevant because the nurse had not been given authority to deviate from the physician's order and, thus, had breached her duty to the patient.

Nurses cannot assume that orders have remained unchanged from previous shifts. They have a duty to check for changes in orders. A Delaware physician wrote an order on the order sheet changing the mode of administration of a drug from injection to oral.[49] When a nurse, who had been off duty for several days, was preparing to give the medication by injection, the patient objected and referred the nurse to the new order. The nurse, however, told the patient she was mistaken and gave the medication by injection. Either the nurse had not reviewed the order sheet after being told by the patient that the medication was to be given orally or did so in a negligent manner and did not note the physician's entry. In either case, the conduct of the nurse was held to be negligent. The court stated that the jury could find the nurse negligent by applying ordinary common sense, so expert testimony was not necessary to prove the applicable standard of care.

When a nurse carries out an order that is neither ambiguous nor apparently erroneous, the order provides significant protection from liability. A Nebraska hospital was unsuccessfully sued when a schizophrenic patient fractured her arm.[50] The physician had ordered the patient restrained the first four days of the admission, then had directed that the restraints be removed. The requests of the daughter of the patient that the restraints be restored had been conveyed to the physician but he declined to do so. The court ruled there was no liability for the nurse because there was no duty to restrain when the physician did not order restraints, and there was no reason to believe the order was so erroneous as to require intervention.

A Montana court ruled that a hospital could not be liable for failing to lock the door of a security room while an irrational patient had an attendant present when the physician had ordered the door locked only when the patient was unattended.[51] The patient had forced himself past the attendant, ran to a window outside the security room, and jumped to the ground 20 feet below. The court ruled that the nurses had to follow the physician's orders unless there was an emergency.

Orders do not excuse the nurse from the duty to use proper care for the safety of the patient and to carry out the orders nonnegligently. A Kentucky physician ordered a patient to be exercised after her surgery.[52] The patient became violently ill at the first attempt. The physician ordered a second attempt, but the patient protested when two nurses tried to carry out the order. The patient collapsed, hitting the floor and suffering permanent pain. The court ruled that the jury could find the nurses did not use proper care for the safety of the patient. Many of the other ways orders have been carried out negligently are discussed in the next section.

Errors in Carrying Out Interventions

Many types of negligent errors in carrying out interventions have led to lawsuits. Some of these interventions were initiated by nurses, and some were ordered by physicians. This section gives examples of errors involving (1) patient identity, (2) patient positioning, (3) changing sheets, (4) medications, (5) injections, (6) sterile technique, (7) catheterization, (8) foreign objects left in the body, (9) incubators, (10) restraints and falls, and (11) patient instructions. This is not a complete list of the areas leading to liability, which can also include such errors as giving the wrong medication to a patient, but it illustrates the range.

Patient Identity

The identity of the patient should be checked before initiating major interventions. A patient scheduled for conization of the cervix was taken to the operating room by a surgical technician at the time a thyroidectomy was scheduled for another patient.[53] The mistake was discovered after the incisions of the thyroidectomy were made but before excision of the thyroid. No one checked the identification bracelet of the patient. They erroneously relied on the patient who had answered to the wrong name. The court found the hospital liable for the failure of the nurse to check the bracelet. The erroneous answer by the patient was not accepted as a defense.

In a Louisiana case, a nurse's aide was sent to the laboratory to obtain two extra units of blood before an operation.[54] The laboratory gave her blood intended for a different patient on a different floor. The circulating nurse checked the number on the blood with the number on the slip accompanying the blood, which matched, but she never checked the name. The O-positive patient received 600 ml of A-positive blood. The hospital was found liable.

Patient Positioning

Improper positioning of a patient for some procedures can result in injuries and liability. A Missouri hospital was held liable when a nursing assistant improperly adjusted a proctoscopic table and improperly positioned the patient, resulting in neck injuries.[55] An employee of a Michigan hospital failed to pad an elbow properly when restraining the patient for an appendectomy.[56] The hospital was found liable for the resulting impairment of the conduction of nerve impulses in the left ulnar nerve that caused numbness in two fingers. One of the grounds of a suit against a Minnesota hospital was that a nurse incorrectly positioned an infant for a lumbar puncture shortly before the infant had a cardiac arrest resulting in a semi-comatose condition.[57] However, there was no liability because the family did not prove the positioning could have caused the cardiac arrest.

Changing Sheets

Even changing sheets can lead to suits and potential liability. A minor patient in a Florida hospital had his leg in traction to avoid any movement that might lead to a fracture because he had a degenerative bone disease that made fractures likely.[58] A nurse pulled the sheets from under the patient without assistance, causing his body to twist. He immediately thought that his leg had broken, which was confirmed later. The court ruled that a jury should decide whether the actions of the nurse caused the fracture.

Medications

Medication errors can arise from giving the wrong substance or wrong dose, using the wrong route of administration, or giving the substance at the wrong time.

Wrong Substance. Liability resulted when a patient was injured because a scrub nurse filled a syringe with a solution different from the one ordered by the physician.[59] In another case, a Maryland hospital and nurse settled a claim arising out of mismatched blood.[60] A physician ordered the nurse to get another unit of Rh-negative blood for a 15-year-old female victim of an automobile accident. The nurse mistakenly picked up a unit of Rh-positive blood and gave the patient 0.5 ml before detecting the error and stopping. The patient had an itching rash for a half-hour and was permanently sensitized so that any pregnancy would be more complicated.

Wrong Dose. A North Carolina patient attempted to prove that damage to his hand and skin was caused by an excessive dose of potassium chloride through an intravenous line into his hand.[61] The trial judge refused to allow a nurse trained in intravenous therapy to testify concerning the cause of damage, so the patient did not have expert testimony concerning causation, and the hospital won. The appellate court ruled that the nurse should have been permitted to testify and ordered a new trial.

An Alaska case involving an overdose illustrates the defense of the statute of limitations.[62] A nurse mistakenly administered an overdose of lidocaine, causing a cardiac arrest. On directions of a physician, hospital records were altered to delete references to the overdose. Despite this cover-up attempt, another physician told the family of the patient about the overdose two days later. The physician who attempted to cover up was suspended from the hospital staff. This was reported in detail in the newspaper, including the reasons and the last name of the patient. Normally, statutes of limitation do not apply during periods of cover-ups. The court ruled that the statute of limitations began to apply when the newspaper reports appeared. Because the suit was not filed for more than two years after that and the time limit for malpractice suits in Alaska is two years, the suit was barred. It is never advisable to attempt a cover-up; cover-ups only extend the exposure to liability and increase the potential liability for this improper behavior.

Wrong Route. Medications can be given orally; by injection into a vein, the skin, or a muscle; or by application to the surface of the skin, as well as by other means. When drugs are given by the wrong route, injuries and liability can result.

A Kansas hospital was held liable when a nurse used a needle that was too short to inject Dramamine into the hip of a large patient.[63] Because the needle was too short, the drug was injected subcutaneously rather than the intended intramuscular route. The injection caused a painful odoriferous wound and recurring back pain. A New York hospital was held liable when a licensed practical nurse who was attempting to inject penicillin intramuscularly accidentally pierced a vein, injecting the drug into the blood stream.[64] The patient died from anaphylactic shock.

Wrong Time. Another type of error is a delay in administering a prescribed medication. Most minor delays will not have serious consequences, but sometimes the results can be substantial. A 1979 Utah case resulted when a nurse did not administer a psychiatric medication until 10 PM, although it had been ordered to be given immediately at 8 PM. At 2:40 AM, the patient broke a window of his room on the sixth floor and jumped to a roof five stories below. He was permanently paralyzed. The trial court granted summary judgment for the defendants. The Utah Supreme Court ruled that the jury should have been permitted to decide whether the delay contributed to the jump.[65]

An Illinois hospital was sued for the death of a 14-month-old child from measles.[66] The two-hour delay by a nurse in administering prescribed medications was one of the grounds of the suit. There was conflicting testimony as to whether this contributed to the death and whether it was a deviation from the standard of care, because other medications were given just before the two hours began. The jury ruled in favor of the defendants.

Injections

Injections can lead to liability for all the reasons discussed in the medication errors and sterile technique sections, plus other reasons unique to injections. A frequent source of liability is damage to the sciatic nerve during injections in the buttocks. For example, an Oregon hospital was held liable in 1980 for a Nembutal injection by a nurse that injured the sciatic nerve.[67] A California court ruled that the jury could apply res ipsa loquitur to a case involving wrist drop that resulted from an injection in the arm by a nurse in a physician's office.[68]

In 1982, a federal appeals court was presented with an unusual case involving an outpatient hemodialysis facility and its nursing supervisor.[69] A patient had used abusive, disruptive, and threatening language with the staff and used an extension phone to eavesdrop on the nursing supervisor's telephone calls. When his dialysis was completed, the nursing supervisor had disconnected him from the machine, called him a "black son of a bitch," and left the dialysis needles in his arm. He refused all offers of assistance from other staff personnel, left the facility, and later removed the needles himself with substantial loss of blood. Staff members at the facility testified that it was not unusual for the needles not to be removed immediately and for other staff members to do so later. The court discounted this testimony because the actions of the nursing supervisor were associated with name-calling, indicating unprofessional conduct. The court held the facility liable despite the extreme provocation by the patient, but allocated 40 percent of the fault to the patient because he had refused other assistance, so the patient received payment for only 60 percent of the damages.

Sterile Technique

In the past, courts found hospitals liable for infections when the patient proved unsanitary hospital conditions. With improvements in infection control and in determining types and sources of infections, courts increasingly have recognized that nurses, physicians, and hospitals cannot guarantee the absence of infections and that infections do occur for many reasons other than negligence. Thus, most courts require proof of a causal relationship between the infection and a deviation from proper practices.

Virtually every state has standards and regulations with respect to infection control. These standards vary widely from state to state, and each hospital must consult the requirements of the state in which it is located. In some states, hospital-licensing regulations are imprecise, thereby allowing hospitals wide latitude in procedures to control infection. In other states, however, such regulations may be very detailed.

A hospital in Washington State was held liable for a staphylococcus infection because the patient proved that nurses failed to take the necessary precautions, such as hand washing, to avoid cross-infection from the other patient in the semiprivate room who was infected with the same organism.[70] The patient who suffered the cross-infection recently had undergone hip surgery, and the infection entered his hip, requiring its fusing into a nearly immovable position.

A jury found a New York hospital liable for the loss of the eye of a patient from an infection after a nurse put a patch that had fallen on the floor over the eye.[71] However, the judge overruled the jury because there was no evidence that that particular type of infection could be transmitted by the patch.

In the past, there frequently were suits when nurses failed to sterilize needles and other equipment.[72] The use of presterilized supplies has reduced both the risk to the patient and the liability exposure. If a patient is infected by a presterilized item, the manufacturer usually will bear the liability unless the item was contaminated by negligent conduct of the nurse or other health professionals or there was a pattern of infection that should have led to discontinuance of use of the supply of the item.

For example, a Georgia physician was found not liable for an infection because an office nurse had properly used a prepackaged, presterilized needle and syringe.[73] However, an Iowa surgeon was held liable for infection from contaminated sutures because he knew they were contaminated when he used them since an earlier patient had become infected through use of sutures from the same supply.[74]

Catheterization

Improper insertion or removal of catheters and failure to catheterize a patient have led to negligence suits. A Utah patient had a series of catheterizations after a hysterectomy.[75] When a nurse performed the 12th catheterization, the patient experienced pain, and later the urine bag filled with blood. There was conflicting testimony concerning the cause of the injury, with one expert saying it could be from a hematoma from the surgery. The jury decided that causation was not proved and ruled in favor of the defendants.

A Florida hospital was held liable when a nurse removed a Foley catheter without first deflating the cup, resulting in bladder damage.[76] An Oklahoma court ruled that a hospital could be liable for the refusal of nurses to catheterize a patient for 22 hours, despite repeated requests from the person.[77] Stitches from a prior operation tore and the bladder fell.

Foreign Objects

When foreign objects such as sponges or surgical instruments are left in patients during surgery, there usually is liability. Most courts apply the doctrine of res ipsa loquitur to such cases. Thus, liability is avoided only when the defendants can show that the injury was not caused by negligence. For example, if the patient has to be quickly closed in an emergency, the failure to make an instrument or sponge count can be justified.

Most foreign object cases center on whether the hospital or surgeon is liable. It is generally recognized that a nurse is responsible for the count of the sponges and instruments. A California court held that a hospital could be liable for a clamp left in a patient even though it was not local practice at that time (1956) to take a count.[78] The court ruled that hospitals should require counts by their nurses.

The hospital, as employer of the nurse, is generally liable in foreign object cases. In the past, the surgeon often was liable as captain of the ship but today generally is liable only when exercising specific control or personally making errors. For example, a Missouri physician was held not liable, while the hospital was held liable, for a laparotomy sponge left after a gallbladder operation.[79] The court ruled that the injury resulted from the failure of the circulating nurse to announce the sponge count correctly. The surgeon had not exercised specific control and could not do so without violating proper sterile technique. (The interrelationship of the liability of the nurse, hospital, and surgeon in the operating room is discussed further in the nurse anesthetist section of this chapter.)

Incubators

Infants have been burned and overheated in incubators. A Georgia court ruled that a hospital could be sued when an infant was burned in an incubator.[80] The nurse placed the infant so that a foot was in contact with a preheating electric light bulb. Severe burns required amputation of most of the foot. The court noted that liability could be based on failure to turn off the preheating bulb and on the incorrect positioning of the infant.

In another case, an infant became extremely overheated in an incubator, was dehydrated, and experienced convulsions and twitching.[81] A few days after discharge, the infant developed central nervous system disorders, cerebral palsy, and mental retardation. When the suit was decided more than 20 years later, the jury decided in favor of the defendants, probably because there was testimony that the condition of the patient was caused by prenatal injuries, not the overheated incubator.

Although incubator design has changed, nurses still need to be aware of potential risks to infants and to take appropriate steps to reduce those risks.

Restraints and Falls

Nurses have a responsibility to provide proper attention for disoriented, disabled, and mentally ill patients. This frequently includes a duty to restrain or provide proper attendance. Although some emergency restraints may be applied temporarily, based on nursing judgment, most restraints—especially for extended periods—require the order of a physician and the consent of the patient or the patient's representative. Such orders provide substantial protection for the nurse, as discussed earlier, if the order is carried out nonnegligently.

Liability generally arises after patients fall or escape and injure themselves or others. Courts frequently take the position that juries do not need expert testimony to establish what the nurse should have done; juries are allowed to apply common sense.

Leaving a patient in a risky situation without an attendant or proper restraint has led to suits and liability. A Louisiana hospital was held liable when a patient fell, lacerating his penis, after a nurse left him unattended in a bathroom.[82] The court held that he should have been attended because he was drugged and had previously had an arm amputated. A North Carolina court ruled that a hospital and nurse's aide could be liable for leaving a patient unattended on a bed pan in an armchair, even though the absence was only for four minutes for the purpose of patient privacy.[83] The armchair was not in reach of a call buzzer. The patient fell, breaking a hip. The court ruled that expert testimony concerning the standard of care was necessary and that expert testimony from a nurse was sufficient.

Courts are especially critical when they believe the nurse has left the patient unattended to do something considered less important. An Ohio hospital was held liable when a patient fell from a bed in the labor room.[84] The patient was under sedation, restless, and repeatedly attempted to climb out of bed. The nurse left the room briefly to do some charting and then agreed to accompany a physician to see another patient because hospital rules prohibited physicians from attending a woman in labor unless a nurse was present.

A Texas hospital was held liable when a patient fell from an emergency department table.[85] The nurse was busy having the father of the patient sign papers and refused to respond when the patient started to turn white and vomit. The patient fainted and fell to the floor, breaking two teeth, fracturing a thumb, suffering a concussion, and bruising a shoulder. The court criticized the nurse for being more attentive to forms than to the patient.

When nurses remove ordered restraints, they need to be particularly careful to ensure attendance. A Wisconsin court ruled that a hospital could be liable when a patient fell breaking his hip, after a nurse removed his restraint and left him unattended.[86] The nurse had removed the restraint to permit the patient to feed himself. The court ruled that expert testimony was not necessary to establish the need for restraints because the patient was confused and irrational.

The nurse does not have to be present continuously when the patient does not need an attendant. In cases in which the need is marginal, the request of the patient to be left alone may excuse the nurse from liability. An elderly patient refused assistance from a nurse while disrobing in a Connecticut physician's office.[87] While the nurse was waiting a few feet away in an adjacent room, the patient fell. The jury found the defendant physician not liable because the patient had refused assistance, there was no physician order requiring an attendant, and the patient demanded to be left alone.

Failure to provide a patient with a signaling device and failure to respond to a signal can lead to liability. A Florida court ruled that a hospital and nurse could be liable for a fall in an emergency department.[88] The patient presented with chest pains, was given medications, and was left lying for nearly two hours on a stretcher in an empty room without a signaling device. When nurses did not respond to his oral calls, he attempted to go to the bathroom unassisted and fell, injuring himself. A Louisiana hospital was found liable when nurses failed to respond to a call light for 15 minutes.[89] A drugged patient attempted to go to a bathroom unassisted and fell, suffering a compression fracture of the vertebra.

There can be liability when restraints are not applied properly. An example concerning a patient restrained during surgery is discussed in the earlier section on patient positioning.[90] Another example is an Arizona case in which a hospital was found liable when a patient struck another patient with a chair.[91] The assailant extricated himself from restraints five times, and the incident occurred after the fifth escape. The court ruled that no expert testimony was needed to prove that properly applied restraints should have precluded multiple escapes.

Patient Instructions

Some interventions require cooperation of or special care by the patient, for which nurses need to give appropriate instructions. However, if proper instructions are given to a competent patient who does not follow them, liability is unlikely unless proper nursing care calls for additional precautions that are omitted.

An Indiana physician ordered a 24-hour urine collection that required all the urine to be transferred into a jug with hydrochloric acid.[92] There was conflicting evidence as to whether the nurse advised the patient how to safely collect the urine and pour it into the jug through a funnel. The patient voided directly into the jug and the acid reacted, burning his penis. The jury believed the nurse had provided appropriate instructions, so it found no liability.

EVALUATION

Evaluation is the review and documentation of the effect of the intervention step to ensure it is completed properly. If further action may be warranted, the nurse returns to the assessment step. Although important, the evaluation step itself seldom leads to liability; liability arises from failure to perform a proper assessment or failure to carry out proper intervention.

For example, a California nurse detected problems when evaluating the effects of an intravenous infection.[93] Her assessment included observation of increased swelling and redness in the area of the intravenous tube. She notified the physician several times of the swelling, but he ordered continuation of the procedure. There was conflicting testimony at the trial concerning (1) whether the nurse had communicated the seriousness of the swelling when it became markedly worse and (2) whether the nurse had the authority to discontinue the intravenous infusion without a physician's order. The court overturned the decision of the trial court in favor of the hospital and physician and ordered a new trial so a jury could determine these issues. In this case, the potential liability arose from the assessment and intervention phases, not the evaluation. Today, a nurse confronted with this situation would either (1) discontinue the procedure if authorized to do so by institutional policy or (2) follow the institutional procedure for reporting apparently erroneous orders.

LIABILITY OF NURSING STAFF

Supervisors

Because the nursing supervisor is not the employer of the nurses supervised, respondeat superior does not impose liability on the supervisor for the negligent acts of those people supervised. Supervisors will be held liable for their own negligent acts or omissions, and the employer will be held liable for the negligence of the supervisor under respondeat superior.

Generally, a nursing supervisor will be held liable for negligent acts of supervision. Liability also can be imposed on a supervisor who is negligent in providing care while assisting in patient treatment on a unit she supervises. For example, in one case, the superintendent of the hospital was acting as a circulating nurse in the operating room when she applied straps to the feet of the patient so tightly that circulation was cut off and the patient developed gangrenous sores.[94] The patient successfully sued the hospital and the nurse as an individual for negligence. In another case, a nursing supervisor whose duties included covering the emergency department as a staff nurse was held by the court to be acting as a hospital employee when she administered an injection to a patient in the emergency department.[95]

The liability of a supervising nurse was involved in another case in which a needle was left in the abdomen of the patient during surgery and discovered after the operation had been completed.[96] The patient brought suit against the surgeons, the hospital, a nurse, and the nursing supervisor of the operating room.

The court dismissed the suit against the nursing supervisor saying, "It appears that she, as supervisor of the operating rooms, assigned two competent nurses to attend the operation, that she was not present at the operation or any other place with the plaintiff, and she had no control or custody of plaintiff. Furthermore, she was acting as a supervisory employee of the hospital in assigning the nurses and she . . . would to be liable by reason of the assignment." The court ruled that the doctrine of respondeat superior is not applicable to the relationship between a supervisor and subordinate employees.

Another case that illustrates the potential liability of a nursing supervisor was decided by a Canadian court in British Columbia.[97] The court found both the supervising nurse and her employer, the hospital, liable for injuries to a woman who was not observed often enough in a postoperative recovery room. The patient had a cholecystectomy without complications and was transferred to the recovery room. The hospital had provided two staff nurses for the area, which the court accepted as adequate staffing, but the supervising nurse permitted one nurse to leave for a coffee break just before three patients were admitted. One of the patients suffered a respiratory obstruction that was not observed until the lack of oxygen caused permanent brain damage.

The court ruled that the supervising nurse was liable for permitting the other nurse to leave the area at a time when she knew that the operating schedule would result in several admissions to the unit. The court said that even if she had not known the operating schedule, she still would be liable for not knowing the aspects of the schedule that applied to the staffing needs of the area she supervised. Because the supervising nurse also provided direct care to the patients in the area, she also was liable for failing to observe the patient more frequently.

The court also ruled that the nurse who left the area would have been liable had she been included in the suit because she should have known the aspects of the operating schedule that applied to the staffing needs of the area in which she worked. The hospital also was liable for the acts of both nurses under the doctrine of respondeat superior.

Two years later, a similar case was decided in the same province in Canada.[98] A 10-year-old boy who had undergone plastic surgery for overprominent ears suffered a cardiac arrest resulting in a permanent coma for more than four years until his death. The cardiac arrest occurred in the postanesthesia area while three of the five nurses assigned to the area were on a coffee break. The hospital was found liable for negligence for the same reasons described in the earlier case.

In a New York case, a patient who had been disoriented was found on a balcony outside a second-story window.[99] After the patient was returned to the hospital room, a physician told the staff to arrange to have the person watched. The charge nurse called the family of the patient to tell them to arrange to have someone do so. The family said someone would be at the hospital in 10 or 15 minutes. By the time the family member arrived, the patient had fallen out the window and was seriously injured.

The hospital was found liable for failing to remove the patient to a secure room, apply additional restraints, or find someone to watch the patient for the 15 minutes. There was one charge nurse, one new registered nurse in orientation, one practical nurse, and one aide on a unit with 19 patients. The court found that all except the aide had been engaged in routine duties that could have been delayed for 15 minutes and that the aide had been permitted to leave for supper during the period. The court said this was evidence that there was sufficient staffing to provide continuous supervision for a patient in known danger for 15 minutes. The failure of the supervising nurse to properly allocate the time of the available staff properly was one of the grounds for the hospital being held liable.

In a 1942 California case, the hospital was held liable for the death of a patient from tetanus after a successful hernia operation.[100] Evidence showed that the patient had demonstrated symptoms of tetanus for some time, the supervisory nurse and other nursing staff knew of the symptoms, and none of them had reported the symptoms. The court said that for a supervisory nurse to permit a patient recovering from a major operation knowingly to suffer symptoms indicating a growing pathology for three days merely because the attending physicians were not available amounted to negligence.

In summary, these cases illustrate that a supervisor can be held liable if

1. The supervisor assigns a subordinate to do something the supervisor knows or should know that the person is unable to do.
2. The supervisor does not provide the subordinate the degree of supervision that the supervisor knows or should know is needed.
3. The supervisor is present and fails to take action when possible to avoid an injury.
4. The supervisor does not allocate the time of available staff properly, for example, by permitting breaks from areas where there are critical needs at times when the supervisor knows or should know that the staff will be needed.

Student Nurses

Student nurses will be held liable for their own acts of negligence committed in the course of clinical experiences. If they are performing duties that are within the scope of professional nursing, they will be held to the same standard of skill and competence as registered professional nurses. A lower standard of care will not be applied to the actions of nursing students. To fulfill their responsibilities to their patients and to minimize exposure to liability, nursing students should make sure that they are prepared to care properly for assigned patients and should ask for additional help or supervision if they feel inadequately prepared for an assignment.

A nursing instructor is responsible for assigning students to the care of patients and for exercising reasonable supervision over the students. The instructor could be held liable for injuries that resulted from the assignment to a patient of a student who is not competent and prepared for the assignment or from the failure of the instructor to supervise the performance of the student adequately.

Traditionally, cases arising from the negligent acts of student nurses resulted in their being treated as employees of the hospital, which was held liable under respondeat superior. In a 1921 case, two student nurses volunteered to work in the pediatric ward to care for a two-and-one-half-year-old child.[101] No trained nurses were available to provide special nursing services for the child because of an influenza epidemic. The child was having difficulty breathing, and a lighted vaporizer containing alcohol and eucalyptus oil was placed in the bed. One of the students left the child unattended for a few minutes, and when she returned the bed was in flames. The child died a few hours later. The court held that, even though the student was acting voluntarily, the authorization of the hospital of her actions amounted to an assignment and she was acting within the scope of employment. The hospital was found liable for damages resulting from the death of the child.

Several other cases imposed liability for the actions of students. In a 1954 case, parents were awarded damages for the death of their infant when a student nurse placed an unshielded light bulb 2 inches from the blankets in the crib.[102] Later, when the student checked the baby, the crib was in flames. In a 1962 case, a student failed to heed a warning on a medication vial to the effect that the drug was for intravenous use only and injected the medication into the buttock of a baby, resulting in serious injury.[103] The parents sued the child's physician and received an out-of-court settlement.

Failure to provide a student with reasonable supervision also can be the basis for liability. In a 1957 case, the court ordered an osteopathic hospital to pay damages to a patient who had been injured by a student.[104] The patient had gone to a clinic for evaluation and treatment of back problems. A student, attempting to treat the patient without supervision, struck him in the back, precipitating a ruptured disk. The court said that a student in a clinical situation must be given reasonable guidance and supervision.

Today, most nursing students would not be considered employees of the agencies in which they receive clinical experience because associate and baccalaureate degree programs generally contract with agencies to provide student experiences. However, nursing students probably will continue to be viewed as agents of hospitals and other agencies (e.g., public health agencies) when participating in patient care at the hospital. Thus, future cases involving the liability of students probably will hold both the hospital or agency and the educational institution potentially liable for the actions of the student.

Students should expect to satisfy requirements of both the college and the agency during clinical experiences and to comply with the policies of each agency in which clinical experiences are obtained. When a nurse employed by the hospital or other agency accepts responsibility to supervise a nursing student, even for a short time, the nurse becomes a supervisor and has the liability exposure described in the preceding section on supervisors. If no one else is supervising a student and a nurse permits a student to aid in the care of a patient, that nurse usually will be considered to have accepted the responsibility of supervising. It is advisable that the nursing staff on any unit where students are in training clarify the roles of the student, instructor, and staff nurse in the care of each patient to ensure that appropriate supervision actually is provided.

Nursing Specialties

Nurses who are certified and/or licensed as specialists in a nursing speciality area generally are expected to meet the higher standard of care of that particular specialist when providing such services. The most common type of nursing specialists in practice are nurse anesthetists, nurse practitioners, and nurse-midwives.

Nurse Anesthetists

It is not surprising that there has been more litigation involving nurse anesthetists than any other subspecialty because of the high risks associated with anesthesia and their longer recognition as specialists. A nurse anesthetist is a registered nurse who has completed a program of clinical training in planning anesthesia, administering anesthetic agents, and monitoring the anesthetized patient. The program most often is university-affiliated, with graduate course work leading to a Master's degree and the ability to take a national certification examination for nurse anesthetists. Successful passage on this certification examination allows the nurse to apply for state licensure as a nurse anesthetist. Nurse anesthetists have several practice arrangements, including employment by a hospital or by an anesthesiologist or a practice made up exclusively of nurse anesthetists.

The earliest reported cases involving nurse anesthetists focused on whether the administration of anesthetics by a specially trained nurse constituted the practice of medicine. A 1917 Kentucky case held that a nurse anesthetist who was employed by a physician and administered anesthetics under the direction of the physician was not practicing medicine within the meaning of the state medical practice statute.[105] A 1936 California case reached a similar result. [106] The court held that a nurse anesthetist was not practicing medicine without a license because she was not diagnosing or prescribing and her actions were under the control of the surgeon. In a 1938 case involving interpretation of an Arizona law that allowed a nurse anesthetist to administer anesthesia under the direction of a surgeon, the court included dental surgeons in the meaning of the statute.[107]

Question of Liability. There has been considerable litigation on allocating liability for negligent acts of nurse anesthetists. They clearly are liable for the results of their own negligence but the legal question has been: Who also is liable? There have been four general results: (1) the employer of the nurse anesthetist has been liable under the principle of respondeat superior; (2) the surgeon has been liable under the "captain of the ship" doctrine or for personal negligence of the surgeon; (3) both the employer and the surgeon have been liable under the dual servant doctrine; or (4) only the nurse anesthetist has been liable.

When nurse anesthetists are employees, the employer generally will be liable for the results of their negligence under respondeat superior. For example, several anesthesiologists were ordered to pay $500,000 for the death of a patient when a nurse anesthetist they employed failed to call for assistance when she had problems ventilating a patient.[108] Similarly, a California hospital was found liable for the death of a child because of errors by a nurse anesthetist it employed who gave the child too much ether during a tonsillectomy.[109]

In the past, when charitable hospitals were exempt from liability, several courts imposed liability on the surgeon for injuries caused by nurse anesthetists employed by the hospital. The courts reasoned that the surgeon was like the "captain of the ship" during the operation and was legally accountable for all actions of the operating crew, including the nurse anesthetist. The courts said that the hospital had loaned the nurse to the surgeon and, as a loaned servant or borrowed servant, was in effect an employee of the surgeon, not the hospital, for purposes of liability.[110]

Today, courts seldom use the captain of the ship doctrine. The surgeon generally is liable only under the general principles applicable to supervisors unless the surgeon actually employs the anesthetist. The surgeon is liable only for personally doing something wrong. For example, an Illinois court ruled that a jury could find a surgeon liable for his personal decisions concerning draping the patient and not remaining in the room until the patient resumed breathing.[111] The court ruled that the surgeon was not automatically liable for the actions of the nurse anesthetist who was a hospital employee.

Similarly, the Ohio Supreme Court ruled that a surgeon could be liable for the actions of a nurse anesthetist when the surgeon "does control or realistically possesses the right to control events and procedures."[112] The court held that there could have been sufficient control in the case because the surgeon had instructed, assisted, and watched the anesthetist intubate the patient before a laminectomy.

When sufficient actual control is not possessed or exercised, courts that apply this approach rule in favor of the surgeon. A New Jersey court overturned a judgment against a surgeon, ruling that it was valid only against the employing hospital because the surgeon did not exercise sufficient control to be responsible for injuries to the teeth and mouth of a mother due to intubation during childbirth.[113]

A few courts have decided that both the surgeon and the employer can be liable under the dual servant doctrine. They reasoned that both have sufficient control over the activities of the nurse, through either direct supervision or through policies and procedures, so each should be legally accountable.[114]

Sole Liability. There are three situations in which nurse anesthetists may not have anyone with whom to share liability: (1) when they are self-employed and the court determines that the surgeon has not exercised sufficient control to have assumed responsibility, (2) when their employer is immune from liability, or (3) when the patient decides to sue only the nurse anesthetist.

In a 1981 Louisiana case, a nurse anesthetist had attempted a nasal intubation that failed, resulting in the death of the patient. The family settled with the insurer of the nurse anesthetist for $264,728. The family then sued the surgeon, but the court ruled in his favor because it found that he had not exercised sufficient control.[115]

In a 1976 North Carolina case, a newborn was burned by a hot water bottle that was under the control of a nurse anesthetist.[116] The court held that the surgeon was not liable because he had not been in control of the heating and was not aware of the problem. The court also ruled that the hospital was immune because it was a charitable institution. This left the nurse as the only defendant. Charitable immunity has since been eliminated in North Carolina and nearly all other states, but it still is possible for governmental hospitals in some states to be protected by sovereign immunity.

When both the nurse anesthetist and someone else are sued for the negligence of the former, if the court holds that the nurse is not liable then it cannot find the other defendants liable for the actions of the nurse. Of course, the other defendants still could be found liable for their own acts of negligence. In a 1969 Virginia case, a patient had died of a stomach rupture because of insufflation of gas.[117] The jury found that the nurse anesthetist had not been negligent and thus not liable. The court ruled that because the jury had exonerated the nurse, the hospital-employer could not be liable for the acts of the nurse. There was no evidence of another basis for hospital liability, so the plaintiff lost the case.

In some cases, the patient chooses to sue only the employer. In a 1982 Missouri case, the patient dropped the claim against the nurse and sued only the hospital. The jury decided that the hospital owed $4 million, but the judgment was reversed on a technicality concerning the trial procedure.[118]

Some plaintiffs have attempted to convince courts that it is negligent for a hospital to permit nurse anesthetists to provide anesthesia services. Their position has been that all anesthesia should be provided by anesthesiologists. Courts have uniformly rejected this position.[119] It is proper to permit properly trained nurse anesthetists to administer anesthesia to most patients under appropriate supervision.

Nurse Anesthetist and Physician Roles. Some cases have made a clear distinction between the roles of nurse anesthetists and physicians and analyzed the duties separately for purposes of liability. In one case, the court said that it is customary for the physician to rely on the anesthetist for the selection and administration of drugs and that the statute that authorized nurse anesthetist practice did not require constant direct supervision by a physician.[120] In another case, the court distinguished between matters of judgment that were exclusively the concern of the physician and those within the duties of the nurse anesthetist.[121] When the physician turns the care of the patient over to the nurse anesthetist, the latter will be liable for any injuries that result from acts that occur while the patient is under the control of the nurse. In one case, a nurse anesthetist was found liable for negligently monitoring anesthesia of a patient undergoing a tonsillectomy when the physician was called out of the room.[122]

The nurse anesthetist also will be held liable for negligence in basic nursing care functions such as reporting, monitoring, and maintaining patient safety. For example, the employer of a nurse anesthetist was held liable for damages when she failed to inform a nurse who was inserting a catheter in the arm of the patient that the patient was under "light" anesthesia.[123] The patient moved his arm when the catheter was inserted, the catheter broke in the arm, and he developed carpal tunnel syndrome. In another case, a nurse anesthetist was held liable for burns sustained by a newborn when she failed to monitor the temperature of water being used to warm the patient.[124]

The standard of care for nurse anesthetists was described in a 1980 Michigan case.[125] The court said that nurse anesthetists are professionals who have expertise in an area akin to the practice of medicine. Because their responsibilities are greater than those of general duty nurses and because those responsibilities lie in an area of "medical" expertise, the standard of care is based on the skill and care normally expected of those with the same education and training.

The standard of care for nurse anesthetists was held to be a national standard in a 1982 Alabama case,[126] in which the nurse had trouble ventilating a patient but did not call for assistance. Expert testimony attempted to show the nurse complied with the standard of care for the city—Mobile. The court said that the local and national standards were the same and that the failure of the nurse anesthetist to call for assistance when she first realized there was a problem was a departure from the accepted standard of care in the national medical community.

A critical element for nurse anesthetists is the duty to seek assistance from a supervising physician when the situation demands it. Other areas in which they must exercise reasonable care are the selection of anesthetic agents, administration of anesthesia, monitoring the patient, maintaining safety precautions on behalf of the patient, communicating with the surgeon about the anesthetic agent being used, and performing procedures.

Nurse Practitioners

A nurse practitioner is a registered nurse who has completed a program in a specialized nursing area such as pediatrics, emergency care, or family or adult health. This specialized area is commonly at the graduate level leading to a Master's degree, although certificate programs also provide such specialized training. Certification examinations in specialty areas are provided through the American Nurses Association. In addition, nurse practitioners are licensed to practice by state boards of nursing and/or medicine. Depending on the individual state nurse practice act, nurse practitioners may have various supervisory, consultative, and/or collaborative management arrangements with a physician(s) and may be self-employed or employed by a hospital, clinic, physician group, or state agency.

Several cases involving nurse practitioners have addressed both negligence and scope of practice issues. In a 1980 case, a patient brought suit against a physician and a nurse practitioner.[127] The patient had a Dalkon Shield intrauterine contraceptive device implanted in 1972. In June 1974, she read an article concerning the shield and subsequently consulted her physician about the risks of pregnancy and infection that the article had described. The physician advised her that he knew of no risks associated with the device. Several months later, in mid-April 1975, the patient began to experience a foul vaginal odor. She called the Harvard Health Plan for an appointment and was told by a nurse practitioner to douche with yogurt. A little more than a week later, the patient called again complaining of intense abdominal pain. The nurse practitioner told the patient that she probably had the flu and to call back if she developed a fever. On April 30, when the patient kept a scheduled appointment with the plan she could hardly walk. She was given antibiotics, and her Dalkon Shield was removed. When she returned on May 2, multiple abscesses were diagnosed, and she underwent a total hysterectomy three days later.

The patient offered testimony by an expert as evidence of negligence. The expert had considerable experience working with a supervising nurse practitioner. The expert stated that the physician and the nurse practitioner were under a continuing obligation to inform the patient of the risks known to be associated with the Dalkon Shield. Failure of the physician to inform the patient in June 1974 probably determined the retention of the device by the patient and contributed to the development of the infection.

The expert said that the management of the patient by the nurse in April clearly was in error, her recommendation being substandard and inappropriate. The delay in scheduling diagnosis and treatment constituted substandard care, and the delay was the factor that caused the need for a total hysterectomy. An expert witness said articles published in both professional journals and the lay press had analyzed problems with the Dalkon Shield. The court found that the expert testimony created sufficient question about the adequacy of care to warrant a trial. The case was remanded for trial.

An interesting feature of this case was the testimony of the expert witness that it was difficult to evaluate the situation because the records were "sketchy." The court said it was difficult to determine how sketchy the records were because many of them were totally illegible. Nurse practitioners, like other health care providers, should keep complete legible records of patient visits and telephone counseling.

A 1981 California case addressed the standard of care for nurse practitioners.[128] A 34-year-old man noticed chest pains several times in a four-day period. He made an appointment at the Kaiser Health Plan and was examined by a nurse practitioner. After taking a history and examining the patient, the nurse gave him a prescription for Valium and told him he was suffering from muscle spasms. The following morning, the patient awoke with severe chest pains and went to the emergency department, where he was given pain medication and again told that he was having muscle spasms. Later that day he returned to the emergency department where an electrocardiograph showed that he had suffered a heart attack. The patient sued the health care provider, alleging that his condition should have been diagnosed earlier and that earlier diagnosis would have reduced the residual effect of the heart attack, which included a reduced life expectancy.

The trial court instructed the jury that the standard of care required of a nurse practitioner is the same as that of a physician. On appeal, the nurse practitioner claimed that this instruction was erroneous, and the court of appeals agreed that the standard of care required of a nurse practitioner is not the same as for a physician. However, the court said that this was a "harmless error" because the patient had sued the employer, not the nurse individually. The employer was responsible for satisfying the standard of care of a physician when a patient was treated in the clinic even though the care actually was provided by a nurse practitioner.

Another case alleging negligence of a nurse practitioner involved telephone consulting of an injured patient.[129] A woman who had stepped on a thumb tack causing a puncture wound in the ball of her foot was treated in an emergency department. Three days later, her daughter telephoned a clinic and told the nurse practitioner on duty that the toes on her mother's foot were turning purple, there was redness around the purple areas, the flesh around the toes was very white, and her mother was very cold. The nurse practitioner allegedly told the daughter "not to worry, that purple was a good color." Four days after this conversation, the mother underwent amputation of two toes.

The mother sued, alleging that the nurse practitioner was negligent in undertaking to provide a medical diagnosis and recommendation, failing to recognize obvious symptoms of infection and gangrene, failing to refer her to a physician, and giving inappropriate instructions concerning her condition. She also sued the clinic, claiming that it was negligent in (1) failing to maintain adequate supervision and control over its employees, (2) failing to establish appropriate standard operating procedures to correct misinformation, and (3) failing to ensure that its personnel were trained to recognize ailments or trained to be aware of their inability to recognize such elements.

Although the court dismissed the case on procedural grounds, the facts raise significant issues of negligence by nurse practitioners. It is clear that they should be very careful in their responses during telephone consultations and should keep accurate records documenting the occurrence of calls and the advice given. Agencies that employ nurse practitioners also should have guidelines to direct them in their handling of such calls.

In one case, the license of a nurse practitioner was suspended for treating patients without the supervision of a physician.[130] The court upheld the suspension for treating two patients by providing medication to one and therapy for the other. Nurse practitioners should be familiar with their permitted scope of practice in their state to avoid liability to their patients and to retain their licenses.

Nurse-Midwives

Midwifery became a regulated, legally recognized profession in some states in the early 1900s. Before that time, it was practiced by women who learned about birth from other women and their own experiences and often practiced without compensation in areas where there were no other health care providers. The first nurse-midwifery education program was opened by the Maternity Association in New York City in 1952; currently, many university-affiliated programs across the country are accredited by the American College of Nurse Midwifery, and most programs lead to a Master's degree. Nevertheless, "lay midwives" continue to practice midwifery, but these individuals have various types of unaccredited training, are often not registered nurses, and need to be distinguished from nurse-midwives.

Authorization for the practice of nurse-midwifery may be found in nurse practice acts, medical practice acts, rules and regulations pertaining to nursing or midwives, public health laws, allied health laws, or separate nurse-midwife practice acts. Depending on the jurisdiction, various state agencies may have regulatory authority over nurse-midwives.

Midwifery practice includes the independent management of essentially normal newborns and women for prenatal, intrapartum, postpartum, and gynecologic care in a system that provides for medical consultation and collaborative management or referral.[131] Generally, state regulations permit the full range of practice, although there have been legislative attempts to limit or restrict nurse-midwifery practice in several states.

The earliest cases addressed the question of whether midwifery constituted the practice of medicine. An 1894 Illinois case sought to penalize a midwife for practicing medicine without a license.[132] The court ruled that the midwife was practicing in violation of the medical practice act. It said that midwifery was an important part of medicine and was recognized as such in the medical practice act and that people who engaged in the practice of midwifery should possess special knowledge and skill. Subsequently, midwives worked to establish a clear legal status for their practice, including the licensure of lay midwives who are not registered nurses.[133]

Liability of nurse-midwives is based on patient injuries resulting from their negligent actions. In a 1925 case, a midwife was attending a patient after delivery.[134] The patient suffered a seizure and a physician was called. The physician ordered that hot water bottles and flatirons be placed on the patient, and the midwife carried out the orders. The patient was burned and sued the physician.

The court, affirming a judgment that the physician was not negligent, said: "Mrs. Frost was a woman of 12 years' experience as a midwife who had been employed by plaintiff's husband to attend her at this time. Wrapping the irons so they would not burn and so the wrappings would remain in place required no professional skill. Mrs. Frost or any person of common intelligence and experience was competent to do it. It cannot be said that the doctor was guilty of negligence in trusting Mrs. Frost to perform this service and in relying on her to perform it properly." In effect, the court said that a physician would not be liable for the actions of a midwife that should have been governed by common sense.

To protect themselves from liability, nurse-midwives should first be sure that they are properly licensed and practicing as legally defined by statute or rule. They must familiarize themselves with the regulations that govern midwife practice in their jurisdiction. In a negligence action, they will be held to the standard of care of other reasonable competent nurse-midwives. As a practical matter, physicians probably will provide the expert testimony on the standard of care.

A significant element in the duty of a nurse-midwife is to refer a patient who requires medical care or to seek assistance when complications arise. Protocols should be developed to specify the circumstances requiring referral by the certified nurse-midwife to a physician. The failure to do so in a timely manner may be the basis for a negligence action, as well as put the nurse-midwife in the position of having to act beyond the permissible scope of practice in the course of providing care. Criminal and civil liability may be imposed on a nurse-midwife who is found guilty of the unauthorized practice of medicine.

School Nurses

Most school nurses are employed by a state department of education or a local school board. Their general duties include health screening, record keeping, planning and implementing health education programs, first aid, and prevention of injuries. The duties also may be described in rules or regulations promulgated by the local or county board of education. These should be examined regularly to ensure that they are consistent with the relevant nurse practice act.

School nurses should have approved procedures for situations that occur frequently. They generally will be held liable for acts of negligence, but their employer also will be liable for damages under the doctrine of respondeat superior unless the school nurse-employee was acting outside the scope of the prescribed duties.

School nurses who are registered nurses but generally not nurse practitioners with an extended scope of practice cannot make a medical diagnosis and cannot prescribe medications. The importance of this rule, although it may seem overly restrictive, is clear when the consequences of incorrect diagnosis or medications are considered. School nurses should seek a statement from their employer detailing the extent, scope, and limitations on their practice as well as the extent of liability insurance coverage extended by the employer.

Several areas have legal consequences and are of particular concern to school nurses, such as child abuse, drug abuse, venereal disease, and parental consent. Parental consent usually is not required for basic health screening. If anything more than measurement or observation is contemplated, parental permission must be obtained unless state law authorizes the minor to consent. If psychological testing or referral is planned, parents must be involved because such tests have the potential for invading the privacy of the family.

Another area of concern to school nurses is access to records. School records generally are not open to the public, so some degree of confidentiality can be maintained. Nurses have a professional and ethical obligation to maintain confidentiality of information received from a patient until legally compelled to disclose the information. However, the records can be subpoenaed, and a nurse or teacher can be compelled to testify about them because in most states no privilege of confidentiality applies to school nurses.

Public Health Nurses

The duties of public health nurses include health screening, teaching, assessment, referral, and planning and implementing programs of health education for individuals and the community. Often, health departments employ nurse practitioners in various specialty areas who provide extended nursing care services consistent with the relevant nurse practice act. In addition, the public health nurse may, in the course of a home visit, perform procedures related to patient care. The employer of a public health nurse may be held liable for the acts of the employee under respondeat superior. If the employer is a government agency, it might not be liable for damages in the absence of a statutory provision authorizing such liability. If government immunity does apply, the public health nurse may be the only party from whom damages may be obtained.

Avoiding liability when working as a public health nurse involves (1) good judgment, (2) careful performance of procedures and screening, (3) appropriate referrals, and (4) clear policies that define the role and appropriate actions for both registered nurses and nurse practitioners providing services in their extended role. Such policies should specifically address documentation, phone counseling, verbal orders, referrals, reporting of patient conditions, and access to records. There should be procedures for basic nursing care tasks performed (e.g., assessment or injections), as well as responses in emergencies (e.g., anaphylactic reactions). There also should be guidelines for how many visits may be made without medical supervision or reporting to the physician of the patient.

Written orders should be obtained for treatments and procedures performed when they do not involve nursing judgments exclusively. Verbal and telephone orders should be recorded and copied and the original sent to the physician for signature. The notes of the nurse should reflect each consultation and order. Written consent must be obtained for treatment, use of photographs, or release of information outside of the agency or treating physician.

Public health nurses should know the extent of liability insurance coverage provided for them by the employing agency. Specifically, they should clarify their protection while traveling to home visits, while using their own or an agency car for transporting patients and equipment, and for their own injuries or those sustained by others.

Public health nurses must keep records that are as accurate and complete as possible. There have been cases in which the records of a public health nurse have been used as evidence in a legal action.[135] Records also may serve as the basis for reports submitted to court on issues such as parental fitness and termination of parental rights.[136]

A 1983 case involved the liability of a public health nurse in a suit in which a couple alleged trespass, conversion of property, and deprivation of civil rights arising out of the destruction of their mobile home.[137] The Iowa Supreme Court affirmed a damage award against a public health nurse because, at the request of the sheriff, she had written a letter declaring the home of the couple a health hazard. The home then was demolished without notifying the owners, who were vacationing out of state. In this case, the nurse was found liable for violating the rights of the couple even though they were not her patients.

Occupational Health Nurses

The nurse employed by a company to administer nursing and emergency services to its employees generally is viewed as an employee of the company, which will be liable for the negligent actions of the nurse under respondeat superior. As a result, in some states the only recourse is through workers' compensation law, because in many states an employer can be sued only under that law.

For example, the Pennsylvania Supreme Court found an employer responsible under the Workers' Compensation Act when a company nurse failed to call a physician although an employee had severe chest pains, vomiting, and chills and was perspiring—and died a few hours later.[138] In other states, occupational health nurses are considered independent contractors even though salaried by the company, so the nurse, but not the employer, can be sued outside the workers' compensation process. For example, an Indiana court ruled that an occupational nurse could be sued for administering a hypodermic injection that damaged the left ulnar nerve of the patient.[139]

Several potential legal problems are associated with nurses practicing in the occupational health setting. First, they must be sure they are within the acceptable limits of nursing practice as defined by statute and rule in the jurisdiction. Second, they must recognize situations in which referral is appropriate. Finally, nurses performing procedures such as dressing or cleansing wounds will be held to the same standard of care as those in the hospital.

In one case, an employee brought a malpractice action against an occupational health nurse and the company that employed her.[140] The employee had sustained a puncture wound in his forehead. The nurse bandaged the wound but did not probe it for foreign objects. After several months, the wound healed, but a small red area remained and eventually became puffy. During this time, the patient visited the nurse several times to point out that the wound did not seem to be healing.

Ten months after the injury, the patient requested that he be referred to a physician. After the examination by the physician, the patient had a basal cell carcinoma removed from his forehead. The court found the company and the nurse liable for damages. The court noted two bases for its finding of liability against the nurse: (1) her failure to examine the wound for foreign bodies, and (2) her failure to refer the patient to a physician when the wound did not heal.

Similar factors were issues in another case.[141] An employee coughed, then felt an intense pain down her leg. A few hours later, she reported to the company nurse, who told her the pain was caused by a sciatic nerve spasm that could be relieved by soaking in a tub of hot water. The nurse also gave the woman two green pills. Several days later, it was determined that the patient had a ruptured disk.

The court affirmed a decision against the patient because the claim already had been litigated and denied under the Workers' Compensation Act. The facts of the case, however, disclose two areas of concern: (1) the nurse did not keep records of non–work-related complaints, and (2) the company had a policy of dispensing mild analgesic preparations to employees who complained of discomfort. To avoid liability, a company nurse should keep records of all visits and should not dispense medications independently unless specifically authorized to do so by state law.

Office Nurses

A nurse who works for a physician or dentist usually will be considered an employee. The employing physician generally directs and controls the work of the office nurse to an extent that will support the application of respondeat superior. Thus, the employer can be held liable for the negligent acts of the nurse. Most lawsuits based on the actions of office nurses are filed against both the nurse and the physician.

The duties of an office nurse generally include assisting with procedures, carrying out orders, charting, recording measurements, and health counseling. They may include history taking, physical assessments, screening examinations, and other procedures. The office nurse must comply with the accepted standard of care for nurses generally when attending to patients or performing treatments and procedures. The office nurse should be especially careful to record and report symptoms and other observations, telephone inquiries, and what information is given to a patient.

Office nurse liability arises from four general areas: (1) failure to assist patients, (2) failure to maintain confidentiality, (3) failure to perform procedures according to the accepted standard of care, and (4) failure to monitor or refer the patient.

In one case, a patient fell down while disrobing at the physician's office.[142] The family sued the physician for the negligence of his office nurse, claiming that they were negligent in failing to assist the patient and in leaving her unattended. The physician knew that the elderly patient had a tendency to fall backward. The nurse offered to help, but the patient refused. The court said that the physician who employs a nurse is liable for any wrongful conduct on the part of the nurse in following the instructions of the physician and in any breach of nursing duty but upheld a finding of no liability because the patient had accepted the risk by refusing assistance while competent to do so.

The failure to maintain confidentiality of patient information can subject the office nurse to liability based on defamation or invasion of privacy. In a California case, an office nurse was found liable for saying that a patient had syphilis when the person actually was being treated for a false-positive test for syphilis.[143] A nurse employed in the office of a physician has a duty not to disclose confidential patient information.

Most cases involving the liability of office nurses occur when nurses perform a procedure incorrectly, leading to patient injury. In one case, a judgment against a nurse and her employer was upheld when the nurse, acting on the orders of the physician, used a Stryker saw to remove a cast from the arm of a patient.[144] While the nurse was cutting the cast, the patient complained, but the nurse told the patient she was only feeling the heat from the blade. In fact, the saw made a cut in the arm of the patient the length of the cast. The nurse testified that she continued to use the same amount of pressure even after the patient complained. The court found that the failure of the nurse to respond to the complaints of the patient did not conform to the standard of care.

In another case, a patient suffering from neck pain underwent a diathermic treatment prescribed by her physician.[145] The physician's assistant placed the electrodes on the patient and turned on the current. The patient immediately complained of a burning sensation, but the assistant took no action and left the room. After repeated complaints, the electricity was turned off but the patient suffered severe burns. The court found that both the physician and his assistant were liable for negligence.

A nurse was held to be negligent in a case in which a woman brought her son in for examination by a physician, and the office nurse requested that the woman help her hold another child for a radiograph.[146] In the process of assisting, the woman was burned by an electric current and injured in a fall. She recovered damages for the negligence of the nurse. In another case, the California Court of Appeals reversed a judgment in favor of an office nurse and her employing physician.[147] A patient suffered injuries to his right arm after an injection given by the nurse. The appellate court held that the jury could have properly been instructed to apply res ipsa loquitur, saying that it is common knowledge among laypersons that injections in the muscles of the arm do not cause trouble unless they are done unskillfully or there is something wrong with the medication.

A patient who suffered punctured ear drums when an office nurse washed wax from his ears was not allowed to recover damages in a 1968 case.[148] The physician was not in the office, and the patient insisted that the nurse wash out his ears. The nurse protested but eventually performed the procedure, stopping when the patient complained of pain. The court found that the patient was contributorily negligent and not entitled to recover. Nurses should not accede to demands by a patient for inappropriate therapy. Under the comparative negligence rule that is replacing the contributory negligence rule in most states, the nurse could be found liable today for a substantial portion of the damages in cases such as this.

In another case, a surgeon asked a nurse to provide him with a 1 percent procaine solution, and the nurse negligently prepared a solution of formaldehyde.[149] Even though the nurse was under the direction and control of the surgeon, the court held that the surgeon was entitled to rely on the skill of the nurse and was not liable for the negligence of the nurse. This case illustrates the proposition that a physician generally will not be liable for the negligence of a nurse when the physician has no reason to believe that the nurse is not competent.

A nurse and her physician-employer were found liable for negligence in the death of a 22-month-old child who died from aspiration after the nurse left him lying on his back unattended.[150] The child had been seen by the physician earlier in the day, and his mother brought him back to the office because she thought he was much worse. The nurse told the physician, who was out of the office, that the child was about the same condition as earlier so the physician had lunch before returning to the office. The nurse went to lunch before the physician returned, leaving a receptionist in charge at the office. The child vomited while positioned on his back and died a few minutes later. The court found both the nurse and the physician liable for negligence. The court ruled that if the nurse had been with the child or available to help, she could have done several things to save the boy's life.

Nurses in Nursing Homes

The general standard of care required of staff members dealing with patients in a nursing home is the degree of care, skill, and diligence characteristic of such facilities. Although some of the rules applicable to hospitals apply also to nursing homes, distinctions must be made between the two because a hospital generally has more extensive facilities, greater control over and access to physicians, and a larger number of staff members. The duties of a nursing home to its patients sometimes are treated as contractual in nature and also are affected by statutes, regulations, and agreements with reimbursement entities. The elements of the contract or the regulations for nursing homes represent the minimum standard of care that must be met.

The general rule in nursing homes is that nurses must exercise the degree of care and skill required by the condition and capabilities of the patient and must take into account their ability or inability to care for and protect themselves. Litigation involving nursing staff members of such homes is based primarily on an alleged breach of the duty to maintain patient safety. The cases fall into three general categories: (1) falls, (2) burns and other injuries, and (3) patients wandering away.

The most common cause of action involves patient injuries in falling. The significant facts include whether the patient was attended, whether the patient was appropriately restrained, and the general condition of the person. Most often, the outcome of the case turns on two questions: (1) would a reasonably competent nurse, in the same circumstances, have taken additional precautions to protect the patient? and (2) would these precautions have prevented the injures? Expert testimony often is used to provide the basis for a judge or jury answering those questions. However, some courts do not require expert testimony for fall cases.

Cases that find liability for negligence on the part of the home are those in which the nursing staff (1) failed to follow a physician's orders to restrain a patient with appropriate consent, (2) left a patient who had a known tendency to fall unattended in a chair, or (3) failed to provide help for a patient who was unsteady.

When safety precautions can be documented, through the record of the patient or through standard institutional procedures, liability generally is not imposed. A patient who falls should be evaluated and observed closely for any injuries. The nursing home was held liable for injuries in a case in which the leg of a patient was broken in a fall but it was not noted until nine hours later.[151] The court noted that the patient should have been watched closely after the fall and that the complaints of pain should have alerted the staff that something was wrong.

Several cases involve burned or scalded patients. Circumstances in which the nursing home staff exercised exclusive control over the cause of the injury (e.g., heat lamps, radiators, or hot water bottles) generally result in a finding of liability against the home. For example, the Alabama Supreme Court affirmed a $500,000 judgment against a nursing home and subsequently treating hospital after a patient died as a result of a scalding in a bathtub in the nursing home.[152] A nursing aide had left the 26-year-old severely retarded patient unattended in an empty bathtub and another retarded patient had turned on the hot water, scalding the first patient. Some circumstances, such as when competent patients smoke in bed in violation of instructions, may lead to a finding of no liability for the institution.[153]

Suits against nursing homes also involve patients who wander away and are injured. In one case, the nursing home was found liable for negligence when it sent an elderly senile patient to the hospital without giving the hospital instructions about his special need for supervision.[154] The patient wandered away from the hospital and was found dead several days later. In some cases, the nursing home may not be held liable, because it is not possible to provide constant supervision of all patients. The responsibility of the nursing home extends to a reasonable standard of care, taking into account the mental and physical condition of the patient.

CONCLUSION

Given the complexity of nursing practice and the variety of speciality roles that nurses assume, it is not surprising that nurses face claims from patients. Most claims against nurses are made on professional malpractice theories, which require a plaintiff to establish that there was a breach of the applicable standard of care by the nurse, damage to the patient, and causation between the nurse's action or inaction and the patient's injury. This general principle of liability is the same regardless of whether the nurse is working in the operating room, floor, or office or is an advanced practice nurse. Nurses who perform more complex roles or procedures will be held to a standard that is commensurate with that role or task.

FOOTNOTES

1. Webb v. Jorns, 473 S.W.2d 328 (Tex. Civ. App. 1971), *rev'd on other grounds,* 488 S.W.2d 407.

2. Thompson v. Brent, 245 So. 2d 751 (La. Ct. App. 1971).

3. New Biloxi Hosp. v. Frazier, 245 Miss. 185, 145 So. 2d 882 (1962).

4. Cooper v. National Motor Bearing Co., 136 Cal. App. 2d 299, 288 P.2d 581 (1955).

5. 262 S.E.2d 391, 397 (N.C. App. 1980).

6. 236 S.E.2d 213 (W.Va. 1977).

7. *Id.* at 216.

8. Washington Hosp. Ctr. v. Martin, 454 A.2d 306 (D.C. 1982).

9. Cline v. Lund, 31 Cal. App. 3d 755, 107 Cal. Rptr. 629 (1973).

10. Delicata v. Bourlesses, 80 Mass. App. 963, 404 N.E.2d 667 (1980).

11. Koeniguer v. Eckrich, 422 N.W.2d 600 (S.D. 1988).

12. 292 So. 2d 382 (Fla. Dist. Ct. App. 1974).

13. Crowe v. Provost, 52 Tenn. App. 397, 374 S.W.2d 645 (1963).

14. Yorita v. Okumoto, 643 P.2d 820 (Haw. Ct. App. 1982); *see also* Goldfoot v. Lofgren, 135 Or. 533, 296 P. 843 (1931) (adult with lung abscess due to aspirated material during recovery); Thomas v. Seaside Mem'l Hosp., 80 Cal. App. 2d 841, 183 P.2d 288 (1947) (eight-month-old died during recovery).

15. Lhotka v. Larson, 238 N.W.2d 870 (Minn. 1976).

16. Newhall v. Central Vt. Hosp., 349 A.2d 890 (Vt. 1975).

17. Nelson v. Peterson, 542 P.2d 1075 (Utah 1975).

18. Sanchez v. Bay Gen. Hosp., 116 Cal. App. 3d 776, 172 Cal. Rptr. 342 (1981).

19. Belmon v. St. Francis Cabrini Hosp., 427 So. 2d 541 (La. Ct. App. 1983).

20. Ramsey v. Physicians Mem'l Hosp., Inc., 36 Md. App. 42, 373 A.2d 26 (1977).

21. Baker v. Warner, 654 P.2d 263 (Alaska 1982).

22. Polischeck v. United States, 535 F. Supp. 1261 (E.D. Pa. 1982).

23. Hiatt v. Groce, 215 Kan. 14, 523 P.2d 320 (1974).

24. Samii v. Baystate Med. Ctr., Inc., 8 Mass. App. 911, 395 N.E.2d 455 (1979).

25. Duling v. Bluefield Sanitarium, Inc., 149 W. Va. 567, 142 S.E.2d 754 (1965).

26. Howard v. Piver, 279 S.E.2d 876 (N.C. Ct. App. 1981).

27. Goff v. Doctors Gen. Hosp., 166 Cal. App. 2d 314, 333 P.2d 29 (1958).

28. Karrigan v. Nazareth Convent & Academy, Inc., 212 Kan. 44, 510 P.2d 190 (1973).

29. Darling v. Charleston Community Mem'l Hosp., 33 Ill. 2d 326, 211 N.E.2d 253 (1966), *cert. denied,* 383 U.S. 496 (1966).

30. 236 S.E.2d 213 (W. Va. 1977).

31. Carson v. United States, 304 F. Supp. 155 (E.D. Pa. 1969).

32. Krestview Nursing Home, Inc. v. Synowiec, 317 So. 2d 94 (Fla. Dist. Ct. App. 1975).

33. Frantz v. San Luis Med. Clinic, 81 Cal. App. 3d 34, 146 Cal. Rptr. 146 (1978).

34. Collins v. Westlake Community Hosp., 57 Ill. 2d 388, 312 N.E.2d 614 (1974).

35. Trichel v. Caire, 427 So. 2d 1227 (La. Ct. App. 1983).

36. Thompson v. United States, 368 F. Supp. 466 (W.D. La. 1973).

37. Gugino v. Harvard Community Health Plan, 403 N.E.2d 1166 (Mass. 1980).

38. Duling v. Bluefield Sanitarium, Inc., 142 S.E.2d 754 (1965).

39. 107 Cal. Rptr. 629 (1973).

40. Jarvis v. St. Charles Med. Ctr., 713 P.2d 620 (Or. Ct. App. 1986).

41. 144 So. 2d 249 (La. Ct. App. 1962).

42. Norton v. Argonaut Ins. Co., 144 So. 2d 249 (La. Ct. App. 1962).

43. Poor Sisters of St. Francis v. Catron, 435 N.E.2d 305 (Ind. Ct. App. 1982).

44. Fraijo v. Hartland Hosp., 99 Cal. App. 3d 331, 160 Cal. Rptr. 246 (1979).

45. Striano v. Deepdale Gen. Hosp., 54 A.D.2d 730, 387 N.Y.S.2d 678 (1976).

46. Lenger v. Physician's Gen. Hosp., Inc., 455 S.W.2d 703 (Tex. 1970).

47. 144 Ga. App. 184, 241 S.E.2d 2 (1977).

48. Toth v. Community Hosp., 22 N.Y.2d 255, 239 N.E.2d 368 (1968).

49. Larrimore v. Homeopathic Hosp. Ass'n, 54 Del. 449, 181 A.2d 573 (1962).

50. Wees v. Creighton Mem'l St. Joseph's Hosp., 194 Neb. 295, 231 N.W.2d 570 (1975).

51. Hunsaker v. Bozeman Deaconess Found., 588 P.2d 493 (Mont. 1978).

52. Arnold v. James B. Haggin Mem'l Hosp., 415 S.W.2d 844 (Ky. Ct. App. 1967).

53. Southeastern Ky. Baptist Hosp., Inc., v. Bruce, 539 S.W.2d 286 (Ky. 1976).

54. Parker v. St. Paul Fire & Marine Ins. Co., 335 So. 2d 725 (La. Ct. App. 1976).

55. Goodenough v. Deaconess Hosp., 637 S.W.2d 123 (Mo. Ct. App. 1982).

56. Koepel v. St. Joseph Hosp. & Med. Ctr., 381 Mich. 440, 163 N.W.2d 222 (1968), *rev'd,* 8 Mich App. 609, 155 N.W.2d 199 (1967).

57. Plutshack v. University of Minn. Hosps., 316 N.W.2d 1 (Minn. 1982).

58. Truluck v. Municipal Hosp. Bd., 162 So. 2d 549 (Fla. Dist. Ct. App. 1964).

59. Hudmon v. Martin, 315 So. 2d 516 (Fla. Dist. Ct. App. 1975).

60. Kyte v. McMillion, 256 Md. 85, 259 A.2d 532 (Md. Ct. Spec. App. 1969).

61. Maloney v. Wake Hosp. Sys., Inc., 262 S.E.2d 680 (N.C. Ct. App. 1980).

62. Sharrow v. Archer, 658 P.2d 1331 (Alaska 1983).

63. Barnes v. St. Francis Hosp. & School of Nursing, Inc., 211 Kan. 315, 507 P.2d 288 (1973); *see also* Su v. Perkins, 133 Ga. App. 474, 211 S.E.2d 421 (1974) (prescribing physician not liable when nurse selects wrong needle size).

64. Rodriguez v. Columbus Hosp., 38 A.D.2d 517, 326 N.Y.S.2d 438 (1971).

65. Farrow v. Health Servs. Corp., 604 P.2d 474 (Utah 1979).

66. Gasbarra v. St. James Hosp., 85 Ill. App. 3d 32, 40 Ill. Dec. 538, 406 N.E.2d 544 (1980).

67. Macy v. Presbyterian Intercommunity Hosp., Inc., 46 Or. App. 791, 612 P.2d 769 (1980).

68. Bauer v. Otis, 133 Cal. App. 2d 439, 284 P.2d 133 (1955).

69. Hall v. Bio-Medical Applications, Inc., 671 F.2d 300 (8th Cir. 1982).

70. Helman v. Sacred Heart Hosp., 62 Wash. 2d 69, 381 P.2d 605 (1963).

71. DeFalco v. Long Island College Hosp., 393 N.Y.S.2d 859 (N.Y. Sup. Ct. 1977).

72. *E.g.,* Kalmus v. Cedars of Lebanon Hosp., 132 Cal. 2d 243, 281 P.2d 872 (1955).

73. Cochran v. Harper, 115 Ga. App. 277, 159 S.E.2d 461 (1967).

74. Shepard v. McGinnis, 251 Iowa 35, 131 N.W.2d 475 (1964).

75. Schmidt v. Intermountain Health Care, Inc., 635 P.2d 99 (Utah 1981).

76. Zack v. Centro Espanol Hosp., 319 So. 2d 34 (Fla. Dist. Ct. App. 1975).

77. Skidmore v. Oklahoma Hosp., 137 Okla. 133, 278 P. 334 (1929).

78. Leonard v. Watsonville Community Hosp., 47 Cal. 2d 509, 305 P.2d 36 (1956).

79. Robinson v. St. John's Med. Ctr., Joplin, 508 S.W.2d 7 (Mo. Ct. App. 1975).

80. Porter v. Patterson, 107 Ga. App. 64, 129 S.E.2d 70 (1962).

81. Horwitz v. Michael Reese Hosp., 5 Ill. App. 3d 508, 284 N.E.2d 4 (1972).

82. Daniel v. St. Francis Cabrini Hosp., 415 So. 2d 586 (La. Ct. App. 1982).

83. Page v. Wilson Mem'l Hosp., 49 N.C. App. 533, 272 S.E.2d 8 (1980).

84. Jones v. Hawkes Hosp., 175 Ohio St. 503, 196 N.E.2d 592 (1964).

85. McEachern v. Glenview Hosp., Inc., 505 S.W.2d 386 (Tex. Civ. App. 1974).

86. Cramer v. Theda Clark Mem'l Hosp., 45 Wis. 2d 147, 172 N.W.2d 427 (1969).

87. Levett v. Etkind, 158 Conn. 567, 265 A.2d 70 (1969).

88. Cavenaugh v. South Broward Hosp. Dist., 247 So. 2d 769 (Fla. Dist. Ct. App. 1971).

89. Leavitt v. St. Tammany Parish Hosp., 396 So. 2d 406 (La. Ct. App. 1981).

90. Koepel v. St. Joseph Hosp. & Med. Ctr., 1381 Mich. 440, 163 N.W.2d 222 (1968), *rev'd,* 58 Mich. App. 609, 155 N.W.2d 199 (1967).

91. Doctors Hosp. Inc. v. Kovats, 16 Ariz. App. 489, 494 P.2d 389 (1972).

92. Chamberlain v. Deaconess Hosp., Inc., 324 N.W.2d 172 (Ind. Ct. App. 1975).

93. Mundt v. Alta Bates Hosp., 223 Cal. App. 2d 413, 35 Cal. Rptr. 848 (1963).

94. Palmer v. Clarksdale Hosp., 57 So. 2d 476 (Miss. 1952).

95. Lewis v. Davis, 410 N.E.2d 1363 (Ind. Ct. App. 1980).

96. Bowers v. Olch, 120 Cal. App. 2d 108, 260 P.2d 997 (1953).

97. Laidlaw v. Lions Gate Hosp., 8 D.L.R.3d 730 (B.C. Sup. Ct. 1969).

98. Krujelis v. Esdale, (1972) 2 W.W.R. 495 (B.C. Sup. Ct. 1971).

99. Horton v. Niagara Falls Mem'l Med. Ctr., 51 A.D.2d 152, 380 N.Y.S.2d 116 (1976).

100. Valentin v. LaSociete Francaise de Bienfaisance, 76 Cal. App. 2d 1, 172 P.2d 359 (1946).

101. Longguy v. Societe Francaise de Bienfaisance Mutuelle, 52 Cal. App. 370, 198 P.1011 (1921).

102. Cadicamo v. Long Island College Hosp., 308 N.Y. 196, 124 N.E.2d 279 (1954).

103. O'Neil v. Glens Falls Indemnity Co., 310 F.2d 165 (8th Cir. 1962).

104. Christiansen v. Des Moines Still College of Osteopathy, 248 Iowa 810, 82 N.W.2d 741 (1957).

105. Frank v. South, 175 Ky. 416, 194 S.W. 375 (1917).

106. Chalmers-Francis v. Nelson, 6 Cal. 2d 402, 57 P.2d 1312 (1936).

107. State v. Borah, 51 Ariz. 318, 76 P.2d 757 (1938).

108. Lane v. Otis, 412 So. 2d 254 (Ala. 1982).

109. Cavero v. Franklin Gen. Benevolent Soc'y, 36 Cal. 2d 301, 223 P.2d 471 (1950).

110. Jackson v. Joyner, 236 N.C. 259, 72 S.E.2d 589 (1952).

111. Foster v. Englewood Hosp. Assoc., 19 Ill. App. 3d 1055, 313 N.E.2d 255 (1974).

112. Baird v. Sickler, 69 Ohio St. 2d 652, 433 N.E.2d 593 (1982).

113. Sesselman v. Muhlenberg Hosp., 124 N.J. Super. 285, 306 A.2d 474 (N.J. Super. Ct. App. Div. 1973).

114. *E.g.,* Tonic v. Wagner, 458 Pa. 246, 329 A.2d 497 (1974) (nursing case not involving a nurse anesthetist).

115. Hughes v. St. Paul Fire & Marine Ins. Co., 401 So. 2d 448 (La. Ct. App. 1981).

116. Starnes v. Charlotte-Mecklenburg Hosp. Auth., 28 N.C. App. 418, 221 S.E.2d 733 (1976).

117. Whitfield v. Whitaker Mem'l Hosp., 210 Va. 176, 169 S.E.2d 563 (1969).

118. Yoos v. Jewish Hosp., 645 S.W.2d 177 (Mo. Ct. App. 1982).

119. *E.g.,* Whitney v. Day, 100 Mich. App. 707, 300 N.W.2d 380 (1980); Starnes v. Charlotte-Mecklenburg Hosp. Auth., 28 N.C. App. 418, 221 S.E.2d 733 (1976).

120. Brown v. Allen Sanitorium, Inc., 364 So. 2d 661 (La. Ct. App. 1978), *cert. denied,* 367 So. 2d 392 (La. 1979).

121. Weinstein v. Prostkoff, 13 A.D.2d 539, 213 N.Y.S.2d 571 (1961).

122. Willinger v. Mercy Catholic Med. Ctr., 362 A.2d 280 (Pa. Super. Ct. 1976).

123. Corson v. United States, 304 F. Supp. 155 (E.O. Pa. 1969).

124. Starnes v. Charlotte-Mecklenburg Hosp. Auth., 28 N.C. App. 418, 221 S.E.2d 733 (1976).

125. Whitney v. Day, 100 Mich. App. 707, 300 N.W.2d 380 (1980).

126. Lane v. Otis, 412 So. 2d 254 (Ala. 1982).

127. Gugino v. Harvard Community Health Plan, 403 N.E.2d 1166 (Mass. 1980).

128. Fein v. Permanente Med. Group, 121 Cal. App. 3d 135, 175 Cal. Rptr. 177 (1981).

129. Flickinger v. United States, 523 F. Supp. 1372 (E.D. Pa. 1981).

130. Hernicz v. Florida, 390 So. 2d 194 (Fla. Dist. Ct. App. 1980).

131. AMERICAN COLLEGE OF NURSE MIDWIVES, OFFICIAL DEFINITIONS (1978).

132. People v. Arendt, 60 Ill. App. 89 (1894).

133. Bowland v. Santa Cruz Court, 18 Cal. 3d 479, 556 P.2d 1081, 134 Cal. Rptr. 630 (1976).

134. Olson v. Bolstad, 161 Minn. 419, 201 N.W. 918 (1925).

135. *E.g.,* McCarthy v. Mason, 134 Conn. 170, 55 A.2d 912 (1947).

136. *E.g., In re* Hoppe, 289 N.W.2d 613 (Iowa 1980).

137. Dickerson v. Young, 332 N.W.2d 93 (Iowa 1983).

138. Baur v. Mesta Mach. Co., 405 Pa. 617, 176 A.2d 684 (1962).

139. McDaniel v. Sage, 419 N.E.2d 1322 (Ind. Ct. App. 1981).

140. Cooper v. National Motor Bearing Co., 136 Cal. App. 2d 299, 288 P.2d 581 (1955).

141. Akins v. Hudson Pulp & Paper Co., 330 So. 2d 757 (Fla. Dist. Ct. App. 1976).

142. Levett v. Etkind, 158 Conn. 567, 265 A.2d 70 (1969).

143. Schessler v. Keck, 125 Cal. App. 2d 827, 271 P.2d 588 (1954).

144. Thompson v. Brent, 245 So. 2d 751 (La. Ct. App. 1971).

145. Wood v. Miller, 158 Or. 444, 76 P.2d 963 (1938).

146. Kelly v. Yount, 338 Pa. 190, 12 A.2d 579 (1940).

147. Bauer v. Otis, 133 Cal. App. 2d 439, 284 P.2d 133 (1955).

148. Brockman v. Harpole, 444 P.2d 25 (Or. 1968).

149. Hallinan v. Prindle, 11 P.2d 426 (1932), *rev'd,* 220 Cal. 46, 29 P.2d 202 (1934), *aff'd in part, rev'd in part,* 17 Cal. App. 2d 656, 62 P.2d 1075 (1936).

150. Crowe v. Provost, 52 Tenn. App. 397, 374 S.W.2d 645 (1963).

151. Powell v. Parkview Estate Nursing Home, Inc., 240 So. 2d 53 (La. Ct. App. 1970).

152. Estes Health Care Ctr., Inc. v. Bannerman, 411 So. 2d 109 (Ala. 1982).

153. LeBlanc v. Midland Nat'l Ins. Co., 219 So. 2d 251 (La. Ct. App. 1969).

154. Krestview Nursing Home, Inc. v. Synowiec, 317 So. 2d 94 (Fla. Dist. Ct. App. 1975), *cert. denied,* 333 So. 2d 463 (Fla. 1976).

Index

A

Abandonment, 110
Ability to pay, 112
Abortion, 203–204
    clinics, 209
    conduct surrounding clinics, 209
    conscience clauses, 209–210
    funding for, 210
    legal status of, 204–205
Accreditation, 19
    educational programs, 27
    standards, medical records access,
        154
Acquired immune deficiency
    syndrome, 113
    access to care, 219–221
    confidentiality issues, 221–224
    disclosure
        health care workers, 222–223
        sexual or needle partner, 223
        third parties, 223–224
    discrimination and, 47
    employment, 39–40
    exposure, infection, 224–225
    medical records access, 138
    OSH Act, 50
    reporting laws, 147–148
    strict liability, 286–287
Acquisitions, 96–97
Action, commencement of, 13

Administrative agency, decisions/rules
    of, 7
Administrative procedures acts, 7
Admission consent forms, 178–179
Adoption, 203
Adult
    competent, 180–181
    incompetent and consent, 181,
        184–185
Advance directives, 244, 251
Advanced practice nurse, 21–22,
    28–31, 108
Adverse impact, 41
Affidavits, 15
Age Discrimination in Employment
    Act, 45, 113
AIDS. *See* Acquired immune
    deficiency syndrome
Alcoholism, 46
American Medical Association
    physician-assisted suicide position,
        243
    supportive care position, 237–240
American Nurses Association, *Social
    Policy Statement*, 20–21
Americans with Disabilities Act, 47, 113
Amniocentesis, 211
Anencephaly, 246
Anesthesia recovery, 309–310
Antitrust statutes, 91–92
    contracts/agreements, 92–96

353